The Enemy Within

*Culture Wars and Political Identity in
Novels of the French Third Republic*

GILBERT D. CHAITIN

THE OHIO STATE UNIVERSITY PRESS
COLUMBUS

Library of Congress Cataloging-in-Publication Data
Chaitin, Gilbert D.
The enemy within : Culture wars and political identity in novels of the French Third Republic /
Gilbert D. Chaitin.
    p. cm.
  Includes bibliographical references and index.
  ISBN-13: 978-0-8142-0231-9 (cloth : alk. paper)
  ISBN-10: 0-8142-0231-4 (cloth : alk. paper)
  1. French fiction—19th century—History and criticism. 2. Politics and literature—France—History—19th century. 3. France—History—Third Republic, 1870–1940. I. Title.
  PQ653.C43 2008
  843'.80935844081—dc22
                                2008015617

This book is available in the following editions:
Cloth (ISBN 978-08142-0231-9)
CD-ROM (ISBN 978-08142-9044-6)

Cover design by Fulcrum Design Corps
Typeset in Galliard ITC
Text design by Juliet Williams
Printed by Thomson-Shore, Inc.

♾ The paper used in this publication meets the minimum requirements of the American National
Standard for Information Sciences—Permanence of Paper for Printed Library Materials. ANSI
Z39.48-1992.

9 8 7 6 5 4 3 2 1

CONTENTS

❦

ACKNOWLEDGMENTS

The research for this book was carried out thanks to grants from the Indiana University Office of Research and the University Graduate School, the National Endowment for the Humanities, and the School of Social Science of the Institute for Advanced Study in Princeton.

I want to express my heartfelt gratitude to those who have supported my project through their recommendations for these research grants, without which I could never have brought this book to completion: David Bell, Oscar Kenshur, Rosemary Lloyd, Gerald Prince, Joan Wallach Scott, and Samuel Weber.

My thanks go to Christophe Charle for his guidance and suggestions at the early stages of my research; to Jane Fulcher for her intervention on my behalf with French scholars; to Christin Ross for her friendship and moral support during my stay at the Institute for Advanced Study; and to Tom Broden for his help in finding a home for this manuscript.

I am especially grateful to Joan Wallach Scott, who has taken the time to read early versions of my manuscript and has given me valuable suggestions for revision, and whose encouragement and confidence in my project has helped to sustain my efforts through the many years it has taken me to complete it.

Portions of this text have appeared in *Australian Journal of French Studies, Cahiers Naturalistes, MLN, Yale French Studies,* and *Revolutions in Writing: Readings in Nineteenth-Century French Prose.*

INTRODUCTION

✢✦❦✦✢

*I*N THE YEARS 1880–1882, Jules Ferry, then minister of public education and president of the Council of Ministers (akin to prime minister),[1] presented a series of laws to the French parliament designed to establish a system of universal primary education that would, according to the political slogans of the ruling party, be "obligatory, free and laic." At the same time, he vigorously defended the bill introduced by his close collaborator, Camille Sée, instituting a nationwide network of public secondary schools for girls. With these actions he raised a firestorm of controversy pitting Catholics against proponents of lay education that would embroil the nation for the ensuing thirty-five years. Culminating in the Dreyfus Affair, which divided the country into two warring camps, roughly from 1897 to 1900, and in the official separation of Church and State in 1905, the internal strife lasted until the beginning of World War I, and the effects of these educational reforms are still felt even today (see Chatin, "'France Is My Mother'" 129).

The linchpin of the curriculum in the new schools was to be its course in "moral and civic education," designed to replace the classes in "moral and religious education" of the Catholic schools. The new system was to be universal not only in the sense of being obligatory for all children but also, and more importantly, in that of being grounded in the principle of universality asserted in the Declaration of the Rights of Man and of the Citizen, issued in 1789 and incorporated into the

1

Constitution of the First French Republic. Branding Catholicism as just one religion among several in France, Ferry and his Opportunist colleagues sought to unify the nation and justify the secularization of the schools under the banner of an "independent morality" allegedly common to all peoples of all times. When inculcated into the children of France, this morality, consistent with the positivist notion of a universally human social sense at the basis of morality, or with the Enlightenment conception of a universal human subject whose personhood resides in the dignity of a rational being capable of moral action and thus of governing himself, and in either case independent of any particular set of beliefs or dogmas, would serve to form true and loyal citizens of the Third Republic, worthy of participating in the self-government made possible by universal suffrage.

From the start, the Catholic opposition argued that a school without God must be a school against God, that is, a breeding ground of vice and iniquity that would destroy national character and unity. In subsequent years, both the nationalist right and the anarchist left asserted that, by ignoring or overriding particulars of history, region, and race, republican universalism eliminated the creative spontaneity of history, the uniqueness of different cultures and individuals, and true human freedom. The abstract Enlightenment subject, they claimed, was nothing but an "empty simulacrum, a philosophical marionette" easily tyrannized by the centralized powers of Jacobin government (Taine, *Révolution jacobine* 9). The education the Republic proffered to its peasant and working classes led to the creation of a mass of *declassés*, people who had lost all sense of their prior identities and who could not find a home among the upper classes either. In short, the new identity of the republican citizen, the enemies of the Republic alleged, signified in fact the destruction of both individual and national identity.

The same disputes between the universal and the particular have often resurfaced in both politics and education until today.[2] Since the Langevin-Wallon report in 1947, professors of education on the left have argued that democratic schooling should balance universality, providing equal opportunity for all pupils, and particularity, developing each child's individual aptitudes to the fullest, in order to serve both the collective good and individual happiness. While endorsing these principles, later educators such as Louis Legrand, Antoine Prost, and Philippe Meirieu have contrasted the increasing democratization of admission to the secondary schools with the ever-growing abstraction, formalism, and theoretical bent of the subjects taught, not only in math and science but in the social sciences and humanities as well. Like their university counterparts, they target the prevalence of universalizing abstract reason as a major source of the crisis in the schools, for technocratic education gives exclusive preference to the "abstract intelligence" that many immigrant and working-class pupils lack, and it ignores the education in multicultural values they believe would fulfill the socializing task of today's schools.

Critics of the center right counter that universalism is the essential characteristic of French schooling, and that it is actually the ideology of the left that supports the technological mentality in the schools that both sides profess to fear and deplore. In the 1980s, Jean-Claude Milner reasserted the main claim of the Ferry schools: that they alone shape the identity of French children into the true republican citizens of the future by providing universal access to the knowledge that guarantees civil rights in a country with neither the Bill of Rights of the U.S. Constitution nor the principle of habeas corpus in Britain. Expanding Milner's argument at the start of the new millennium, Denis Kambouchner constructed the problem as a quarrel between the "schools-that-teach [content, knowledge]" and the "techno-pedagogues" of the left, who worry about principles and methods at the expense of subject matter. He contrasts Condorcet's universal humanism with the 'German Romantic' particularism of ethnicity, in order to argue that attention to the multicultural backgrounds of the pupils will inevitably detract from the cause of national unity it is supposed to support.

Criticism of higher education has followed a similar pattern. The modern French university system was created at the turn of the twentieth century and modeled on the German system initiated by Wilhelm von Humboldt in Berlin at the beginning of the nineteenth century. The Idea of the University, as scholars are fond of calling it, is the Enlightenment ideal of the independent, disinterested practice of universal reason with the aim of producing objective research and individual development (*Bildung*).

Social critics such as Pierre Bourdieu have argued that the universalism of the university is an illusion; in reality, it represents the values and interests of the bourgeoisie of a particular period in history, and therefore excludes, or at least dooms to failure, the majority of farmers and working-class students (*Reproduction*). Jacques Derrida points out that the rights asserted by the Declaration of the Rights of Man are not in fact 'natural' and therefore not universal, but are performed by the declaration itself, in a particular language and in a particular historical and social context. As a result, the university can never actually attain the autonomy of its Idea; there will always be a tension between the

University and the State (*Right to Philosophy* I). Jacques Lacan sees the universalizing Discourse of the University as a mask hiding and serving the domination of the Discourse of the Master—that is, as a means of control rather than a path to liberation (*The Other Side of Psychoanalysis*). And François Lyotard, referring to Ludwig Wittgenstein, argues that there is no metalanguage, and therefore no possibility of a universal reason that could, in all cases, adjudicate disagreements among competing claims; there is only a multiplicity of heterogeneous, incommensurable, and therefore irreconcilable language games. As a result, the rug has been swept out from under the foundations of modern educational systems—emancipation of the people through learning in the French tradition (*Postmodern Condition*).

Attacks against the universalism of bourgeois republicanism similar to those of right-wing nationalism at the turn of the nineteenth century have been renewed in recent decades by critics and theoreticians who identify themselves as belonging to the political left. Unwittingly echoing Anatole France, Cornel West has characterized this "cultural politics of difference" as the tendency "to trash the monolithic and homogeneous in the name of diversity, multiplicity and heterogeneity; to reject the abstract, general and universal in light of the concrete, specific, and particular; and to historicize, contextualize and pluralize by highlighting the contingent, provisional, variable, tentative, shifting and changing" (19).

A decade earlier, Edward Said denounced the cultural imperialism of nineteenth-century orientalism that privileged 'vision' over 'narrative,' by which he meant the universalizing and reifying categorization of the colonized designed "to wipe out any traces of individual Arabs with narratable life histories" (229), eliminating both sensuous particularity and historical contingency. And while Lyotard found that it is narrative—the grand Enlightenment narrative of human emancipation—that effects universalization, the thrust of his critique of modernism is to open a path toward 'little stories' that would preserve the identity of minority groups or colonized cultures. For Homi Bhabha, "the aim of cultural difference is to rearticulate the sum of knowledge from the perspective of the signifying position of the minority that resists totalization" (162). In this stance we can hear echoes of the Lacanian valorization of the nonnarcissistic Other as well as of the deconstructive critique of that philosophical notion of truth as presence which acts to marginalize and ultimately to repress difference. Shoshana Felman summarized "Derrida's . . . critique . . . of traditional philosophy," in the assertion that "Western metaphysics is based on the totalitarian principle of so-called logocentrism, that is, on the repressive predominance of 'logos' over 'writing' . . ." (22). Others claim that the totalitarian principle has arisen not from Western metaphysics in general, but more specifically from the "Enlightenment's universalism and rationalism." In "Feminism, Citizenship, and Radical Democratic Politics," Chantal Mouffe has described these twentieth-century attacks on "the idea of a universal human nature, of a universal canon of rationality through which that nature could be known as well as the traditional conception of truth" (369–70).

An important segment of feminist thought has participated in this movement, as can be heard in the call that Julia Kristeva issued in 1979, in "Women's Time": "[T]he struggle is no longer concerned with the quest for equality, but, rather, with difference and specificity . . . in order to discover, first, the specificity of the female, and then, in the end, that of each individual woman" (196). Luce Irigaray put the negative case in forceful terms: "Any universal [other than that of the natural economy] is a partial construct and, therefore, authoritarian and unjust. . . . [O]ur identity cannot be constructed without a vertical and horizontal horizon that respects that difference between the sexes" (205). Sandra Bermann concluded that American feminists have been even more radical opponents of the universal, more committed proponents of the particular that grounds cultural diversity in "specific feminist histories, in which differences of race, religion, class, ethnic group and sexual preference are foregrounded" (105). In short, as Joan Scott has observed in her book on the parity movement, for these "first wave" feminists, Enlightenment ideology was a false universalism, for the allegedly neutral figure of the abstract subject was in fact "imagined as male" (*Parité* 4).

Champions of universalism have not remained silent during this time, starting with Julien Benda's epoch-making *La trahison des clercs* (*Betrayal of the Intellectuals;* 1927; see also Chaitin, "Education and Political Identity"). Writing in the aftermath of World War I and during the rise of fascism and Nazism, Benda bemoaned the fact that even intellectuals, including leading writers and university professors, had abandoned the universalist principles that make the disinterested pursuit of truth possible in favor of practical and political interests. Those modern intellectuals who not only love the particular but raise it to the level of a divinity in a new practical religion assuage the consciences of the politicians and the citizens who indulge in the worst forms of egotistical passion, the love of self writ large that constitutes modern nationalism. In the early 1960s, Jean-Paul Sartre chimed in with his attempt to reconcile universalism and particularism, G. W. F. Hegel and Søren

Kierkegaard, via his concept of the "singular universal," according to which man is the being who brings forth the universal by transcending (*dépasser*) the absolute singularity of the contingent events of life and history, giving them meaning (*le sens;* "L'universel singulier" 174–75).

Once particularism had shifted to the left, voices from the right, most notably Alain Finkielkraut in his *Defeat of the Mind* (*La défaite de la pensée;* 1987), adopted Benda's arguments to fuel a frontal attack on the anticolonial ideology of UNESCO and on the particularist aspects of structuralist, poststructuralist, postcolonial, and postmodern thought. His basic argument is that, in rejecting European universalism as a disguise for ethnocentrism and colonial domination, in emphasizing difference and cultural identity at the expense of Man and the real person in place of the abstract individual, the 'decolonizers' have reverted to the ideas of Johann Gottfried von Herder and Oswald Spengler, espousing the narcissistic love of self in the form of one's ethnic or class identity and destroying any sense of a legitimate hierarchy of values (58). The logical result of this reasoning is that the peoples of the former colonies have now become the slaves of their national identity (95 French ed.; 69 English ed.). For the Enlightenment, freedom was impossible for the ignorant (168 French ed.; 125 English ed.). One became an individual in overcoming appetites, self-interest, and prejudices. For consumer society, on the contrary, freedom and culture are defined by the satisfaction of needs; thus the idea of distancing oneself from "instinct and tradition" has been lost (169 French ed.; 125 English ed.). With the current challenges to the Enlightenment, the ideas that form the basis of our modern schools—only thought confers autonomy and only self-exertion produces thought—have fallen by the wayside (169–70).

Bourget and the Lessons of Literature

The attempt to create a new national identity of loyal citizens of the Republic based on universal secular morality rather than God-given commandments produced a trauma in the national psyche that gave rise to culture wars very similar to those of today in France, the United States, and elsewhere. In undermining the Catholicism that had offered easy answers to the questions at the root of identity, the reforms created an existential angst to accompany the political and social anxiety resulting from the upheavals and wars since the Revolution, above all the devastating military defeat in the Franco-German War of 1870–71 and the bloody civil war of the Paris Commune in 1871. Now both education and identity became political matters. What might seem at first sight to be narrow questions of pedagogy such as curriculum or teaching methods became, therefore, entangled in what might be called the first experiment in postmodern performativity, a complex effort on a hitherto unprecedented scale to alter the identity of a modern nation. For that reason, disputes over education produced a kind of ideological polygamy in which, as Mona Ozouf so happily put it: "[P]edagogy was married to law, politics, economics, metaphysics and morals" (18).[3] And, I would add, to literature as well.[4]

While it was primarily in the schools that the determining battles were waged from the 1880s until well after the turn of the century, it was in narrative that the human implications of the issues raised by the education wars were articulated, appraised, and dramatized (on the role of the serial novel, see M. Ozouf 18). In his highly influential *Essais de psychologie contemporaine* (1883) and the *Nouveaux essais* (1885; see Mansuy 372–76), Paul Bourget puts narrative in opposition to education, but as its rival as much as its negation. His opening gambit is to establish the parallel and thus the implicit competition between literature and institutional forms of education such as religion and the public school system. In the forewords to both volumes he justifies his "psychological" analysis of literary works, rather than the normative aesthetic judgments or the biographical accounts customary in the criticism of the times, by setting up literature as a powerful force in the moral education of the young, in overt conflict with parental upbringing and traditional influences ("Avant-Propos de 1883" xvi; "Avant-Propos de 1885" xx).

The novelist as educator was in fact a common theme in nineteenth-century France. Jules Vallès made the point more succinctly and more brutally than Bourget in "Victimes du Livre," an article reprinted in *Les réfractaires* (1876)—"The Book Will Kill the Father"—as well as in his novel *L'enfant* (1878). A few years after Bourget, Maurice Barrès would describe his antiauthoritarian *Culte du Moi* novels as a work of edification ("Examen des trois romans idéologiques" 17). Alphonse Lamartine, Victor Hugo, George Sand, Émile Zola, Bernard Lazare, and many other writers agreed that their mission was to educate the public.

Literature is a powerful educational force, yes—but, according to Bourget, in the wrong direction. Unfortunately, the moral lesson of the major writers of the preceding generation, those who exercise the strongest influence on present-day youth, is the loss of traditional values compounded by the failure to replace them. The present generation in

France suffers from a sense of pessimism and depression that is not just the effect of Arthur Schopenhauer's philosophy but betrays the existence of a deep crisis, a "moral malady" ("Avant-Propos de 1885" xxii). Having enumerated the symptoms of the modern illness of decadence, Bourget proceeds to diagnose its profound cultural causes rendered visible in the literature of the Second Empire: dilettantism, nihilism, and cosmopolitanism; the perversions and impotence of modern love; the effects of science; the conflict between democracy and high culture. Ultimately he isolates two pathogenic bacilli under his cultural microscope: science and democracy. It is they that have dried up the wellsprings of moral life, without having found a way to replenish them (xxv). Now, under the Third Republic, the infection is being spread by the schools, the main effect of whose teachings is to undermine the identities of their pupils (166–67).

Bourget conjures up the fantasy of an army of nihilists launched on a crusade of negativity, destroying everything in a paroxysm of rage at being unable to find certain knowledge (*Essais de psychologie contemporaine* 84). Contingency has thus invaded the bastion of belief, with one set of ideas being considered just as valid as another, and its agents provocateurs are science and democracy abetted by the diversity of 'races.' The insidious march of contingency is not content with planting its black flag of anarchy in heaven, earth, and society; it inflicts a similar fate on identity in the writings of Gustave Flaubert. Adapting the power of romantic prose to describe the concrete details of decor, costume, and the representation of character, he succeeded in giving fictional realization to the English conception of the inner self as an "association of ideas," by depicting the series of images that pass through the heads of his characters and capturing the rhythm of their recurrence (165).[5] With this unique blend of romanticism and science, Flaubert depicts the 'ego' as the 'collection of little facts' of Hippolyte Taine's theories (166). As Bourget explains in his essay on Taine, the basic problem is that this notion of the self as a series of events jettisons the idea of an abiding "substance" behind mental phenomena and thus that of an immortal soul (226). In the realm of the self multiplicity is not only the archenemy of unity, order and harmony; its very presence calls into question the necessity and perpetuity of being.

The only island of certainty in this sea of skepticism is the science Taine espoused in his philosophy. Here at last is a single principle of cause and effect capable of unifying all of nature by means of the inductive logic that makes it possible to subsume the observations of particular phenomena under larger and larger general laws. The trouble is that this system, which exalts the power of the human mind, at the same time abases the individual will before the inexorability of the supreme forces of the natural and social milieus. The only sensible counsel in this situation is the ethic of resignation preached by Spinoza or Goethe. For Bourget, although not for Taine himself, the inevitable effect of science is once again a kind of nihilism (242–43). In literature, this conception has led to the reduction of the self to a kind of nothingness caught between instinct and milieu in the fiction of the naturalist school of Zola and his disciples, just then at the height of their influence in the aftermath of the *Soirées de Médan* manifesto and the polemical essays of the *Roman Expérimental*.

Literature produces devastating as well as salutary effects, precisely because art is the great competitor of life. The tragic flaw of the contemporary adolescent is the desire to know and experience everything, a desire he can satisfy in no other way than through reading. The idyllic unity and energy of his childhood self and world are consequently swamped by an uncontrollable tide of disparate ideas and forces—causal, critical, educational, political, and international.

The hero of this tragic tale is ostensibly the youth whose sensibility is educated through his contact with literature, but Bourget intimates clearly that in fact its vicissitudes recount the fate of reading in general in modern France. Instead of preparing us for experience or substituting for it, reading distorts experience, prevents us from enjoying or even from having it, as with Emma Bovary. The constant bombardment of heterogeneous ideas isolates us from nature, society, and the unconscious wellsprings of personality, precluding the formation of a stable, unified, and forceful self, secure in its relation to other people and the world. Reading must therefore be added to science and democracy as the third scourge of modern society. Narrative may be our best source of knowledge about the moral life understood in its widest sense as the life of sentiments and values, as Bourget repeatedly asserts, but it is also, he continues, at least in its present decadent and naturalist forms, a teacher of demoralization and despair.

The Novel of Ideas

In his essay on the Goncourt brothers, Bourget contrasts their objective "novels of observation" with the distortion of reality found in the "thesis novels" of Sand (*Essais* II 155–56). Although Bourget does not dwell on the topic, his little phrase *roman à thèse* was destined to become a catchword in the succeeding decades, precisely because it came to stand for everything that was considered worst in the myriad attempts to carry out the program of merging politicized morality and the fictional representations of identity in the literature of the Third Republic. Indeed, the very name of this subgenre has remained a term of opprobrium to this day, a curious and possibly unique fact of literary history that is all the more surprising in an era that prides itself on having abandoned, at least officially, the notion of a hierarchy of genres. (See, for instance, the passages by Sartre and Simone de Beauvoir quoted in the *Grand Robert* dictionary's entry under "roman à thèse").

The solidification of the name 'thesis novel' with its henceforth inseparable stigma occurred as a result of the convergence of developments both within the field of literature and outside it in the culture at large.[6] The crucial precondition for this process was the transformation of the literary field during the Second Empire, which was increasingly dominated by *l'art pour l'art* on the one hand, and the positivist notion of realism on the other. The first condemned the novel of ideas for besmirching the purity of art, which should maintain its autonomy by excluding all supposedly external discourses such as those of politics, philosophy, religion, or morality—the ability to incorporate, which critics from Friedrich Schlegel to Mikhail Bakhtin have singled out as the defining characteristic of the novel form. The second redefined the concept of proof in keeping with the empiricist method of induction from the observation of a multitude of particular cases to general truth, rather than the illustration of a predetermined general idea, as was the case in the classical conception. However contradictory the two movements may have been in certain regards, they came together in defining a new meaning of objectivity as disinterestedness, according to which the subject—the perceiving, feeling, and thinking mind—can reach truth only by refraining from injecting itself into the phenomena it surveys or the art it is creating. From this perspective, the problem with the thesis novel was not the fact that it contained an idea but that it inserted an unwanted subjective meaning into its representation and consequently departed from objective presentation.

The progressive hardening of the theoretical category of the thesis novel would not have taken place had it not been for the simultaneous proliferation of novels that, in the eyes of the critics, deviated from that standard and therefore had to be defended or attacked, depending on the commentator's point of view. Writing in 1908, Jean Charles-Brun accumulates quotations on the subject by Bourget, Flaubert, Ferdinand Brunetière, Jules Lemaître, and Léon Blum, not to mention lesser lights such as Édouard Rod, René Doumic, Victor Marguerite, Jules Bois, Marius-Ary Leblond, Eugène Montfort, Adolphe Brisson, Jean Viollis, and others. He concludes that the recent proliferation of thesis novels and social novels results from the democratization of literature combined with the increased pressure of the social environment on contemporary novelists, and he adduces as evidence the fact that the two eras that produced the most such novels were those that witnessed the most widespread debates about social issues—the period around the Revolution of 1848 and that of the Dreyfus Affair (*Le roman social* 53–54, 57). Several years later, Marcel Proust would look back on the Dreyfus Affair as a time when, urged to come down from their ivory towers, writers used this excuse to "assure the triumph of right, [and] rebuild the moral unity of the nation" rather than perform the "true" function of literature (*The Past Recaptured* 206). Susan Suleiman makes a similar point in her influential treatise on the thesis novel. Noting that the Dreyfus Affair divided the country into two political groups that had virtually nothing in common, a division that lasted all the way to the Vichy government in 1940, she asserts that it's not by chance that this period of ideological polarization produced so many thesis novels: "The thesis novel is a genre in which ideological polarization is manifested both as a basic theme and as an organizing structural principle" (*Authoritarian Fictions* 69).

The literary culture wars that accompanied this polarization had already begun in the 1880s, in reaction to the Ferry educational reforms and the Opportunists' attempts to separate Church from State. Octave Feuillet's *La morte* (*Aliette*) (1886) and Bourget's *Disciple* (1889), both of which focus on the disputes between supporters of the Church and partisans of secularization, mark the onset of this new series of novels of ideas. Each of the other major novels of education I study in this book—Barrès's *Novel of National Energy* (in addition to *The Disciple*) on the political right, France's *Contemporary History* and Zola's *Truth* on the left—was at least partly composed in reaction to the ideological issues raised during the Affair. While the first volume of Barrès's trilogy was published a few months before the Dreyfus case became a national affair, it already broaches several of the main political and social themes that would form the program of Barrès's nationalism in the succeeding years; and the two other volumes reinterpret earlier events, such as the phenomenon of Boulangism (1886–1889) and the Panama Canal graft scandals (1892–93), in light of the Affair (see Sternhell, *Maurice Barrès* 217–20). France's tetralogy was also overtaken in the middle by the Affair, which cast a different light on the earlier volumes. It starts out as a critique of the republican leaders' complicity with the Church during the 1890s, after Pope Leo XIII called on the French Church to "rally" to the Republic and the government had instituted the policy of the "new spirit" of reconciliation with the Church, before the Affair (see appendix A). In the later volumes, however, the Affair swallows up the earlier plot and appears, retrospectively, to be the logical outcome of those earlier phenomena. In writing his novel after the general amnesty had quieted the most violent passions of the Affair, Zola constructed his fictional transposition with the aim of drawing the social and political lessons the government was trying to squelch by pardoning all parties involved, even those guilty of deception, fraud, forgery, and perjury.[7]

In her "Notice" to the Pléiade edition of France's *L'anneau d'amé-thyste,* one of the four novels comprising his *Histoire contemporaine,* Marie-Claire Bancquart states that the writer was responding to the same "neurosis of national identity" that inflated the Dreyfus case into a national affair. Indeed, the structure of French national identity, already shaken by the defeat at the hands of the Prussians and the Ferry educational reforms, was shattered to the core by the Affair.[8] For those on the left, it was clear that the nation had abandoned its historical mission, and with it, its national identity of spreading human rights and liberating the peoples of the world from their tyrants. Dumbfounded by this turn of events, France's spokesperson in the novels, Professor Bergeret, imagines that the brains of his countrymen have been mysteriously lobotomized. Zola put the case forcefully in his "Declaration to the Jury" at his trial for libeling the authorities who framed Dreyfus for treason:

> The Dreyfus Affair has become a petty matter at this point . . . compared to the terrifying questions it has raised. . . . Now we need to know if France is still the France of the rights of man, the nation that gave liberty to the world and which should give it justice. Open your eyes and see that, if it is so helpless and confused, the French soul must be stirred to its inmost depths in the face of such redoubtable perils. A people cannot be subject to such distress without its very moral life being in danger. (*Vérité en marche* 79)

Those on the right perceived the same crisis of national identity but attributed it to the temerity and lack of patriotism of those who challenged the verdicts of the military courts that condemned Alfred Dreyfus and exonerated Ferdinand Walsin Esterhazy (the real perpetrator of the treason). By undermining the credibility of the army and its courts, the 'intellectuals' who defended Dreyfus represented a mortal threat to the very idea of the homeland (speech by former minister of war Eugène Cavaignac, December 1, 1901, cited in Girardet 174–76). Barrès claimed to discover the source of this antipatriotic evil in the Kantian universalism taught in the schools and universities of the Republic.

> Verbalism that distances the child from all reality, Kantianism that uproots him from his soil and his dead, overproduction of high school graduates that creates what we've called, after Bismarck, "a proletariat of degree-holders," those are our reproaches to the University, those are what make its products, the "intellectuals," enemies of society. . . . The philosophy that the State teaches is responsible . . . for people think[ing] it is intellectual to scorn the national unconscious and to cause the intellect to function in [the realm of] pure abstraction, beyond the plane of reality. (*Scènes et doctrines* 45)

The Kantian universalism of the Republic is destroying the identity of its citizens, based on their regional, racial, and historical heritage. These rootless intellectuals have become enemies of society who place their individual ideas above the cause of national unity. They are "individuals who convince themselves that society should be founded on logic and who fail to recognize that it rests in fact on prior necessities that are perhaps foreign to individual reason" and thus fail to content themselves with their proper role in the social order (38).

The birth of the Republic, with its universal suffrage, universal education, and the influential role of public opinion in an era of expanded journalism and publishing, provided an advantageous context for the abundance of novels of ideas (Masson 7). In a democracy, however imperfect it may be, the writer has a special role to play in the fight to establish the meaning of events in order to sway the public toward the policy or candidate she favors (see Barrès, *Mes cahiers* 139–40).[9] Moreover, although traditional criticism, from Plato on, has often seen an unbridgeable gap between the particularity of narrative and the universality of cognitive discourse, critics at the turn of the twentieth century asserted that the novel was well adapted to convincing readers of the validity of general ideas precisely because its very particularity gave it, like life itself, "the violence of the concrete" (René Johannet, quoted in Charles-Brun 49–50). If the critics justifiably perceive many thesis novels as authoritarian, that is because such texts magnify the ever-present but more hidden coercive force of every symbolic system that functions within or like a language.

The Enemy Within

Given the widespread view under the Third Republic that the schools and teachers possessed the enormous power to control the welfare, the destiny, and the very being of the nation, novels about education were inevitably, and in many cases explicitly, conceived to be examinations of the formation of national identity. My emphasis is therefore on texts in which the emotionally charged relation between teachers and pupils, at one level or another of the educational hierarchy, plays a major role in representing specific ideological systems of education current in the national debates instigated by the Ferry reforms. The four novels I examine in this book respond to the trauma of identity by uncovering what I would term the erotics of politics: the subjective roots of political and social arrangements and the central fantasies that structure the relation of the subject to social realities entailed by competing ideological positions. In order to make their political programs appealing and those of their adversaries abhorrent, these texts deploy fantasy scenarios that mobilize the fears and desires awakened in the public by the attempt to replace the Catholic Other with that of the Republic.

The perceived loss of an absolute source of truth and guarantor of social cohesion in the form of Catholicism and the monarchy awakened in French consciousness a sense of the contingency of symbolic systems, of the Other's feet of clay. In each of the four model novels I will examine a rent is opened up in the fabric of the regnant symbolic system that threatens to expose the traumatic Real that system serves to shield from view. For Bourget and Barrès, it is Enlightenment science and universalism that rings hollow; for France and Zola it is God, Catholicism, and spiritualism that are mere covers for emptiness. As Ernesto Laclau argues, by affirming the lack in the Other's Other, these texts imply the existence of an impossible plenitude, the utopia of an unfulfilled demand from society. Each, then, offers to fill the void, and thus to shore up the nation's identity, in the battle to name and thus constitute what Lacan calls the a-object, that whose possession would confer complete fulfillment on its possessors (Laclau 96–100). Taking on the role of educators of the nation, the four writers intervened in the national debate, redefining its terms by dramatizing the formation and destruction of the ideological fantasies that structure social reality and sustain the representation of imaginary communities (see Žižek, "Sur le pouvoir politique" 43).

The most visible theme common to these works as to the polemics of republican and antirepublican forces was the need for unity, a unity supposedly lost through the machinations of the other side and recoverable only if the correct group were permitted to direct national education according to its principles. The unspoken presupposition is that unity is equivalent to identity, for both the person and the nation. While the sources of disunity are identified differently by writers of the left and those of the right, the fundamental fantasy underlying each political program is the conviction that the adversarial party, the primal enemy, has somehow penetrated within the bastion of the self; indeed, as conceptualized in Lacan's notion of the 'extimate,' that the very root of its existence comes from outside the self. On the national level, the homeland is portrayed as striving to rid itself of an alien element which is, in fact, as Barrès puts it in a telling passage, "the most intimate part" of itself.

CHAPTER 1

Universal Education, Culture Wars, and National Identity

❧❦❧

A Matter of Life and Death:
Secular Education versus the Catholic Church

The laws on educational reform introduced in 1880–82 constituted the first major set of legislation pushed through by the loose coalition of republican groups who, under the leadership of the so-called Opportunists—Léon Gambetta, Ferry, and others—had captured the majority of seats in the lower house in the elections of 1877 and in the Senate in 1882,[1] thus ratifying the victory of the Republic over its traditional opponents, the legitimist (Bourbon) and Orleanist monarchists, and the Bonapartist supporters of a new Empire-style dictatorship. Like most legislation, whatever its ostensible goals or actual effects, the reform laws were meant to serve a political purpose, first and foremost, that of ensuring the long-term survival of the still very much embattled Third Republic (see Chaitin, "'France Is My Mother'" 130–31). As Ferry put it in a speech delivered some ten years earlier, education was a matter of life or death for the Republic: Democracy must choose between science and the Church (Salle Molière speech of April 10, 1870; reproduced in Legrand 237). The legislation attacked the power of the Church, now allied with the old oligarchy of aristocrats and an important segment of the traditional bourgeoisie, and at the same time was designed to allay fears of a new social revolution by the working classes—which is why the socialist parties, still weak from the bloodletting through which the self-appointed Versailles government had annihilated the Communards in 1871, gave it only lukewarm support (M. Ozouf 84). Above all, it was designed to give the republicans a foothold in every village and rural area in the land, essential to combating the influence of the local priest and thus to attaining political power in a regime of universal suffrage, as Gambetta had seen as early as 1871.

The role undoubtedly played by strategies of power politics and crass political calculation should not obscure the importance of the specific ideological content of the proposed reforms or the sincerity of the convictions of those who promulgated these reforms. While they were no doubt conceived to justify the program to potential members of the political movement and to respond to the economic realities of the modern industrial world (Eros 258), the goal of safeguarding the longevity of the Republic required something more than concocting a program that would increase the party rolls and win the upcoming election. It entailed the attempt to create something new in the world, a large body of loyal republican citizens who would no longer be susceptible to the dictates of the Church or to the seductions of authoritarian dictatorship—"Caesarism" in the catchword of the enemies of Bonapartism (see Albanese, *Molière à l'École républicaine* 3–6).

The novelty and enormity of the task confronting this effort at cultural revolution can be properly measured only against the backdrop of the social realities of France in 1870. Although united administratively, most of the country had none of the characteristics of a modern nation as defined by the nationalist rhetoric of Ernest Renan or Maurice Barrès, or by the standards of more recent social theorists. As Eugen Weber emphasizes,

> [O]utside the urban centers, over much of France there was no "common history to be experienced as common," no "community of complementary habits," little interdependency furthered by the division of labor in the production of goods and services, and only limited "channels of social communication and economic intercourse." (486)

The slogans for this program had been devised and the program worked out in the waning years of the Second Empire and the beginning of the Third Republic, but the fundamental ideas went back, as Ferry noted more than once, to the Revolution and the "principles of 1789," especially as applied to education in the writings of Condorcet. If a significant portion of the public became receptive to them in the first decade of the Republic, it was not because the ideas were new at that time, but

because so many of the country's leaders attributed the disastrous outcome of the war against Prussia to the superiority of the German school
system. (See Gambetta's Bordeaux speech of 26 June 1871, in *Discours
et plaidoyers choisis* 67.)

During the Empire, the Church had begun to operate essentially as
a political party, first in support of Napoleon III, who realized at the
beginning of his reign that, like his namesake, he needed its cooperation in order to consolidate his hold on power, and then in opposition
to his regime as the latter leaned farther and farther toward the pro-
democratic and anticlerical forces among the ruling group, especially
insofar as they backed the fledgling Republic of Italy in its conflicts with
the papacy. Although it had a liberal wing headed by Bishop Dupanloup
and the Duke de Broglie,[2] and a reactionary faction whose most outspoken proponents were Bishop Freppel and the notorious polemicist
Louis Veuillot (the model for Zola's rabid Catholic journalist, Vuil-
let, in *La fortune des Rougon*), throughout the first two decades of the
Republic, until Pope Leo XIII's encyclical in 1892 calling for Catholics
to "rally" to the Republic and even beyond, the political arm of the
Church aligned itself with one form or other of monarchy and against
the Republic.[3] In reaction to the collusion between the Church and the
dictatorial Empire, liberal proponents of democratic freedom claimed
to perceive the same authoritarian principles in Catholicism that they
found in the rule of Napoleon III, and they proceeded to denounce the
moral teachings of the Church and the schools in which those tenets
were disseminated.

While education had always been a point of focus for republican
politics in France, the issue took on a new urgency after the passage
of the Falloux laws under Louis-Napoleon's aegis as president of the
Second Republic in 1850, which, under the guise of the "freedom of
education," had delivered virtually the entire French educational system into the hands of the Church.[4] In reaction, Edgar Quinet issued
the polemical pamphlet that Jules Ferry would later call "my breviary"
(Eros, 277 n25), *L'enseignement du peuple* (1850), which argued that
there was an inextricable contradiction between secular and religious
education, for political freedom is possible only in countries where
freedom of thought and conscience are protected, while the Catholic
Church prohibits both. Moreover, in order to ensure civil peace, the
modern State has a vital interest in teaching a "social morality" of religious tolerance,[5] while the Church, with its claim to be the unique
possessor of truth, must instruct, and does in fact instruct, its pupils
to condemn other religions as invalid. Pierre-Joseph Proudhon's *De la*

justice dans la Révolution et dans l'Église (1858) pitted the revolutionary ethic of individual freedom and equality, founded on the 'new idea' of Justice, against the morality of indignity and resignation to the evils of this life, based on the old dogma of original sin. A few years later, from 1865 until the war with Prussia, Proudhon's call for a new republican ethic independent of religion was given widespread currency in the journal *La Morale Indépendante,* founded by the former Saint-Simonian Alexandre Massol. In a similar spirit, the comparatively liberal minister of education, Victor Duruy, had introduced in 1865 a "neutral"—that is, nonsectarian—course of moral education into the so-called special secondary schools, which offered professional training in commerce and business. In the meantime, the philosopher Étienne Vacherot, following Proudhon and recalling the ideas of Jules Michelet and the republican opposition to the July Monarchy, made liberty the basic principle of all law, rights, and justice, and stressed that the most fundamental freedom is that of thought. Sheltered from legal control, this freedom is nevertheless subject to inhibition by ignorance and superstition. As a result, in a democracy this liberty creates the essential duty for families and for the state to provide education and moral training to its citizens (*La démocratie* 5). This was also the profound belief of Jean Macé, a socialist journalist of 1848 turned schoolteacher, who founded the Ligue de l'Enseignement in 1866 to promote popular education via the principle of free, obligatory primary schools. The way was thus prepared for Gambetta's strategy in his electoral campaigns of 1869 and 1871: In order to create citizens of the Republic, we must combat ignorance, but in order to combat ignorance we must combat the Church, since the Church fosters ignorance (Chaitin, "'France Is My Mother'" 132–34). To the working-class population of Belleville, he promised "primary education, laic, free and obligatory" in 1869 (Mona Ozouf 30). In 1871, he returned to the theme, insisting that the moral training in the Congregationist schools was designed to make the children hate the modern republican values of free inquiry, science, tolerance, and humanity and thus divide the country into two warring factions (report of speech in Gambetta's newspaper, *La République Française,* November 25, 1871, in Mona Ozouf 27).

Gambetta's defense of free inquiry and science indicates the other main intellectual source of his educational policy, the positivism of Auguste Comte and Émile Littré. Proposing a remedy for the defeat at the hands of the Prussians and the annexation of Alsace-Lorraine in his pivotal speech in Bordeaux on June 26, 1871, he mapped out a strategy for "regenerating the country and founding a free government" that combined the Proudhonian concern for the emancipation and well-being of the peasants and working classes with the positivist principles of modern education and scientific progress into a policy that would form the basis of the radical republicans' platform for the subsequent decade. Its key planks were the avoidance of violence, concentration on one issue at a time, and designation of rearmament and universal national education as the essential first steps in the establishment and consolidation of the Republic (*Discours et plaidoyers* 66).

But of what, precisely, will this universal education consist? First and foremost, of science, especially the 'exact sciences'—mathematics and the natural sciences (72). No longer is there a reason to be afraid of spreading such knowledge to the hitherto unenlightened population, Gambetta continues, attempting to allay the fears of the traditional bourgeoisie, whose conviction that critical rationalism leads to social unrest had prompted them to support the Falloux laws since the 1850s (Weisz 98). On the contrary, we must show the upper classes that it is in their best interest to have an enlightened populace of workers and peasants; the disastrous results of the war demonstrate that it is vitally important to cultivate this as yet untapped source of energy and abilities. Moreover, once the peasants understand the advantages they have already derived from the republic and the benefits they can expect from it in future, starting with the fact that it was the Revolution that made it possible for them to acquire the land they now possess and gave them the right to own it, they will be eager to support the government rather than seek to overturn it. Similarly, we must teach the working classes that their government is not a greedy, external master but a legitimate emanation of their own sovereignty, while allowing them to benefit from the advances of modern science and civilization. Moreover, the scientific method of thinking can liberate the minds of all citizens, regardless of social class. At the same time, the objectivity of that method, its alleged disinterestedness, ensures the equal treatment of citizens and the lack of bias of the republican government, which alone makes objective reason rather than class interest the basis of its policies. In short, such education can provide liberty, equality, and the pursuit of happiness for all citizens. In fact, when Paul Bert, a pupil of the renowned physiologist Claude Bernard and a member of Gambetta's editorial team on *La République Française,* introduced the Opportunist law on universal primary education to the Chamber of Deputies in his speech of December 6, 1879, he listed the same conquests of the Revolution to be included in the new civics course curriculum (*L'instruction civique à l'école* 6).

Gambetta also implies that acquaintance with the exact sciences has a greater role to play in the establishment of social order. Here he was perhaps thinking of Comte's three organizing tendencies of the positive spirit: (1) the mind grows accustomed to submitting to facts and demonstrations; (2) it acquires the habit of always seeking orderly laws within phenomenal appearances; and (3) it develops the custom of considering that all phenomena are regulated by laws. For Comte, then, the study of science inculcates a belief in the rational order of the universe, a conviction that, when transferred to the social world, convinces its holders of the impossibility of sudden change and thus of the fruitlessness of coups d'état and social revolutions. Here again, Paul Bert made this argument quite explicitly in his speech to the lower house of Parliament in 1879, and in a way that reveals clearly the object of the tacit polemic contained in Comte's principles (8–9).

It might seem incongruous to invoke the name of Comte as the ideological savior of the Republic, since he developed his doctrine specifically in order to counter the "anarchy" of the revolutionary spirit he considered to be a dangerous "metaphysical" illusion, thought that parliamentary democracy was an expression of the "individualist and revolutionary" spirit, and had therefore gladly welcomed Louis-Napoleon's dictatorship (see Legrand 49–51). By the 1870s, however, most of his disciples had gone over, often reluctantly and with strong reservations, to the republican side (Eros 255; Legrand 49, 54). In the aftermath of the uprising of the Paris Commune and with the memory of the civil strife and class warfare of the short-lived First and Second republics fresh in everyone's mind, the leaders of the republican factions recognized that the Third Republic would be successful only to the extent that they could convince large segments of the population, and especially the new industrial bourgeoisie, that it was the regime best capable of establishing public order, for the virtue of positivist education, in addition to promoting progress, was precisely that it would assure national unity by inculcating the same ideas in everyone, thereby combating "mental" and "social anarchy" and guaranteeing "social order" (Legrand 47–48, quoting various authors from the two main positivist journals, *La Philosophie Positive*, edited by Littré, and the *Revue Occidentale*, run by Pierre Laffitte).

Comte with Kant: The Moral Is the Political

Positivism made a second claim to be the guarantee of social unity: It asserted the existence of a natural and hence universal "social sense" that acts as the primordial social bond counteracting selfishness and uniting mankind. In the latest version of his theory, Comte insisted that this social feeling is the true source of morality and should therefore be cultivated in children by parents, teachers, and civic leaders[6] (Comte, *Discours sur l'ensemble du positivisme* 166–67; cited in Legrand 37). It was this positivist notion of morality as a fundamental and autonomous human feeling that Jules Ferry adopted as his own in his speeches to the Freemasons in 1875 and 1876. In the first, Ferry repeated Comte's arguments: that the heart is more powerful than the intellect, that sympathy is as natural an affection as selfishness, that sentiments must be cultivated and developed, and that religion is a particularism, since, as opposed to the universality of true, i.e., positivist, morality, it teaches selfishness in the form of concern for one's individual salvation (Legrand 182). In the second, he proclaimed that morality is universally human and thus distinct from any metaphysical beliefs (245); it follows that the state has no need for any divine or transcendent source of moral and political legitimacy.

It was quite logical, then, that armed with this conception of the source, nature, and function of morality, Ferry should move its teaching to center stage when proposing his educational reforms for the primary schools to the legislature in the 1880s. The teaching of morality in the public schools became a political issue because it combined the endeavor to establish a new republican national unity with an attack on the Catholic Church's hitherto unchallenged monopoly on morality and moral training. While positivism had only lately become associated with the republican cause, Ferry could point to a predecessor, Condorcet, whose similar plan for school reforms during the Revolution authenticated the claim that Ferry's program was consistent with the "principles of 1789." Before the Chamber of Deputies on December 20, 1880, Ferry pointed out that, like the Positivists, Condorcet asserted that morality is based on natural sentiments and reason, attributes shared by all people regardless of their social class or religion (*Officiel de la République française* 130). "Forming men and citizens" rather than "dialecticians and preachers"—that was the aim of Condorcet's project and the rationale for his recommendation that the new schools he envisioned should teach the sciences in place of rhetoric and the classics (Salle Molière speech of 1870, in Legrand, *L'influence du positivisme* 225). The phrase "men and citizens" here (which explicitly includes women for both Condorcet and Ferry) indicates people whom society has raised above their natural condition of fatality and inequality. Education is thus a means toward the political end of establishing equality among people, and equality in turn can be instituted only by ensuring their liberation from natural constraints. To this end, social institutions should free society's members from "natural" differences due to birth as well as to physical constitution. Democratic education should nurture a sense of dignity in the members of all social classes and allow all members of an egalitarian society to share the same ideas and opportunities ("Discours" 218–22). Hence the call for teaching the sciences, for the latter include not only mathematics and the natural sciences, but also *les sciences morales,* whose first lessons reveal to the child that he belongs to the great family called the homeland (225). Teaching morality is thus the nexus in which fraternity, the construction of national unity through the cultivation of the "social sense," is knotted with equality, society's rectification of natural inequities, by means of liberty, from the constraints of birth and nature.

In Ferry's 'breviary,' Quinet had argued that while liberty is the fundamental political value of the modern state, political freedom cannot exist without freedom of thought (*la liberté d'examen*). Science, the result of this freedom and the intellectual basis of modern society, has its own certainty, which has no need of religion's seal of approval. Ferry reiterated this claim before the Senate on November 22, 1880, when defending the teaching of independent morality in the new secondary schools for girls (Robiquet 15). Reversing the Church's age-old claims to universalism, like Condorcet and Comte, Quinet strove to reduce Catholicism to the status of a particularism. Science "exists by itself, independent and free. It is the general, universal, absolute religion. Particular dogmas manifest the spirit of sectarianism" (*L'enseignement du peuple* 119). In a society composed of members of several religions, the tenets of any one of them will appear as a form of particularity when measured against the whole. The only way to guarantee the continued existence of such a society is to transmit its basic spirit from generation to generation through a laic education that eschews any "particular dogma" (120). As Ferry will do later, Quinet clinched his argument by citing Condorcet who, already in 1792, opposed morality to the "principles of any particular religion" and used this opposition to call for the separation of religious and secular national education (153).

In short, for these republicans the moral is the political. Independent morality is equated with universality, interpreted as (human) nature, science, society. And universality guarantees autonomy, understood as human independence from nature; as the independence of human nature from the rest of nature; as the independence of individual thought from external control; as the independence of the whole of society from the domination of any part of itself; as the independence of secular education from religious authority; as the independence of human society from transcendent origins, legitimation, or regulation. As Quinet put it when refuting the Church's demand in 1850 for "freedom of education," that is, the right to run their own schools at all levels and everywhere in the country: Freedom is not the solution, it's the problem; how can society establish and maintain liberty? (*L'enseignement du peuple* 139).

But if for some republicans the moral was the political when it came to education, for others the political was the moral. Instead of deriving a plan for moral education from what they held to be good for the collectivity, the republican nation, these thinkers took as their starting point the dignity of the individual, claiming that this fundamentally moral conception of humanity is, or should be, the basis of republican politics and hence of democratic education. In place of Condorcet and Comte, wittingly or unwittingly they hark back primarily to Immanuel Kant as their intellectual forefather.

The philosopher and educator Étienne Vacherot (former director of studies at the École Normale Supérieure) argues that democracy is the only true—that is, ideal—form of government, for it alone guarantees justice, the protection of the rights of its citizens. But we become aware of our rights only because of our consciousness of our duties, a realization made possible by the fact that, as human beings, we have reason and free will and are therefore persons in the strict sense (4). At bottom, then, it is freedom that constitutes the essence of being human and the basis of personhood, and it is freedom that democracy must protect. Now what distinguishes democracy from other forms of government? Self-government. Here the notion of autonomy reappears, as in the previously cited arguments, but with one great difference. For Vacherot as for his model, Kant, true autonomy does not simply mean that which comes from within, as opposed to submission to external forces. Real freedom requires legislating for oneself, giving oneself a law: in short, obeying one's reason, acting in accordance with the moral law (understood in the singular; see Kant 100–1). In the same way, democratic government requires a nation to give to itself and to obey its own laws. In order to guarantee liberty, it must also have equality in the form of universal suffrage, to ensure that each citizen does indeed participate in legislating, even if only indirectly.

The link between morals and politics is therefore asserted to be the concept and practice of self-government. But how can a nation rule itself if its members remain incapable of exercising their reason? Hence the need for universal education (Vacherot 5). And Vacherot quotes Proudhon's famous lapidary phrase with approval: "Démocracy is demopaedia" (in *Démocratie* 90). His acceptance of Proudhon is not limited to the sole need for education. Through Proudhon's concern for workers and peasants, Vacherot is able to extend the logic of Kant's notions of freedom and dignity to economic issues. The democracy he is proposing is not simply the idea of Enlightenment liberalism, for when you put liberty first, you can condemn the laissez-faire that leads to economic as well as social and political privileges and servitude (13). With Proudhon he insists that poverty is one of the most potent abridgments of liberty (14). Enlightened socialism acts on the basis of freedom, morality, human dignity (14). Body and soul, matter and spirit are tightly connected in humans. Therefore, in order to free the mind, you must first liberate the body. (During the Third Republic, Vacherot would retreat from this advanced social position.)

In the final years of the Empire, the cause of independent morality was spread by means of the journal of the same name. One member of Massol's editorial team, Clarisse Coignet, was to become an influential exponent of the new educational system established under the Third Republic. A convert to Protestantism, under the influence of Charles Fourier's brand of socialism since her youth, and a former member of the Conseil d'Administration of the Lemonnier schools for young women,[7] during the early days of the Republic she spoke out vehemently for laic education, asserting that Catholicism "is the most powerful expression of intellectual despotism the human mind has ever presented," while laic schools are the forerunners of a secular society, the new Republic, the rights of man, individual liberty, universal suffrage, and self-government. The choice is then clear, either Catholicism or modern society ("De l'enseignement laïque en France et en Angleterre" 928–31). The position Coignet states in this article is one she had worked out in detail in the book she wrote during her collaboration on Massol's journal, *La morale indépendante dans son principe et dans son objet* (1869). Like Massol, she makes liberty "the human fact par excellence," the foundation of right (*le droit*) and thus of both morality and politics (5). Interestingly, she explains that by making right depend on a personal experience accessible to everyone rather than a conception of universal reason or an external natural law, independent morality ensures respect for the human person, thus avoiding the "crimes and follies" that result from theories that make the ends the ultimate criterion of right as well as those that take the self-interest of the majority as their gauge (5). Without naming them directly, she takes her stand against utilitarianism, positivism, social Darwinism, and communism all at once. With acknowledgments to Aristotle, Kant, and philosophical "criticism," Coignet proceeds to remove natural science from the field of morality by claiming that nature is the domain of blind necessity and bloody struggle, while metaphysical (i.e., religious) notions of morals, like science, make people dependent on a higher external order. By thus eliminating individual autonomy and responsibility (41), both ultimately lead to despotism (55). In their place, she endorses the tenets of Kant's practical reason: the freedom in question is that of justice, a liberty that governs itself according to a law that it freely gives itself and then follows in action (6).

One of the early contributors to *La morale indépendante* was Charles Renouvier, the most renowned proponent of Kant's philosophy in France in the nineteenth century. Already famous in republican circles for his *Manuel républicain de l'homme et du citoyen* (1848), a kind of laic, but not antireligious, catechism in democracy composed for the schoolchildren of the Second Republic at the request of the minister of public education, Hippolyte Carnot (see Agulhon, "Introduction"), Renouvier exercised a decisive influence on the teaching of morality and civics in the educational system of the Third Republic through the dissemination of Kantian ideas in *La Critique Philosophique* (abbreviated as *RCP*), the journal he edited along with his collaborator, François Pillon.[8] The editors marked the occasion of the publication of the review's second volume with a resounding statement whose title sums up their mission: "Republican Doctrine: or What We Are, What We Want to Become" (2.1.1 [August 8, 1872]: 1–16). In it they asserted that the country was in dire need of a "republican philosophy" that would carry on its tradition of lofty principles and rigorous consequences, affirm the human need to believe in the rule of moral law in the universe, and start from a first principle that would lead directly to the doctrines of liberty and equality (1).

After criticizing just about everyone else in sight—the Catholics, the monarchists, the old bourgeoisie, the two Napoleons and their followers, the socialists, the Positivists, and above all the Jacobins—who allegedly betrayed the principles of freedom and equality they claimed to be defending by importing into the Revolution the principles of the Old Regime, imposing artificial unity, extreme centralization, and rule by force, in order to ensure the domination of the majority by an active minority—Renouvier and Pillon announce their first principle, drawn from Kant's *Critique of Practical Reason:* "the right of the person . . . the respect due the person," which comprises the foundation of the republican principles of liberty and equality ("Republican Doctrine" 5). Since the old habits and traditions of France have been largely uprooted, the country needs a new point around which to rally the nation, and that point should be a true ethics that can be taught in the schools and put into practice in political action (8).

Once the fundamental principle has been accepted of treating people as ends rather than means due to the presence of reason in every human being, everything else follows logically. Conscience and self-interest unite in opposing any universal rule based on selfish or vicious motives; the notion of justice, which requires reciprocity, equal exchange, and the correlation of rights with duties, derives directly from that premise, and freedom is the means necessary for reason to accomplish its moral duty. Hence we must postulate the existence of a real subject of this freedom, both moral agent and citizen. They acknowledge that this is a vicious circle, but, they argue, that is inevitable since first principles can never be proved (12).

For Renouvier, the Kantian scion of the old patrician bourgeoisie (Agulhon, "Introduction" 10–11), the law was the foundation of freedom and equality. This notion of the supremacy of the law, especially when used to oppose socialism along with Caesarism, made his policies appealing to the basically conservative, bourgeois Opportunist republic of the following decade. Yet, unlike the common run of what John Scott has called the "neo-Girondist" conservatives, Renouvier had learned from his contacts with the socialist writings and followers of Saint-Simon, Pierre Leroux, Proudhon, and above all Fourier, from whom he adopted the right to trade unions and producer cooperatives, a right forbidden by law until 1884 (John Scott 70). Unlike the majority of conservatives of the seventies, he attacked the bloody repression of the Communards and protested vigorously the patently unjust treatment of those who had survived the hecatomb of 1871 by the government and courts of the period ("La raison d'État en 1872"). Some twenty years later it would be this notion of the supremacy of the law that would rally many younger intellectuals to the cause of Dreyfus.

Renouvier's Kantian liberalism was able to produce real effects through its penetration of all levels of the republican educational system (John Scott 76–77). In fact, Kantianism dominated the philosophy departments of French higher education until well after the First World War. Its influence was felt equally in the secondary schools, whose last year included a special course on philosophy. Looking back on the decades since the founding of the Republic and citing the teachings of Renouvier and Jules Lachelier, the philosopher Alphonse Darlu asserted in 1895 that philosophy, specifically Kant's doctrine of practical reason, had become a social force in France (249).[9]

Kantianism was, if anything, even more influential in the primary schools than in the higher levels of the educational system. While the sponsors of the bills that created the new schools were mostly positivists, those Ferry appointed to formulate and carry out the directives mandated by the laws and the educational commissions they called into being were thinkers heavily indebted to Renouvier or to parallel radical Protestant theology equally under the sway of Kant's doctrines. Ferdinand Buisson, philosopher, director of primary education, and Ferry's most trusted adviser on educational matters (and eventual winner of the Nobel Peace Prize in 1927), Félix Pécaut, pastor, inspector-general of public education, and first director of the École Normale Supérieure at Fontenay-aux-Roses, and Jules Steeg, pastor, inspector general of the Université (i.e., of secondary schools),[10] director of the Pedagogical Museum, and second director of the newly established École Normale Supérieure for women primary schoolteachers and principals at Fontenay-aux-Roses. All three men had been involved in establishing a liberal Protestant Church in Neuchâtel at the end of the Empire (Acomb 55). Although they believed in a personal God, all rejected religious dogmas and, most important, believed in the existence of a universal and eternal independent morality shared by all peoples in all periods of history.[11]

To these educational leaders must be added Mme. Jules Favre (Julie Charlotte Velten), a Protestant from Wissembourg appointed first director of the newly founded École Normale Supérieure at Sèvres, designed to prepare principals and teachers for the new secondary schools for women (F. Mayeur 116). In this capacity she set the tone of the entire system for many years. Author of a study of the Stoic philosophers, she combined their morality with that of Protestantism in her philosophy of education: Teaching is not a mere profession but an apostolate whose mission is to contribute to the regeneration and moral emancipation of the members of the Republic. Mme. Favre strove to inculcate into her pupils the practice as well as the theory of self-rule, allowing them much more freedom of movement than was common in those days in schools for young women, and strongly encouraging them to exercise freedom of thought and independence of action. In the course she herself taught on law, while emphasizing the social advantages of voluntary obedience to the laws of the state, she put the cultivation of the spirit of justice above all utilitarian considerations. Thus she constantly looked at what she took to be the prejudices of her society with a critical eye. She approved of "free"—that is, purely civil—marriage; thought illegitimate children should have the same rights as others; and, in matters of conscience, taught that passively submitting to paternal authority undermined the freedom and dignity of our moral being (see Réval, *Les Sèvriennes*). Above all, as Françoise Mayeur points out, she demanded full equality for women, disavowing the officially accepted programmatic phrase of the times for women's education, "equality in difference" (121).

Beyond their disputes about the priority of rights or duties, of freedom or the moral law, and beyond their differences of focus, all the thinkers and educators we have discussed agreed that it is the notion of rational self-government that spans the gap between the individual and the state, between morality and politics (Coignet, *De l'éducation dans la démocratie* viii). The moral sovereignty of the individual becomes the model for the political sovereignty of the people in the republic.

As a result, the greatest challenge Ferry faced in defending his reforms in Parliament was to substantiate the assertion that universal morality does in fact exist. In the Senate session of July 2, 1881, trying to stave off an amendment that would have reinstated the teaching of religious (i.e., Catholic) morality in the girls' secondary schools, he proclaimed that Catholic, Protestant, evolutionist, positivist, utilitarian, and independent moralities are all the same: "True morality, grand morality, eternal morality is morality without qualification" (Robiquet 175). He continued: "It's the morality of duty, ours, yours, Gentlemen, Kant's morality, the morality of Christianity" (176). In his famous letter to the primary schoolteachers of the nation of November 17, 1883, he explained that duty, that is, the universally recognized set of maxims of applied morality, is what counts, a matter independent of the various theoretical bases of ethics (*Lettre aux instituteurs,* cited in Legrand 156).

The tight relationship between ethics and politics was not just a matter of principle for the Opportunists. In 1871, Gambetta had already accused the Congregationist schools of using moral education for political ends. It was consistent with this view that the bill on primary schools Ferry's government brought before Parliament in 1879–80 sought to remedy that situation by requiring not simply the teaching of "morals" but explicitly giving pride of place in the new curriculum to "moral and civic education" (Ferry, cited in Reclus 213). In justifying the new civics curriculum before the Chamber of Deputies in 1879, Bert stressed the rationale of inspiring national unity through the teaching of the nation's "reasons for existence and principles of life," what today we would call its culture (*L'instruction civique* 7).

Bert was also quick to add that this instruction is especially necessary since many schools nowadays—meaning the Congregationist schools, of course—teach just the opposite. Ferry himself was not so subtle when responding in the Chamber on December 20, 1880 to charges from the right that a "school without God would be a school against God." (Note that Bishop Dupanloup had already argued in his diatribe against Littré a decade before that positivism would undermine morality and social unity.) Claiming that the notion of laic schools implies only that they will be nonsectarian, he argued that the purpose of this measure was to ensure the security of the republican state. We must safeguard the primary school system from falling into the hands of the "prelates who have declared that the French Revolution is a deicide . . . [and] that the principles of '89 are the negation of original sin" (Robiquet 126).

Disparities between Opportunist Theory and Practice

In a country where changes of regime were as frequent as in France in the nineteenth century, in a republic that was barely ten years old in name and scarcely three years old in fact, the republican form of government was just as much a particularism as Catholicism was, in Ferry's words, "a particular dogma." If he and his fellow republicans insisted so heavily on the universality of their civic morality, it must have been in part because they knew that in reality the ethics and the politics they championed comprised just one of several possible systems competing for supremacy in France.

The inherent tension between the ostensible universality and actual particularity within republicanism existed on several levels in the ideology we have been examining and played itself out historically in many guises during the subsequent years of the century. Its most obvious manifestation, of course, was the clash between secular and Church institutions of learning. Much less visible but even more widespread and fateful was the virtual elimination of local peasant cultures in France, effected mostly in the years from 1880 to 1914 in an attempt to create and enforce the national unity so prominent in the pronouncements of thinkers, educators, and politicians alike (Weber 9). The Opportunists made no secret, either, about the fact that their universalism did not extend beyond human and civil rights to the domain of economics; hence the widespread perception that their policy was intended to placate the bourgeoisie by avoiding measures designed to alleviate the condition of the working classes.

The most glaring contradiction between theoretical universalism and practical particularism occurred in the differential distribution and significance of moral and civic instruction. During the Third Republic, the moral teaching aimed at reforming the conduct of children from their first days in school, the instruction that permeated every aspect of the curriculum and drew its examples from everyday life—in short, the lessons designed to create the new citizens of the Republic—were taught only in the primary schools and the new girls' secondary schools. In the traditional boys' secondary schools, independent morality entered the curriculum only as a theory in the philosophy class taken in the last year of study. Practical moral training was deemed unnecessary for these pupils because of the high cultural value the French attributed to the Greco-Latin humanities taught in the secondary schools, the study of which was assumed to be sufficient to immunize pupils against all baseness (Bouglé 11).[12] The reason for this difference is not far to seek. The primary schools, free of charge and located in every commune in the country, enrolled the children of the people, while the secondary schools catered almost exclusively to the sons of the bourgeoisie. For the children of the people, despite all the lofty talk about the autonomy of the moral person—or, in a sense, because of it—the thrust of the new moral and civic education was to teach them resignation to their lot in life and obedience to authority (Prost 10; Katan 436).

Children of the people were not the only category whose members were somehow less than universal. As is well known, women were subject to much more significant restrictions on their participation in the benefits of universal rights and moral sovereignty, since under the Third Republic they were once again deprived of the right to vote. In the narrower world of education their allegedly natural differences from men served as the rationale for their unequal treatment. In order to preserve the institution of marriage and secure the "unity of souls" of husband and wife, we must have enlightened women who will second their husbands' progressive beliefs rather than cause dissension in the family as is now the case due to the nefarious influence of the clergy on ignorant women. It is women who have the greatest educative influence on future citizens, in their role as mothers. In short, it was as wives and mothers, not as citizens in their own right, that educated women were needed to protect the Republic, primarily, as with the primary schools, by weakening the hold of the Church over them (Ferry, Salle Molière speech, in Legrand 235–37; Ferry, defense of Sée bill in Senate, December 10, 1880, in Robiquet 10–15; see also discussion in F. Mayeur 58–60).

While educators of all stripes agreed that moral habits of thought and action must be learned first through practice, and that the example set by the teacher is of primary importance, the main bone of contention among the schoolteachers (*instituteurs*) was the status of moral theory. At first the teaching was based purely on the intuitive sense of conscience. Already in 1883, however, Louis Liard, rector of the Academy of Normandy and about to be named director of higher education in the Ministry of Public Education, called for a rational demonstration of duty in his primary school textbook, *Morale et enseignement civique à l'usage des écoles primaires* (*Morals and Civic Education in the Primary Schools*), a proposal ratified in a directive issued to the school inspectors in October 1888. Jules Payot, whose *Avant d'entrer dans la vie: aux instituteurs et institutrices, conseils et directions pratiques* (*Before Starting out in Life: Advice and Practical Directions for Schoolteachers*; 1897) was the most popular teachers' manual until the First World War, insisted that morality is as evident a science as geometry, and, like the mathematical discipline, must be demonstrated logically to the pupils (15 n1). Unfortunately, the inspection reports since 1889 showed that both the teachers and the students were at a loss when it came to providing rational, Kantian proofs of the concepts of morals (16). The problem was that morals are a matter of practice, not theory; hence they require a pragmatic justification as is provided for in positivist sociology.

Here, in the distinction between the rational and the scientific, lies the crux of the disparity between the Kantian and the positivist views, at least as it was perceived by the vast majority of the thinkers of the period. In the simplified terms utilized in journalism, politics, and pedagogical polemics, science means starting from the observation of empirical reality in order to arrive at general laws through the process of induction. Rationalism means starting from a priori principles combined according to logical operations in order to arrive at an understanding of things at the level of phenomena. The one is concrete, the other abstract—and young children, it was argued, are not capable of grasping abstractions. Like scientists, they learn first through the use of their windows onto the world: their five senses. The first project of the educator should therefore be to enhance and train their capacities of observation, to teach them to "observe well" (Payot 16–17). Only later will they be able to move on, as the scientist does, from observation of particulars to seeing the relations among things by abstracting general conclusions from the similarities noticed in comparing multiple observations (17). Instead of lectures, teachers should provide concrete examples in the form of "object lessons" (*leçons de choses*).

Spiritualist Particularity versus
Republican Universality

It is evident that in crucial respects positivism and Kantianism are totally incompatible. And yet it is equally apparent that, beyond or in spite of their disparities, the two were somehow combined as the quasi-official doctrine of the Third Republic. In "Métaphysique et morale" (1893), the mission statement that led off the first number of the *Revue de Métaphysique et de Morale,* the spiritualist philosopher Félix Ravaisson, for many years the dominant force in the philosophy department of the Sorbonne, objected to the recent trend in philosophy to condemn metaphysics as a useless and impossible preoccupation, a trend he attributed to both Comte and Kant (6).

Ravaisson's manifesto was the spearhead of a more general counterattack usually known as the revival of French spiritualism, which would soon crystallize right-wing opposition to the "new Sorbonne." This new spiritualism, despite the noisy drumbeating of Ferdinand Brunetière with his visit to the Vatican ("Après une visite au Vatican," *RDD* [January 1, 1895]), was a far cry from the doctrines of Victor Cousin or Jules Simon, let alone official Church dogma of the period. As with positivism, there was a lag of several decades from the time of its development, in the 1870s and 1880s, to that of its emergence as a political ideology. One of the founders of the movement was Émile Boutroux, for two years the philosophy teacher at the rue d'Ulm of its most famous exponent, Henri Bergson,[13] and also a friend of the influential writer Paul Bourget (Mansuy 305, n154). Like that of Ravaisson, whom Bergson was to acknowledge as an important antecedent to his thought (Thibaudet, *Le bergsonisme* 39), the polemical thrust of Boutroux's doctrine was directed against both positivism and Kantianism. His point of attack, however, was not so much their common denial of the possibility of metaphysical knowledge as their shared emphasis on universality. As the title of his thesis—*De la contingence des lois de la nature (On the Contingency of the Laws of Nature*; 1874)—announces, he set out to break the ironclad concatenation of universal natural laws that rule the entire universe, according to the fundamental scientific premise of his times. Defining science as the attempt to eradicate the multiplicity of experience by reducing it to the one of generality—the type, the concept, the essence—and to eliminate the changeable—history—by reducing it to the immutable—natural laws—he argues that if those laws are not necessary in the philosophical sense of the term, then they must be dependent on something other than themselves. Spontaneity in the universe is not simply an illusion based on our ignorance of the conditions determining phenomena, but bears witness to the existence of causes outside the laws of nature.

In his demonstration, Boutroux does not challenge science per se; rather, he locates the element of contingency first in the relation between the laws that govern the various levels of natural phenomena. In other words, he claims it is impossible to deduce or derive in any causal or logical fashion the rules of chemistry from the laws of physics, those of biology from those of chemistry, and so on. He concludes that even in the natural world, "everything is thus radically contingent" (*De la contingence* 29), and when it comes to human beings, where history and individual experience play a much greater role, "acts entail essence, far from essence being able to explain acts. . . . Man is the author of his character and of his destiny" (Boutroux 145). Human behavior is not predictable, for it is not determined in advance by an essence or nature which would act as its cause. In short, as Sartre would reiterate in his own antideterministic arguments in "Existentialism Is a Humanism," existence precedes essence. The contingency of things is an external sign of this fundamental freedom, which ultimately derives from a purely voluntaristic God—that is, one who, in the last analysis, is not constrained by the laws of logic or rationality.[14]

While it might seem that this defense of freedom was entirely compatible with Kant's philosophy of practical reason, in fact Boutroux opposed the latter because, by relegating freedom to the realm of the "intelligible," the unknowable thing in itself, it leads either to a liberty unrelated to action and morality (the noumenal self outside the empirical world), or to a kind of determinism (of the person as phenomenon in the determined world). His doctrine, on the other hand, entails its real and active presence within the fabric of the known and knowable worlds (149). In this respect, Boutroux is indeed attacking the antimetaphysical bias of Kantianism. But the crux of his argument here, even more so than with regard to positivistic science, turns on the disregard for particulars, for those aspects of individual phenomena and experience that escape from the general categories and laws they deploy as the only knowable reality. At bottom, both modern science and Kantianism postulate a subject of knowledge and action devoid of any contingent subjective conditions that differentiate one rational being from another, as Kant put it, whereas for Boutroux God and people are 'personal,' in the sense of being distinct from one another and at least potentially free of any general rule.

It was Bergson's doctoral dissertation, *Essai sur les données immédiates de la conscience* (*Time and Free Will: An Essay on the Immediate Data of Consciousness*; 1889), that did most to reinvigorate French philosophical spiritualism. Like his predecessor, he responds to the claims of both positivism in its mechanist and associationist branches and Kantianism, with its assertion of a moral freedom in the world of the 'thing in itself' outside the domain of temporality, by developing his notion of duration, according to which contingency was tantamount to a freedom opposed not only to any determinism, but to any universal law in general. The core of his opposition to Kantianism, as to scientific predictability in the human realm, is his insistence on the inextricable link between freedom and singularity, what today we would call difference.[15] His basic argument is that human action can neither be predicted in advance nor subsumed under any general law, because to do so one would have to translate mental states into some language, and any language necessarily deals only with generalized abstractions: Words are like numbers or algebraic notation in that they can be applied to whole classes of objects, precisely because they ignore all the concrete, sensory, and historical aspects of things. But each mental state, like the moments of the history of a nation, is unique in its genre, and will never again be reproduced. The qualitative multiplicity of such moments represents "phases of our real, concrete duration, of heterogeneous duration, of living duration" (181).

The new spiritualists all agree, then, that at a very fundamental level, that of the abstract, rational subject of science and of moral action, positivism and Kantianism are one. As we shall see in more detail in chapter 3, however, this perceived unity did not preclude a political alliance of certain strains of spiritualism and positivism against parliamentary democracy and the Third Republic. Right-wing nationalism and racism had no trouble amalgamating the emphasis on uniqueness and contingency in Bergson with the similar stress on particularity present in positivism whenever the latter found it convenient to distinguish its own method of empirical observation from the abstract logic of rationalism. When applied to the human realm, as in Renan's early *L'avenir de la science* (*The Future of Science,* composed in 1848), this reliance on empirical data was translated into respect for the uniqueness of historical change and of bodily life (*Future* 264, English ed.). The goal of this brand of positivism becomes the appreciation of the ethnic differences produced by this spontaneity. In its reverence for life, for individuality, for the creative spontaneity of history, positivism thus took over, from the comparative study of national literatures and the philological study of languages, the leading themes of Romanticism, both German and French.

All that was needed for the emergence of the full-blown nationalist ideology of "the soil and the dead," and its even more sinister offspring, the fascist "blood and soil," was the admixture of the conservative anti-rationalist arguments of Edmund Burke, the German Romantics' reinterpretation of J. G. Herder, and the indigenous doctrines of Joseph de Maistre and Louis de Bonald, accomplished in Taine's multivolume *Origins of Contemporary France*. The crux of their arguments was that in its basic function—namely, voting—democracy treats people as pure abstractions, mere numbers divested of their individual histories, experiences, and feelings, and that this inhumanity is consistent with the Kantian assertion of abstract humanity at the expense of individual sentiments and interests—the "pathological" in Kant's language—and even with the worst excesses of the Reign of Terror in that there too the life of individuals was sacrificed to abstract principles.[16] It is this alleged contradiction between democracy and liberty that presided over the union of antirationalism and right-wing politics and made their proponents adopt Bergson's arguments about freedom and contingency.[17] Once he makes contingency the bastion of freedom insofar as each of us has a unique history that escapes any attempt at characterization through universals, once he describes freedom as acting solely in accord with one's self as given in duration—the synthesis of that past experience—rather than with any external law, then each region or nation can understand its freedom to consist in its respect for and adherence to its own past, its ancestors, its land, its communal experience, in opposition to and exclusion of everything and everyone it considers alien.

The Crisis of Authority:
France Is My Mother, the Republic My God

Opportunist ideology ignored many of the disparities between Kant and Comte because it was of course meant first of all to unite the largest number of people possible behind the new republic. But in order to do so, along with the concrete rewards it held out to its supporters, it had to convince them and potential converts of the legitimacy of its claim to authority, if only to assure them that it had indeed become the party most capable of ensuring national order and regeneration. The emphasis on independent morality, with its peculiar blend of freedom, autonomy, obedience, and conformity, was a versatile weapon in this battle, allowing the Opportunists to combat Catholicism while at the same time demonstrating their own adherence to a strict moralism that could assuage their compatriots' sense of guilt and allay their fears of renewed social rebellions.

Like most weapons, however, this one had its drawbacks. As reactionary critics had been complaining since the beginning of the Revolution, with the fall of the monarchy authority had become part of the problem of government, instead of its solution. Bonald had argued that power and law must precede society, since without them no society could ever be formed. Social order must be separate from human will, since it precedes human action (Bonald 95, 151–52). Burke had already proclaimed in 1790 that the existence of society often requires that people's individual as well as collective passions and wills be controlled and even thwarted, and "this can only be done *by a power out of themselves*" (151; emphasis in original). Joseph de Maistre's similar analysis of the insufficiency of authority in constitutional monarchies and republican governments, due to the lack of a "superior authority," clearly threatens the moral and political principles at the heart of Opportunist ideology also (2; see Gauchet 32–33). By making the source of morality immanent rather than transcendent, the liberals left it open to the charge that it was a partisan matter, to be determined in fact by a particular segment of the population in accordance with its own lights and interests.

It was in order to protect their principles from this kind of attack that the Opportunists insisted so heavily on the universality of their morality and on its foundation in a realm outside the fray of social, economic, and political contention, even if not removed to a domain beyond the world of human life. If the same moral principles had existed forever, in all places and among all human groups, then it could not be argued that they were the result of particular interests. Hence the recourse to the universality of human reason as the basis for republican ethics and politics among the Kantians. Alternatively, if morality was a sentiment engraved into human nature or a fact of social evolution, as the positivists contended at one time or another, then it was independent not only of religion but of any set of ideas or beliefs whatsoever, and therefore all the more universal, albeit in a slightly different sense of the term. In either case, whether based on the authority of reason or of fact, the control of morality was thus put out of reach of any individual group. In short, universality was supposed to assume the role, formerly filled by the transcendence of rule by divine right, of supplying a fixed point from which action could be judged according to an objective criterion independent of the play of contingent forces.

Now one of the major tenets of this universal morality was the assertion of individual freedom, the basic principle of republican politics, both as the freedom of thought that justifies the autonomy of the voter and as the foundation of sovereignty understood as self-rule. While this capacity was of valuable assistance in combating religious dogma and "metaphysics," it had the unfortunate potential of inciting criticism of the Republic's authorities, as well as of its social and political arrangements. It was for this reason that the moral education offered in the primary schools emphasized duty, that is, obedience, before broaching the question of freedom. The main remedy for this problem inscribed into the new curriculum was the coupling of moral training with civic education.

"Moral and civic education," in the consecrated formula of the educational reform laws, was to furnish the necessary compromise between individual freedom and social responsibility. On the simplest and most evident level, civic instruction was a matter of creating an informed electorate capable of exercising the vote in a mature way (to use Kant's term for the enlightened person). Thus Bert begins by contrasting republican Enlightenment with monarchical and dictatorial benightedness in explaining the rationale for civics education in his speech to the Chamber of Deputies on December 6, 1879 (*Instruction civique* 5–6). By this contrast, Bert intimates that Enlightenment is a process of struggle. In the list that follows of topics to be covered in civics classes, he openly invokes the Revolution as the historical and ideological matrix of that conflict, implicitly portrays the present Republic as its dutiful heir, and explicitly characterizes it as the worthy object of its children's respect and gratitude. Two years later, in his defense of this law before the Senate, Ferry would make the same connection between the Third Republic and the Revolution (see Chaitin, "'France Is My Mother'" 143–52).

There is a striking similarity between the emotions the Republic is supposed to arouse in its children and the obedience, gratitude, and respect toward their parents the primary school textbooks on morality aim to inculcate in their pupils. Bert and Ferry complete the parallel with sentiments of filial piety when they cap their rationale for civic instruction by adding love to the equation. The first lessons in Bert's civics textbook treat the virtues of the army and the duty of military service, explaining that the *patrie* is a great family, telling the children in direct address that it is "your mother."[18] The child, Bert argues in his speech to the Chamber, must know why he should love France so that he will give himself to it entirely, so that he will defend the homeland and the "principles whose triumph has made of him a free man and a citizen" (6). Strange as it may seem, the notion that you can induce people to love by teaching them why they should do so was also a commonplace in the lessons on children's attitudes toward their parents in the school ethics texts of the times (Renouvier, "Petit traité" 129).

The justification for the new civics lessons was thus structured by a series of metonymical and metaphorical substitutions: The Revolution becomes the name of the Third Republic (which, of course, came to power not through revolution but thanks to a military defeat followed by a series of proclamations and votes, and which confirmed its existence by crushing a revolution), and the Republic that of France (when the country was still divided fairly evenly between republicans and antirepublicans); at the same time, the Republic was equated with the beneficent parent to whom its citizens owed their very existence (as free men and citizens) as well as a host of other blessings that make life worth living, and to whom they owe in return gratitude, obedience, respect, and ultimately a love whose supreme proof is the willingness to sacrifice their very lives.

Moreover, according to Coignet, only members of free countries really have a homeland, because as citizens they exercise governing functions and make sacrifices for the nation ("Instruction secondaire des jeunes filles" 81). Here she clearly and unequivocally links republican citizenship and autonomous morality to the citizen's sense of identity. Like the family, the free state becomes the ideal object of both self-love and altruistic love, for, as with the family, the members of a democratic state both have it and are it at the same time. The homeland is not simply France, then, but the Republic, for in it alone personal identity and national identity can coalesce.

In order to ensure social cohesion and responsibility, the new civics instruction relied much more heavily on subjectifying the citizen's relation to the state through identification and the cultivation of love than on producing the uniformity of ideas recommended by the positivists. The idea of deriving feelings from universal moral principles, rather than the reverse, was consistent with Kant's doctrines and was also symptomatic of the more general Enlightenment belief in the power of reason to inform and reform not only people's conduct but their very being. The primary reason, however, why the idea of teaching people to love was unquestioningly presupposed by the authors of laws and textbooks, and so easily accepted by the public, was that it was a simple restatement of traditional religious teachings, particularly the catechism, with the reasons for loving the Republic and acknowledging its authority to be legitimate replacing of those for loving God and obeying His commandments.

In fact, as many scholars have pointed out, Third Republic education strove to make "the homeland [play] the role reserved for God in the Catholic schools" (M. Ozouf 114).[19] By the end of the century, the

schoolteachers of the Republic had become "lay monks," "lay mission-
aries of the truth," "apostles of progress," "priests of a religion of love"
who would "sow the good word in the tender souls of the children" so
that their "successors will see the harvest of the ideas of justice and fraternal solidarity germinate" (Laville 332–34; the last quotation is from
Payot's manual for schoolteachers). In her study of Zola's *Truth,* Béatrice Laville points out that the drive for secular education was painted
as a veritable religious crusade, in which Charles Péguy's famous *hus-
sards noirs de la république* (black Hussars of the Republic) were to lead
the holy war to replace the dying religious faith of the people with the
ideals of science and make the schools into the new Church of free
thought (334).[20]

Nor was it through the schools alone that the Republic strove to
make patriotism into a second religion for the masses. Jean-Marie Mayeur, summarizing the conclusions of several important scholarly works,
reminds us of the concerted efforts of the regime to orchestrate a series
of representations of the Republic through the construction of sculptural
monuments; the elevation of various figures to the status of national
heroes; and above all the public festivals, celebrations, and events of the
1880s, which he calls "the rites of a veritable republican liturgy" (83).
In 1880, the year July 14 was made into the French national holiday,
the Municipal Council of Paris declared that schoolchildren should participate in the official ceremonies in order to rid them of the "practices
of superstition." Like the First Republic, the Third wanted to combat
the "old dogmas" by creating a civic religion, and while the Goddess of
Reason was not revived, the figure of Marianne gave the Republic a face
and a body to worship in place of the Virgin (84; see Agulhon, *Marianne au pouvoir*). In those early years, the July 14 celebrations aroused
special fervor in the popular sections of Paris and the other big cities,
where they took on the flavor of "political liturgies" (J.-M. Mayeur
84).

As this last example shows, it was not the *patrie* as such, but the
Republic, that took over the role of God. Perhaps it would be more
accurate to say that the modern idea of the homeland as object of love
and veneration was the invention of the Republic. By putting this new
version of the homeland into the place of a deity, the Republic strove to
construct an "imagined community" characteristic of modern nations
(see Anderson, *Imagined Communities*), not so much to replace real
human communities destroyed by modernization (although that would
become the case more and more as the century came to a close), but to
supplant the communities that still existed at the time.[21] The community

of republican patriotism was not only 'imagined' in Anderson's sense of a group created by the discourse of the nation spread primarily in the unified languages made possible by the print media; it was above all 'imaginary' in Lacan's meaning of the term, designed to make the individual dependent for his identity, his very being, on the Republic, conceived as a transcendent Other that guarantees that identity in return for sacrificial devotion. By producing the impression that the new regime stood outside the flux of time and thus above partisan divisiveness and earthly incompetence and corruption, it meant to prove itself worthy of the subjective allegiance, identification, and love of all its inhabitants. The transcendence promoted in the civics curriculum thus was to complement the universalism of the moral education in establishing a firm foundation for the authority of the still extremely fragile Republic.

The Conflict of Identities

The new patriotism, then, was an attempt by a particular regime to identify itself with the universal existence of the nation, of an individual class to represent the interests of the nation as a whole, of a specific set of principles to express the will of the entire people. In order to accomplish this feat, it had to convince all its citizens that its interests were their interests, that its heroes were their heroes, that its culture was their culture, that its principles were their principles: in short, that they were it and it was they, and yet at the same time that it was worthy of assuming the parental role, while they should be happy to devote their filial piety and loyalty to it. The fundamental contradiction between the universal and the particular inscribed in this program, which was considered necessary for the very survival of the Republic yet flew in the face of a host of facts, inevitably led to a multileveled civil war of identifications.

The greatest blessing of the republic was supposed to be freedom, autonomy, self-rule. Yet just as the Republic put itself in the position of God in its civics courses, so its educators adhered to the same authoritarian notions and methods as the Congregationists. With Kant's assertion of the basically evil character of human nature and Comte's equally strong distrust of the selfishness of the individual, it is not the least bit surprising that the republican schools should have adopted this attitude toward children's education, nor that Durkheim should proclaim that education is a "work of authority" almost on a par with hypnotic suggestion (*Éducation et sociologie* 85–87). Although there were a few voices raised for the principles of Jean-Jacques Rousseau and his successors such as Johann Heinrich Pestalozzi and Friedrich Froebel, as Prost explains persuasively, the child's spontaneity was generally seen as a danger rather than a promise, a source of potential insubordination that must be curbed by strong discipline (9). Independence of mind was a fine ideal for adults, but the goal of children's education was to indoctrinate them with the proper convictions. Hence the use, in more than one textbook (e.g., Renouvier's *Manuel;* Bert's *Instruction civique*), of the same method of questions and answers as in the catechism. The strongest advocates of free thought did not allow children to doubt the word of the teacher. As Renouvier puts it in his "Petit traité," children will be raised to the status of adults, that is, of moral persons worthy of respect and capable of self-government, only when they have learned obedience to duty (*RCP* 4.49 [January 6, 1876]: 367). He has no trouble reconciling this conception with his liberal principles since, according to him, the authoritarian teacher in fact merely "lends his voice" to reason and conscience (367).

The contrast between an ideology of sovereignty and the reality of impotent obedience was not restricted to children and the schools. As the century wore on, it became most blatant in the case of the growing urban proletariat, aware of their powerlessness in the face of an anonymous and impersonal state. It was this impression that Zola succeeded in capturing so forcefully in *Germinal* and other novels of the eighties. But his portrayal of the effects of industrial and commercial capitalism omitted one aspect of the situation that exacerbated its action a hundredfold: namely, the sense of real powerlessness was compounded by the promise, new with the Republic and specific to it, of partial control over government through participation in the electoral process.

On the theoretical level, the problem was that the war of identifications took place within the ideology of the Republic itself. The conflict between the universal and the particular emerged in the two incompatible foundations the Republic was trying to use to establish its legitimacy: the abstract, impersonal, universal subject of modern science and autonomous morality and the image of itself as a parental deity modeled after the age-old notion of the God of Christianity. The flaw in this imitation was that the Republic could not portray itself as a personal god without betraying the most fundamental principles of democracy as they were understood in France at the time. The series of authorities going from parents to teachers to the state left no room for a monarch, dictator, or even a president possessed of real executive powers who could serve as the concrete representative of the state. But is it possible to identify with an immaterial principle rather than with a tangible fig-ure? Can the abstract moral agent stripped of all contingent properties and obedient to reason alone insofar as he acts morally or politically in a democracy at the same time remain the human individual endowed with feelings of pity and gratitude, respect and loyalty?

The most ingenious, even if most evident, attempt to reconcile these opposites was the inscription of the Revolution at the heart of the myth of the Third Republic. The obvious purpose of this maneuver was to provide the fledgling republic with distinguished predecessors, identi-fying it as the continuation of the historical mission of France. More significant, however, was the endeavor, in imitation of Christianity once again, to redefine history in general in terms of the Revolution. Like the advent of Jesus, it was conceived as an occurrence both within history and outside it, a meeting point between the universal and the particular, the event in which the eternal and universal principles of reason and justice interrupted the flow of history by manifesting themselves in a set of human actors in a specific time and place.

The crisis of authority gave rise to a similar contradiction in the efforts of the Republic to manipulate the identity of its citizens, styl-ing itself a transcendent Other that can guarantee the existence of its members in order to gain legitimacy and obedience while indoctrinating them at the same time with the conviction that the democratic State is a manifestation of themselves as autonomous, self-governing beings: in short, that they are the State. As a result, the educational project of the Republic provoked a predicament of representation similar to the one which occurred simultaneously in the realm of literature, and for much the same reasons. In this dual crisis of representation and identity, the opposing parties enlisted fiction in their polemical campaigns.

CHAPTER 2

The Disciple,
by Paul Bourget

❦

A Dangerous Experiment in Education

Nation and Mutilation

In 1886, the struggle between Catholic and republican education became the subject of *La morte* (*The Deceased*), a novel by the society writer Octave Feuillet that sparked an outburst of controversy by the country's most notable critics—among them Jules Lemaître and Paul Bourget in France, Walter Pater in England—who attacked or defended it on aesthetic, philosophical, and political grounds, often using the one as a guise for the others. Sabine, a freethinker raised and trained in the ways of positivism by her uncle, Dr. Tallevaut, murders Aliette de Courteheuse, the good Catholic daughter of a provincial nobleman who traces his ancestry back to the time of William the Conqueror, in order to have for herself Aliette's husband, the equally aristocratic but considerably less Catholic Bernard de Montauret, Marquis de Vaudricourt, a modern fellow who is delighted to have freed himself in his youth from his religious "superstitions" and his belief in God. The success of Sabine's project does not end the story, however, for, as Bourget points out in his review, the main subject of the book is the conflict of religious beliefs between marital partners. Sabine's plan succeeds, but her marriage to Bernard soon goes sour, as he comes to realize the profound incompatibility between his conception of life and marriage and that of his liberated spouse. Upon discovering the truth about his first wife's murder and learning that the latter said nothing because she thought he was in on the plot, Bernard is overcome with guilt, and on his deathbed he converts back to the faith of his youth. Thus Feuillet can conclude his opus with a triumphant, albeit melodramatic flourish: "He wanted to die in Aliette's religion. Alive the poor child had been vanquished: dead she triumphed" (305–6; all quotes from *La Morte* are my translations from the French).

Present-day historians of literature generally dismiss Feuillet in an icy phrase or two as the epitome of the bourgeois writer, if they deign to mention him at all. In this disdain they are only following the lead of the most respected novelists of the times—Flaubert, Zola, and the Goncourts. Yet Feuillet was highly respected (see Hauser, 4: 58–59); indeed he was the first novelist ever elected to the Académie Française (in 1863). While his style is a pale imitation of Mme. de Lafayette and his characters stereotypes, Feuillet does abandon, to an admittedly limited extent, the Manichaeism that plagues so many thesis novels, by attributing only the most noble motives and actions to the archpositivist Dr. Tallevaut. He can allow himself this show of magnanimity toward his ideological opponents, because he then blackens them by painting the sorcerer's apprentice as evil incarnate.

The choice of a woman to commit the crime, although it was not without precedent in nineteenth-century literature and would soon become a commonplace of decadent fiction, was something of a novelty in 1886. Feuillet found the connection between the two themes of the dangers of positivism and the education of women in an essay on the great positivist Littré by his longtime friend and admirer, the spiritualist philosopher Elme Caro (see Caro's flattering portrait of the writer in *Poètes et romanciers*). In *M. Littré et le positivisme* (1883), Caro dwells on the positivist's lengthy training and practice as a medical student (although he never completed the degree), the many articles he wrote and treatises he translated on medical topics, the free medical treatment he provided for the peasants living in the country village where his summer home was located, and his modesty in speaking about this service. Littré's relationship with his daughter was a mirror image of Tallevaut's with Sabine. As Tallevaut raised his niece, Littré himself raised his daughter, and she became his faithful helper when she grew up. But, out of a spirit of tolerance and respect for his wife's piety, he gave the girl a Catholic upbringing despite his own atheist convictions, and even abandoned his plan to have her choose between his beliefs and her mother's when she was old enough to understand such a choice, for fear of causing his wife pain (Caro, *M. Littré* 24–25, quoting an unnamed essay by Sainte-Beuve). Seen in the light of Littré's actions,

La morte appears as a kind of mental 'experiment,' as Bourget called it in his review, designed to show what would have happened if the positivist had raised his daughter according to the tenets of his own philosophical and antireligious persuasion.

For Caro's study is marked by a peculiar ambivalence. He describes Littré the man as a paragon of personal virtue, yet as laudatory as Caro is of Littré's character, that is how harsh he is in his judgment of the implications of his philosophy. The philosopher's overarching thesis is that positivism is in reality the negation of everything that is not a perceptible phenomenon or a law derived from the latter: namely, the rejection of theology and metaphysics. The impetus for his book, with its hundred or more pages of detailed analysis and point-by-point refutation, is his fear that, under the Opportunist Republic, positivism "is in the process of becoming through its negations the official philosophy in France" (Caro, *M. Littré* 197). The main political and social problem of his times, the struggle between the secular State and theological beliefs (167), is therefore the question of the proper foundation for the education of humanity: "Is positive science up to the task of being the only teacher of humanity, the arbiter of its ideas and its mores?" (201). His answer, of course, is no. Morality in the West has ever depended on the ideas of a personal God, the immortality of the soul, and absolute duty, independent of human conventions, races, and climates, whereas positivism assumes that happiness depends solely on this present life and that no being, power, or law transcends the forces of this world. Caro's first conclusion is that the positivist idea of evolutionary progress is simply a form of "universal fatalism," which relieves both individual and collective moral responsibility (131–32). He follows this up with a statement of the typical Catholic (and also Kantian) reproach to the positivist's creed of accepting the laws of nature: Nature is the reign of brute force and selfishness, whereas, as Caro puts it in a phrase Huysmans will remember the following year, "guided by admirable instincts, humanity works against the grain [*au rebours*] of nature" (188).

More interesting for our purposes, because more specific, more inventive, and closer to the experiential form of novelistic representation adopted by Feuillet, is his argument about the relation between morality and happiness. For the positivist, the only force to pit against individual happiness is the general happiness. But why should he sacrifice his present happiness for so distant and impersonal a goal as the future well-being of the human race, an "abstract being" that has no separate existence, consciousness, or personal sensation? 'Sympathy' is the positivist's response (Caro, *M. Littré* 242). In everyday life, however, sympathy and disinterestedness, although real phenomena, are generally incapable of overcoming self-interest. Moreover, this grandiose general happiness resembles nothing so much as the sum of individual happinesses—but if that's the case, why should I sacrifice mine to it? The response is that it is also the guarantee of individual happiness, of social order. Perhaps—but maybe I don't think the goal is worth the renunciation. How can anyone prove empirically that my idea of my own happiness is mistaken (250–51)?

Feuillet had simply to distribute the two aspects of Caro's analysis among the two positivist characters of his novel in order to represent his indictment of republican educational policy. Dr. Tallevaut received all of Littré's positive character traits (with an admixture of some features from other renowned positivists such as Taine, Renan, and Comte himself), while Feuillet transformed Caro's abstract critique of positivism into the personal characteristics and base actions of the young woman the doctor raised, "to serve by turns as his office secretary and his laboratory assistant" (*La morte* 157). Tallevaut inherits Littré's concern for his family in the person of Sabine: his high moral standards, his charity toward the peasants, his selfless devotion to science. Feuillet even endows him with an attribute Caro refused to positivism, if not to Littré himself: a religious belief in the promise of science for "the moral and religious future of humanity" similar to the "religion of humanity" and progress Littré wanted to substitute for traditional 'theological' religions (208). Without such an "ideal belief," man would seek only "base and facile pleasures; thus he [would] descend, little by little, under his civilized patina, to the moral level of the negro [and then] still lower" (211). Despite all Tallevaut's admirable qualities, the aristocrats in the country to which he has retired think poorly of him and his ward (156). The physics and chemistry experiments he carries out in his laboratory add to the aura of mystery and evil that hovers over him, inducing Aliette to call his residence "the alchemist's house" (157).

Feuillet's novel was but a minor blip on the radar screen of the antinaturalist reaction, whose gaudiest splashes were Ferdinand Brunetière's *Le roman naturaliste* (1883), Eugène-Melchior de Vogüé's *Roman russe* (1886), Théodore de Wyzewa's *Nos maîtres* (1887) and the assault on Zola's *La terre* (*Earth*) titled "Le manifeste des cinq" (The Manifesto of the Five) (August 18, 1887, *Le Figaro*). Yet *La morte* did have a far-reaching although indirect effect on the world of letters through the role it played in inspiring Bourget's novel *Le Disciple* (*The Disciple;* 1889), a resounding success and a powerful influence on the younger generation.

Like Feuillet, Bourget had been impressed by Caro's book on Littré (which he reviewed in *Le Parlement*) and had accepted his thesis that positivism leads to despair (Mansuy 263), but, unlike his predecessor, Bourget had long been an ardent advocate of positivism and had a sophisticated understanding of its philosophy, psychology, and ethics that he used to advantage in portraying the character and career of his counterpart to Tallevaut, the philosopher Adrien Sixte.

The story and the moral lessons of *The Disciple* are extremely close to those of Feuillet. The protagonist, Robert Greslou, is a "villainous disciple" (to use Bourget's own characterization of Sabine) whose actions lead to the suicide of his innocent mistress of a single night, even if he is not legally guilty of a crime. Greslou's confession, which makes up almost two-thirds of the text, is, so to speak, an enormous expansion of the confrontation scene between teacher and pupil in *La morte*, in which the young man strives, like his model, to throw all the blame for his misdeeds onto his teacher by demonstrating that they were the direct result of the positivist doctrine that forms the nucleus of the mentor's identity. As with the commission of the crime, here too Bourget mitigates both the pupil's allegations and their impact on the educator: Greslou looks to his confession for absolution from guilt, where Sabine took a vicious pleasure in turning her tutor's own philosophy against him; Sixte's self-assurance is shattered, but he is left to contemplate his future, while Tallevaut pays with his life. In both cases, however, teacher and doctrine are made to bear a heavy load of responsibility: that is, both novels constitute indictments of the ideological justification of republican educational policies. In sum, the resemblances between the two are so striking, and the differences are so clearly adumbrated in Bourget's review of the earlier work, there can be little doubt that the master's text served as an essential intertext for the disciple's novel.

Bourget's admiration for Feuillet and the spiritualist lesson of *La morte*, made evident in his defense of it as a legitimate 'novel of ideas' rather than a 'thesis novel,' only underlined his dissatisfaction with the weak connection the author constructed between the story and its message. Both Bourget and Lemaître protest in their reviews that Feuillet has not convinced them of the necessary link between Sabine's positivist upbringing and her crimes, and they wonder whether another type of education might not have produced similar results (Bourget, "Réflexions sur Octave Feuillet" 118; Lemaître, review of *La morte*). Bourget goes so far as to claim that a novelist with the opposite ideology could easily have written a similar novel in which the Catholic girl is a materialist and a criminal, the freethinker pure and devoted ("Réflexions"

120). No doubt disturbed by his own imaginings, he pinpoints what he takes to be the reason for Feuillet's artistic failings and suggests a remedy for them. The problem, as Bourget sees it, is that the author has departed from the method of careful psychological analysis he had used so successfully in earlier novels such as *M. de Camors* to provide convincing evidence of the general principle he wanted to illustrate, if not demonstrate, through his story. In short, there should be an undeniable relation between the principles Feuillet is defending and their alleged consequences, and the author should have supplied a whole series of 'small human details' to make the development of her thought seem inevitable (120).

In *The Disciple* Bourget strives to do just that, in the form of the lengthy confession Greslou writes while in prison awaiting his trial. In order to prove his theorem, or hypothesis, as he prefers to call it, the writer must give the reader a view of the internal development of the disciple's ideas and feelings sufficient to show the effects of the character's education on his desires, beliefs, and behavior. The factor lacking in the Feuillet novel that Bourget is most exercised to furnish is the relation between education and the formation of identity.

In *La morte,* that relation is simplistic: Despite Feuillet's professed belief in freedom of the will, he represents education as a mechanical process of imprinting, in which identity is automatically stamped onto the person once and for all. In contrast to Feuillet's emphasis on the end results of his characters' upbringing, Bourget focuses on the dynamic processes that shape his characters' personalities and give rise to their actions. The lives of his main characters are changed by their youthful educational experiences, both reflect on the nature and practice of education, and both are themselves educators by profession—Sixte, the scholar who acts as (anti)spiritual guide to Greslou, then, by extension, to the youth of France; and the disciple himself, who is as much a teacher as a pupil, for he not only becomes the tutor of the young Lucien de Jussat, but also undertakes the sentimental education of his eventual victim, Charlotte. Where Feuillet treats his characters' identities like inanimate objects, Bourget narrates the many 'small human details' that constitute their family life, their upbringing, and both their formal and informal educations, and he structures his entire text around the moments of crisis in their lives in which their identities are thrown into jeopardy.

In good Balzacian fashion, then, the text alternates between detailed accounts of the characters' past histories and dramatic scenes in which radical transformations in their lives become the pretexts for soul-searching self-analyses. The story opens with the disruption of Sixte's rigid daily routine, a disturbance that provokes a stupor in the shopkeepers of the Latin Quarter similar to the sense of an impending upheaval in the civilized world produced in the inhabitants of Koenigsberg when Kant changed the path of his daily walk upon hearing news of the outbreak of the French Revolution. The obvious disproportion between Kant's concern for the world-historic event of the Revolution and Sixte's fear for his own well-being when called before the magistrate investigating the death of Charlotte de Jussat, combined with the description of the fanatical regularity of Sixte's comings and goings, his inability to deal with the realities of everyday life, and his withdrawal from normal human relationships, creates a mock-epic tone that continues the satirical tradition of the unworldly professor seen in the writings of Alphonse Karr, Champfleury, or Vallès. But just as Sixte's life is interrupted by the series of events that triggered Charlotte de Jussat's suicide, so the ironic style gives way to the serious tone of drama, if not of tragedy. The visit of Greslou's mother, Sixte's reading of the young man's "Memoir," and the ensuing trial all force the philosopher to call into question, in a way Tallevaut never does, the validity of the credo around which he has built his entire life. In similar fashion, Greslou introduces his "monograph on the present state of [his] self" by explaining that "the crisis from which [he] suffer[s]" is a kind of geometric resultant of a series of vectors: his parental heredity, his childhood environment, and his stint as tutor in the unaccustomed aristocratic milieu of the Jussat household (93),[1] which brought him into contact with his antithesis, Count André, the military officer who is the older brother of his pupil, and with their sister, Charlotte, the young woman he sets out to seduce. This transplantation, as he calls it, throws him into a turmoil that stretches the fibers of his being in ways his early life never had.

As we know, Bourget had already meditated on the themes of education and identity in his *Essais,* particularly in relation to the power of literature. Commenting on the author's childhood enthusiasm for reading fiction, Michel Mansuy remarks that he was destined to become one of Vallès's victims of the book (Mansuy, *Un moderne* 14). However that may be, there is no doubt that Bourget had read Vallès's famous article, since he refers to *Les réfractaires*, in which it was republished, in a footnote to his essay on the Goncourts. It is therefore quite likely that Bourget's theory of literature as a potent rival of formal education in shaping the self derived as much from Vallès's piece as from the writer's personal experience. Likewise, his emphasis on these themes in his novel seems to be modeled in part after the first two books of the Vingtras trilogy, for which he expressed his admiration in reviews appearing in the journal *Parlement* (Mansuy 262, 265) and again in the essay on the Goncourt brothers, where he praises *L'enfant* (*The Child*) and *Le bachelier* (*The High School Graduate*) for their accurate description of student mentality during the Second Empire. In *The Disciple* itself, he has Greslou recall Vingtras along with Julien Sorel (the hero of Stendhal's *The Red and the Black* [1830]) and Lucien de Rubempré (protagonist of Balzac's trilogy *Lost Illusions* [1835–1843]), when he is about to present himself for the first time in the Jussat household.

In fact, Bourget had held Vallès in high esteem since their first meeting during the Commune, with which the future monarchist strongly sympathized as an eighteen-year-old student at the Collège Sainte-Barbe (Mansuy 114–15, 265 n23). The most fateful encounter between the two writers, however—one that had profoundly troubling effects on both the men and their fiction—may never have taken place in reality but only in the repercussions in the real world of their theories of the power of literature to shape identity. In the original 1862 version of Vallès's article "Victimes du Livre," the author states: "Every murderer in a frock coat, every suicide in a worker's smock, victim of the Book"; and he declares that women who killed their husbands or children were inspired by reading novels (Bellet 190). But when, in 1866, the defense lawyer of two men who had murdered an old lady not only made the same argument but cited this very article in support, Vallès was aghast at the power being attributed to his own literary construct—the theory of the causative force of the literary. Unwilling to shoulder the burden of responsibility for the crimes, in an article published in *L'Événement* on February 26, 1866, he jeered at the claim that their act had been inspired by their reading of a serial novel, and he decided to omit the offending passage from the *Réfractaires* version (Bellet 191). Bellet gives evidence that although Vallès never formally repudiated his theory, the question of the relation between reading and crime always continued to haunt him (190, 191).

Did Bourget know the earlier version of Vallès's article? Had he read the subsequent retraction in *L'Événement*? It is impossible to answer these questions without having access to Bourget's private papers. What is certain, however, is that a decade later something very similar happened to Bourget, but in this instance the writer was much more deeply implicated than Vallès had been. On January 25, 1888, a twenty-two-year-old law student named Henri Chambige was found unconscious in a villa near Constantine, Algeria, with two bullet holes in his cheek. His mistress, Mme. Grille, a thirty-year-old married woman from a rich and well-connected Protestant family, lay nearby with several gunshot wounds to the temple. He survived, but she did not. At his interrogation, he declared that having decided to end their lives together, he had shot her and then himself. While in prison awaiting trial on charges of murder, Chambige wrote a long confession recounting his past and indulging in minute self-analysis. In the fall of 1888, when the case came to trial, the proceedings were widely reported in the Parisian press. A multitude of commentaries about the sensational case appeared, starting with the reflections of André Bataille, the legal reporter for *Le Figaro* and a colleague of Bourget's, on the court sessions and the wider implications of the affair in that paper's editions of November 2 and 8. As it became known that Chambige had had literary ambitions and that he was an amateur of contemporary philosophy and psychology, conservative and Opportunist republican journalists had a field day with the affair, laying the responsibility for the tragedy directly at the doorstep of "decadent" literature in general, and Bourget in particular. On November 7 and 8, a journalist named Paul Bluysen penned a two-part article in *La République Française* titled "Un drame décadent" (A Decadent Drama), in which he explained that the events were decadent because the killer had committed "a literary crime . . . in his capacity as a disciple of Schopenhauer, Herbert Spencer, Stendhal and a few contemporary past masters in analyses of cruel enigmas whose names you can guess." In case the allusion to Bourget's most famous novel at the time was not clear enough, later in the article Bluysen mentions the author by name and speaks of André Cornélis (the eponymous protagonist of a lesser-known work by Bourget) and Fyodor Dostoyevsky's Raskolnikov as possible inspirations for the crime.

This was only the first of a veritable explosion of articles about the literary dimension of the affair. Maître Trarieux, the public prosecutor in the Chambige case, attacked the creators of Werther, Julien Sorel, and especially Raskolnikov in his speech for the prosecution as well as in his article "L'Affaire Chambige" (The Chambige Case), in the *Gazette des Tribunaux* of November 9, 1888: A few lofty spirits armed with especially robust willpower may be capable of entertaining "certain" philosophical doctrines (i.e., atheism), but for the great mass of weak mortals, such ideas are noxious. Two young writers soon destined to become heavy hitters weighed in on opposite sides of the controversy a few days later. No doubt feeling himself under attack due to the obvious similarities between Chambige's explanation of his actions and the tenets of Philippe, the hero of his recently published *Sous l'oeil des barbares* (*Under the Barbarians' Eyes*), Barrès showed considerable sympathy for the young man's attitudes and actions, such as his disdain for the ordinary laws of life, his 'experimentation' with the outside world—beautiful scenery, science, women—the cultivation of his inner emotions, and his easy acceptance of death (see Carassus 116). Barrès was willing to concede that the heightened sensibility that led to the crime was indeed inspired by high literature, but, he claimed, Chambige had ignored the remedy his masters taught in those same works—the power of "splitting oneself in two," of distancing oneself from one's feelings. Like scientists working with dangerous substances, sensitivity makers should not let their experiments loose in the world ("La sensibilité d'Henri Chambige" [Henri Chambige's Sensitivity]).

The same day, Anatole France took up the conservative cudgels in his piece for *Le Temps,* "Un crime littéraire—l'affaire Chambige," arguing that Chambige was especially despicable for trying to glorify his crime by draping it in the aura of literature. "Wretched, wretched, wretched man," he exclaimed, "the Muses are always innocent." *La République Française* returned to the charge with an anonymous article the following day, "Le crime littéraire" (The Literary Crime; November 12), attributing responsibility for the crime to the "nihilism" of contemporary decadent literature. The republican newspaper followed up this attack on November 13 with a response to Barrès from an influential Opportunist deputy, Dionys Ordinaire, who heartily mocks 'psychology' and wonders rhetorically whether in future the words 'vice' and 'virtue' will have lost their meaning. (One wonders whether he had read the introduction to Taine's *History of English Literature* or Zola's preface to *Thérèse Raquin*.) The legislator launches a direct attack on Barrès and the 'literary school' he represents for encouraging the young to wrap themselves in their self, to make it a 'citadel' of individual enjoyment and selfish pleasures. For Ordinaire the Gambettist, as for the other republican writers, Chambige was merely another victim; the ultimate responsibility for the crime rested with the literary school of Bourget and Barrès. If ever there was a "victim of the Book" in the eyes of the public of 1888, Chambige was it.

In making this argument, Ordinaire was simply continuing a debate about the evils of pessimism and decadence that he and Francisque Sarcey, the most noted theater critic of the times and a staunch supporter of the Opportunist line, had engaged against Bourget and company in 1885, when the novelist vaulted to the forefront of the European literary scene with the enormous success of *Cruelle énigme*. Citing the growing popularity of Schopenhauer and Eduard von Hartmann in French intellectual circles, the publication of Henri Amiel's *Journal* (*Diary*) and Joris-Karl Huysmans's *A rebours* (*Against the Grain*) in 1884, and that of Guy de Maupassant's *Bel Ami,* Édouard Rod's *La course à la mort* (*Race to the Death*) and *Cruelle énigme* in 1885, both had warned that the spread of pessimism was corrupting the youth of France, both had accused Bourget of leading the decadent pack with his *Essais* and his latest novel, and both had asserted that there was in fact nothing to worry about now that the Third Republic had brought democracy and prosperity to the land (Mansuy 401–3)! The political background of this controversy was the growing disarray of the republic, suffering from a series of economic crises and, with the fall of Ferry's ministry in 1885, the appearance of such great governmental instability that many Opportunists shared the sentiments of Paul Cambon, a close friend of Ferry, who wrote that year to his wife that he feared the Republic had less than a year to live (letter quoted in J.-M. Mayeur, *Vie politique* 120). It was this atmosphere that gave rise that same year to the phenomenon of Boulangism. The worst fears of the republicans seemed on the verge of being materialized in 1888, when General Boulanger, the minister of war whose political movement threatened to topple the Third Republic, won election after election throughout the country. This, then, was a political as much as a literary battle, whose subtext was the ongoing dispute over the educational policies of the Republic. Ordinaire was quick to claim the Chambige case as a direct corroboration of his accusations against one of the most vocal opponents of the regime, the decadent 'literary school,' and therefore as a victory for Opportunist educational ideology.

Incredible as it may seem in light of the far-reaching similarities between the stories and mentalities of Chambige and Robert Greslou (Mansuy 481–88), as between the ideological disputes surrounding the case and those enshrined in the novel, in his preface to *The Disciple* Bourget denied that this affair had any influence on his conception of the work, and he continued to do so until his death (see Autin 37–38; Mansuy 488). He insisted instead that the idea of *The Disciple* was suggested to him by what *Le Petit Journal* called at the time "the mystery of the rue Poliveau," otherwise known as the Barré-Lebiez case, which had occurred some ten years earlier. On April 6, 1878, two packages were discovered in the room of a medical student named Lebiez on the rue Poliveau, each one containing an arm and a leg from a woman's body. It turned out that Lebiez and his good friend Barré, desperate for money, had murdered a dairywoman and stolen her securities on March 23. Barré, clerk in a notary's office, had crushed her head with a hammer blow and later cashed in the securities. The medical student had cut up her body. The two murderers were given the death penalty in July and were executed September 7 of that year. What interested Bourget about the case and had fascinated the public at the time was the fact that the two offenders both came from 'good' families, both had their baccalaureate degrees—a mark of distinction in those days—and had been brilliant students at the *lycée* in Angers they had attended together. Between the discovery of the body and the identification of the victim and the murderers, Lebiez gave a public speech in a hall on the rue d'Assas titled "Darwinism and the Church," in which he explained the theory of the survival of the fittest and applied it to human societies, arguing that in life the stronger has the right to 'Caesarize,' that is, in the political parlance left over from the days of the Second Empire, to dominate the weaker (see Autin, chap. 4, and Frandon, "Fait divers et littérature," for accounts of the affair and references to sources published at the time of the events). Albert Autin, an ardent fan of Bourget in the latter's Catholic monarchist period, summarizes the tenor of the speech as substituting the "law of the jungle" for the "ancient morality of fraternal charity" (50). The scholar adds that Lebiez repeated the same argument during the trial, using science to justify his crime (50).

A more recent occurrence may very well have formed a bridge between the two cases in Bourget's mind. In 1886, the same year in which de Vogüé's influential studies of the Russian novel were published in book form, Barrès wrote an article for *La Revue Illustrée* titled "La mode russe" (The Russian Craze), in which he calls Barré and Lebiez "Darwinist murderers" who justified their crime "on scientific principles" and compares them to Raskolnikov, who of course used Darwin to construct his own theory of the right to kill the old pawnbroker in *Crime and Punishment* (Barrès, "la mode russe" 125). The link Barrès establishes among Barré-Lebiez, Darwin, and Raskolnikov does suggest a path that opponents of the Opportunists could later follow in order to put a rhetorical spin on Chambige's act radically different from that of Maître Trarieux and Ordinaire. Both groups invoke Raskolnikov for obvious reasons, but one sees him as the scion of the antisocial principles of Romanticism and its Nietzschean sequel, the other as the natural offspring of science in its social Darwinian form. Instead of reading Chambige's crime as the result of antirepublican decadent literature, they could parse it, as in fact Bourget would do in his novel, as the consequence of the republic's own positivist doctrine.

Nevertheless, it is obvious that the Barré-Lebiez story lacks many of the distinctive traits of similarity between the Chambige affair and *The Disciple,* above all the seduction of a forbidden woman, the love-death pact that motivates the killing, the hero's literary ambitions, the confession he writes in prison, the visits of pupil to master, not to mention the evident differences in the presence of two murderers, the brutality of the crime, and the public speech. Mansuy implies that Bourget wanted to avoid the shame of appearing to capitalize on the sensationalist press reports of a criminal case (488–89), but then why admit that the idea for the novel was stimulated by another, equally sensational case? It would seem much more likely that Bourget disavowed his preoccupation with the Chambige affair because he was loath to divulge the extent of his personal involvement with the young man and the traumatic effect it had on his life.

According to all the evidence, news of Chambige's crime fell on the writer's head like a bolt out of the blue, disrupting his life just as Greslou's indictment and confession did to Sixte. Bourget returned from Italy toward the end of September 1888 with the manuscript for his latest novel, *Cosmopolis,* well under way (Mansuy 467). Yet when press coverage of the Chambige affair picked up in anticipation of the trial, he immediately dropped that project and started work on the new manuscript that would become *The Disciple.* There is good reason to believe that Bourget's sudden change of direction was motivated by his sense of complicity in—if not responsibility for—Chambige's offense. For the fact is that Bourget knew him quite well before the criminal case, precisely in the role of master to disciple. Like Greslou with Sixte, the young man had come to see him several times while a student in Paris a few years before, to submit articles and stories to him and to discuss his plans to write psychological novels under Bourget's inspiration (A. Bataille viii; cited in Mansuy 482). And, like Sixte, Bourget's first reaction when he was publicly accused of being the instigator of Chambige's crime was to deny all responsibility for it. In words that echo those of Vallès a decade earlier, Bourget wrote that literature can have a detrimental impact only on those readers who already suffer from some moral defect (Bataille ix; cited in Mansuy 484 n61).

In fact, the novel was first titled *Adrien Sixte* in September of 1888 and was supposed to describe the philosopher's impressions of the criminal and the effect on the older man of seeing the impotence of science to console the prisoner faced with death. This was basically the position Bourget found himself in during the fall of 1888. But after reading Chambige's confessions—presumably in Bataille's *Causes criminelles*— Bourget had a change of heart. No doubt, again like Sixte, he now understood that his influence on the student had been much greater than what he had been willing to admit, to others or to himself, when he first read about it in the newspapers. He more or less confesses as much when he has Sixte read a nasty newspaper article that strangely echoes the reproaches made against himself and Barrès in reaction to the Chambige case. It condemns "modern phlosophy and its doctrines, incarnated in Adrien Sixte and in several other savants," and makes Greslou's fate an example of the evils of decadent literature (*The Disciple* 313). As a result, in February 1889 Bourget changed the title of his book, shifted its emphasis to Greslou, and greatly expanded the latter's memoir, filling it with details from his own life to amplify and disguise those of Chambige's.

For Bourget had been going through an upheaval of his own that must have made him especially sensitive to the student's predicament. After his father died suddenly in August of 1887, Bourget began to flirt seriously with a return to the religious faith of his youth (Mansuy 443–45). At the same time, he broke off relations with Marie, the woman he desperately loved and against whom he had frequently raged, who had deceived him once again with another man. Extricating himself from her milieu of Jewish high finance, from which he had long felt a sense of alienation, may have recalled his experiences as a young tutor in the family of a rich jeweler and the fantasies he then formed of seducing the fourteen-year-old sister of his pupil. This project would have satisfied his sexual longing, his rise from his subaltern position in the family, and the overcoming of his sense of isolation through incorporation into the otherwise indifferent or hostile milieu in which he found himself (Mansuy 166–67).

Was it due to the reactivation of these forbidden desires that Bourget recognized himself in Chambige? Was it the resulting sense of responsibility for the latter's crime that led him to begin at that time to question the moral responsibility of the writer? In any case, in "To a Young Man," the prefatory essay to *The Disciple,* the writer announces that any man of letters should "tremble with responsibility" at the idea that the future moral life of the nation depends on what his young readers find in his books, and he proclaims that this text is "the study of one of these responsibilities" (vii).

As a result of these upheavals, Bourget came to make Greslou as much a part of himself as Sixte. As though to indicate the underlying identity of the two characters, Bourget took the original first name of the younger man, Adrien, and bestowed it upon the philosopher (whose name in the earliest notes was to be Firmin Vialle; Mansuy 531–32). Sixte and Greslou became a concrete example of the theory of the divided self about which they speculated in the text and which

Taine, Ribot, Barrès, and Bourget himself did so much to popularize in the latter years of the century. Each represents a facet of the author's psyche, as is shown by the ample borrowings from his own life Bourget used to describe their lives and personalities, but their combination does not add up to the unified self that was Bourget's ideal. On the contrary, the shock of the Chambige affair, the eruption of the incomprehensible Real into the seemingly calm surface of the Symbolic, forced the writer to confront the fissures in his own self, which he then assimilated to those of the nation, as he insinuates in "To a Young Man": "[Y]our moral life is the moral life of France itself" (vii).

Experimental Education:
The Personality under Siege

In this novel of transition, the focal point is not so much the question of the alleged dangers of science for morality, as it was in Feuillet's text and in the most vocal critical controversy in the contemporary press, that between Brunetière and Anatole France.[2] In *The Disciple,* the emphasis has shifted from the relation of science to morals per se to what Bourget had called in his *Essais* "the personality under siege" by education: that is, the traumatic effect of the secularization of education on individual and national identity. It is the fear of disruption more than corruption that haunts Bourget's representation of the perilous process of reeducating the members of an entire nation to experience themselves as rational citizens with specific rights and duties first, as members of their village, clan, social class, or church second. *The Disciple* is thus worthy of critical attention due to its exploration, through its structure, its narrative technique, and its ideology, of the trauma allegedly created, on educators and educated alike, by the inculcation of the system of independent morality based on universal rationalist principles.

Bourget's concentration on crises of identity was not, therefore, a simple matter of pumping up the theme he found in *La morte* by applying to it the technique of the "psychological novel." Infusing the standard reactionary critique of republican moral principles with Vallès's acute sensitivity to the havoc republican education might wreak on the citizen's sense of self, on every level *The Disciple* transmits the experience of violent upheaval. The turmoil in Bourget's personal and professional life reverberates through the abrupt swings in the protagonist, from routine to crisis, from theory to practice, from innocence to guilt, from conviction to uncertainty, and, in the text as a whole, through the jumps from satire to drama, from third-person narration to first-person memoir, from Sixte to Greslou, from the freethinking Parisian university to the provincial Catholic nobility. The basic rhythm of the novel likewise consists of placid stretches of routine calm punctuated by sudden moments of feverish excitement.

As for the technique of narrating an accumulation of myriad "small human details," it is not merely a spiritualizing adaptation of naturalist technique to the depiction of the causes of the inner life of thought and emotion, and it is more than a procedure for describing gradual developmental processes. Regardless of specific content, in itself the method signifies a primary concern for the concrete particularities of human life. Bourget's novel begins and ends with third-person narrations that pose the problem and then draw, if not claim to prove, general conclusions from the 'empirical evidence' presented in the middle section, composed of Greslou's first-person memoir. A demonstration in action of an inductive theory of the subject,[3] it thus constitutes an edifying narrative in the empiricist mode.

The conflict between the inductive and deductive modes of procedure, which formed the crux of Bourget's ongoing debate about the thesis novel (in his essay on the Goncourts and his review of *La morte,* as well as in later writings), is in fact thematized in the two main characters of the novel, Sixte and Greslou, as well as in its structure. The dividing line between master and pupil is no longer that of two equally possible interpretations of the conduct to be derived from the same doctrine— the one idealistic, the other materialistic, as in Feuillet's Tallevaut and Sabine—but rather, as in the conservative philosophies of the later Taine and Bourget's contemporaries, Boutroux and Bergson: that between the one who dwells in a purely theoretical realm of abstractions, cut off from social relations and practical experience, and the other who, in attempting to live by the teacher's general principles, brings them into acute conflict with the realities of concrete particularity. Sixte's single-minded devotion to his education as a youth, followed by his fanatical reduction of life in his maturity to the sole activity of thought, isolates him from human association and real experience, "predispos[ing] him to misread philosophical propositions as if they were identical with the complex realities of human life" (Ringer 129). Even though the narrator compares Sixte at one point to Littré, the "Lay Saint" (*The Disciple* 29), unlike Tallevaut, Bourget's philosopher is neither a laboratory scientist nor a practicing physician. Bourget emphasizes this distinction by entitling the first chapter of the novel, in which Sixte is presented, "A Modern Philosopher," not "A Modern Scientist." The narrator repeatedly refers to him as a "metaphysician" (12); a "great abstract intellect" (67); one of those "singular minds" for whom "it is abstraction which is reality, and the daily reality is only a shadow" (35); one of those "generalizing minds, that never more than half verify the ideas upon which they speculate" (72). In a note dictated to his wife, Bourget insisted that this disregard for practical realities was the most important characteristic of his philosopher (Mansuy 498 n101, and 496 n95).

Why, then, did even the best-informed readers, such as Brunetière and France, invariably interpret the novel as an attack on science, and on positivism in particular? In one sense the answer is obvious: In the opening portrait of the philosopher, Bourget links Sixte's ideas—mechanism, determinism, evolution, atheism, the divided self of 'experimental psychology,' the rejection of metaphysics even, despite calling Sixte a 'metaphysician' elsewhere—directly to those of Taine, Ribot, Spencer, and Littré, and behind them to Kant, who denies the possibility of theoretical knowledge of God, and to Spinoza's ethics of the individual's submission to the universal order of things. Sixte recalls these same doctrines when, in the final sections of the book, he agonizes over the possibility that he and his teachings might somehow be responsible for Greslou's evil deeds (318). Moreover, Bourget makes the connection between republican positivism and moral deterioration quite explicit in his preface to the novel. Starting from Renan's premise that universal suffrage is the "most monstrous and the most iniquitous of tyrannies" because based on the brute force of numbers (*The Disciple* x), he divides those who lack "ideals" into two groups: the cynical 'nihilist' intent upon success at all costs, who has borrowed from contemporary evolutionary theory ("the natural philosophy of the times" xiii) the 'law' of the struggle for life ("*la concurrence vitale*" xiii); and the refined intellectual epicurean, who, lacking all belief in religion or anything else except his own sensations, thinks of the 'human soul' as a mere 'mechanism' (xiv). Indeed, the whole purpose of writing the book was to bring to light the villainy hidden beneath the total selfishness of this second type, among whom he counts all young people at some point in their lives, himself included (xiv).

The guilty parties in the preface are positivism and sophism, which manifest themselves in the forms of universal suffrage, social Darwinism, and mechanism. But it is not at all evident how these banal complaints of the Catholic right square with the actual events of the narrative. Surely the abstract rationalism Bourget embodies in the person and teachings of Sixte were not restricted to proponents of modern science or democracy. As Bourget well knew, it was positivism itself that objected most violently to rationalist thought, for its deductive method and its lack of concern for empirical observation. In fact, he has Sixte not only reject the Revolution because it was based on a false, Cartesian conception of mankind, but, going even further than his model, the Taine of *Les origines de la France contemporaine* (*The Origins of Contemporary France*), he portrays Sixte as a monarchist in the lineage of Bonald and de Maistre.

Mansuy claims that, lacking an authentic scientist to balance out the image of Sixte, who constructs mere "philosophical romances" (*romans philosophiques*) on the basis of unproven hypotheses, the novel remains ambiguous in its judgment of science. It is highly unlikely that Bourget would have composed Greslou's confession according to the rigorous methods of positivist psychology if he had intended the book as a frontal attack on positivism (Mansuy 499 n102). Moreover, in various notes, the writer remarked that he never accepted limitations on scientific inquiry (499 n102) and that the aim of his work was not to assert that science was 'guilty,' but that it was 'insufficient': The fatalistic doctrine of Spinozan resignation to the inevitabilities of the physical and psychological universes prevents science from bolstering its proponents' courage and healing their emotional wounds. Only the belief in free will, with the consequent possibilities of repentance and redemption, is capable of performing that task (498–499; 499 n103; *The Disciple* 312).

This is certainly a far cry from Bourget's indictment of modern scientific philosophy in his preface and a much weaker claim than those pressed in Feuillet's novel: Science is not directly responsible for criminal behavior, and the value of religious belief is in overcoming guilt rather than in making believers moral. For Mansuy, the resolution of the apparent contradiction between the assertions Bourget made in his preface and those in his unpublished diaries is to be found in the question of what Herbert Spencer called "the Unknowable." From the outset, the text emphasizes that Sixte's thought is distinguished from that of his famous positivist contemporaries by his determination to destroy, in a kind of ultra-Kantian critique, what he considers to be the last illusion of metaphysics, the notion found in Spencer that this Unknowable is real and living, and contains both thought and feeling: in short, that it is the kind of mysterious but personal God whose disappearance Baudelaire bemoaned in his poetry, according to Bourget (*Essais* 16–17). Mansuy concludes that salvation for Greslou would result from an "optimistic interpretation of the Unknowable" (500), belief in a God who would be the source of morals and who would guarantee that "the world has a meaning analogous to our soul" (Bourget, note on *The Disciple* of November 1, 1888; cited in Mansuy 500). For Bourget, then, belief in God's existence answers society's practical need for order and patriotic action as well as the sinner's psychological need for redemption. His position differs from that of most of his contemporaries in that he proposes a reconciliation of science and religion, neither sacrificing science to religious belief, as did most of the idealists, nor denying religion in the name of empirical observation, as did so many positivists (Mansuy 502).

This explanation clarifies Sixte's reaction after reading the memoir Greslou has written while in prison—guilt at his complicity in his disciple's depravity, even though the same doctrines could have led to entirely opposite actions in another person, and a sense of impotence at his psychology's inability to furnish an adequate response to Greslou's cry for help (*The Disciple* 311). But on this account, Bourget's novel is a failure when judged by the criterion he himself sets up in his critique of *La morte:* that there should be an undeniable relation between the principles the writer defends and their alleged consequences, and that the author should provide a whole series of "little human details" to make the development of the pupil seem inevitable. Moreover, just as there is no genuine scientist in the novel, so is there no representative of true Catholic morality, either. Sixte is the most ethical character in the novel, while the apparent 'hero' of the book, Count André, commits the only actual crime in the story: murdering Greslou in cold blood. While this may be considered by some to be a justifiable act of loyalty, honor, or revenge, one that presumably represents monarchist *revanchard* patriotism in the political arena,[4] it hardly counts as an example of the morality supposedly instilled by Christian belief.

Faced with the ambiguity of the novel's position on science and the difficulty of finding a specific model for Sixte (as opposed to a few traits or ideas taken from this or that philosopher, such as Taine or Ribot), or an identifiable philosophical problem at its center, Pierre Citti finds a solution that takes account both of Sixte's role and of the effect his teachings have on Greslou. Sixte represents an attitude rather than a particular doctrine, namely, the position of the intellectual (Citti 61). The real target of the criticism is the "man of letters," the writer, and especially the esthete of the new generation, such as Barrès, as Bourget indicates more or less explicitly in his preface (Citti 61–62; *The Disciple* 8–9). Bourget's aim is not to destroy the authority of the philosopher or thinker, but to ensure that the latter will weigh the possible effects of his teachings carefully (Citti 62).

Citti's most telling point is that the central situation of the novel, Sixte reading Greslou's confession, is the image of the older writer reading his disciples' imitations and applications of his methods of writing, specifically that of Bourget reading Chambige's prison confession. The effect of the master's teaching has been to turn his disciple, like Larcher (the writer in Bourget's novel *Lies*) and the decadent writer in general, into a tortured modern 'double consciousness.'

In echoing the reproofs directed against Bourget and Barrès in the Chambige case, Citti implies that the radical change in Bourget's literary career marked by *The Disciple*, which formed a turning point in the conception and practice of the novel of the entire period, was primarily the result of authorial self-criticism and self-correction. As Bourget complains in his *Essais*, it is the fragmentation of the divided self that undermines the identity of the younger generation and thereby renders its members incapable of assuming responsibility for their lives. But of course this notion of the self is not the sole prerogative of decadent literature. On the contrary, it results both from the basic tenets of the experimental novel of naturalism, in which the human being is the pawn of instinctual and environmental forces, and from the new experimental psychology represented by Ribot in France, which forms the backbone of the psychological doctrine that Sixte finds so wanting in *The Disciple*.

There is no necessary contradiction, then, between the interpretation of the novel as a statement about the responsibility of the writer and that which sees it as a critique of a certain lack of responsibility on the part of science. In fact, Fritz Ringer combines the two when he asserts that "the idealized *homme de lettres* [evoked in Bourget's preface] would presumably have succeeded where the narrowly 'academic' scientist [Sixte] was bound to fail" (129). The good writer is better equipped than the abstract, metaphysical psychologist to fulfill his responsibilities to his public, precisely because the former deals in the concrete and thus knows how people feel, think, and act in real life.

This reconciliation is tenable, however, only if we assume that Bourget is tarring both realist fiction and positivist psychology with the same brush: He blames the tendency toward abstraction for the lack of moral responsibility found in both. As a matter of fact, critics from Brunetière to the present have indeed lauded or lambasted *The Disciple* for reintroducing morality into French fiction, in opposition to the reign of the morally neutral art for art's sake and naturalist movements, with their principles of objective observation and narration (cf. Wyzewa's introduction to the 1908 edition of *Le disciple;* Autin; Citti; Loué). In reality, morality had always been the centerfold of mainstream, bourgeois fiction, and literary criticism during the Second Empire (Hauser 67). Nevertheless, Bourget did make morality respectable once again in high literature, by clothing Feuillet's middlebrow writing with a veneer of patriotism and then wedding it to a clever interrogation of the philosophical and social implications of the two basic tenets of the positivist education touted by the Opportunists as the source of morality and national unity—experimentation and disinterestedness. The key, then, is to recognize that in *The Disciple* Bourget does not aim to incriminate science per se but the ideology of positivism (and naturalism) that remains independent of empirical observation.

The central situation of the novel that Citti has isolated—the master reading his pupil's application of his ideas—acts as a *mise-en-abîme* of both the writer's relation to the public and the philosopher's relation to his pupils, for, as we have seen, for Bourget both are educators. For all their theorizing about the freedom of inquiry inherent in the experimental method, their emphasis on the observable universality of the innate social sentiment and their polemics in favor of the pedagogy of experience and object lessons in the primary schools, the Opportunist politicians and educators never confronted head-on the relation between the ideology of experimentation and their own project of instituting a system of republican national education. In his critique of *La morte,* Bourget had already formulated a definition of the novelist adopted from Zola's theory of the experimental novel: "What is called a law in psychology or sociology is only the sum, the abstract expression of an experiment that is more or less extended. And what is a novel, if not the imagination of a human experiment?" ("Réflexions" 116). His author of *romans philosophiques* in *The Disciple* extends that notion to the theory of positivist education in his replies to the magistrate investigating Greslou's case.

Both the writer and the educator undertake experiments; the only difference is that the one conducts them on fictional characters in the realm of the imagination, while the other carries them out on real people in real life. Sixte completes his theory of education by combining the positivist ideas of the child as tabula rasa and morality as a set of conventions arising from social need rather than a rational or transcendent principle, with the early Taine's claim that vices and virtues are simply the results of certain psychological laws. The logical conclusion is that we ought to run experiments with childen, varying the conditions of their upbringing in order to discover those that will nourish the socially advantageous dispositions we call virtues and those that will eliminate the socially damaging tendencies we call vices. Unfortunately, it is unlikely that such experiments would be allowed (*The Disciple* 58–60; the English translation consistently gives "experience" for the French *expérience,* a misleading rendition at best).

Experimenting on children may seem unworkable to the bookish philosopher and unthinkable to the virtuous reader, but those are the very words his more enterprising disciple echoed in describing the project he undertook with the young Charlotte de Jussat. The action that motivates his anguished appeal for absolution from his master consists, he writes, of "the cold resolution . . . to seduce that child . . . from the pleasure of governing a living soul" (173; translation modified), a plan he later describes as "the programme of the experiment [*expérience*] which I proposed to attempt upon the mind of Mlle. de Jussat" (187; translation modified). Although his official task is to act as tutor to Charlotte's ten-year-old brother, Lucien, Greslou spends much of his time educating the girl's sensibilities and stimulating her desire, first by telling her "a long, touching romance of false confidences" (188) devised according to the principles of Spinoza, Ribot, and Sixte, then by reading Balzac's *Eugénie Grandet* aloud to her (and her family). He administers the coup de grâce by drawing up a list of other novels for her to read, based on his own fascination with books that satisfied his desire to assimilate emotions not yet experienced in life, as well as on Sixte's theory of imitative emotion, especially in regard to literature: "the Literary Mind . . . this unconscious modeling of our heart to the resemblance of the passions painted by the poets" (204).

Greslou's fault, then, lies in overstepping the bounds of the writer's thought experiment by taking on the role of the educator. Indeed, the tutor articulates his moment of no return in terms of the distinction between imaginary and real experimentation. In transgressing this boundary, Greslou commits the mistake that Barrès had described in his article on the Chambige affair, letting his experiment loose on the outside world rather than containing it within his self.

On the political level, it is thus the disciple who represents the real educational experiment undertaken by the Third Republic, while his master, Sixte, represents the theoretical guidance the Republic sought from the scientist principles of Spinoza, Comte, Taine, Ribot, and Littré. It is in Greslou's confession, therefore, that Bourget formulates the specifics of his critique of the Opportunist reforms.

Education as Seduction:
'Bestial Desire' and the Ethics of Experimentation

As Mansuy suggests, the target of Bourget's criticism was the insufficiency of scientific fatalism, but in his *Memoir* Greslou expresses two complaints against the ethics of science that, going well beyond the inability to provide a source of courage and redemption, strike at the heart of the ideology of experimentation: When applied to human beings, scientific objectivity becomes an excuse for callous indifference to the feelings and dignity of the individual, while the ethic of universality, far from liberating us from our passions, increases our enslavement to them.

By the time he writes his confession, Greslou is appalled by the fact that he embarked on his project without loving the girl, as an intellectual experiment calculated in advance to satisfy his psychological curiosity about the "mechanism" of passion, his desire to manipulate another person, and his greedy urge to acquire a new *"expérience"* (*The Disciple* 173). "Tell me that I am not a monster," he pleads with his mentor, for undertaking the seduction with no regard for his victim's feelings and with no feelings of his own (293). Yet when he first arrives at the Jussat's house, he prides himself on his scientific goal of observing the members of the family and of taking apart, "cog by cog," the mechanism of their psychology, an aim he deems quite superior to the selfish ambition for riches and social advancement of other young men in situations similar to his, such as Julien Sorel at the Rênals' or Lucien de Rubempré at Mme. de Bargeton's. Once he has decided to carry out his experiment, he even boasts that, like the great scientists Louis Pasteur and Claude Bernard, who vivisect laboratory animals, he will "vivisect at length, a human soul" (188). In short, he takes himself to be the model of the disinterested quest for pure knowledge and the careful attention to detail that define the scientific observer. When he moves from the stage of observation to that of experimentation, ostensibly in order to verify the accuracy of the psychological "laws" he has induced from his observations—or, more likely, has learned from his master—he therefore feels justified in claiming that he undertook his seduction of Charlotte not for personal motives but "dictated by pure reason [*pures idées*]" (210), a fact that ironically underscores the obtuseness of the examining magistrate and the male members of Charlotte's family, who are convinced that Greslou seduced her in order to gain money and social status by forcing them to consent to a marriage.

If his experiment was not motivated by self-interest, why, then, does Greslou later find his actions so repugnant? Why does the lack of personal feelings toward his subject change from a sign of intellectual superiority at the beginning to the mark of base perversity at the end? What has provoked this complete about-face in his attitude toward scientific objectivity between the time he arrives at the château and the time he is imprisoned? On one level, it is of course the end result of the experiment that arouses his horror, the simple facts of Charlotte's death and his survival. Behind that outcome lie the factors he considers responsible for his failure, the conviction that the universe is ruled by ineluctable laws and the attitude of scientific objectivity itself. When his inner voice asks him whether he has the right to treat Charlotte "as a simple object of [his] experiment" (236; translation modified), he resorts to the 'scientific' ethics of Spinoza and Sixte with their Darwinian resonances, according to which our rights are limited only by our power, and which claim that in the moral world, as in the physical universe, it is a law that there are always predators and prey. In this context, the project of vivisecting a soul appears to be motivated by a sadistic lust to inflict pain and control the will of a powerless victim. Indeed, as early as his opening portrait of Sixte, the narrator had already associated scientific psychology with cruelty by characterizing the latter's method of critical analysis as being "keen to the point of cruelty" (24; translation modified) and remarking acerbically that the philosopher never gave charity, because he agreed with Spinoza's dictum that "pity, for a wise man who lives according to reason, is bad and useless" (28). The vaunted objectivity of the scientific attitude is here equated with heartless unconcern at best, cold cruelty at worst; it becomes the antithesis of Kant's moral law, treating people as objects and thus as mere means to an end, rather than as subjects, that is, as ends in themselves.

In linking objectivity to objectification, Bourget associates Greslou with the stock figure of the half-crazed and usually sadistic scientist prominent in the horror stories so widely circulated in Romantic literatures, as seen in characters such as Faust, Frankenstein, Victor Hugo's Claude Frollo, and Balzac's Balthazar Claës.[5] Greslou's cruel lust for power is demonstrated by his decision to use hypnotism in his experiment, about which he learned in Sixte's *Anatomie de la volonté* (*Anatomy of the Will*) as well as in Ribot's *Maladies de la volonté* (*Maladies of the Will*; 1883). Like Faust with Gretchen, Greslou has recourse to this scientific equivalent of black magic in his effort to make his defenseless subject love him, especially in the chapter on the "singular phenomena of certain moral dominations" (*The Disciple* 192).

It is through his second line of attack, however, that Bourget distinguishes himself from his predecessors and establishes his claim to originality. Not only does scientific experimentation destroy rather than sustain human dignity, it also demolishes the very freedom it is supposed to guarantee. Whereas Caro, Feuillet, and the leading Catholic politicians of the period contended that the lack of a transcendent guarantor of morality would leave society unprotected against the evil 'instincts' of the individual, Bourget strives to demonstrate that this lack leaves the individual unprotected from his own worst impulses. Whereas Sabine revels in her lust and desire for power, Greslou is horrified by the presence of these urges in himself and looks to science to quell this enemy within his self.

For Greslou's sense of self-loathing does not originate in the qualms he eventually begins to feel when he is sure that before long Charlotte will yield to his seduction; they are a repetition of powerful emotions he had already experienced well before he undertook his experiment. In his seventeenth year, Robert "ceased to be pure" (134), seduced by a working-class woman of thirty named Marianne who was often called to his home to perform household tasks. This first sexual experience awakens "an inexpressible disgust" in the formerly pious boy, who has lost his faith in the religion he learned from his mother. Yet he is unable to protect himself from "the shame of a new fall into the abyss of the senses" (135), at which time he experiences "a beastly frenzy" followed each time by the same "mortal disgust" (136). Now he discovers, alongside the pious boy and the imaginative dreamer within himself, a third personality, "a sensual being, tormented by the basest desires [bassement brutaux]" (134). And now he finds himself engaged in a violent struggle against 'temptation,' but no matter how hard he tries to resist Marianne's image, he always succumbs to the strength of his desire (136–37). In this painful initiation into adult sexuality, it is neither his self-interest nor his lack of sympathy for human suffering that arouses Robert's self-hatred but a more formidable adversary, his 'bestial' desire (Loué 50). (Unfortunately, the prudish English translation simply omits two pages of French text [135–36] in which Greslou describes in graphic detail his sexual initiation, his repeated inability to resist sensual temptation, and the powerful feelings these experiences arouse within him. All translations in this paragraph without page references are therefore my own.)

Not until Robert enters philosophy class in his last year of high school and discovers Sixte's scientific psychology does he find a remedy for his disgust with himself. In Sixte's *Theory of the Passions,* he learns that his relapses into sensuality, like everything in life, are the necessary result of ineluctable laws of nature. Scientific knowledge becomes the liberating force that saves him from his feelings of "remorse so severe" (141). More specifically, it is the conviction that his individual experience could not have been other than it was, and that, in general, particular events are governed by universal laws, which eases his conscience and allows him to feel at one with himself and the rest of humanity.

It is not surprising, then, that the same inner conflict should be provoked when he begins to realize that his experiment with Charlotte threatens to unleash the 'impure animal' within him once again. In striving to manipulate her by educating her desire, Greslou in fact falls prey to the vagaries of what the psychoanalyst would call countertransference, for scarcely has he launched his experiment than he finds himself responding to the girl's response to his manipulation. The loss of disinterestedness involved in the effort to redefine his identity is not just a reversion to self-interest but results in a powerful source of enjoyment.

His original attitude of pure psychological curiosity and disinterestedness thus quickly gives way to one of implication in the situation he has initiated. At the height of his desire, Robert loses the capacity of doubling, or looking at himself from the outside, so to speak, and playing a role outside his usual self, a talent on which he had prided himself as a means of avoiding the limiting of the self the philosophers call 'determination.' Despite his protestations of scientific detachment, Greslou becomes carried away, *emballé,* as Barrès put it, apropos of Chambige and his experiment, and, like the sorcerer's apprentice, once he begins to put his master's lessons into practice, he can never again regain control of the situation or of himself. It is for that reason that, in complete contradiction to his repeated apologies for seducing the girl without loving her, Greslou reproaches himself most bitterly for the opposite, for having been unable to maintain his attitude of cool objectivity and, above all, his self-control.

Nor is it surprising that, as with Marianne earlier, Robert should turn to the scientific teachings of his mentor in the frantic attempt to shield himself from his sense of self-disgust. The two situations are not entirely comparable, however, for this time he looks to science not to justify the existence of his desire but rather to quell it, so that he may maintain his autonomy. He wants to think that "I was not in love [*pris*], that the philosopher ruled the lover, that myself . . . remained superior, independent and lucid" (235; translation modified). Science has taught him, after all, that "one ought to be able at will to direct the life of the soul. If he could exactly know its laws" (234). When Charlotte leaves the Jussat mansion out of fear of her own love for Greslou, he desperately tries to master his feelings for her and recapture the superior position he had occupied before launching his experiment, by invoking the ethical teachings of Spinoza, Goethe, Taine, and of course Sixte. We can learn to detach ourselves from our passions by "evolving from the accidents of our personal life the law which unites us to the great life of the universe" (246; Greslou referring to Goethe and to book 5 of Spinoza's *Ethics*). In order to free oneself from bondage to the vicissitudes of life, Sixte recommends that one should "consider one's own destiny as a corollary in this living geometry of nature, and as an inevitable consequence of this eternal axiom whose infinite development is prolonged through time and space, [and] is the only principle of enfranchisement" (247).

The fact that Greslou, the would-be scientist, becomes implicated in his own experiment indicates the impossibility of remaining objective when that experiment involves controlling the attitudes and feelings of human subjects. The disciple's loss of disinterestedness, his surrender to the enemy within, functions as a critique of the Third Republic's claim that by applying the principles of positivism and Kantian universalism to educational reform, it can remain above the fray of interested parties struggling to assert their particular vision of morality and government. Without having to broach the question of the universality of secular morality directly, Bourget succeeds in undermining the Republic's pretensions to objectivity, impartiality, and universalism in its educational goals and policies by showing that however lofty the principles and intentions of the reform, once it moves from the abstract plane of theory to the practical world of action, it will inevitably become an interested party itself.

Bourget's critique of republican education is not limited to this demonstration of the inevitable loss of objectivity that ensues once it moves from the level of abstract principles to that of practical application. By focusing on the dialectic of desire between teacher and pupil, he challenges the most basic claims of the republic to provide its citizens with unprecedented autonomy, freedom, and self-determination. Bourget's choice of the plot of Greslou's *Memoir*, however much influenced by the reality of the Chambige case, clearly indicates the accusation that the new education is a form of seduction. The aim of Greslou's experiment was to arouse his pupil's desire, to make her love him, just as the Opportunists wanted to instill a love for the republican homeland into the pupils of the primary schools. In so doing, they or their representatives, the schoolteachers of the new laic primary schools, must be drawn into an emotional relation with the pupils they are trying to indoctrinate, thereby sacrificing the very autonomy the republic claims to offer its citizens, without being able to supply an effective means of regaining the freedom its own practice has forfeited.

The Enemy Within: Identity and the Motherland

The alien forces that threaten to take control of Greslou's emotions and behavior do more than cast doubt onto his responsibility; they endanger the core of his identity. In keeping with the latest developments in empirical psychology (which was called 'experimental psychology' at the time), the entire novel is strewn with allusions to dark powers that threaten to usurp control of the mind. Foremost among these *Maladies of the Will* was the current rage of hypnotism. When Robert can no longer bear the paroxysm of suffering caused by his unsatisfied passion for Charlotte, he decides to commit suicide—or rather, as he puts it, he "hypnotizes himself" and goes like a "sleepwalker" to the pharmacy to buy the fatal poison. In the ensuing pages he multiplies the fashionable terms designating uncanny powerlessness: He feels as though an alien force is operative in his mind, as though he is living a "waking dream," a "lucid automatism," and he diagnoses himself as suffering from a nervous disorder similar to madness due to his *"idée fixe"* (266–67).

Moreover, it is not only his sexual desire that overwhelms his conscious intentions and governs his actions toward Charlotte; his determination to seduce her is motivated as much by his hatred of her brother André as by his attraction to her, and he discerns at the bottom of that feeling "the probable trace of an unconscious atavism" (159). Greslou comes from Lorraine farmer's "blood," while André's family is "of a pure and conquering race" (159). In attributing his hatred to unconscious atavism, Greslou is espousing a system of interpretation widespread in both naturalist and antinaturalist scientific, philosophical, and literary circles in the later years of the century. Zola, for example, who takes his cue from various supposedly scientific theories of heredity, accounts for the outbreak of violence during the miners' strike in *Germinal* in the same manner, and he uses the notion of atavism to rationalize the many stories of identity imperiled by ghosts (*revenants*) he models after Hugo and the other Romantics. Caro, as we have seen, couches his fear of the 'hereditary ferocities' that might overcome the moral force of positivism's altruism in the same terms, as did Bourget in his novel

Cosmopolis. As for the notion of the unconscious, Sixte and his disciple adopt the views of the English experimental psychologists and their French proponents Taine and Ribot, according to whom the conscious will is not a faculty of the soul, as in traditional spiritualist psychology, but an unstable composite, the mere resultant of tendencies of which we remain largely unaware (cf. Mansuy 493). Inserting the pseudobiological notion of atavism into an historical theory of the period, which claimed that the ancestors of the French peasantry were the peace-loving, bucolic Gauls, whereas the aristocracy descended from militaristic Germanic invaders, Bourget concocts a racialist, if not outright racist, conception of class hostility to explain Greslou's loss of control.

With this theory, Bourget rewrites the story of the ambitious young social climbers to whom Grelou compares himself—Julien Sorel, Lucien de Rubempré, and Jacques Vingtras—and whose lives he had analyzed in his essay on Stendhal as a parable of nineteenth-century society: the young 'plebeian' who uses seduction as a means of penetrating the upper classes (*Essais* 319–27). In Bourget's updated right-wing version, this is no longer the tale of the legitimate aspirations of the new classes but, as in *La morte,* an example of the corruption of the purity of the race by a noxious alien invader (see Borie, *Mythologies de l'hérédité* 197–98). No longer motivated by individual ambition and self-interest alone, in Bourget's interpretation the social climber is actually an unwitting *revanchard,* avenging the defeat of his ancestors; he is a helpless pawn in an age-old hereditary battle between hostile races that persists into the present day as the conflict of the 'two Frances.' On the one side, the virtuous nobility represented by Count André, the true defenders of the homeland whose actions are motivated by honor and self-sacrifice; on the other, the ignoble lower classes empowered by the democratic principles of the Republic, who act out of selfishness, envy, and base desire. In this narrative allegory, it is of course the women who represent the stakes of the battle, that is, the two competing versions of the homeland. It is certainly not by chance that Robert is first seduced by a working-class woman driven by pure lust whose name is precisely Marianne, the symbol of the Third Republic. Her counterpart is the noble, pure, and innocent virgin, Charlotte, who acts out of true love.

In turning to science for protection from his desire, Greslou is seeking more than control over his emotions; he is desperately grasping at a life raft to save his very sense of self from the flood of unconscious forces he feels are about to swamp him. What he fears most is a kind of psychological death. For him, science was the object around which he had constructed his tenuous identity, the support of his existence

against the threat of dissolution into the void of madness. No wonder, then, that he should take the teachings of science to task for the
horrible failure of his experiment. Behind those ideas stand the two
paternal figures in his life, his actual father, the civil engineer who first
initiated him into the world of scientific thinking, and then his mentor,
Sixte, who replaced the Catholicism he had learned from his mother and
saved him from his desire for Marianne. (Bourget insinuates the idea
of Sixte's paternity by having the gossips of his neighborhood intimate
that Greslou is the philosopher's illegitimate son.) For Greslou, as for
Michelet and so many other proponents of Enlightenment progress,
science represents the republican version of the patriarchal social order,
whose primary aim should be to protect him from enslavement to the
feminine, understood here as weakness of the will, instinctuality, uncon-
sciousness, and ultimately death. The alternative Bourget proposes is an
antidemocratic (but not yet explicitly monarchist) patriarchy that relies
on a personal God (who is not yet the God of orthodox Catholicism),
and whose protective strength is embodied in Count André.

By raising the character's motives from the individual to the collective level, Bourget gives the story a political twist (see Loué 56, for a
similar view), justifying the repression of the working classes—André's
murder of Robert—simultaneously as the legitimate defense of the
honor of the noble homeland—Charlotte—and as the suppression of
the nation's base republican instincts—Marianne. Indeed, as in the new
republican civics textbooks, Bourget specifically equates the homeland
with the mother in his preface, admonishing his young readers that, in
twenty years' time, "you and your brothers will hold in your hands the
destiny of this ancient country [*patrie*], which is our common mother"
(vii). While Charlotte may seem less appropriate as a maternal figure
than the older and more experienced Marianne, Bourget places sufficient
evidence in the text to allow the reader to understand that Greslou is
trying to transfer his mother love onto the younger woman. Her name,
first of all, inevitably evokes that of the eminently maternal heroine of
Goethe's *Werther.* Moreover, soon after Robert's arrival in the Jussat
household, his pupil Lucien informs the tutor that his sister has been
asking whether he needs anything for his room. He is deeply touched
by this mark of interest, if not affection, in a place that until then has
seemed forbiddingly cold and utterly indifferent to his welfare, and he
continues immediately with the thought that "I missed my mother so
much, although I might not wish to confess it! And it was this act of
simple politeness which made me regard Mlle. de Jussat with more
attention" (176–77; translation modified). Even if one did not recall

that Greslou's model, Julien Sorel, has the identical feelings when he learns of Mme. de Rênal's motherly concern for the state of his wardrobe, Robert makes it clear that he would like Charlotte to fill the void left by his separation from his mother in this foreign milieu.[6]

The fantasy of filling the void left by the disappearance of the mother—the lost object, in Lacan's terminology—forms the most explicit link between Greslou's narrative and Bourget's solution to the tension between science and religion he sees as the source of the 'two Frances.' On the cosmic scale, it is Spencer's Unknowable that plugs the noumenal gap behind the world of observable phenomena available to scientific investigation. In his cautions to the youthful reader of *The Disciple,* as in his piece on Baudelaire, Bourget raises the specter of the abyss, but here he lays it to rest immediately: "Have the courage to respond to those who will tell you that beyond this ocean is emptines, an abyss of darkness and death; 'You do not know that'" (xvi). Today, Bourget protests, science recognizes that beyond its limits lies not the nothingness of the abyss, but the very real domain of the Unknowable, which forms the foundation upon which observable reality rests, thus reconciling the phenomenal with the noumenal. On the personal level, Bourget indicates that belief in the reality of this Unknowable will preserve the life of his readers' souls, for in the next sentence he urges them not to let their souls die before they themselves do. For Greslou, who in this respect is a small-scale model of French society, this armistice between the religion of his mother and the science of his father could establish a peaceful and harmonious union between the warring maternal and paternal identifications threatening to tear his self apart. Mansuy's interpretation of the novel is thus vindicated, but with the crucial addition that, more than repentance and redemption, at stake is the guarantee of existence offered as a barrier against the abyss of psychological dissolution and death.

In his warnings to French youth, Bourget lists a second type of ideas dangerous to the life of their souls: those that diminish the ability to love. The prime example of the latter in the text is Sixte's rationalistic atheism, one corollary of which is his rejection of the Christian principle according to which the social order should be based on love. By doing so, Sixte argues, Christianity has opened the way for capricious and arbitrary rule. The political implication of this attack on love as social principle was no doubt clear to Bourget's contemporaries. In "Le principe d'autorité" (The Principle of Authority), an important article in one of the first numbers of Renouvier's neo-Kantian republican journal, *La Critique Philosophique,* Pillon, the coeditor, had made exactly the same point. Catholicism is an authoritarian religion, fundamentally opposed to the concept of human rights based on reason due to its reliance on charity and love as social principles (145–46, 150). Basing the social order on a policy of love rather than on reason inevitably leads to inequality and unpredictability in its application, since it is the contingencies of particular situations rather than established, universal law that govern the decisions of those who implement that policy. For the rationalist, love is in fact the antiprinciple par excellence.

Greslou finds that out as he tries to fathom Charlotte's feelings in order to control them. Like Julien Sorel, he learns that the love he succeeds in arousing is not the result of his plans and calculations; on the contrary it is what Stendhal called the *imprévu* (unforeseeable), entirely spontaneous and unpredictable, beyond all rationalistic psychological laws. Robert does not set out to stimulate the feeling of pity that acts as a wedge into Charlotte's affection, nor can he control the drama of love and death that plays itself out within her. Nor does he foresee that she will read his papers after he refuses to carry out their suicide pact, precisely because, in his rationalistic way, he reflects instead of observing. Furthermore, he realizes that she still loves him even after becoming engaged to another man, not as a result of 'analysis' but of a sudden, inexplicable 'intuition.' He concludes that it is instinct, not the intellect, that rules us.

The ideological significance of Bourget's *imprévu* differs, however, from Stendhal's. For the author of *The Red and the Black* and *The Charterhouse of Parma,* in addition to indicating the limits of rationalism, it designates resistance to and superiority over the conformism that governs the conduct of the majority due to obedience to authority, fear of embarrassment, greed, self-interest, or simple lack of imagination. In *The Disciple,* as in the writings of Boutroux and Bergson, it signifies the reign of 'instinct' over reason, free will over determinism, the contingent over the universal, and, above all, the intimation of Littré's 'ocean of mystery' beyond the ken of science, to which Bourget alludes in his preface (10), a transcendent realm that can be plumbed only by the superrational power of intuition.

In Bourget's text, there is a strict analogy between the relation of the subject to the Unknowable noumenon and that of the subject to other people. Charlotte's thought and will are just as unfathomable to Robert as the Unknowable is to science. The entire novel is in fact strewn with examples of the unknowability of the otherness of other people: Robert's mother does not understand him for lack of imagination; Charlotte fails to comprehend Robert due to an excess of imagination; André and his father misunderstand Greslou's motives because they judge them according to their own desires and fears; the examining magistrate understands neither Sixte nor Greslou because he assumes that everyone acts for the basest of reasons; Sixte grasps nothing of the magistrate's strategies of interrogation because they do not coincide with his unworldly preoccupations; Sixte and Mme. Greslou are completely deaf to each other's needs and concerns, at least at the beginning of their encounter; and of course Sixte fails utterly to foresee his own influence on his would-be disciple.

Greslou is so strongly attracted to Sixte's theories because he sees in them a way out of the psychological isolation that results from the unknowability of the Other. The plot of the novel is meant to demonstrate, on the contrary, that, far from providing a social bond as the positivists would have it, science condemns the subject to solitude, either as Sixte's ideal and practice of cutting off all social relationships or as Greslou's purely sadistic relationship with Charlotte. The predictability promised by the discovery of rational laws of behavior is exposed as a sadistic effort to coerce the will of the Other, an effort that proves to be illusory, moreover, since they do not really control the Other. Belief in determinism does not liberate the subject from the desire of the Other, as Robert hopes; it makes him even more dependent on the Other, because it is in reality the solipsistic attempt to understand that desire in terms of his own ideas, just as rationalism, according to the empiricists, is a futile attempt to understand independent nature in terms of the categories of the human mind.

Bourget's polemic against the positivist ethic culminates in the quasi-matricidal fantasy of Greslou's confession. The question of responsibility broached in the preface concerns his implication in Charlotte's death as much as Sixte's liability for Robert's actions. It is certainly not by chance that it is precisely Greslou's mother who blames Sixte for his incarceration, nor that it is she whose suffering for her son's misdeeds the text depicts most graphically to the readers. The responsibility for which the man of letters must tremble is to save the mother from the son's sadistic impulses.

While science is unable to protect the subject from his own worst instincts, by the structure of his novel Bourget implies that literature, and particularly the novel of ideas, can do so. The man of letters responsible for *The Disciple* shoulders his moral responsibility by containing the potentially subversive 'scientific' fantasy of matricide recounted in Greslou's *Memoir* within the two third-person narratives that frame it. The latter of these manages to gratify the reader's presumed sense of outrage while exhibiting the moral superiority of the nobleman's code of honor over the scientific ethic, by first displaying Count André's moral probity when, after a bout of soul-searching, he brings himself to testify honestly in court that Greslou did not murder his sister, then showing its higher capacity for effective 'action' and defense of the family honor, when, after Robert is exonerated, the count shoots the commoner dead in the street.

With the shot that excises the alien intruder from the land, the text repudiates the matricidal fantasy it had satisfied in its center. The moral responsibility touted in the preface thus turns out to be an act of self-mutilation as punishment for that criminal fantasy. Bourget thereby announces his break with his own criminal desires, which he associates with the philosophical and social experimentation of his comparatively liberal past. Having already demonstrated through his portrayal of scientific disinterestedness the supposed dangers of doing away entirely with the pathological object, as Kant recommends, he proposes instead an alternative maternal object of a political nature—the homeland. Like the Opportunists he opposes, Bourget advocates transferring maternal love to love of country, and like them he calls on the youth of France to make nationality henceforth the core of their identity. But in his preface it is not so much the love of the homeland inculcated by the secular republican schools that he urges, as total identification with her: The homeland is our common mother and your soul is her soul. Patriotism thus becomes entirely equated with self-love. Moreover, he implies that these prospective disciples of his should also transfer their sadistic enjoyment from the field of sexual desire to the rooting out of the enemies of the motherland, cloaking this witch-hunt under the banner of morality rather than treating it as a matter of pride, revenge, or political and economic need. Through patriotism, they will be able to satisfy their aggressive impulses without feeling the guilt and remorse Greslou experiences. And in the novel, André's killing of Greslou is prefigured by his heroic exploits during the Prussian war, volunteering for the military and then killing a Prussian soldier. The implication is that his murder of the internal enemy—the 'lower classes,' who stand for their uncontrollable forbidden impulses, and their representatives, i.e., democracy—is as honorable and as heroic as his wartime defense of the homeland. It is this sinister twist to republican patriotism that will be elaborated and carried much farther by Barrès and the right-wing nationalism just beginning to emerge from the Boulangist movement.

CHAPTER 3

The Novel of National Energy, by Maurice Barrès

✦

Maurice Barrès Protofascist?

Barrès without Kant

French fascists of the twentieth century such as Pierre Drieu La Rochelle and Robert Brasillach were great admirers of Barrès in their youth (Soucy 18, 162, 283–99), and Georges Valois, leader of the first French fascist party, Le Faisceau, looked on Barrès's nationalism as the major precursor of his movement, as did several others who slid from integral nationalism to fascism in the 1920s (e.g., Taittinger, Renaud, La Rocque, Doriot; Soucy 20). Barrès's son's edition of his works proudly displays a photograph of Adolf Hitler's ex libris and the dedication to the Führer of a book by Walter Frank, *Nationalismus und Demokratie im Frankreich der dritten Republik,* which Hitler had in his library in Berchtesgaden and which contained a lengthy study of Barrès (*L'oeuvre de Maurice Barrès,* vol. IV, n. pag.). It was Barrès, after all, who invented the term "National Socialism," and his brand of nationalism included the "leader principle" along with a heavy dose of mob violence, xenophobia, and anti-Semitism. For the same reasons, recent antifascist scholars, such as Robert Soucy, Zeev Sternhell, and David Carroll, who takes his cue from Philippe Lacoue-Labarthe and Jean-Luc Nancy's *Le mythe nazi,* have examined Barrès's writings in order to discover the roots of the later movement in the ideology of the virulent revolutionary nationalism he developed around the turn of the century, just before and during the Dreyfus Affair (1897–1902).

Paradoxically, whereas Sternhell and Soucy contend that it was Barrès's abandonment of rationalist humanism that made him the bridge between nineteenth-century conservatism and twentieth-century fascism, Carroll takes just the opposite view, namely, that it is the persistence and exacerbation of the philosophy of the autonomous subject that explains his fall into totalitarianism. From the one perspective it is his betrayal of the tradition of the Enlightenment, from the other his fidelity to that heritage, that precipitates him into the abyss of protofascism. While both these explanations have much to recommend them—there certainly was an important strain of irrationalism in Barrès's politics of cultural heredity, the strong leader and the masses on the one hand, the assertion of the prerogatives of the autonomous subject in his identification with national heroes, the valorization of sameness evident in the insistence on national unity and totality leading to racism and xenophobia on the other—each suffers from the flaw of overgeneralization. The major tenets of Barrès's 'irrationalism' were in fact commonplaces of the rationalist scientism of his times. Comte, Taine, Durkheim, Gabriel Tarde, Gustave Le Bon, Théodule Ribot, and Jules-Auguste Soury all believed in some form of hereditary determinism as well as in the subordination of the individual to the group. Like Schopenhauer, Hartmann, Wilhelm Wundt, Sigmund Exner, and Georg Lichtenberg among German thinkers of the period, the last three also upheld the anti-Cartesian view that affect and instinct take precedence over individual reason and that thought itself is the product of the impersonal forces of a collective unconscious, a stance they condensed in the pre-Lacanian catchphrase *Il pense en moi* (It thinks in me). Moreover, as discussed in chapter 1, the anti-individualist social theories of that same positivism were combined in a strange alliance with the philosophy of the subject derived straight from Kant and the Enlightenment via Condorcet, Quinet, Proudhon, and Renouvier, among others, in order to serve as the ideological basis of the very Opportunist Republic Barrès's nationalism and later fascism were designed to overthrow. To put it bluntly, there was a republican irrationalism that nevertheless did not condone mob violence, and a patriotic subject of national unity that did not sanction legalized racism, anti-Semitism, and xenophobia.

The problem, then, is that while each of these theories brings out aspects of Barrès's ideology that might otherwise remain hidden from view, neither distinguishes adequately between protofascism and republicanism, since the very traits they emphasize, even those that appear to be mutually contradictory, were in fact constitutive of republican ideology. Such a differentiation can be effected, I would suggest first, by examining Barrès's texts from the time of the Dreyfus Affair in light of Lacan's notion of "extimacy," his neologistic mode of escaping from the polar opposition of the interior and the exterior that so often haunts the discourse of identity at the heart of republican, nationalist, and fascist ideology (see Miller, "Extimacy," for a detailed explanation of this term).

What makes Barrès's texts of this period especially interesting—and frightening—are his perceptions of the more or less covert fears and gratifications that constitute the emotional force of the striving for identity in fin de siècle nationalism beyond, and often against, the self-interest advertised in political campaigns and the rights and duties described in political philosophies. While Barrès articulated the main themes of his program in the polemical prose of his *Scenes and Doctrines of Nationalism*, a collection of speeches and articles written between 1898 and its publication in 1902, I would argue—and this is my second thesis—that it is in the three novels of *Le roman de l'énergie nationale* (*The Novel of National Energy*), *Les déracinés* (*The Uprooted*; 1897), *L'appel au soldat* (*Appeal to the Soldier*; 1900), and *Leurs figures* (*Their Faces*; 1902),[1] much more than in his political pamphlets, that Barrès allows the full range and complexity of the tendencies that make up nationalist identity, and, above all, the contradictions within them, to surface and interact freely. It is likewise in the novels that what distinguished his nationalist solution from that of others and made it especially dangerous emerges most clearly.

It was the pedagogical stance Barrès assumes in these texts that has provoked critics from Gide to Suleiman to their harshest condemnations of the writer and of the authoritarian genre he practices. The target of their objections is the didacticism of the nationalist *roman à thèse*, Barrès's narratorial pose as the schoolmaster who, like a teacher driving a lesson home to his pupils, defines and delimits the meaning of his fiction and then constrains his readers' freedom of judgment by imposing that univocal and unilaterally defined interpretation onto every episode and circumstance of his narrative. Now while fascism certainly cannot be reduced to authoritarianism, both do involve a will to dictatorship, so that the criticisms leveled at the latter would also apply to the former.

The equation between didacticism and authoritarianism in Barrès is, however, not quite as straightforward as these criticisms would imply, for he did not wait until *Les déracinés* to assume the role of teacher. Already in his first, outspokenly anti-authoritarian novels of the *Culte du Moi* (*Cult of the Ego*) trilogy, he had insisted on the edifying function of his fiction ("Examen des trois romans idéologiques" 17). From the start Barrès considered literature to be in ideological competition with other forms of education. It is not the pedagogical impulse per se that gives *Les déracinés* its authoritarian aura but—and here is my third thesis—the specific, transferential role it confers on the educator that distinguishes it from other didactic works, including Barrès's own early fiction.

In fact, the novel takes explicit aim at the ideology of the ruling authorities of its times, the Kantian doctrine the author claimed was the official State philosophy of the government of the Third Republic and of the school system whose task it was to disseminate that system among future citizens. Like its predecessors, the novel presents itself as a challenge to a certain conception of authoritarianism, personified in the character Bouteiller, who goes from government scholarship student to *lycée* philosophy professor to politician and deputy in the lower house of the French parliament. In a sense, then, Barrès pits his narratorial voice against the teachings of Bouteiller. But *Les déracinés* is a novel of education in every sense of the term, recounting the schooling and young adulthood of its protagonists, during which time they come under the sway of a series of potential masters that includes both fictional characters and real historical personages such as Taine, Hugo, and Napoleon. The question of the relation of education to authority, freedom, and interpretation is thus posed on all levels of the work, explicitly thematized in character, plot, and ideological discussion as well as presented as a function of narratorial discourse; consequently, any attempt to evaluate the political significance of the novel must take all its levels into account.

As the title of the book indicates, personification is not its only rhetorical strategy; the plot is primarily designed to enact before the reader the concrete effects of the 'uprooting' produced by Bouteiller's tenets on the lives of seven of his pupils from Lorraine who decide to seek their fortunes in Paris after completing their baccalaureates at the *lycée* in Nancy. Two of them—Racadot, grandson of a serf freed during the Revolution, and Mouchefrin, whose father is a poverty-stricken photographer—end up very badly, murdering a beautiful young Armenian woman named Astiné Aravian for her jewels. A third, Renaudin, son of a petty civil servant and a scholarship student like Mouchefrin, engages in the most unsavory journalistic practices of the period, and in a later volume of the trilogy is nearly killed in a duel provoked by his betrayal of the cause of General Boulanger. The four others, Roemerspacher, Sturel, Saint-Phlin, and Suret-Lefort, with higher social status, some independent means, and greater intellectual ability, are successful in varying degrees, but only after suffering from their transplantation to the metropolis. Moreover, they all share, to a greater or lesser extent, at least some complicity in Racadot and Mouchefrin's crime. As with Bourget's *Disciple,* the question of the teacher's responsibility is at the heart of this novel, and behind the issue of individual ethics is that of the ideology he teaches, but whereas Bourget wanted to challenge the regime indirectly by attacking the system of ideas that, he claimed, undermined the bases of morality and identity, Barrès's primary targets were, as Ringer has astutely observed (130), the social and political institutions themselves that promulgated the views he opposed. That is why Bourget could tell his story in terms of the fates of a handful of individuals, while Barrès must follow the lives of a whole group of characters as they interact with each other and with the culture and society of the times.

A cursory reading of the opening chapter of *Les déracinés* gives the impression that the ideological argument of the novel will consist of what was by the end of the century the standard right-wing attack against the universalism of the Republic in the name of particularism. On the one hand, Kantian universalism, with its categorical imperative and rationalist abstraction (*Les déracinés* 504, 510); on the other, the empirical consideration of the particular conditions of real life, everything that Kantianism allegedly ignores (502, 505). Barrès uses the expression 'members of humanity' in Taine's sense (which echoes that of de Maistre and Tocqueville): paper constructs, "abstract men, empty simulacra, philosophical marionettes" (*Révolution jacobine* 9); while his 'citizen' indicates people who have lost their selves, their ties to their ancestors, to the land where they were born and raised, and to their cultures; they are victims of synthetic theory and artificial law, imposed upon them by physical or mental violence. The "purity" of reason consists, in the eyes of Kant's adversaries, in turning one's back on the natural, social, and cultural conditions of real life.

There is of course a certain truth to these criticisms; Kant certainly did make the purity of reason consist of its independence from all empirical involvement. However, he did so not in order to ignore empirical reality but to discover its necessary basis for human cognition, what must be the case in order for it to appear to us as it does. One might be tempted to imagine that Barrès, not being a trained philosopher, would have overlooked this aspect of Kantianism, or at the least would have omitted it from a work of fiction meant to appeal to a wide public. Not at all. In fact, Bouteiller's earliest lessons deal not with the ethical teachings of the *Critique of Practical Reason,* but, following Kant's own chronological and logical order, with the limits of knowledge delineated in the *Critique of Pure Reason.* His pedagogical purpose in employing this stratagem is to impress upon his students that the categorical imperative alone can save them from utter skepticism. He sees Kant's first *Critique* as an extension of Descartes's radical doubt, and, like so many French neo-Kantians of the nineteenth century, treats the former's ethics as the sole remedy for the disarray of total uncertainty.

Unfortunately, while Bouteiller's pupils are completely persuaded by the demonstration of the limits of knowledge, they cannot appreciate the compelling force of the categorical imperative. Perhaps that is because neither Bouteiller nor the narrator bothers to explain the logic of the neo-Kantian argument, not even in the inaccurate but more accessible form Coignet gave it: namely, that human freedom is an undeniable fact of which conscience makes each of us aware; that this freedom consists in the ability to give to oneself and to obey one's own law of reason, the expression of which is the categorical imperative; and that the resulting autonomy conveys upon all human beings a dignity worthy of the respect of all others. Bouteiller does summarize the conclusion of his course by reminding his class that he has shown them how Kant reestablished the principle of certainty by saying, "A reality exists, the moral Law" (506), but there is no explicit mention of his reasoning in either dialogue or narration. Be that as it may, to the pupils, universal moral rules are the sort of thing about which teachers tell their charges but which they don't really believe themselves, since the idea seems to contradict everyday experience. In short, Bouteiller has transmitted the malady but not the cure. Deracination, in the first instance, is therefore a matter not of physical or social displacement but of mental upheaval. Like Socrates, the professor has undermined his students' childhood beliefs, the cultural doxa of their social classes and family milieus.

Strangely enough, this loss does not perturb the young men in the slightest. On the contrary, they look upon it as a heady liberation. They are much more impressed by the example of Bouteiller's career than by the ethical side of his teaching. For them, he is associated with the living symbol of the Republic, Victor Hugo, and with the Republic itself. Thanks to the Republic and the new spirit of the École Normale, Bouteiller has risen from the obscure poverty of a provincial working-class family to the rank of professor, first in Nancy and then in Paris. With the support of the government, he is able to disregard the social hierarchy with impunity, mocking the school principal and the *lycée* inspector when they visit his classes, and purposely slighting the grand-mother of his noble pupil, Saint-Phlin. He seems to be living the mod-ern-day version of Julien Sorel's romance, and like him will no doubt soon be able to say: "My story is ended, and all the credit is mine."

But of course Barrès does not see Bouteiller's story the same way. For him, the professor's behavior toward the 'natural' social order is scandalous. In any case, his rise, even if it were to unfold according to the ideal model, entirely uninterrupted by setbacks or failures, is merely a grotesque parody of Julien's struggles, just as the republican model is a debased pastiche of the glories of Napoleon, or even of Rousseau, which inspired the young Sorel. Following the style of conservative ideology of the 1890s, Barrès repeatedly uses the term 'nihilism' to characterize the skepticism the young men derive from Kant's critique.[2] Bouteiller teaches them that it is not possible to tell whether our sense of space and time or our idea of causality corresponds to anything real; what they receive from this notion is "the most acute sense of nothingness" (500). Feigning ignorance of the future, the narrator puts himself in the place of the reader and wonders whether this overdose of negation might not lead them to devise for themselves "a kind of cruel nihilism" (500). He reinforces this impression in a crucial scene later in the novel by attributing the same idea to a voice of authority, the philosopher Taine: "The philosopher took a few moments to meditate on the nihil-ism or rather the void expressed in such simple terms by a young fellow [Roemerspacher] who seemed neither base nor mediocre" (595).

Between Stendhal's Julien Sorel, Balzac's Lucien de Rubempré, and Barrès's François Sturel comes Turgenev's Bazarov, the nihilist protago-nist of *Fathers and Sons*: "[T]he nihilist is the man who bows down to no authority, who accepts no principle as an article of faith, no matter how much respect the principle is given" (Vogüé, *Roman russe* 187; quoting *Fathers and Sons*).[3] As Bazarov demonstrates, nihilism is not a simple belief, nor even the lack of belief, but a critical attitude and a code of action. The worst effect of Kantianism on the adolescents from Lorraine is that, in robbing them of their certainty, it also deprives them of all socially accepted goals and means of attaining those goals. The only meaningful motive for action that remains for them is therefore themselves, their own survival, well-being, advancement, 'vanity.' One will naturally object that this conclusion in no way follows from Kant's or Bouteiller's teaching. Barrès's response is that Bouteiller could have foreseen this outcome if he had paid attention to the particularity of his students and their backgrounds (*Les déracinés* 502), so that, albeit indirectly, it is universalism nevertheless which is responsible for their nihilism. The cruelly paradoxical result of the Kantian universalism that ignores individuality is thus a renewed and reinforced individualism.

Bouteiller is himself the moldering fruit of the same educational system he is foisting on his pupils. As such, he serves as the instrument of Barrès's criticism of that system as well as of the parliamentary government that has created him and which he embodies, in his actions as in his doctrine. An orphan removed from his 'natural' milieu at an early age, he is literally the child of Third Republic pedagogy, "a child of reason, foreign to our traditional local or family habits, completely abstract and truly suspended above the void" (503).[4] His only ties of affection and gratitude going to the government that has raised and supported him, he interprets the universality of the categorical imperative to mean that the citizen's duty to society overrides all conflicting claims to individual rights. Like Auguste Burdeau, whom Barrès quotes directly in the text, Bouteiller asserts that the individual owes complete and entire allegiance to the State, in his fortune, his efforts, his thoughts, his blood, his very heartbeat (503). Yet his own actions repeatedly betray his words: When his personal convictions or welfare are at stake, he has no qualms about ignoring or disrespecting the authorities of the State to which he is allegedly devoted, as we see in his contemptuous attitude toward the principal and school inspector. When called to teach in Paris, Bouteiller cloaks his private ambition in a cloud of duty to society and has his pupils ratify his decision to leave in a sham vote determined by the false impression he gives them and by his personal prestige. Some time later, when he has the opportunity to apply the categorical imperative in practice to a real situation—his protector, Gambetta, wants one of his former students, Renaudin, to accept a job with a socialist newspaper as a government spy—he caves in to pressure and advises Renaudin to take the job. This moral failure is only a foretaste of the act that leads to his downfall, his involvement in the Panama Canal scandal that rocked the Third Republic in the 1890s, which Barrès describes in detail in the final volume of his trilogy of "national energy," *Leurs figures.*

The brunt of Barrès's assault is directed toward the potential for abuse inherent in the Kantian ethic. Like the Catholic morality the Third Republic sought to replace, it delivers the individual up, bound hand and foot, to the central power—only in this case, it is the State that has taken the place of the Church (cf., Taine, *L'école* 260). Once again Barrès is following, in broad outline, the arguments of Taine, who, in his *Origines,* portrays a continuity among the throne and altar of Louis XIV's absolute monarchy, the homeland of the Jacobins, and the centralized empire of Napoleon I. Wittingly or unwittingly, both are repeating Hegel's claim that Kant's ethic is just as tyrannical as the dogmatic morality he wishes to supplant; he has simply replaced the external despot with an inner dictator, the moral law. According to both writers, the ultimate guilt for this subjection falls on the shoulders of universalization. Barrès argues that Bouteiller's behavior toward Renaudin, oscillating between "respecting a soul" and "serving the State" (*Les déracinés* 522), shows up a fundamental flaw in the categorical imperative, for the principle of making one's conduct into a general rule does not provide a sure criterion for deciding between the welfare of the individual and that of the State. It therefore fails to supply any argument to defend the rights of the individual and makes it an easy matter for Bouteiller to parse Kant's absolute duty as a call for blind obedience to the State (505, 507). Once the individual has thus been made vulnerable, it is an easy matter for the actual State, or those who run it, to manipulate people for the benefit of the rulers, that is, the bourgeoisie of finance and industry who stood to profit from the Panama Canal deal and the members of Parliament who represent their interests, in every sense of the word. The allegedly universal ethic of society as a whole turns out in fact to promote the interests of a single segment of that society. Via this route, Barrès's analysis of Third Republic moral universalism approaches Karl Marx's critique of the false universalism of the bourgeois class.

Endemic hypocrisy and nihilistic egotism are not the sole results of Kantian universalism. As an enemy of abstraction, Barrès is equally concerned with the positive actions that philosophy is likely to enjoin upon its followers. Judging by Bouteiller's conduct, it induces in its disciples a moral quietude that only increases the tyrannical potential of universal ethics (504), for the true believer need not cudgel his brains to find the right course of action, no matter how complicated or delicate the particular case may be. While this calm assurance may seem to contradict the assertion that the general rule cannot decide between the claims of the individual and those of society, in a chilling passage in which Barrès seems to foresee the "ethics" of an Adolf Eichmann, the narrator affirms that obedience to the rule in fact solves every moral dilemma by dictating a single acceptable choice, provided that choice conform to the principle of total responsibility to the collectivity (505). Knowledge of the universal rule, moreover, guides action in a second way, by inciting the knower to apply that standard to other people, ostensibly for their own good, in actuality in order to dominate them (505).

Arboreal Ethics

Barrès's answer to what he finds most odious in Bouteiller, according to the majority of scholars, is the fictionalized Taine who appears in the famous chapter VII of the novel titled *L'arbre de M. Taine* (*Mr. Taine's Tree*). Curious about the author of an admiring newspaper review of his *Origins of Contemporary France*, Taine pays a visit to Roemerspacher's lodgings in the Latin Quarter. In response to the older man's inquiries, the student advises him that the younger generation, informed by Kant's critique, no longer believes in either the spiritualism that reigned in French schools during the July Monarchy or the materialism championed by Taine and his generation during the Second Empire. Untroubled on the level of epistemology, they are nevertheless disturbed by the lack of an absolute morality, unable to accept the categorical imperative that ignores the fact, which Taine himself, after Pascal, has demonstrated so well, that in varying periods and climates different laws and morals become just and necessary (*Les déracinés* 594). Taine replies to the student's tacit request for guidance with his own declaration of faith. The key to moral life is sociability: Everyone should act in accordance with the customs of the social order (595). In consequence, he recommends that Roemerspacher should join with his comrades from Nancy to form an organized group (595).

The text characterizes this 'Goethean' philosophy as the strongest possible contradiction to Kant and Bouteiller, and as a viable alternative to the attempt to reorganize society on the basis of pure reason, which Taine criticizes heavily in his *Origines* (*Les déracinés* 596). The fact that Barrès has previously neglected to mention human dignity in the novel, especially its glaring omission from his depiction of Bouteiller's lessons on the Kantian ethic, makes it plausible to assume that he approves of this defense of "the spontaneous vitality of regional and social 'milieus' against the deracinating influence of the Republican administration" (Ringer 133). All the more so, since Taine finds his ideal of human and social dignity embodied in the arboreal image of a plane tree growing in the Place des Invalides. A product of the mysterious, unifying, creative forces of nature, it develops according to its own inner law, its destiny, without the need for any external direction or control. Never having been uprooted, the tree has managed to preserve the autonomy that lies at the root of dignity. The "expressive image of a beautiful existence," it is an organic unity bursting with health, a "rustling federation" of branches, leaves, and trunk, with no part dominating the others nor any artificial French symmetry. Above all, it images forth the ethical principle that has guided Taine in his philosophy and throughout his life, the acceptance of the necessities of life (*Les déracinés* 597). When confronted with external obstacles to its development, it adapts to those conditions as best it can. Eventually, having attained its state of perfection, it will succumb to the same natural forces that had presided over its birth.

The lessons Roemerspacher draws from this living metaphor are evident. Individuals have a humble, dependent place in society and in history. Each person being like a leaf on the tree, it would be of divine nobility if each of these leaves recognized its dependence on the tree, and the limitations placed upon its individual fate by the destiny of the whole tree that controls it. People would profit from knowing that they are at first produced identical to their predecessors and successors by a natural force, and that they will later be detached from their branch by a similar force. Contemplation of these problems of universality and unity leads to a feeling of inner joy and religious tranquillity that derives from understanding the laws of nature that govern the lives of the individual and of society and from the satisfaction of submitting to those laws.

From the time of the novel's publication in 1897 to the present, most commentators have taken this fictional character Taine to be the representative of Barrès's views in the text. Ringer, for instance, states that in *Les déracinés* the philosopher "is an intellectual counterweight to Kant and Bouteiller, and a spokesman for Barrès himself" (132). Already Bourget's review of the novel in *Le Figaro* of November 7, 1897, significantly titled "L'arbre de M. Taine," reprinted in "Théories politiques," proclaims that Barrès owed the philosopher his most essential ideas and the best aspects of his method ("Théories politiques" 168). Indeed, it was in Taine's *L'école* that the novelist found the fundamental idea for the entire book, the increasing discordance between school and life due to the excessive centralization of the French *Université* designed to eliminate any trace of local tradition from school and *lycée* (169–70). Above all, Bourget sees in Taine's tree the political lesson of the vital energy of thought (*la sève pensante*) "which causes the same spirit to circulate through many souls in the same era," and which thus can provide the national unity that is so critical if France is to overcome its alleged state of 'decadence' (171).

In the ensuing decades, Ernst Curtius, Pierre-Henri Petitbon, Soucy, and Sternhell also assumed that Barrès endorsed Taine's ethic of acceptance, often citing the unambiguous pronouncements in favor of acceptance Barrès made in *Scenes and Doctrines*: "[W]e are enslaved by the transmissions of the past"; "our dead give us orders which we must obey; we are not free to choose"; "nationalism is the acceptance of a determinism" (*Scènes et doctrines* 12–15). There is certainly much in the novel to support this view of Taine's role. The philosopher is described in glowing terms and the narrator shows his ethic to be superior to that of Kant. Moreover, like Taine in *L'école* (296–97), the narrator explains the errors of his seven students as the result of being subjected to a totally unrealistic education that has deceived them about the realities of the world, causing their imaginations and sensibilities to run wild. Unrealistic, they never think to consult and submit to "[the] conditions imposed by circumstances" (568).

It is this same lack of realism, this same preponderance of imagination over evaluation of the particular empirical facts, inculcated by the schools in accordance with the neo-Kantian rationalism of the Republic, that governs the two main plots of the novel and has induced many readers to see the work as an updated version of Balzac's *Lost Illusions*. Inspired by Taine's principle of association, Roemerspacher incites Sturel and the others to join together in what turns out to be the disastrous decision to start a newspaper. Because of the inadequate funds at the young men's disposal combined with their lack of business and journalistic experience, this project eventually leads Racadot, who has lost his entire inheritance in it, and his friend Mouchefrin, for whom the paper represents the only means of escape from his life of dire poverty, to murder Astiné.

The author shields Taine's teaching from potential blame for its fatal effect by maintaining that, without particular examples as a guide to the correct method for putting a general principle into practice, each person may interpret it differently, according to his own mentality (*Les déracinés* 596). Although Roemerspacher senses that Sturel's plan does not really correspond to Taine's teaching, he nevertheless reluctantly gives in to his friend's urging, carried away by the penchant for the marvelous he acquired as a child raised on fairy tales and crime stories, a taste he maintains through his habit of reading novels of the imaginary before going to bed each night (604).

As it turns out, Sturel has received a similar education of the imagination, first as a child of four or five to whom were read stories of the "Orient," and then, after his arrival in Paris, from his Armenian lover, Astiné, whose exotic tales of her life in Russia and the Caucasus reawaken his childhood reveries (545). In Sturel's case the narrator puts the blame for the corruption of the young man's imagination squarely on the shoulders of the University rationalism that separates him from the realities of his native land and mentality (554). If his hereditary vital forces had not been weakened by Bouteiller's teachings, he could have resisted these dreams of the Orient, "that cup of poison" (553).

If Sturel fails to lift a finger to aid Astiné in her time of need, watching motionless while Racadot and Mouchefrin drag her off to her death, if he avoids turning Mouchefrin in to the police after the crime has been committed, it is because, swept up in the communal life he experiences during Hugo's public funeral ceremonies, he has finally learned the lesson of Taine's ethic of acceptance. Hugo's works and the crowd remind him of the mysterious unity of all the manifestations of life, which leads him to conclude that acceptance is the only reasonable solution (730). Only in view of the totality is each individual justified by his necessity. And that is precisely the Spinozan formula that Taine reproduces in his article on the philosopher in his *Philosophes classiques*. The postulation of absolute determinism guarantees the unity of the whole of Nature, each and every part of it causally related to the rest. The universe is "a hierarchy of necessities" and therefore "a unique, indivisible being, of which all beings are members" (370).

Finally, as Curtius, Soucy, and other critics emphasize, it is the lack of this sense of order and concomitant resignation which motivates the murder that Racadot and Mouchefrin commit. Like their comrades, the two refuse to submit to circumstances, and after the killing the narrator wonders rhetorically whether the "educator Bouteiller" and the spirit of their society "could have caused Racadot and Mouchefrin not to prefer a crime to the collapse of their ambitions" (*Les déracinés* 708). His conclusion, foregone, is that the government and its minions (like Bouteiller) are indeed responsible for Mouchefrin's and Racadot's failure to be "transplanted," delivering them up to "anarchy, a mortal disorder" (738). The University and the Republic are thus found guilty of Astiné's murder, and all because, far from teaching their charges the proper sense of order and resignation, they incited them to aspire beyond their social, financial, and intellectual means.

Voluntary Determinism

Not all readers are so firmly convinced of Barrès's complete adherence to Taine's principles, however; nor do they necessarily accept the notion that Barrès's nationalism is the strict equivalent of Taine's conservatism. Moreover, while many critics, whether hostile (Suleiman) or favorable (Petitbon), see the trilogy as all of a piece, others claim to perceive serious inconsistencies in its ideology and fissures in its narrative surface.

Virtually all the disputes turn on the question of the relations between determinism, ethics, and political action. To what degree does the author accept Taine's ethic of acceptance? What is the latter's relation to determinism? And to what extent are both doctrines compatible with an active political program of nationalism?

Ringer points out the inherent contradiction in Taine's parable of the tree (133): How can the voluntaristic theory of sociability and the formation of associations, which leads toward the politics of regional nationalism that Bourget took to be the primary message of the novel, be reconciled with the doctrine of causal environmentalism illustrated by the tree's "acceptance of the necessities of life"? An expert on the development of ideology in Germany during the period, Ringer notes that the metaphors of organic growth in the tree allegory bear only a superficial resemblance to the German conception of *Bildung,* for the diversity implied is that of "conditioning environments" rather than of "self-defining individuals," with the result that the unstable equilibrium between voluntarism and social determinism is soon upset, the former giving way to the latter (133). Underneath this observation seems to lie the reproach several "humanist" critics (e.g., Curtius, Soucy, Stern-hell), who correctly see Barrès's attacks on Kantianism as assaults on the humanist principles they hold dear—"the mental anarchy, called humanism, that the *Université* put into [Sturel et Roemerspacher]" (*L'Appel au soldat* 775)—level explicitly at Barrès: by denying the autonomy of the subject, he eliminates the possibility of free will and thereby of any genuine morality, which must of necessity be universal. In its place, he leaves only the relativist pseudoethic of nationalism: "resolve each question in relation to France," a grotesque parody of the categorical imperative and formula for amoral intolerance at best (Curtius 168, who wrote before the rise of Nazism), a source of xenophobia, racism, and brutality at worst (Soucy and Sternhell, writing after World War II).

The ethical and political stakes are high, then, in the controversy over what at first might have appeared to be the merely logical inconsistency involved in advocating both voluntarism and determinism at the same time. It is therefore essential to ascertain how Barrès attempts to juggle these two disparate principles. Now the very fact that Roemerspacher and friends could, as we have seen, "misapply" Taine's voluntaristic principle indicates that there is a clash between it and an underlying determinism. The proof of its erroneous use is not, after all, a matter of logic but of "empirical" consequences. It is the plot that gainsays the idea of the newspaper association. In other words, the issue in question is not the abstract dilemma of 'determinism versus free will,' but rather the correlation between voluntary action and its outcome. The mistake in the utilization of the principle is that it went against the realities of the situation—the background, education, experience, social class, and financial status of the participants, and the conditions of journalism in Paris at the time. The implication is that, if associating in groups can be done poorly, it can also be done properly, where 'properly' means 'in agreement with the underlying determinism of the situation.' Once again it is Barrès's empirical and historical particularism that unlocks the door to understanding the ideological and narrative structure of the novel.

The specific facts and conditions, however (and in this respect Barrès remains quite faithful to Taine and the entire tradition of French positivism), must be organized into a general 'law' in order to furnish a complete explanation of phenomena. The name of that law is included in the title of the work, "rootedness." It is the students' deracination and their subsequent inability to achieve a happy 'transplantation' in the capital that prevents them from taking accurate cognizance of the situation and condemns their enterprise to failure. Had they not been "detached from the soil, from all society, from their families" (512) by the *lycée* environment and by Bouteiller's teaching, which led to their ensuing immigration to Paris, they would presumably have been better able to implement Taine's doctrine of assembly, for they would have remained in contact with the national consciousness, their land and their history (513).

While the critics and the public of the late 1890s welcomed or condemned Barrès's shift from the earlier *Cult of the Ego* to the nationalism of *Les déracinés* as a radical break in his career, in fact, as the author himself protested and as several more recent critics have acknowledged, despite the obvious disparities, the major propositions of deracination form part of a theory he had been developing at least since the end of the previous decade. As early as 1891, in his retrospective "Examen" of the *Cult of the Ego* trilogy, he had asserted that Philippe, the hero of *Un homme libre* (*A Free Man*), sees himself as part of a tradition that gives meaning to his life, and, by means of that tradition, plunges himself into the collective unconscious of humanity, of universal life. Barrès refers the reader to Schopenhauer and, above all, to Hartmann's *Philosophy of the Unconscious* (translated into French in 1877; Barrès, "Examen" 20–21).

The way has been prepared for exalting the immersion of the individual in the group, and it will only require a few reversals in order to arrive at the nationalist position: the 'necessary law' of positivism will be redefined as the operation of heredity, and the group will become one's ancestors. Already in the third volume of the series, *Le jardin de Bérénice* (*Berenice's Garden*), written just after his own election as *député* from Nancy in 1890, Barrès had conferred a political meaning onto this theme through the Platonic move of assimilating Hartmann's Unconscious to the "soul of the people." This popular soul acts as the conditioning matrix of temporal evolution, since, by virtue of its function as the repository of the past experiences of the "race," it contains the roots of the future as well (*Le jardin de Bérénice* 229). The word "race" is still understood here in the cultural sense of Herder, equivalent to that of the English term "a people," that was customary in the first two-thirds of the nineteenth century, especially among writers of the political left; but Hartmann's unconscious has provided a bridge between the psychological and the physiological realms which will soon facilitate the transformation of the social being into the biological entity of Barrès's later racist ideology (230). It is instinct rather than reason that shapes the future, for the unconscious is the creative force of the world (229–31). Nevertheless, for the time being at least, this creative energy remains an attribute of humanity at large rather than the property of a specific race.

While there is no logical necessity for this idea to evolve into a theory of deracination, it does provide a natural connection to the later doctrine in that it implies the existence of a ubiquitous instance whose force must be either recognized and abetted or ignored and thwarted. Consciousness, and with it education, comes back into its own somewhat in the guise of guardian or gatekeeper. Keeping the genie in the bottle, failing to recognize the sense of the unconscious, can only result in disaster, whereas acknowledging its existence and framing one's wishes in accordance with its inherent direction will lead to the outburst of creative energy. In sum, this soul of the people has become the dominating force in human affairs, the native soil in which alone the tree of humanity can prosper.

The superior intuitive knowledge and creative force of the popular soul only emerge, however, when the members of the people are fused together in large gatherings, a crowd (*Le jardin de Bérénice* 236). Unlike Zola or Gustave Le Bon, who generally fear and distrust the mob, and in total opposition to Taine, who makes it the very principle of Revolutionary evil, Barrès not only welcomes it but sees in it the sole path to political salvation. As individuals, the members of the people are just as dominated by reflective self-interest as those of the other social classes. Only by shedding one's rational outer coating can one liberate the instinctive core of "energy" imprisoned underneath that same "foam" of education identified with the "barbarians" in his first novel, and this effect can best be attained through the mutual influence Le Bon a few years later would call suggestive "contagion."

In reality, Barrès had not simply abandoned the ethics of individuality in favor of the politics of crowd passion; rather, he had dislodged the self from its position of mastery, displacing it within the psychological and social fields. Plumbing the depths of the collective unconscious will allow his "real" self to surface from behind the false ego of education, and thereby make it possible to act in accordance with the sense of history. While this theory may seem more fatalistic than deterministic in the scientific sense, Hartmann's instinct played a role homologous to that of Taine's determinism, and the German philosopher went to great pains to give it a scientific, physiological basis. A similar tension reigns between it and voluntary action, and Barrès resolves this conflict in a way not so different after all from Hugo, Goethe, or Renan, not to mention Marx: The first goal of the *Moi* must be to attune itself with the determining force of the unconscious; the energy liberated can then serve to fuel voluntary group action, but this associative activity will be successful only on condition of taking account of and working in harmony with the underlying potential of instinct.

Toward Nationalism

Well before *Les déracinés,* then, Barrès had found a modus vivendi that allowed voluntarism and determinism, rationalism and irrationalism, not only to coexist side by side but to reinforce each other, albeit at the price of endorsing the politics of the crowd that Taine feared and detested. As he moved toward the later nationalism, he felt obliged to distance himself from other Tainian doctrines as well. The promotion of a certain irrationalism and the politicization of the masses, the latter easily assimilated to the rapidly growing urban proletariat created during the economic recovery of the late 1880s and 1890s, were compatible with various forms of socialism and Boulangist populism vying for power with the bourgeois republic in the last decades of the nineteenth century. Lacking still were the specific elements that would shift Barrès's program from a variant of socialism to the virulent revolutionary nationalism of the turn of the century that recent scholars have portrayed as a kind of protofascism. Those ingredients were supplied by Jules Soury, professor of physiological psychology at the École des hautes études of

the Sorbonne and a violent anti-Semitic pamphleteer during the Dreyfus Affair. Barrès attended his lectures from 1893 to 1897 and soon
enjoyed numerous private conversations with him.[5] Indeed, as Sternhell
has shown in great detail, "Jules Soury was Barrès's true intellectual
guide when he wrote the *Novel of National Energy*" as well as *Scenes and
Doctrines of Nationalism* and *Bastions of the East* (254). It was Soury's
scientific theories of physiological determinism, influenced by Darwin,
Haeckel, and Spencer, which transformed Barrès's long-standing anti-
Semitism into something approaching a biological racism, and it was
those same notions that allowed the writer to amalgamate Hartmann's
instinctual unconscious and Taine's determinism into the principle of
cultural heredity that reigns in his nationalist program.

It would be a mistake, however, to see this shift as a change from
scientific rationalism to protofascist irrationalism (cf. Sternhell, *Maurice
Barrès et le nationalisme français* 16–20, 259–62, 269–71). Even before
the publication of *Les déracinés,* Barrès announced publicly his rejection
of Taine's belief in the autonomy and power of individual reason, in
"Taine et le philistin," which appeared in *Le Figaro* of December 19,
1896 (*Taine et Renan* 101). In that same article he already espoused
Soury's principle of the automatism of thought resulting from the invol-
untary reactions common to all those living in a given milieu (101).
On the other hand, in *L'Appel au soldat* the narrator declares that both
Soury and Taine embraced the same principle of natural and historical
development (767). And in the text of *Les déracinés* Barrès quotes with
approval the expression that had come to symbolize the repudiation of
autonomous reason that had become a commonplace in the German
physiology of the period: "Intellect, what a small thing on the surface of
ourselves! Certain Germans do not say, 'I think,' but, 'it thinks in me';
in our depths we are affective beings" (660).

This is not simply an isolated assertion; the dynamic principle of
the novel is the ruling force of the nonrational in human affairs. From
the start, Bouteiller's students are influenced by his person, his style, his
career, and the images of the Republic with which he coalesces in their
minds, much more than by the ideas he advocates. In accordance with
the views of Ignatius Loyola or Le Bon, it is the nonrational image, as
opposed to the idea, that plays the dominant role in the key nationalist scenes of the work, when the students gather around Napoleon's
tomb and when the country mourns the passing of Hugo. Likewise,
during his conversation with Taine, Roemerspacher discovers that the
thinker is not just a set of ideas, methods, and abstractions as he had
previously assumed, but a body, an animal (598). It is this physicality,

this animality, corporality, and mortality that inspire him and Sturel to form their association with the other students, for "the idea of death and their animality . . . like an aphrodisiac, injects into their blood the frantic desire to live right away" (605). Most telling is the fact that the narrator introduces the passage quoted above about the feebleness of intelligence compared to affect in order to downgrade the power of Roemerspacher's rational analysis and to confirm the validity of Sturel's intuitive assessment of the situation in France (660).

Note that Barrès does not call into question the rationality, the intelligibility, of the world but only the capacity of individual reason to attain knowledge of it. In this respect, he is simply following the lead of standard conservative thought. Burke, for instance, says exactly the same thing in order to justify his dismissal of the rational principles of the Revolution in favor of the policy of basing human (i.e., British) law on the "natural" principle of inheritance: "[T]his policy appears to me to be the result of profound reflection; or rather the happy effect of following nature, which is *wisdom without reflection,* and above it" (119; emphasis added). Barrès's repudiation of Taine in this passage could not be more evident, for, in "L'influence de M. Taine" (*Le Journal* March 6, 1893), the writer precisely singled out "analysis," ascertaining the causes of a series of phenomena, as the key to Taine's "method" and therefore as one of the two elements of his success (*Taine et Renan* 64–65).

In short, it is clear that Barrès had already been converted to Soury's ideas by the time he wrote *Les déracinés.* Yet this brand of irrationalism could not have been the motivating force behind Barrès's attempts to overthrow the Republic, still less the justification of those efforts, since it was a widespread cliché of the scientistic thought of the times and even formed part of the official ideology of that very Republic. As we have seen, Jules Ferry, following the positivist theories of Comte and his disciples as well as of Spencer's *On Education* (translated in 1878), justified teaching secular morality in the schools with exactly the same "irrationalist" ideas as Soury. The heart is more powerful than the intellect; the 'instinct' of sympathy, which is the basis of morality, is as natural an affection as selfishness; sentiments must be actively cultivated and developed; and the goal of ethical instruction in the schools is to teach the individual to subordinate himself to the group, and above all to national unity in order to combat "intellectual anarchy."

Champions of scientific rationalism and the Republic such as Émile Durkheim argued that the individual is unimportant without the group (Weisz 292), and that society "lives and acts in him" (quoted in Weisz

294). Alfred Espinas, a philosopher appointed in 1894 to the newly created chair in the history of social economy at the Sorbonne and thus a quasi-official spokesman for the Republic, announced in his inaugural lecture that "human action was largely based on irrational beliefs and desires" (Weisz 293).

Similar "irrationalist" claims are found in the writings of Ribot, Le Bon, and a host of others (see Sternhell, *Droite révolutionnaire* and Nye, *Origins of Crowd Psychology*). They all show that not only is a certain anti-individualism and irrationalism compatible with a certain rationalism, and specifically with various types of determinism, but that the particular brand of irrationalism to which Soury and Barrès adhered in actuality derives directly from rationalism itself. Ribot's first important work, *La psychologie anglaise contemporaine* (*Contemporary English Psychologie*; 1870), was a presentation to the French public of the psychological theories of the British empiricists, from Locke to Spencer, most of whom attacked the notion of free will in the name of determinism and attempted to separate it from morality. The arguments of John Stuart Mill, whom one can hardly accuse of being a wild-eyed irrationalist let alone a protofascist, are characteristic: Morality is independent of freedom; we judge someone moral if they are beneficent to others, immoral if they are not (Ribot, *La psychologie anglaise* 143). Moreover, necessity, in the literal sense, does not apply to human motives and causality (in Mill's conception of the term). Even in a fatalistic view (which Mill did not hold), responsibility subsists and so does punishment (143). This was precisely Taine's position in response to *The Disciple,* and Barrès's in *Les déracinés.*

But it is not only nineteenth-century empirical scientism that led to these principles. Spinoza, the rationalist's rationalist, had long since derived similar conclusions about the unity of nature and the subjection of the individual to the totality from what he, and Taine after him, considered to be purely logical, a priori considerations. Indeed, it is not by chance that rationalism leads to irrationalism—the denial of free will and autonomy—via determinism. The basic premise of Spinoza's line of reasoning is, in a sense, reason itself, that is, the ultimate intelligibility of the universe. We can only understand that which we can explain causally, and there is no way to arrest the chain of causes before we reach the totality of the world. Individuals are merely parts of the whole, so that the only sensible attitude for us to take toward life is to accept our role in the system of necessities. What appears to be irrationality from our individual perspective turns out in reality to be ultimate rationality when considered under the aspect of eternity, as Spinoza's famous phrase has it.

We must acknowledge, then, that important elements of Barrès's irrationalism are, in the writer's view at least, perfectly compatible with certain aspects of Taine's rationalism, which in turn come directly from the principles of the Enlightenment, such as the belief in the fundamental intelligibility of the human as well as of the natural worlds, the existence of general causal "laws" governing the various series of observable phenomena, and the conviction that all are subject to the familiar Tainian determining categories of race, moment, and milieu; and that the hereditary determinism Barrès took from Soury was in fact a commonplace of the scientistic doctrines of the era. In short, to admit that it is impossible to separate rationalism from irrationalism neatly and without overlap, and that, as a result, fascism cannot be explained as the consequence of antihumanistic irrationalism.

Dialogic Ethics

How, then, do these solutions to the tension between voluntary action and determinism, rationalism and irrationalism, affect Barrès's attitude toward Taine's ethic of acceptance? The external evidence is unequivocal. In private Barrès was quick to reject the claim, made by Bourget in his *Figaro* review, that he was indebted to Taine for all the ideas espoused in *Les déracinés* (*Oeuvres* XIII 138; entry of November 13, 1897). He had already made the same stand public in his response to a survey of opinions about Taine's works published in *La Revue Blanche* in the summer of 1897, precisely at the time when the last installments of *Les déracinés* were appearing in the *Revue de Paris*. While generally praising the philosopher's ideas, he had denounced the ethic of acceptance they implied as lacking energy and encouraging timidity (*Taine et Renan*). In fact, in an early draft of the novel, Barrès had included a passage of commentary which explicitly condemned Roemerspacher's visitor for glazing "the fatalistic and cruel doctrines issued forth from Spinoza" with a patina of morality. Although the logic of Spinoza's ideas ought to condemn morality as a religious survival, for a novice like Roemerspacher there is something intoxicating about the idea that necessity governs both nature and history (*Romans et voyages* 1377 n266).

The fact remains, however, that Barrès chose not to include this comment in the final version of the work, and we might well wonder why not. It cannot be that he simply changed his mind, since his remarks in the *Revue Blanche* survey appeared after the completion of the manuscript of *Les déracinés*. Indeed, his critique of Taine's pusillanimity does emerge within the novel, but not in the form he had first envisaged. While Barrès was rarely shy about expressing his views directly in this work, in the case of Taine's ethic of acceptance the writer chose to present them in dialogue rather than in explicit narratorial interventions. His brain overheated by the blaze of new ideas and the sheer excitement of Taine's visit, Roemerspacher cannot wait a moment to relay everything to his friend Sturel. The latter is genuinely happy for his comrade, but is less than enthusiastic about his message: "In what you are reporting to me and what I discern in M. Taine, there is something sad and humble; excuse me, Maurice: something servile . . . it's the doctrine of renunciation" (602). Sturel goes on to explain that of course he prefers Taine's stoicism to the mentality of exploitation he senses in Bouteiller, but his ideal is an "intellectual"—this was written before the Dreyfus case had become a cause célèbre—who is not afraid of life, who is willing to take risks and confront unexpected dangers; someone who would renounce nothing but rather "absorb" everything that comes his way and integrate it all into a new and unique unity. For Sturel, thought has value only insofar as it stimulates action, as it inspires and mobilizes his creative energy (602–4).

There are several good reasons for thinking that Sturel acts as Barrès's spokesperson here. The simplest is that, if anyone is the "hero" of this novel, it is Sturel. The main love interest involves him, Astiné and a young woman named Mlle. Alison, who lives in the same boarding house as he does. It is he who, like Barrès, becomes the champion of the Boulangist cause in the Chamber of Deputies in the second volume of the trilogy and its would-be avenger via the Panama Canal scandal in the third. It is in his mind that the culminating scenes of *Les déracinés* are focalized, the mass funeral ceremonies for Hugo intermingled with the condemnation and execution of Racadot and a confrontation with Mouchefrin and Racadot's mistress, Léontine, after which he becomes the main actor and center of consciousness in the following two volumes. Moreover, Sturel's ideal recapitulates Barrès's ideology of the "Cult of the Ego" and the "energy" that gives its name to the trilogy. Indeed Barrès deliberately situates this dialogic conflict of "two contradictory ethics" in the symbolic setting of the Place des Invalides, in which Taine's plane tree is juxtaposed to the tomb of that "professor of energy," Napoleon I (608), and the author dubs it "the dialogue of the Plane Tree and the Dome" (600).

There are equally good reasons, however, for thinking that, while Sturel may be the main character in the sense of capturing the limelight and acting out the writer's inner conflicts, it is Roemerspacher who represents the author's ideal and receives his final approval. Petitbon points out that it is he who gets the girl from Lorraine, Mlle. Alison, whom Sturel could not keep (90). Curtius mentions that it is Sturel's misplaced enthusiasm for Napoleon and Caesarism that leads to the founding of the newspaper and, indirectly, to Astiné's murder. To complicate matters further, Soucy maintains that, while Sturel is the main character, the denouement of the plot proves that Roemerspacher's realism is right, Sturel's idealism wrong. The latter's heroic allegiance to Boulangism come what may is admirable but ultimately misguided, leading only to disappointment and lost illusions, as the general's failure amply demonstrates. In politics, only success has value, and success depends on a realistic assessment of the situation and the willingness to bring one's wishes into conformity with that reality (257). Yet Barrès also continued to criticize Roemerspacher's overly passive determinism: "The perfect hero, Barrès implies, would be someone who would combine the best features of both men, the vigorous activism of Sturel with the social consciousness of Roemerspacher, the dome of Les Invalides with Taine's plane tree" (205).

Is it possible to harmonize these conflicting views with each other? Must we conclude that Barrès's text is shot through with irreconcilable contradictions? A telling clue to an answer is provided by the fact that Barrès chose to frame the debate about acceptance as a dialogue between the two major characters of the novel. This fact would indicate that a purely ideological reading of the work, one that ignores its narrative character, will inevitably overlook important evidence of the degree of validity the text imputes to the ideas expressed. In this particular case, we know that Barrès began with a single character modeled on a friend named Audiat, but soon decided to split this prototype of Sturel into several independent personae in order, precisely, to be able to present "multiple points of view" (Germain 35, quoting from an early draft by Barrès).

It was the concept of the absolute ego, derived from his early reading of Fichte, Feuerbach, and Stirner, that led simultaneously to the rejection of everything that was "*not-I*" and to the conviction that each person sees the world from his or her own individual perspective (Frandon, *Barrès précurseur* 51–54). Barrès found the same idea expressed in Bourget's summary of the mentality reigning in the fin de siècle due to the "dilettantism" of Renan and the "analysis" of Taine. The importance of point of view combined with the deprecation of narratorial intervention had of course been essential tenets of the discourse of the novel since Flaubert. But it was the symbolist reaction against the naturalist novel that led to the new conception of fiction that Barrès helped to initiate in the first books of the *Cult of the Ego* (Ouston 55, and n37). If Barrès decided to present the conflict over Taine's doctrines as a dialogue between two sympathetically drawn characters rather than in narratorial commentary, it was precisely in order to leave the debate open, at least for a considerable time. By doing so, he could show the divergent views at work, not merely as an abstract dispute between opposing ideas but as dynamic forces that govern the way Sturel and Roemerspacher understand the world and hence the way they live their lives.

It is therefore not at all surprising that the question of the author's acceptance of Taine's ethic of acceptance should be open to so many conflicting appraisals. Assessing the didactic import of these characters cannot be restricted to purely ideological considerations. As Suleiman eventually concedes (*Authoritarian Fictions* 205–8), mythos does not surrender to logos so easily. Even in a *roman à thèse,* at least in this one, plot and character do not merely "illustrate" ideas, for the simple reason that any judgment of *what the thesis actually is* must take into account the literariness of the text, distinguishing the nuances of voice and focus, heeding the qualifications of statements and the complexities of tone, and, above all, examining the relation of the ideological positions claimed to the events recounted. In sum, it must scrutinize each relevant passage individually and carefully in light of the entire text if it is to determine accurately the political thrust of Barrès's explanations and their possible relations to the theory or practice of fascism.

It is true that the narrator of the *Novel of National Energy* never wavers from his thesis on the evils of uprooting, but, as the conflicting interpretations cited above demonstrate, it is not at all clear what the implications of this thesis are in every case, and particularly in that of Taine's ethic of acceptance. Nor is it always a simple matter to determine which character acts as spokesperson for the author. A closer reading of the admiring descriptions of Taine in chapter VII indicates, for instance, that they bathe in the aura produced by the impressions of the young Roemerspacher, who, quite obviously, is deeply honored and touched by the celebrated thinker's visit to his room. In several passages of this chapter, the prevalence of the character's point of view is indicated only by the use of the free indirect discourse perfected by Flaubert and Zola, in which it is difficult to distinguish between narrator and character, since the narrative voice continues to be that of the narrator using the third person, while only subtle verbal or contextual hints attest that the feelings, ideas, or impressions are actually those of the character. When Roemerspacher hears the knock on his door and cries, "Come in," for instance, the text continues: "A stranger, almost an old man, rather short, with a serious and unaffected look, appeared" (591). Clearly the term "stranger" conveys the student's impression, not the evaluation of the narrator (or author), and it is the young man who notes the philosopher's "serious and unaffected look." After Taine introduces himself, the text reads: "Obviously, the illustrious philosopher, interested by the work of this unknown writer, had gone to the newspaper's office" (591). Here again, the "obviously" introduces, in free indirect discourse, the student's reconstruction of the process by which Taine was able to locate his residence. Similarly, the passage summarized above describing the lessons imparted by the tree image are placed under Roemerspacher's aegis in a kind of free indirect discourse typically introduced by a verb of perception or thought: "What he glimpses immediately is . . . " (599). Even the passage insisting that Taine's "Goethian" morality of sociability is the very antithesis of Bouteiller's neo-Kantianism may be taken either as the narrator's voice or as free indirect discourse representing the student's ruminations, since the paragraph in which it appears is introduced by a sentence indicating the impression of the character: "This point of view is so new that the young man doesn't know how to relate to it" (595).

Of course, the mere presence of free indirect discourse does not automatically prove that the narrator is distancing himself from the ideas expressed. Indeed, some scholars maintain that the style always marks a fusion between narrator and character. Moreover, not every passage in the chapter is in free indirect discourse. In certain cases the narrator speaks directly in his own voice; in others, the thoughts are explicitly those of the student alone. The only certainty to be deduced from the key passages in chapter VII, however, is that it is Roemerspacher who admires and approves wholeheartedly of Taine's ideas. Insofar as it is reflected in the narrator's expressed attitudes, the author's stand at this point is not so much ambiguous as simply left open.

After the explicit pronouncements of the narrator, a second major narrative criterion for determining the thesis is the account of the education of the central characters, who can be expected to discover and expound the "truth," espousing the "right" values and rejecting the "wrong" ones (Suleiman, *Authoritarian Fictions* 76–78). Whether or not the outcome is predictable because fixed in advance, this learning entails a temporal process in which, under the test of experience, the characters' beliefs and values undergo one or more changes during the course of the story. That even Roemerspacher's belief in Taine's teaching is deeply shaken is demonstrated by his experience as a student in Germany, in *L'Appel au soldat*. In speaking of the "law of continuity and universal determinism" in his letter to Sturel (*L'Appel au soldat* 771), the young man claims that it is the Germans who embrace Taine's idea, in stark opposition to the French, who allegedly believe in free will. He is horrified to think that he was about to adopt principles which seem to justify the "thousands of Taine's plane trees" he has come upon in Germany (which he then decides to call "German oaks") in their conviction of German supremacy and French inferiority (771). In other words, he recognizes that both the Darwinian idea of development in nature and history, which the narrator briefly evokes in introducing the letter (767), and the ethic of acceptance, imply an acquiescence in the status quo of political forces which contradicts his French patriotism and thus the very nationalism he, Taine, and Barrès are supposed to be promoting in this novel. He manages to quell his misgivings only when he comes to the conclusion that each nation possesses its own truth derived from the facts of its history and inculcates its own ideal into its members, so that it is as natural for the Germans to believe in their own superiority as for the French to act to ensure the survival of their collectivity (774–75). If it is essential that the individual accept his role in the national collectivity, it is just as important that he *not accept* the claims of rival nations. In short, the 'truth' that Roemerspacher discovers, the ultimate ethical principle, is national survival. Even for this supposedly model Tainian, acceptance is good only to the extent and in the manner that it furthers the cause of nationalism. No wonder that in his letter Roemerspacher ends up by revolting against the status quo and embracing revanchist claims to Alsace-Lorraine.

Roemerspacher applies this new understanding of acceptance to the Panama Canal scandals in *Leurs figures,* although it is difficult to decide at that point whether his principle is Tainian or anti-Tainian. While Sturel is intent on exposing those involved in the corruption and bringing them to justice no matter what the cost, Roemerspacher takes the view that his friend is a budding anarchist who is more interested in his own ideas than in the good of society (1197). This may be cynical *Realpolitik,* provoked by Barrès's resentment over the failure of Boulangism and his subsequent defeats in parliamentary elections, as Soucy argues (112–13), or, just as likely, a coded justification for valuing the army over the truth, Barrès's basic anti-Dreyfusard stance during the Dreyfus

Affair, but does it represent an unequivocal acceptance of Taine's ideas? It will be recalled that in *Les déracinés* Roemerspacher had played the same 'good of society' card in order to justify the rejection rather than the acceptance of criminality, labeling Racadot and Mouchefrin "venomous dust," and "wolves to be slaughtered" in order to protect society (725–26). If we take the signifier "Taine" to mean the good of society as opposed to the claims of the individual, then Roemerspacher remains consistent in these two apparently opposed stances; if it signifies instead acceptance, then he has reversed his attitude from the first to the last novel.

Are we supposed to take him at his word, without second thoughts? Earlier Sturel had expressed the strong suspicion that Roemerspacher's attitude toward justice in the Panama affair was the result of his own petty self-interest rather than of any broad concern for the well-being of society (1068). Afraid that his career and his liaison with Mme. de Nelles (the former Mlle. Alison) might be compromised if he supported Sturel's efforts to bring the truth to light, Roemerspacher accuses the latter of anarchism, that is, of attacking the social order out of exaggerated individualism, in order to cover up his own egotism and cowardice. For Barrès, Taine's acceptance connotes careerism and pusillanimity as much as a genuine concern for the welfare of the body politic.

Roemerspacher's final lesson in the trilogy is that intelligence does not have the importance he had previously attributed to it. About to be married to Mme. de Nelles, who has obtained a divorce from her husband thanks to Sturel's last-minute agreement not to publish his list of *chéquards* (the members of Parliament who had taken graft in return for support of financing the Panama Canal) which included the name of M. de Nelles, Roemerspacher announces to him: "'Intelligence, bah! We are affective beings in our depths. Emotivity is the great human quality," without which intellect must remain sterile (1197). Now, in these novels the signifier "Taine" stands precisely for excessive devotion to intellect. It is certainly not by chance that his main philosophical treatise is titled *De l'intelligence,* as any contemporary reader would have recalled. More important, as Curtius emphasized from the outset, in the trilogy Roemerspacher represents the primacy of the intellect, while Sturel exemplifies that of the life of feeling (81). Upon hearing his friend quote Soury to him in this way, Sturel indeed recognizes that Roemerspacher has come around to the way of thinking that has motivated his, Sturel's, involvement in Boulangism and the Panama affair.

A recognition scene in the Aristotelian sense, this moment marks the perception that the two aspects of life must be combined, the emotional leading to heroism, the intellectual to determinism, as Soucy maintains (206). Roemerspacher had declared (paraphrasing Soury): "Every great discovery, every lofty and powerful thought, is always accompanied by extraordinary emotivity. That's what I failed to recognize for years" (1197). And Sturel concludes that his own political commitments have resulted from high-minded reasoning about the nation's destiny "pushed to a degree at which intellect joins and confirms the instinctive passions" (1197).

Sturel's development is no more conclusive a vindication of Taine's ethic of acceptance than is Roemerspacher's self-serving collectivism. In *L'Appel au soldat*, Sturel makes a pilgrimage through his native Lorraine guided by his friend Saint-Phlin, during which he and the narrator wax sarcastic over the sluggishness of the German peasants in the Moselle area of Trier and Koblenz, and their lack of any superior people who might stir up "disorder." Sturel and Saint-Phlin are dismayed by the French-speaking tavern keeper, who has no sense of responsibility toward the war of 1870, the siege of Paris, or the occupation of his country, and they remark derisively that the fellow accepts all events with the "resignation of a serf" (958). In a note, Rambaud indicates sensibly that this episode betrays Barrès's hesitation between 'order' and the 'disorder' of genius and revolution, referring to the article in *Le Journal* (1900), "La maison natale de M Taine." In sum, the trip does convince Sturel of the value of reverence for one's ancestors, of "soil and the dead" nationalism, but by no means of acceptance.

In fact, after the tour of Lorraine he parts ways with Saint-Phlin, irritated at the latter's smug willingness to settle for the mediocrity of everyday life, marrying the girl next door and raising a family rather than joining Sturel on the path of adventure fighting for the Boulangist cause. Of course there were still one and a half novels to go before the end of the trilogy, so Barrès could hardly afford to complete his protagonist's education so early. But beyond this practical consideration emerges the sense that the writer wants above all to preserve Sturel as the man of desire—the 'enemy of the laws' as the title of Barrès's earlier novel has it—by having him refuse to submit to any law, whether it be the social law of marriage or the intellectual law of a fixed ideology, even that of nationalism. Indeed, throughout the last novel of the series, Sturel resists the sermons on nationalist acceptance he receives from Roemerspacher and especially from Saint-Phlin. It is only at the very end of the book, when he has lost his father and given up his campaign against the *chéquards* out of love for Mme. de Nelles that he finally acquiesces, grudgingly, to arboreal logic. Unable to bear the idea that he alone might be responsible for all his failures, "[he] saw the individual subjected to circumstances, attached to large groups, like the leaf to the oak shaken by the storm" (1199). But the admission that he is merely an extension of his parents and ancestors is a bitter pill for him to swallow, one that induces a kind of drugged torpor (1199). This hardly qualifies as a resounding endorsement of the nationalist politics of soil and the dead!

As in *Les déracinés,* the final pages of *Leurs figures* are devoted to Sturel's ruminations, about the past and the future. He goes for a walk in the parks of Versailles on his thirtieth birthday in 1893, a year when the right lost heavily in the elections. Now, contemplating the dying leaves, thinking of his friends' successes and his own defeats, he begins to convince himself of the circumstantial interpretation of those failures, slowly reconciling himself to the idea of acceptance (1208). He does not do so, however, in the spirit of a Roemerspacher or a Saint-Phlin; on the contrary, inspired by the poplars reaching toward the sky, he defiantly refuses to give up his desire, his idealism (1208–9).

The last scene of the trilogy is an encounter between Sturel and Bouteiller, both licking the wounds suffered in their parliamentary battles (Bouteiller, compromised in the Panama scandal, has just lost his seat to Suret-Lefort). Well before Derrida's *Glas,* Barrès juxtaposes their reflections about the future in two parallel columns on the same pages. Whereas Bouteiller can think of nothing but appeasing the elite of his political party, Sturel's soul-searching leads him to decide that he should not accept the definition of himself as a failure, which others want to attach to him like children tying tin cans onto a dog's tail. Here he reverts to the main theme from *Sous l'oeil des barbares,* in which the Fichtean ego of the protagonist takes on the divinity described by Spinoza as the lack of any limitation from outside itself, that is, of any definition (*Barbares* 73–77). The problem for Sturel is the same: If he accepted that definition, it would mean that he had taken his inspiration from outside not from within. He concludes by essaying a combination of autonomy and necessity, of individualism and collectivism: "My heroic resolutions have value only if they proceed from a deep inner necessity, from something ethnic" (1211).

I will give myself over to my inner necessity. If I maintain my tradition, if I prevent my chain from being unlinked, if I am the son of my dead ones and the father of their grandchildren, I may not bring the plans of my race to reality, but I will maintain their potential. My task is clear: become more and more a man of Lorraine, to be Lorraine so that she can traverse intact this period when decerebrated and dissociated France seems to suffer from general paralysis. (1211)

CHAPTER 4

The Novel of National Energy

ᴇ᷎⟨◉⟩᷎ᴏ

Nationalism, Identity, and the Transferential Novel

Extimate Identity

Sturel's tour de force in his final acceptance of acceptance, or perhaps his sleight of hand, is to harmonize the apparent contradictories that have plagued not only himself but the entire novel. He has accomplished, or at least talked himself into believing that he has accomplished, what Barrès claimed in his "Réponse à M. René Doumic" (1900) as the major achievement of his writing to that point in his career: showing that "the individual ego was completely supported and sustained by society" (181). Far from contradicting his *Cult of the Ego*, the collectivism of the *Novel of National Energy* represents the logical development of the "constant opinions" he expressed in *A Free Man*. It is easy enough to poke holes in this argument: Barrès's attitude toward Lorraine, its inhabitants, and his ancestors underwent a reversal from the early novel to the later nationalist period, from loathing to adoration, as he abandoned his former cosmopolitanism in favor of regional nationalism (Rambaud 1259 n235; Soucy 75). When confronted with this sort of objection, Barrès responded that perhaps he did not follow the arid logic of the schools, but he did at least adhere to "the superior logic of a tree seeking light and yielding to its inner necessity" ("Réponse à M. René Doumic 179).

This last statement sounds very much like an endorsement, or rather a repetition, of Taine's tree parable, but it differs from the latter by the single word "inner." Taine's tree followed its own internal law, but yielded to the necessities imposed upon it by the external environment; Barrès's, on the contrary, yields to an inner compulsion. When Barrès finally sings the praises of acceptance, as he does in his "Réponse" (182) and in the contemporary *Scènes et doctrines* (19), he is accepting what he takes to be an internal pressure. This is precisely the same difference that Sturel insists upon in resisting Roemerspacher's notion of necessity, for in it resides the key to his—and Barrès's—sense of identity. Barrès's nationalism is the acceptance of a determinism (12, 13), but it is a determinism that aims to preserve the freedom of its adherents. The contradictory nature of these two requirements is evident, as Jules Renard noted with glee (Soucy 208); yet they do have a certain hidden coherence similar to that already adumbrated in Barrès's exaltation of the collective unconscious in *Le jardin de Bérénice*. For the nationalist Barrès as for Sturel or the nameless hero of *Barbarians*—but also for Spinoza, Kant's pupil Fichte, or for Kant himself—the enemy is the Other, otherness in any form, like definition, constituting the negation of autonomy. In Kant the subject is free to the extent that it obeys reason, giving itself its own law, determining its own action in competition with, if not in downright contradiction to, the external law of physical determinism. Likewise for Barrès in his nationalist phase, insofar as one's ancestors are experienced as forming the core of one's inner being, accepting their "determinism" is the ultimate expression of the freedom of the self. It is in this context that Carroll's astute remark should be read: In this conception, the others which the self is, its ancestors or fellow countrymen, are not really other, for they are felt to be "affinities" (*Réponse* 181), that is, the same as the self (Carroll 27).

When Barrès protests in his response to Doumic that in the *National Energy* trilogy he has merely developed the tendencies laid forth in *A Free Man,* in this respect at least he is telling the plain truth. The social self that forms the base of the individual self resists domination by what it conceives to be the external just as strongly and in just the same way as the self of the *Cult of the Ego.* Moreover, the social self is not the simple opposite, nor even the adamant antagonist of the individual, at least not in France, for, according to Barrès, the individualism enshrined in the Declaration of the Rights of Man during the Revolution forms an integral part of French historical tradition and therefore of French identity (1904 preface to *Un homme libre* 93–94). He is even open to foreign influences, of a sort: namely, he will take, and has taken, from foreign cultures that which can be divested of its otherness and "transformed" into something compatible with the self, the way a plant assimilates the minerals with which it nourishes itself (93).

What has changed is that formerly Barrès's protagonists believed there was an authentic, natural inner self hidden beneath the social self, waiting to be unearthed and cultivated, whereas now he claims to have discovered that, somewhat as in Barthes's image of the onion, when the various layers of the self are peeled away through continued analyses, eventually one finds nothing—absolutely nothing.

> In *The Uprooted*, the free man discerns and accepts his determinism. A candidate for nihilism pursues his apprenticeship, and, from analysis to analysis, he experiences the nothingness of the Ego. [1904 preface to *Un homme libre* 93]
>
> [I] observed that the "Ego" is destroyed [*s'anéantit*], when subjected to conscientious analysis. . . . But the "Ego" is destroyed in a still more terrifying way if we can recognize our automatic reflexes. . . . We are not the masters of the thoughts that arise within us. They are ways of reacting that translate very ancient physiological dispositions. ("Réponse à Doumic" 182)

At stake in Barrès's denial of the power of personal consciousness here is not merely the individual's claim to independent reason, however crucial that may be, but rather his hold on existence itself. It is this distress, this dread of the total loss of self, that imparts such dire urgency to that lust for being that Barrès knew as the Spinozan desire to "persevere in our being" and that we most often call euphemistically the quest for identity.

It was the shadow of annihilation that gave Barrès's long-standing nationalism its peculiar virulence at the end of the century. While he mentioned the cult of the soil and the dead as a possible solution to the disarray he claimed to perceive in himself and in his country at the time of *The Uprooted*, it was the demise of his father in the following year, 1898, that threw him into the turmoil which frightened him into fully embracing that ideology as the only viable life raft in the ocean of randomness and contingency (Rambaud 1351 n48). Reinforced by the death of his mother a few years later, this reaction was a kind of rejection of mourning, a desperate attempt to "save" his parents from the grip of death (*Mes mémoires* 26), just as the theoreticians of reaction in France, de Maistre and Bonald, wanted to rescue the ancien régime from the oblivion threatened by the Revolution.

Barrès explained his conversion to rootedness in his retrospective account of the motives that impelled him to champion the anti-Drey-fusard cause: "I realized that I was they [my parents] and that it was my destiny, my necessity to maintain them as long as I could. . . . I didn't give a damn [*Je me foutais*] about the universe as soon as I was in agreeement with their memory" (*Mes cahiers,* I 43). Like Lacan's Antigone in his *Ethics of Psychoanalysis,* during the Dreyfus Affair Barrès refused to sacrifice his parents, in all their undefinable singularity, to any universalizing law of truth or justice. And indeed, in his own analysis of the Greek tragedy, Barrès praises the heroine for refusing to bow to the "foreigner" Creon, who applies the laws with his intellect, whereas she succeeds in reconciling her city by listening to her heart and obey-ing her sense of veneration for her "profound heredity," that is, her race (*Scènes et doctrines* 14). Unlike the Lacanian heroine, however, Barrès maintained his stance not through the acceptance of death, but through the denial of it.

Neither Barrès's novels nor the nationalist movement he led would have had the resonance they did, especially among the literati, if this had been a purely personal reaction to a private event. Raoul Girardet cites Barrès's fears of annihilation along with Charles Maurras's dread of being the "last of the French" as evidence that the fear of death seemed to obsess the entire nationalist movement of the times (*Le nationalisme français* 17). The Dreyfus Affair, of course, played a preponderant role in the spread of nationalism after 1897, but the nationalists were neither the first nor the only ones to suffer from this anxiety in the so-called *belle époque.* At the root of the decadent movement, whether considered as a positive or negative phenomenon, were the same fears of death and disintegration, that is, of castration both mental and physical. Nor did they have confidence in the universalist humanism so closely associated with the quasi-official doctrine of the Republic, which Barrès attacked as Kantianism.

For Barrès the solution lay in "making his relativism absolute," as Rambaud pithily expresses the matter, by privileging the point of view of his forebears, the only one, the writer claimed, that makes things appear in their proper proportions to a Frenchman; otherwise, lacking any universal basis, our choice of ethics would be a matter of pure chance (*Scènes et doctrines* 15; Rambaud 192). In order to negate the death of his parents while maintaining contact with the living, he adopted the ideological move typical of reactionary thought of the nineteenth cen-tury (but by no means restricted to the right): assimilating society to the ancestors, and both to the self. Each time he insists on the annihilation of the self, he adds that underneath its nothingness lies society, the collectivity that supports and thereby reassures the disappearing self ("Réponse" 181–82; préface to *Un homme libre* 93). Barrès found his barrier against death first through the dissolution of his individuality in the relative eternity of ancestral continuity ("Réponse" 182).

Unlike the earlier apologists for the monarchy, Bonald and de Maistre, or the contemporary royalists, Bourget and Maurras, Barrès refused to jettison what he considered to be the ideals of the Revolution, a certain conception of democracy, individualism, and the rights of man. The populism of the collective unconscious he had proclaimed in *Le jardin de Bérénice* opened up a second avenue into the disintegration and subsequent rehabilitation of the self: merging with the all-encompassing spatiality of the collectivity. In his reminiscences about his involvement in Boulangism, Barrès reveals that, although the movement lacked a "great idea" to solidify its program, its strong appeal for him derived from the sensation of being a member of the herd (*troupeau*) (*Mémoires* 24). The "instinctive" character of this experience recalls the encomium to the national unconscious of mass meetings in *Berenice's Garden,* but now it is a matter of enjoyment of the mob in the present rather than the emergence of an ideal for the future as it was then. Not just the result of guilt or a cause of fear, then, the dissolution of the individual self has also become a source of *jouissance.* Barrès promises a similar enjoyment to those who participate in his ideology of "the soil and the dead," assuring them of the "delightful giddiness" aroused by the sensation of finding oneself again in the family, race, and nation whose continuity cannot be negated by death ("Réponse" 182).

In either case, whether fusing with the spatial or the temporal collectivity, it is by reveling in the death drive that Barrès's nationalism professes to nullify death. The death of the ego was thus only a provisional condition, a way station on the road to the total recovery of the self. Society served not only as a support underneath the nothingness of the conscious self but also as a kind of manhole cover shielding from view the even darker abyss of physiological heredity and processes whose ancient instinctual compulsion threatens to annihilate the Ego "in a still more terrifying manner."

The Barresian, then, must cling to his national identity for dear life because group identity was his dear life; the innermost core of his being was, at the very same time, outside of his self. Ringer was therefore only half right to contrast Barrès's doctrine to the German idea of *Bildung,* for the French writer does not simply abandon the ideal of the development of the inner self; he concludes rather that the inner self is, at the same time, outer. Unable to endure the tension entailed by this confrontation with what Lacan calls 'extimacy,' however, he immediately recuperates the otherness within by making it over into a new dimension of the same. This oddly Kantian conception entailed a new duty, designed to replace Kant's categorical imperative. In Saint-Phlin's words: "[E]ach of us must fall back on his hereditary reserves and seek his rule there" (*Leurs figures* 1172). This duty not only justified the xenophobia and racism typical of modern nationalism, it obligated its adherents to safeguard the purity of the nation by extirpating all foreign elements from the greater body of which they strove to be a part. Otherwise, as Sturel puts it in *L'Appel au soldat:* "Then I feel French nationality diminishing, disappearing; that is, the substance that sustains me, without which I would vanish" (901).

Enjoying Your Thesis

If there were nothing more to Barrès's nationalism than this recycled Herder, Burke, and de Maistre, there would be little reason to believe that examination of his writings might provide fresh insight into fascism. Sternhell has accurately pinpointed its most important innovation on the political level: the populist use of anti-Semitism as a political concept, rather than a simple xenophobia or anti-Jewish reflex (*Maurice Barrès* 231), making it an essential tool in the mobilization of the new urban masses against the Republic, or at least against parliamentary democracy (Sternhell, *La droite révolutionnaire* 24–25, 80–81; see also Soucy, chap. 4, "Vitalism, *Massendemokratie,* and Racism"; and Viereck 62). Previously in France, from the Revolution to the Commune, as Taine and Le Bon complained loudly, the working-class crowds had intervened to support the radical left, while in Germany the nationalist ideas of the *Volksgeist,* racism, and the cult of the land were put in the service of rural reaction against industrialization (see Mosse chaps. 1 and 3).

What Barrès has added to that equation is the sense of enjoyment involved in identifying with the national ancestors and the nationalist herd, and it is this *jouissance* that he explores in his *Novel of National Energy.* On one level, belonging to the herd was a paradoxical reaction against the discourse of the Republic, whose insistence on national unity through universalism both intensified the desire for local identity and heightened the craving for adherence to the group, whether crowd or ancestors, and its power. On another, however, it was an ironic, populist extension of the republican lessons in morality and patriotism. That most distinguished spokesman for republican values, Michelet, asserted the solidarity of the living and the dead in the preface to volume I of his *Histoire du XIXe siècle* (1872): "[The dead] now live with us who feel ourselves to be their relatives, their friends. That is how a family is made, a community of the living and the dead." In "Qu'est-ce qu'une nation" ("What Is a Nation?"; 1882), the famous speech at the Sorbonne announcing his newfound support of the Republic, Renan proclaimed that "the cult of ancestors is the most legitimate of all: our ancestors have made us who we are" (quoted in Girardet 65). Moreover, the Republic's ethics of universality depended on and enforced the sameness of all citizens as of humanity in general, thus encouraging the dissolution of individuality. Herd action became a kind of living parody of republican universalism, a theatricalized performance, for the benefit of the Other, of the inadequacy and persistent externality of republican identity for those members of the intelligentsia or of the proletariat who felt that in reality they were excluded from participating in it.

The Kantian universalism of the Republic instituted what Lacan called the senseless obscenity of the superego on two fronts: first, by instilling a notion of duty unmotivated by any goal or purpose and thus incomprehensible (as the primary schoolteachers quickly discovered—see chapter 1), and, second, by promoting a notion of individual rights that relied on the uniformity of all persons. If Freud was right to assert that morality results from the renunciation of aggression, that "the categorical imperative of Kant is thus a direct inheritance from the Oedipus-complex" ("The Economic Problem of Masochism" 264), and not the force that mandates that renunciation, then it makes sense that the imposition of the republican superego would increase citizens' need to find substitute objects for their sadistic impulses. The herd mentality thus complies with the more or less covert lesson of *jouissance* taught in the schools, by the behavior of the pupils and the tacit encouragement of the authorities who embodied the democratic superego: Conform or suffer exclusion. In exchange for the renunciation of all particularity, individuals received the sensation, if not the reality, of control and group identity, to compensate for their sense of impotence in the face of a distant, vast, and impersonal bureaucracy on the national level. Worst of all, this perception of actual powerlessness was magnified a thousandfold by the promise of power—the citizen as sovereign—held out in all the Republic's civics textbooks. Hence the reveling in the sheer power of the mob (Soucy 117–18).

In the *Novel of National Energy,* the seductive power of Barrès's nationalism is not simply asserted or described as in his political and journalistic pamphlets; it is dramatized as scenarios of *jouissance,* especially in Sturel's life. It is in Sturel's development that Barrès brings out the hidden implications of his nationalist program and its relation to the earlier *Cult of the Ego:* the threads leading from the extimate to the ambivalence toward acceptance, the giddiness of merging with the crowd, and xenophobia. His enjoyment of the crowd is nowhere more evident than in the mob scene around the Lyons train station in *L'Appel au soldat* (786–87; see Soucy 118). Dismissed from his post as minister of war, forced to leave Paris and go into exile, Boulanger is hailed by a crowd of screaming supporters and carried off in a whirlwind of humanity. In a description whose images and ambiguous focalization are reminiscent of Hugo or Zola, but whose tone betrays a rapt admiration for sheer power alien to his predecessors, Barrès metaphorizes the crowd into an "immense wave," an "animal" with "formidable undulations," and explains: "Obscure feelings, inherited from our ancestors, words these combatants could not define, but through which they recognize each other as brothers, have created this delirium . . . these . . . forces of the national subconscious," while Sturel "took a few moments to enjoy the emotion that these torrents of humanity aroused in him" (*Appel au soldat* 787).

This scene is the counterpart to the climactic sequence of *The Uprooted,* in which the public outpouring of emotion during Victor Hugo's funeral ceremonies sends thrills running up and down Sturel's spine, while he alternately represses and broods over his complicity in the crime of Racadot and Mouchefrin. In both scenes the narrator follows the young man as he observes the throngs surging around him, so that the thoughts, impressions, and feelings described can be attributed equally plausibly to the narrator or to the mind of the character. In both, the protagonist's emotions lead him up the blind alley of following a movement that has no grand idea to direct it. By its open evocation of death, however, both in the apotheosis of the national hero's body at the foot of the Arc de Triomphe and in the intermittent recalls of Astiné's gruesome murder, the chapter describing Hugo's memorial services, tellingly titled "The Social Virtue of a Corpse," elicits much more forcefully the delectation that constitutes the reward for those who allow themselves the luxury of dissolving into the mob. The exhibition of his corpse in front of that "door to the void," as the Arc de Triomphe was called in those days when the city ended there, brought home to the people of Paris the reality of death whose thought they usually try to elude, for, they reflect, if even the great man can die, then so will I. Thus transformed into the gateway to "nothingness and mystery" (728), the Arc becomes the visible image of that wintry fear of death and the unknown at the bottom of every effort to grasp at a solid identity. Like Roemerspacher when confronted with Taine's mortality, in reaction to this dread the crowds of people flooding the Champs-Élysées from the Place de la Concorde to the Arc de Triomphe soon become drunk with the furious desire to live; elevating the poet to the status of a god, they devote a veritable orgiastic cult to the product of their creation.

> Like all cults of the dead, these funeral ceremonies exalted the sense of life. The lofty idea the crowd had of this corpse . . . swept a strange ardor through their veins. The benches along the Champs-Élysées, the shadows under the bushes were the scene of a vast orgy that lasted until dawn. (728)

The other death evoked in this passage is that of Astiné. The chapter opens with Sturel's mortal battle with himself over the guilt he feels for his implication in the murder and the sense of obligation he harbors toward his friend Mouchefrin. After he decides he must turn the killer in to the police, he breaks out in a cold sweat at the image he conjures up of himself as a traitor dragging his friend down into the sewer (723). But he is even more horrified when, half delirious, he pictures his double turning his face away from the sordid spectacle of Billancourt, where he witnessed the murder, in order to contemplate the beauties of nature (an indirect reminder of his feeling for Thérèse Alison). The ostensible purpose for the juxtaposition of the two fatalities is of course to provide a determining reason for Sturel to conclude his otherwise interminable vacillation between loyalty to a former friend and the obligation to denounce a criminal. The national grandeur and unity manifested in the civil ceremonies of Hugo's funeral chase away his somber thoughts of death, replacing them with acceptance of Taine's message: "After walking all day with organized France, with her elected powers, official celebrities and corporate bodies, he recognized the great spring of life, in which his own was just a tiny stream" (737). Now able to step back from his individual predicament and see things under the aspect of eternity, feeling the mysterious unity of life that Hugo displays in his poetry and the crowd manifests in its exhilaration, Sturel renounces all desire to seek remedies or wreak vengeance for "the atrocity committed" (la chose atroce accomplie): "There are ignoble moments, but together they add up to a noble eternity" (730).

Carroll discerns another function in this combination of plot elements: The assassination of Astiné and the trial of Mouchefrin and Racadot, which surround the narrative of Hugo's burial, represent a purification of the nation, the eradication of the "foreign," whether external or internal, being a necessary preparation for the exaltation of Hugo as national hero (Carroll 39). "The logic of the novel is unambiguous and brutal; the elimination of the foreign and the construction of the Nation-Subject justify any means used to accomplish them" (39). No "sacrifice," as the narrator later calls the failure of the two criminals, is too great in the service of the noble goal of national unity. Martine Reid goes even further in this direction, arguing that Barrès's overt political explanation of Astiné's murder hides a series of repressed meanings. While Barrès states that her death benefits the remaining students by bringing them face to face with reality, careful perusal of the text shows that it also serves the darker and more hidden purpose of slaying everything the author hates and fears: "Admirable scene of a very personal 'theater of cruelty,' Astiné's murder brings together all the elements of Barrès's political unconscious" (Reid 387). With the "eternal feminine" that she represents must perish the entire "unthought" (*impensé*) of the novel, the whole textual chain of elements associated with her figure as foreign, starting with the subject matter of Bouteiller's teaching, the philosophy of Greece and Germany (385; Carroll notes the same connection between Bouteiller and Astiné).

Reid refers to the fact that the author's long-standing anti-Semitism finds *revanchard* expression in Sturel's visit to his hometown of Neufchâteau, now "invaded" by bands of Jewish refugees from Alsace and the annexed portion of Lorraine (see Reid 386–87). They would have made a touching spectacle in the Frankfurt ghetto, he thinks, but their foreign gestures bring only ugliness to Neufchâteau (*Les déracinés* 660).[1] The narrator then "clarifies" his character's ideas about the psychological defeat of France, adding that in previous times the country was strengthened by integrating foreigners into herself, whereas "nowadays these vagabonds are making us over in their image" (661). This interpretation is just the forerunner of the noxious anti-Semitism Barrès will take over from Soury during the heat of the Dreyfus Affair (Sternhell, *Maurice Barrès* 253), when he will trumpet the defamations later repeated by the Nazis: "The Jews have no homeland in the sense that we understand the term. For us the homeland is the soil and our ancestors, it is the land of our dead ones. For them it is the place where they find their greatest self-interest" (*Scènes et doctrines* 72).

Lacoue-Labarthe and Nancy point out that Hitler and Alfred Rosenberg extended this argument to conclude that the Jews, supposedly living only in the world of abstractions such as philosophy, science, and democracy, were the 'anti-type,' destructive of all identity (*Mythe Nazi* 58). What they don't mention is that Barrès was merely repeating the ancient Christian attacks on the Jews: "They [the Jews] do not observe the Passover, for how can they? They have no place, but wander everywhere" (Athanasius of Alexandria, "Festal Letter" of January 16, 329). In fact, the Jew is not a human being at all, according to Barrès, and therefore has no claim to be treated according to ethical or legal standards. Being of a different species, Jews should be exhibited in an ethnology department as an 'object lesson' (*Scènes et doctrines* 153).

According to Reid, Astiné acts the role of scapegoat as defined by René Girard: through her the author violently purges the "substance" of the country of all difference, of every kind of alterity in the name of the self-identical (Reid 387)—the foreign, whether Greek, German, or Jewish, but also the feminine that weakens men, and philosophy, literature in the form of stories, fiction, and, above all, exoticism, "his bête noire, Romanticism along with the whole Orientalist hodgepodge" (386–87).

While Reid's and Carroll's observations are both accurate and penetrating, there is one dimension of the crime they scarcely discuss: Sturel's profound complicity in it and the enjoyment his vicarious participation betrays. It is he who precipitates the bankruptcy of Renaudin's newspaper, and in a most hypocritical way. Through a complex set of events designed to expose the corrupt underside of the newspaper business of the times and its hidden collusion with the powers that be, the author leads Sturel into the situation of traitor. By preventing the newspaper from receiving a government subsidy, allegedly out of fear of compromising its independence, Sturel destroys Racadot's last chance to recoup his money. As a result, Racadot becomes desperate and persuades Mouchefrin to help him kill Astiné in order to steal her jewels. Sturel's high-minded protestations cannot hide the fact that his primary motive is selfish: He reacts so violently to the news of this request precisely because he is embarrassed in front of Mlle. Alison, the woman he loves, or at least wants to impress. Although Sturel is not present at the moment when the two men begin to rush Astiné off into the darkness, the author takes great pains to make it clear to the reader that he did witness another part of the scene without intervening on Astiné's behalf. That evening, he, Mlle. Alison, her mother, and the owner of the boarding house where he and Thérèse live are on an outing in the Bois de Boulogne when they notice a woman trying to hail a cab while two men lurk in the background. Sturel recognizes the three immediately, but refuses to acknowledge them or admit that he knows them to

Mlle. Alison. Despite the fact that he reads the "unutterable anguish" on Astiné's face, he does nothing to grasp the "hand of the drowning woman in the night" that she seems to hold out toward him (702–3).

The message these scenes convey is that Sturel inadvertently but inevitably must do everything in his power to rid himself of Astiné in order to be able to possess Thérèse Alison. On the level of political ideology, his behavior signifies, as the critics point out, the removal of the foreign and the return to the regional, the national, Thérèse being from Lorraine. The accidental nature of his involvement in the motivation of Racadot's crime, the quasi-hypnotic character of his paralysis at the time of Astiné's need, and above all the fact that he never recalls either event during his anguished debate with himself in the aftermath of the crime—all this intimates the presence of an unconscious motive as well. A great part of Astiné's attraction for her young lover derives from the stories of her Oriental origins she recounts to him, and it is these tales that awaken in Sturel an insatiable desire that tears him away from his 'roots,' indeed, from reality itself (Les déracinés 554).

The names of the areas where her family had lived—the Euphrates, Mesopotamia, Persia—awaken deep stirrings within him, for when he was four or five, his imagination was created through listening to stories of these legendary places (545). In Mes mémoires, Barrès reveals that it was his own mother who performed this service for him in reality by reading him Richard the Lion-Hearted in Palestine when he lay ill as a child. At that moment, "my imagination grabbed hold of a few delightful figures that would never again leave me; the angelic young women and the Orient would go to sleep in the depths of my mind along with the voice of my young mama and wake up at the time of my adolescence" (Mes mémoires, O. C. XIII 8). Astiné, the widow, the older, experienced woman who initiates Sturel into sexuality, the "Oriental" whose very exoticism recalls the most intimate memories of the child, is thus an avatar of the mother from whom Sturel must liberate himself in order to reach the emotional autonomy and sense of reality without which he will never attain the identity he seeks.

The private oedipal situation is thus transposed onto the politics of nationalism, although it should be noted that this is not a necessary connection, desire for the exotic woman having already served in L'ennemi des lois (The Enemy of the Laws) the contrary ideological aim of attacking "narrow" nationalism (307–8). The same motif of separation from the matrix, which seems so contradictory to nationalist immersion in the group, recurs twice in the space of a few pages, the first time in the narrator's commentary on the lesson Hugo offers Sturel in his poetry, the second in the narration of Sturel's visit to Mouchefrin's room the night of Hugo's burial. On the one hand, the narrator casts the murderer outside the pale of the human race, describing him as "a reptile trying to attain full being, to differentiate himself from the mire, the fevers of chaos in which he moves" (733); on the other, like Michelet, he exalts the power of the word, of Hugo's poetry, to make us participate in the fraternal communion of our common heritage as we rose out of the darkness of undifferentiated nature (720), just as he had admired Michelangelo's Promethean figures "who tear themselves out of their blocks of marble" ("Du sang, de la volupté et de la mort," *Romans et voyages* 449). Fraternity in the collectivity is therefore the remedy to nondifferentiation, in the same way that belonging to society is meant to protect us from the abyss of pure nature that represents dissolution into the sheer nothingness which preceded the first glimmerings of identity.

The nationalist and oedipal themes of xenophobia and separation are not the only significant aspects of Astiné's murder, however. It becomes the proof par excellence of the immorality of the positivist education touted by the Republic. Ida-Marie Frandon gives convincing evidence that Barrès used several aspects of the Barré-Lebiez case as models for the crime: first of all, the gruesome murder of an older woman for her money by two well-educated young men in dire poverty; the use of the term 'Caesarize' in Sturel's discourse to mean 'dominate'; and, most important for the educational message of the text, the public lecture on Darwinism by the medical student Lebiez and the use of the notion of the survival of the fittest in the pair's legal defense ("Fait divers et littérature"). Barrès adapted these events in having Racadot give a public speech attacking Hugo and justifying his crime, before his involvement in Astiné's murder is discovered. Racadot's theory is a kind of parody of Spinoza, Darwin, Taine, Roemerspacher, and Sturel combined, in which he states that Hugo's promise of making mankind happy through education is false and that the "instinct" for survival should replace Hugo's idea of 'duty,' which in reality is just a rehash of every priest's sermons. Nature teaches us to live at the expense of others (*Les déracinés* 713).

The other face of the crime is the mask of enjoyment. The entire murder scene is tinged with sexual overtones. Mouchefrin especially, who has earlier tried in vain to make the Armenian woman his mistress, is excited by frustrated desire, whipped up into a frenzy by Astiné's insulting sneer at his size as he pulls her along: "You can see very well that you're still too little to hold onto a woman except by her apron strings" (704). "Luxurious creature, with her contemptuous body she has whipped up their blood with desires. She is being killed by two poor men who are also proud males. These two characteristics, when they don't exclude each other, form an explosive mixture" (705). The narrator takes obvious delight in the detailed, sensual, and rhythmic description he gives of her dead body:

> Ce beau corps, cette gorge de vierge qu'elle avait gardée, et que baigne le fleuve d'un sang encore vivant, ces jambes adorables. . . . Ce cadavre, ce sang et ces beautés découvertes . . . c'est l'éternelle Hélène . . . qui . . . attise dans notre sein une ardeur que rien ne satisfera. . . . pour que soit complète l'atmosphère de volupté, il ne manque pas au tableau l'appareil du carnage. (706)

Here is a literal translation of the passage that conveys its sense, if not its sensuality: "That beautiful body, that virgin's breast she had preserved and which is bathed in a river of still living blood, those adorable legs. . . . That corpse, that blood and those uncovered beauties . . . she is the eternal Helen . . . who fans in our breast the flames of an ardor that nothing will satisfy. . . . To complete the voluptuous atmosphere, not even the trappings of carnage are missing from this tableau."

In a word, Astiné *is* desire: insatiable, unquenchable desire; the perpetual desire for "something other," as Baudelaire once put it, the void at the center of the subject that can never be completely filled.

At the same time, as Suleiman and Reid have argued, Barrès tries to exorcize the temptation of sadism and disorder by throwing all the blame, scientifically—"We are botanists" (708)—on the two allegedly primitive characters and the universalizing education that has deracinated them from the social ties that prevent other men from acting out their violent instincts (738). Yet the description of the act tells another story. "Frightful debauchery"; "[t]he profoundly horrible thing is that this spectacle is quite exciting! Men love to bite, and desire makes their mouths run dry when they see frightful things" (705). No other characters being present at the fatal moment, it must be to the reader that the narrator addresses his exclamation; Barrès thus invites his public to participate imaginatively in the sadistic pleasure aroused in contemplating this sight. Despite the narrator's overt disavowal of Racadot and Mouchefrin, then, he makes their act appealing to the reader in order to demonstrate the kind of covert gratification he can expect from participation in nationalist pogroms designed to exterminate the foreign. As her decapitation testifies, Astiné is the figure of the first, terrifying phase of imaginary "castration" in the Lacanian sense of the term. The graphic description of her murder represents a kind of sexual climax, a covert satisfaction of incestuous desire that combines the refusal to renounce the maternal object and to take on the mutilation of the self such renunciation entails, with the attempt to throw all the suffering of being onto the other, all of this staged for the benefit of the Other, a position occupied in this case by the politicized readers who together form the Nation (see Lacan, "Kant with Sade" 65).

Suleiman makes the interesting suggestion that the strong emotional reaction evoked by these descriptions overflows, as it were, the didactic intention of the author manifested in the analytic tone of his scientific explanations (*Authoritarian Fictions* 209). Certainly, the charm Astiné exercises on the reader as on Sturel is not dissipated by the narrator's classification of her as the evil alien, the virus or poison (Barrès's terms for her, e.g., *Les déracinés* 554) that must be extracted in order to restore the national organism to health (Reid; Carroll). As Suleiman points out, Astiné's influence on Sturel, like Bouteiller's, is mentioned in the later volumes of the trilogy, long after her murder (*Authoritarian Fictions* 125). Her argument is based on the premise that Astiné is "a character whose value in the ideological supersystem of the work is strongly negative" (206), but there is good reason to wonder whether the appealing character of the Armenian woman actually contradicts the narratorial value system. In fact, as strange as it might seem in light of her foreign ethnicity and exotic lure, each time the narrator mentions her lingering seductive power over the young man, it is to support rather than negate the nationalist ideology he espouses elsewhere in the novels. It is not only the "text," in Suleiman's sense of the rhetorical play of narration, action, and description, that exceeds the narrator's "reductive interpretation" of Astiné's significance, it is the narrator's interpretations themselves that cannot be so contained. In short, the contradiction, if contradiction there be, lies within the system of interpretation, not outside it between text and interpretation. For the lesson Astiné taught Sturel is the same one he learns from the crowds at Hugo's funeral and from the poet's writings, the very notion of acceptance that is supposed to constitute the heart of Barrès's nationalist doctrine, the ethic of acceptance (*Les déracinés* 730).

Nihil humani mihi alienum

It is true that the spirit in which Sturel decides to accept the "atrocity committed" differs from the attitude of the scornful voluptuary she had inculcated into him (730), but the metaphysical distance he attains does not prevent Astiné's ghostly presence from reasserting itself years, and several hundred pages, later in the same manner. Sitting in a café, plotting vengeance for the Panama scandal with the anarchist Fanfournot, Sturel ponders the similarity between the profiteering *chéquards* and the anarchists who steal Panama bonds to finance their political activities. The two groups use identical pretexts to justify their appetites. Overcome by the atmosphere of the place, Fanfournot's stories, and too much absinthe, Sturel plunges into a kind of trance, in which he contemplates "this abject society of enjoyment" under the same aspect of eternity he had reached during Hugo's burial. Individuality, however real, becomes irrelevant in this perspective; all people are united in their fundamental animality, in the very instincts the narrator invokes in describing Racadot and Mouchefrin attacking Astiné: biting, grasping, tearing apart (1146). Lurking beneath the pleasant glow that society projects over life, Sturel muses, reign the "Mothers" of Goethe's *Faust* Part Two, and this idea inevitably calls to his mind the image of Astiné with her "proud humility" and her "clairvoyant slave's resignation" (1146–47). Like her, the Mothers, as Mephisto explains to Faust, counsel total acceptance, and like Sturel, Faust resists this temptation: "Go; I do not seek my salvation in torpor" (*Leurs figures* 1147). With a shudder, Sturel pulls himself out of his stupor, but just as Barrès never loses his fascination with and taste for the "Orient" or for Romanticism, despite his sometimes violent criticisms of both (cf. Reid 387), so he will memorialize the call of the earth in his political slogan of "the soil and the dead."

In this whole scene Sturel is described as a drowning man being sucked down into the depths of a whirlpool whose overwhelming force derives from the almost irresistible attraction of the sheer nothingness of the prehuman, presocial self attached to Astiné and the earth Mothers. It is the surreptitious attraction of that nothingness, the love of death designated under the term "nihilism," that unites the apparently disparate and unmotivated set of associations the text attaches to Astiné. Her assassination aims not only at eliminating everything foreign, as Reid and Carroll observe; it also strives to eradicate that which is most intimate.

For in fact, Astiné never did die; the foreign element of desire lives on forever within the future nationalist hero. During the murder and again in the description of the Hugo ceremonies, the narrator insists that Astiné, "that foreigner . . . mixed into his thoughts and modifying all of them" (703), "still lived within him [Sturel]. She had deposited in him elements forever amalgamated with the young man from Lorraine's own nature," so that henceforth there exists "that intimate part of Sturel that is essentially Astiné" (730). Nihilism, the fascinating seduction of nothingness, is "Astiné's poison acting in his [Sturel's] blood. Wherever he goes, he carries it within him" (703). It is this nothingness that forms the core of Sturel's identity and constitutes at the same time the rationale for Barrès's "scientific" condemnation of Astiné and the voluptuous charm that causes both the rhetoric and the ideology of the text to overflow the "reductive interpretation" of her.

The internalization of the foreign via Astiné is also not without its larger political significance. For the first time since the Revolution, in Barrès's nationalism there was the perceived danger of an "inner enemy," because in the Third Republic everyone (every adult male, that is) was a citizen on an equal footing, a human being, at least officially, whereas in previous times the Jews, the Protestants, and other religious and ethnic minorities were clearly and officially (at different times) demarcated from the mass of the French. As a result, the inner enemy became still more important than the external enemy for nationalism and, later on, for fascism. The purification of the nation arose from the effort to define and delimit national identity in the face of this internal invasion. Ironically enough, the only previous direct parallel to this situation had occurred during the Revolution. Fin de siècle nationalism was thus a repetition of the Jacobin Terror, whose revolutionary 'energy' Barrès refused to renounce, in its fight against the internal enemies of the Republic, the "traitors in our midst."

When Barrès links Astiné's "Oriental" poison to German thought in general and to Kant's philosophy in particular, he is not succumbing to some *impensé* of the text; rather he is following a trajectory through a network of associations joining Germany, the Orient, and nihilism plotted out by leading French thinkers of the nineteenth century. Barrès need have looked no farther than Bourget's article on Renan in the *Essais de psychologie contemporaine* to find that the various strains of neo-Kantianism recalled "the magnificent hypotheses of ancient Ionia" (*Essais* 51–52). In *L'orient de Maurice Barrès,* Frandon has traced the development of Barrès's thought on this system back to his reading of Quinet, who argues that there is an ancient connection between the Germans and the orient, since the language of the former shows that they are descended from the Medes (*Génie des religions* 61), while their Protestantism led them to study the Bible and thus Judaism and Hebrew poetry (Herder); from there it was an easy step to cultures farther east, like Persia and India (Goethe, Ruckert) (Quinet, *le génie des religions* 63–65).

Renan, Bourget, Vogüé, Taine, Leconte de Lisle, Soury—Barrès connects them all in one way or another with the new French *mal de siècle,* as Vogüé once called it, amalgamating the ideas of fatalism, nihilism, the orient, and Germany (Frandon, *L'orient de Maurice Barrès* 39–42). The Eastern religions of Hinduism and Buddhism form the major bridge between nihilism and German thought. In "L'oeuvre de Leconte de Lisle," Barrès describes the poet's evocation of the uselessness of all feeling and effort, of the nothingness and nirvana in Brahma (122–23). The novelist seems to have accepted Vogüé's contention that nihilism came to France from the Hindu nirvana via the Russians— think of Kutuzov's fatalism in *War and Peace*—and the Germans (41). Anatole France reminds his readers of the link between Buddhism and the thought of Schopenhauer, probably the best-known representative of German philosophy in France during the period ("Bouddhisme" 331). And many French commentators, from Charles de Villers in the eighteenth century (Munteanu 142) to the symbolists and decadents, often via a detour through Wagnerism, interpreted Kant's doctrine of the forms of intuition and the categories of understanding as a kind of subjectivist skepticism or nihilism. The two major aspects of Bouteiller's teaching that Barrès attacks, Kant's universalism and those "Oriental perfumes of death" filtered through German thought the professor wafts over his pupils, are not unrelated, as it may seem at first sight (cf. Carroll 32). Nothing could be more universalizing, indeed, than the utter uniformity of nondifferentiation at the instinctual level Sturel perceives in his hallucinatory descent into the chthonian realm of the Mothers. The equivalence Barrès establishes among Bouteiller, Astiné, and Hugo is thus not at all far-fetched, once the notion, the dread, and the desire of nihilism are factored into the equation.

The motto of the Barresian nationalist (with apologies to Terence) thus could be: "I think the nothingness of humanity is the foreign within me." This extimacy is not quite the same thing as the assertion that "the individual is nothing without the group." Like Barrès and the nationalists of those days and our own, the critics would like to make a neat division between inside and outside: between the others who are in fact the same (see Carroll 27)—Barrès's "affinities"—and the Others who are genuinely alien, foreign. The problem is that the enemy also resides within the self, not just outside it. And it does so due to the subject's own desire. Astiné's murder aims at eliminating everything foreign, as the critics rightly observe, but to do so would be to eradicate that which is most intimate within Sturel. The nationalists' bargain is the reverse of Faust's pact with the devil: He was eager to sell his soul for one moment of total fulfillment, while they are willing to kill their desire in order to acquire a solid identity (see Lacan's analysis of university discourse in *The Other Side of Psychoanalysis*)—willing, but, at least in the exemplary case of Sturel, not able. For to eliminate "that intimate part of Sturel that is essentially Astiné" (730) would be to eliminate the desiring core of his self. Secretly convinced that the Other, the foreigner, holds the key to *jouissance,* the nationalist Sturel—the "true French"—cannot live with her, yet he (and they) cannot live without her. The nationalist solution to this paradox—which is the main paradox of present-day multiculturalism and its discontents—is instead to embalm her within him, to preserve her, but as dead.

From this perspective, a third reading of the function of the juxtaposition of the two deaths emerges: Sturel is able to exorcise the foreign only by making it an essential 'part' of himself. It is not simply that the nationalist subject defines himself by his difference from the other, as some postcolonial theory has it; rather, by the paradoxical logic of the extimate, the act of murder functions to immortalize the (M)Other, preserved in vitro, so to speak. As Sturel watches Astiné about to be hauled off to her death, the narrator opines:

> In truth, at this moment, if she has accomplished her inner [*propre*] destiny, she can enjoy an extension of her life in Sturel. And perhaps it is her appetite for self-destruction, her perpetual gift of herself in the midst of her debauchery, which will earn this rare woman the possibility of surviving herself. (703)

The permanent installation of Astiné in Sturel's mind is a refusal of mourning, in every way comparable to the institution of Barrès's nationalist identification with the race in reaction to the death of his parents, and to the intoxication with death that characterizes the *jouissance* of Barrès's nationalism.

After her death, Astiné is transported through her murder from the real to the symbolic, becoming the element of suture for the discourse of rootedness and nationalism. Once dead, she functions as the signifier of the excluded element—the foreign, the Other, the *nihil*—the signifier that makes it possible to incorporate the alien into the nationalist system *as that which is excluded from nationalism,* and that, like Frege's empty set in the realm of the logic of number theory, is required to allow that system to achieve closure (see Miller, "Suture").[2] Her use as suture constitutes the desperate attempt to assimilate the unassimilable, to guarantee the unity so obviously contradicted by her very existence.

Unlike a purely logical system, however, a political engine like nationalism must constantly be fed and stoked in order to be maintained; hence the insatiable need, characteristic of fascism, for ever more victims to persecute and eventually to exterminate. An infinite series of human signifiers representing the Other, the foreign, the exotic must be lined up and purged, but not in order to purify the system totally, getting rid of them once and for all. Rather, they must be inhumed and embalmed within the system, like dead butterflies skewered onto the pages of an entomologist's album. For ultimately, the closure and the sense of autonomy achieved by killing desire are illusory: The sense of incompletion and the recognition of loss inevitably return, to haunt the nationalist and to reactivate the secret allure of nothingness. Rootedness may very well have "provide[d] an intellectually respectable solution to the problem of nihilism and decadence which plagued so many intellectuals at the fin de siècle" (Soucy 113), but it did so by enshrining the very nihilism whose troublesome persistence it was meant to eliminate.

Readability and Transference:
Barrès and the Fiction of Teaching

The choice of the *roman à thèse* genre was governed by the same dialectic of nihilism and assertion. In a move typical of conservative political strategy (see Charle, *Paris fin de siècle* 169), the trilogy presents itself as a remedy for the anarchy resulting from the alleged loss of values and certainty produced by the Third Republic's adoption of Kantian universalist doctrine and the practices of collusion and corruption in the alliance of "foreigners," big capital, and parliamentary democracy that ideology supposedly favors. Bourget had already depicted the fear of "intellectual anarchy" produced by the multiplicity of points of view simultaneously admitted in the fin de siècle. Barrès did not simply reject this multiplicity, however; on the contrary, he espoused it as the only notion of truth appropriate to the contemporary world and hence to modern literature. A major corollary of this perspectivism, which the humanist critics like to call 'relativism' and which Barrès termed 'skepticism' or nihilism, is that, since all phenomena demand interpretation, they also therefore run the risk of receiving divergent interpretations. Now, unlike the realist novel, which imagines that reality wears its meaning on its sleeve, and in contrast to the modernist novel, which supposes that meaning can be subverted, if not entirely avoided, the *roman à thèse* knows this problem exists but reveals its difference from its symbolist brothers in that, intent upon promoting a specific ideological program, it sees that risk more as a danger than as an opportunity. The self-contradictory antidote for this peril adopted by the thesis novel, as André Gide points out, is to attempt, through narratorial commentary, to restrict the very freedom of judgment it acknowledges by dictating the one "correct" interpretation of its stories (30). The special role of the narrator of the ideological novel is to enunciate the thesis and to communicate it to his readers; in short, it is that of the 'master' Barrès always aspired to be, the teacher, the authoritarian instructor who tells his charges what to think.

As with all exemplary tales, then, in order to bring home its lesson and to support its call for action, the thesis novel must make "the interpretation . . . 'superior' to the story, as the general is to the particular, the universal to the singular, or truth to its manifestation" (Suleiman, *Authoritarian Fictions* 30). This result is always paradoxical, since it undermines the very purpose of employing stories in the first place, the supposed ease of understanding and more immediate appeal of narrative over abstract ideas. But it is doubly paradoxical in the case of Barrès's trilogy, since the latter's purpose is to discredit universalism: The general lesson its narrator sets out to impose is precisely the distrust of the general. Indeed, that is one of the primary reasons for which *The Uprooted* takes on the structure of a novel of education. The good teacher has the duty to understand the diverse living conditions of his pupils, and to "distribute truth" in proportion to the individual truth of each pupil, which entails studying their biographies as well as the particularities of the Lorraine character (502).

Biography is particularity, in both the temporal and the spatial dimensions. Recounting the life histories of his protagonists is therefore not simply a matter of 'illustrating' his thesis by tracing the results of the 'deracinating' education Bouteiller dispenses to his pupils, but of the obligation to respect and demonstrate the particularity of life the Barresian narrator claims is trampled upon by the republican professor's Kantianism.

The more general function of Barrès's education novel is also a matter of particularity, in that it consists of the search for identity. As Georg Lukács explains in his *Theory of the Novel*, in the contingency of the modern world there no longer exists an accepted source of transcendent meaning; hence individual identity is no longer a given but becomes the object of a quest. The hero seeks adventure in order to discover his own essence. Barrès's novels have gone a step further than the traditional *Bildungsroman*, however, for they presuppose not only the lack of transcendent meaning but also the absence of the inherent, immanent meaning implied in the positivist position and entailed by the dominant forms of realist and naturalist literary representation. They participate in the general fin de siècle breakdown in representation that gives rise to a modernism much more radical than the mere distrust of the expressive capacity of language repeated by writers from Rousseau through the Romantics to Flaubert.

Since we can never get beyond some particular point of view, it is an illusion to imagine that observation, no matter how careful, can arrive at an objective knowledge of things, that is, one in which they have the same significance for everyone. As a consequence, events, whether fictional or real, can never express their own meaning; each is always and unavoidably subject to a variety of interpretations. Moreover, a person's reactions to situations, events, and the actions of other people will depend on his or her understanding of those occurrences. Although Barrès oscillated between an individual and a collective subject, he was in basic agreement with the subjectivist notion of perception popular in antipositivist, symbolist, and decadent writers such as Bourget, Vogüé, and Wyzewa. While Barrès's first novels adhered to the decadent credo described by Michel Raimond, "For the novelist, the world is no longer *a field on which to bring passions into conflict but a set of appearances to be elucidated*" (76; emphasis in original), *The Uprooted,* with its wider ambitions than the *Cult of the Ego* novels, brought the two models of the novel together, recounting Balzacian conflicts of passion and interest with a social and ideological import, but showing that those clashes result from the opposing points of view of the multiple characters whose lives the story follows.

The juxtaposition of these two strains in the same work throws into relief the fundamental crisis of fin de siècle narrative brought to light by the educational thesis novel. By underscoring the fact that the events in the world of fiction can no longer contain their own meaning, the genre threatens to expose the traumatic void lurking beneath the apparently seamless surface of everyday life smoothed over by the ready-made meanings of the prevailing symbolic system. In order to counter this danger, the narrator must rush into the vacuum, supplying the meaning from outside that world, transgressing the barrier between fiction and reality established in the realist and naturalist novels. There is thus an exact parallel between the situation of the genre, that of the Barresian subject unable to bear the knowledge of its own nothingness and therefore eager to cover it over as soon as possible by finding solace in the illusory warmth of mass existence, and that of the death of Astiné, whose lack of meaning becomes the kernel that allows nationalist meaning to emerge.

In responding to the potential encroachment of the real made possible by the crisis of representation, the thesis novel strikes out in opposite directions at once. On the one hand, it makes overt what the realist novel tries to hide, the fact that, as Bakhtin has so convincingly demonstrated, the novel has always been a fundamentally ideological genre. In it, not only are form and ideology one (259), but every utterance, whether of narration, description, or narratorial interpretation, is directed toward a reader who may have a different conception of the subject matter evoked (281–82). On the other hand, according to the same principle of detachable signification, the narrator will be unable to guarantee the reader's acceptance of the meanings he supplies. For how can a teacher (read: 'novelist'), however authoritarian, expect to control the lesson (read: 'thesis') she wants to transmit to her pupils (read: 'readers'), if each of them necessarily interprets it in an individual way, according to his or her particular history, education, or 'instinct'? Indeed, the text betrays an awareness of teaching as an 'impossible profession,' as a result of the difficulties inherent in attempting to impose one's preferred interpretation on people and events. Like *The Disciple*, *The Uprooted* contains a kind of negative *mise-en-abîme*, staging the principle of its own failure in the hopes of forestalling the failure of its principle. As the narrator tells us,

> From a professor or a book we receive only what our instinct recognizes as its own, and we take strange liberties with our interpretations. [Bouteiller] would no doubt have been stupefied to observe the repercussions of his words in these young brains. . . . He sows his grain with a bountiful motion but is totally unaware of what his seed becomes. (502)

If these words sound familiar, it is not only because of the irony directed against Bouteiller's (and Barrès's) idol Hugo, but also because we have already listened to a similar invitation to contemplate the melancholy disparity between the *saison des semailles* (season for sowing) and that of the *moisson* (harvest), this time directed against the other model teacher of the novel, Taine (596).

While the narrator's comments about the unanticipated effects of Taine's teachings on his prime pupil, Roemerspacher, do not constitute a disavowal of Taine's 'thesis,' they do call into question his capacity as a teacher. It is, after all, Taine himself who fails to take into account "the mental constitution of those who interpret and apply" his principle. The philosopher is therefore guilty of the same crime of *lèse-particularité* as the professor he is, in other respects, supposed to counterbalance, for the responsibility of the teacher is to foresee the probable effects of the abstract ideas he instills in them. Taine has no better understanding of how his views on voluntary associations will affect Roemerspacher than Bouteiller does about the results of his exposition of Kantian critique and morality on his high school students. The novel thus draws a distinct parallel between Bouteiller and Taine despite their genuine differences, for both contribute to the calamitous events of the story, even though it is not their doctrines per se (as contradictory as they are) that are responsible, but the students' faulty application of those principles.

Moreover, the parallels between the two masters do not stop there. In his original description of Bouteiller's character and principles, the narrator takes him severely to task for blindly following his "categorical imperative" even when he was still a schoolboy, lodging a formal complaint against a classmate who stole a watch and insisting the boy be dismissed from school, heedless of the circumstances—the transgressor had returned the timepiece and the victim had forgiven him—as of the disproportion between the offense and the consequences of his denunciation. The reason given for his action is that "he had deemed it inappropriate for a careless pupil . . . to keep something rotten in the collectivity" (505). This is precisely the idea of Taine's disciple Roemerspacher, when Sturel asks him whether he should turn Mouchefrin in: "Society ought to slaughter [Racadot and Mouchefrin], the way it slaughters wolves and wild boars in winter in the Neufchâteau woods" (726). As if to remove any lingering doubts about the partial interchangeableness of the two doctrines, Barrès has Roemerspacher announce in his last meeting with Sturel in *The Uprooted* that he has discovered the fundamental identity between Bouteiller's ethic and Taine's:

> After giving it a lot of thought, I've come to admit that the principle Bouteiller gave us five years ago . . .
> Oh! Bouteiller . . .
> I'm speaking of his words, not his actions. "Always act in such a way that you can want your action to serve as a universal rule." Act in a way that is profitable to society. . . . (744)

If Taine is no more reliable a model than Bouteiller, at least when it comes to the act of teaching, then it would appear that it is that act the author is calling into question. Furthermore, if we are to accept Roemerspacher's change of heart, we must at the same time reject the earlier narratorial assertion of the radical opposition between Kant and Taine as false, mistaken, or deceptive. It would seem, then, that at the time of writing *The Uprooted*, Barrès still harbored nagging doubts about his role as professor of national energy. All the more so, because the split between phenomenon and meaning tends to undermine political leaders as well as teachers. Contrary to the prevalent critical readings of Napoleon's role in the novel, and despite the praise the narrator heaps upon the Emperor for his charismatic ability to "electrify" people, the author leaves no doubt that, in the last analysis, in choosing Napoleon as their professor of energy, the students commit a serious error, succumbing to "napoleonitis" (610).

The image of Napoleon gives people energy but is incapable of giving them direction. As an imaginary entity, this figure fits into the same category as the stories Sturel and Roemerspacher were told as children; it takes no more account of reality than the students' other desires, ambitions, and plans. But that is exactly the narrator's criticism of Bouteiller! "The education [that Bouteiller gave them] . . . developed energy in them" (513). "Powers [the students from the Nancy lycée] were going to move through the world, to whom [Bouteiller] had given an impetus, without succeeding in steering them [in the right direction]" (512). Barrès explained the failure of the Boulangist movement in the same way: The general's defect as leader was that he was capable of arousing the energies of the masses but lacked any principle that could generate a specific political program for the nation.

Imparting force without controlling direction, all these teachers, models, imaginary figures, and charismatic leaders seem to show that the split between phenomenon and meaning, application and idea, event and thesis—that is, between the particular and the universal—is not only irreparable but potentially dangerous. Real power resides in the concrete, and when the concrete escapes the limited domain of personal experience, it can be conveyed best in images and stories; the question is whether the energy thus awakened can be channeled in the right direction by the right idea.

Consistent with this belief in the force of narrative is the fact, which Carroll notes with his customary acuity, that the tradition Barrès extols as the source of identity is transmitted in the form of stories. Only a living link to the past can guarantee the nation against dissolution, the ultimate loss of self, and that link is supplied by narrative and aesthetic culture (taste) handed down from past generations (Carroll 31). These stories, recounted by close relatives and contained within themselves, tell the young what they should be. The great danger, then, to the preservation of national identity, is foreign counternarratives. Viewed from this perspective, the agon of the novel takes the form of a battle between native and alien stories. To a certain extent, Bouteiller already manifests the peril by his eloquence and his poetic power to stir the imaginations of his pupils with 'Oriental' and Germanic tales of Kant and the Ionian philosophers. His influence is continued and reinforced by Astiné, whose attraction for Sturel is increased by the fact that she herself is Ionian (as Carroll and Reid point out; *Les déracinés* 545). It is the foreign names she invokes and the exotic stories she recounts that make her even more dangerous than Bouteiller, for she represents the seductive threat of cosmopolitanism, "that is, 'the dangerous faculty of borrowing the tone and the allure of each milieu'" (Carroll 34; inner quote from *The Uprooted*).

Although the thesis novel generally expends more energy in attacking its enemies than in defending its friends, Barrès does balance his assault on the universalist education of the Third Republic in the first volume of the trilogy with a counterproposal for a new nationalist instruction in the last book. Ironically enough, the overall structure of Barrès's trilogy thus adopts the same strategy that Bouteiller employed, unsuccessfully, in his lessons on Kant: first destroy meaning via critique, then rebuild it through practical reason. Except our author has substituted regional/national identity for universal ethics. In a letter to Sturel, Saint-Phlin offers a program of immersion in local culture designed to replace the allegedly deracinating universalism of Bouteiller. Convinced that a nation is "a territory in which people have memories and mores in common and an hereditary ideal" (*Appel au soldat* 960), he attributes to education the task of safeguarding this national mentality against domination and eventual assimilation by any foreign people. It is more than a little ironic that this staunch French nationalist should here echo the declarations of Herder in his struggle against French domination of the Germanic peoples, in asserting that the substitution of "their" language for "ours" is equivalent to replacing our mentality with theirs (*Appel au soldat* 960). It doesn't seem to occur to him that this rationale for *revanchard* claims to Lorraine at the same time would justify the German claims to Alsace!

Be that as it may, the important point is that in contrast to virtually all previous pedagogical notions, his basic presupposition is that the primary goal of education is to develop and maintain individual and collective identity (the two being equivalent for Barrès, as we have seen).

Saint-Phlin emphasizes the value of regional identity, because for him national identity is the sum of the particular identities of the various regions rather than a universal synthesis in which regional differences would be submerged in a homogeneous whole. When he espouses the program of on-site visits and "object lessons" promulgated by empiricist educational reformers of the period, it is not for the purpose of appealing to the child's interests, nor in order to overcome the latter's limited ability to grasp abstractions. It is not to counteract the traditional authoritarian methods of lecture and dictation nor even for vocational training; no, for the nationalist concept of education the sole purpose is to promote regional and national cultural identity, by acquainting the pupils with "the particular conditions in the midst of which our little people of Lorraine has grown up and participates in French culture" (*Leurs figures* 1173). As Barrès himself, quoting Saint-Simon, had pointed out many years earlier, nationalism is simply narcissism on a broad scale ("Examen des trois romans idéologiques" 1220 n12). In this sense nationalism is indeed the "Cult of the Ego" writ large, as Barrès protested to Doumic. The goal of education is not to bring something new to its charges, but to awaken within them the "subconscious" that contains everything past generations have accumulated "in order to create a soul for us" (1174). In short, what children need to learn about above all is themselves, insofar as they are their ancestors and their territory. Knowledge of the regional history that constitutes their continuity with their parents will "regenerate" them, for the "human plant" grows to be vigorous and fertile only in the conditions that have nourished its "species" over the centuries.

Because the tradition of Lorraine is not a series of inanimate assertions but a way of judging life, of feeling and of reacting, Saint-Phlin conceives of this education, before Pavlov (but after Soury), as the activation of a set of conditioned reflexes that build upon innate predispositions (1175). Once the Lothringers have acquired these automatic ways of feeling and reacting, they may leave their native region with impunity, confident that their regional identity will allow them to master any alien influences rather than be dominated and thus deracinated by them. In fact, on the plane of European history, the role of Lorraine has always been to protect the cultural identity of Latin civilization, before and since the advent of the French nation, from being "denatured" by Germanicism (1175).

Saint-Phlin's program does retain one aim in common with the positivist plan of educational reform whose concrete methods it adopts: the goal of bypassing all commentary and interpretation, that is, all teaching per se. Pupils should come into direct contact with their subject matter without the intervention of the teacher's explanations, just as the reader of realist fiction is supposed to apprehend the fictional world without having her vision obscured by the narrator's commentary. This insistence on achieving the immediate presence of the concrete would seem to be the very antithesis of the thesis novel, which must rely on the mediation of the narrator/teacher in order to present the thesis. At this point the struggle between nihilism and certainty has reached its utmost paroxysm: the contradiction between using the universality of the thesis to instill in his readers the doctrine of the particular threatens to tear apart the very fabric of the work.

It is here that Saint-Phlin invokes the one genuinely antirational aspect of Barrès's nationalism, itself an outgrowth of the reactionary scientism of the period. Admitting that he lacks the expertise to formulate specific pedagogical methods, he adds that, in any case, it is neither method nor curriculum that will determine the outcome of his program but a feeling (1173). The child intuitively senses, or fails to sense, the reverence for the race that should permeate every moment of the teacher's lesson, and it is this intuition that makes the lesson effective or ineffective.

In the last analysis, nationalist education has only one content—love and respect for the soil and the dead—and this content cannot be conveyed through any amount of description, explanation, or commentary alone (1173). Like the subject matter of the object lessons and field trips, it must be experienced directly. In contrast to the theory of total immediacy, however, it not only leaves room for, but absolutely requires the presence of an intermediary, a teacher or narrator who mediates between child and regional identity by transmitting to his charges, through his attitude rather than by the meaning of his words, his own sense of the value of local tradition and the continuity with the ancestors.

Saint-Phlin is proposing, then, a system of 'direct mediation,' so to speak. Such a system had already been described by Le Bon under the name of "suggestion." Today we would call it, thanks to Freud, a transferential theory of pedagogy.[3] It was in fact transference that made Bouteiller's pupils into his disciples, at least for a time. His influence over them did not derive from the subject matter of his lessons but, as the etymology of the term indicates, from his presence in the classroom, his manifest aplomb and independence, his career, his ability to mobilize their "unused ardors" that made him appear to them as a "young god of the intellect" and enabled him to attract to his person all the prestige of Hugo and the Republic (*Les déracinés* 495–99). It was his eloquence, the seductive power of his narratives that brought them under his spell, rather than his ideas about philosophy, which, it will be recalled, they absorbed only to the extent that they fit in with their own previous ideas, impressions, and desires. Similarly, due to the transferential effect, the result of Bouteiller's teaching is just the opposite of his intent to tie his students to the democratic State: The unforeseen consequence was that he bound them to himself instead (511).

This whole description of Bouteiller reads like a passage out of Le Bon's earliest formulation of crowd psychology, in which 'fascination' plays the role of domination over the listeners he would later, no doubt under the influence of Tarde, attribute to 'suggestion' (*L'homme* I n396; quoted in Nye 47). As a device for wielding the power of 'fascination,' the poetic power to spin tales of the Orient constitutes one of Bouteiller's primary means of attracting his students' "unused ardors"—Freud might have called it 'free-floating libido'—onto himself, a significant aspect of the transference overlooked by Le Bon but not by Barrès. Saint-Phlin expects that the nationalist teacher's manifest love for 'the soil and the dead' will act as a lightning rod to captivate his pupils' feelings, just as Bouteiller's intense admiration for Victor Hugo and the Republic had done with himself and his comrades at the lycée in Nancy. The ability to evoke the transference of his listeners is the one characteristic held in common by the teacher and the storyteller, as well as by the political demagogue.

Transference is the antithesis of critique; it induces uncritical acceptance of the authority of the object by reducing the subject's emotional and intellectual distance from it to zero. Little does it matter if the recipients fail to accept or even to grasp the specific content of the message; what counts is that they be united in a common identity based on their love for the authoritative figure and the resulting desire to become like that which he loves. If Barrès's novel is authoritarian, it is not because its narrator insists on attaching his thesis to every event, nor because it asserts in discursive form a simple ideological system in which good and evil are clearly demarcated, nor even because the plot and characters are simplified in order to reinforce that system; no, it is because it aims to impose the transferential prestige of the storyteller onto the reader and then to use that power for political ends. Like exemplary tales and parables, the thesis novel aims not merely to use story and interpretation to teach a lesson but to arouse its receivers to action. But the rhetorical method of its narrative, at least that of Barrès, is not persuasion but seduction. That is no doubt why the most successful teachers in the trilogy are those whose pupils are motivated by love: Roemerspacher indoctrinates his fiancée, Thérèse de Nelles, and Astiné, who gave Sturel his first lesson in sexual experience as well as in exoticism, maintains her hold over him long after her death. Indeed, if Saint-Phlin has such a difficult time convincing his friend Sturel of the virtues of domesticated nationalism, it is no doubt that, being of similar age and social status, he lacks the prestige of an authoritative figure, and banking on mere friendship, argument, and even the object lesson of their trip along the shores of the Moselle, he must grapple with the posthumous power of Astiné's ghost. Even Bouteiller preserves his influence on Sturel at the end of *Their Faces,* despite the two men's intense hostility in the political arena.

The Barresian narrator does not, for all that, simply abandon all appeals to reason, logic, and evidence. On the contrary, he enlists them, alongside his stories, in his effort to elicit the hypnotic attention of the reading public. Like the storyteller ('narrate' comes ultimately from the same root as 'gnosis'; Latin 'gnarus'), the interpreter is the one who claims to know; in Barrès's case, this claim to authority derives from the assertion that he occupies a privileged point of view, the only standpoint from which reality, justice, and identity appear in their true proportions to the French (*Scènes* 15).

Authority has thus been transferred from the objective truth, open to any careful, unbiased observer, to the narrator, who no longer needs a transcendent inspiration in order to claim special privilege for himself. Now his authority ultimately comes from his self, insofar as he is part of the "nation," and therefore capable of seeing things from the perspective of the ancestors. According to this nationalist logic, it follows that if he really does occupy this privileged position, his French readers, who presumably share his history, ancestors, and way of judging and reacting to life, will interpret events the same way he does once he shows things to them from the proper vantage point, precisely because once he has succeeded in tearing down the misguided universalist system of meaning and has replaced it with the nationalist conception, they will rely on their instinctive, idiosyncratic point of view. Like the pupils of Saint-Phlin's good nationalist teacher, his readers will have changed themselves in order to conform to the model he proposes as worthy of reverence and love. In this overtly dialogic model of the novel, story and interpretation will dovetail perfectly in those whom the narrator holds in his spell.

Luckily for the novel and for France, only a minority of the public did so.

CHAPTER 5

Contemporary History, by Anatole France

❧ ⟨◉⟩ ❧

The Memory of the Present

A Chronicle of Contemporary History

If Barrès's goal in his *Novel of National Energy* was to shape the crowd around the neatly embalmed corpse of the Other in order to merge with it all the more completely, Anatole France's aim in his *Contemporary History* tetralogy was to combat the indifference of the crowd on every level. It is not surprising, then, that although they shared a friendship and many convictions, including contempt for the Opportunist Republic and a certain traditionalism and anti-Semitism, the two writers should have ended up as dire enemies, on opposite sides of the chasm opened up by the Dreyfus Affair. The four volumes of the series—*L'orme du mail* (*The Elm-Tree on the Mall*; January 1897), *Le mannequin d'osier* (*The Wicker Work Woman*; September 1897), *L'anneau d'améthyste* (*The Amethyst Ring*; February 1899), and *M. Bergeret à Paris* (*Monsieur Bergeret in Paris*; February 1901)—published in the same years as Barrès's trilogy, record the shift in France's political stance from right to left in response to the same "neurosis of national identity" (Bancquart, "Notice" to *Amethyst*) that inflated the Dreyfus case into a national affair. At the same time, and for the same reasons, they chronicle the writer's movement from the position of the isolated intellectual, "aristocrat of thought," to the intellectual actively engaged in the clashes of public life (Bancquart, "Notice" to *Bergeret* 1210), or, as

Jean Levaillant succinctly put it, from "politics as spectacle" to "politics as salvation" (441).

France records these final steps in his long migration from his father's royalism, to an Epicurean anarchism, to a militant socialism close to that of Jaurès or the Clemenceau of this period, through the development of the character who eventually emerges as the central figure of the series, the classics professor M. Bergeret. His role in the story and his relation to his pupils, however, differ radically from those portrayed in the novels we have studied to this point. We almost never see him teaching, nor do we follow the careers of his pupils, who generally function only as more or less passive listeners to his ideas. This is not a *roman d'apprentissage,* or rather it is a kind of inverted *Bildungsroman,* in that it is the educator who receives an education in this novel, and it is the student who betrays the teacher rather than the reverse, as in so many education novels (*Aliette, The Disciple, Truth*), when M. Bergeret's prize pupil, M. Roux, has an affair with his wife. Neither the victims of a pernicious doctrine nor the hope of national renewal, his students represent one aspect of the 'crowd,' whose unreflective and stereotyped views the professor is constantly exercised to refute.

Unlike the standard novel of education, *Contemporary History* plots the curve neither of the downfall of the wrongly educated nor of the rise to true enlightenment of the young hero(es). Indeed, it plots no curve at all, having neither beginning nor end in the Aristotelian sense: It is all middle. Almost all the contemporary reviews of *Elm-Tree* and *Wicker Work Woman,* both favorable and unfavorable, wondered whether they were really novels at all. Narrative action is supplanted by various discrete short forms—dialogues, walks, essays, conversations, and so on. Moreover, the plot, such as it is, gets lost among the plethora of digressions, and in any case it is too disjointed. As for the contents, the social analysis and commentary outweigh the concern for realistic characterization and the representation of the passions expected in fiction (see Gier 227 and 239 for a summary of the critical reception of the two volumes). Typical of contemporary reviewers, Fernand Gregh, one of the most highly respected critics of the times, expressed his dismay over the novel's many disparate aspects and ended up calling it a "chronicle" rather than a novel (Review).

In fact, France published the texts he would later patch together into his novel under the heading of the chronicle (*chronique*) rather than of the serial (*feuilleton*), as would have been expected for a novel, first in *L'Écho de Paris,* then, after taking his public stance as a Dreyfusard, in *Le Figaro.* The immediate occasion for the first of these articles was the publication of Brunetière's piece "Après une visite au Vatican" (After a Visit to the Vatican), in January 1895. France read this proclamation as a confirmation of the "new spirit" (*esprit nouveau*) of republican conciliation with the Church announced the year before by Spuller, the minister of cults, in response to Pope Leo XIII's encyclical of 1892 calling for the Church to "rally" to the Republic. While Spuller seemed to be genuinely concerned to heal the widening rift between the clericals and the anticlericals threatening to tear the country apart, Anatole France was convinced that the new spirit of peaceful coexistence touted by the Church would remain peaceful only if the Republic would kowtow to its authoritarian demands. Certainly, the text of the encyclical was enough to give any reader pause, expressing as it does the aim of combating the "progressive abuses" of republican legislation. Moreover, shortly after Brunetière's article appeared, Félix Faure was elected president, and the new rightist government he shepherded in overtly opposed the Ferry laws, high on the list of "progressive abuses," and allowed the Congregationist schools to reopen (Bancquart, *Anatole France* 217–18; Levaillant 467–69). While France held no brief for the various governing parties that had succeeded one another since 1875, he was even more vehemently opposed to the power of the clergy, which he feared would undermine the Republic from within if the French were to allow themselves to be gulled by the new rhetoric of reconciliation.

Instead of entering into a polemical exchange with Brunetière, as he had done with the dispute over *The Disciple,* France decided to respond to the policy of the *esprit nouveau* with a series of short stories, first titled "Ecclesiastical Stories," portraying Church types he considered dangerous to the Republic (Bancquart, *Anatole France* 218). Right in the opening scene he sets the tone for the series, when with one stroke he indicts both the Church and the Republic. Archbishop-Cardinal Charlot is dictating a pastoral letter to his vicar-general, M. de Goulet, praising the 'new spirit' of peace, reconciliation, and submission to "the powers that be." When the latter objects to the conciliatory language of his speech, due to the present "decline of parliamentary predominance," the archbishop notes with satisfaction that the spirit of cooperation now works in both directions. After all, despite the Ferry laws, the prefect, M. Worms-Clavelin, looks favorably on the Congregationist schools (*Elm-Tree* 3).

France strengthens the connection between *ralliement* politics and education by associating the two main ecclesiastics with a seminary, the one as director, abbé Lantaigne, and the other as professor of eloquence, abbé Guitrel, who are competing for appointment as bishop of Tourcoing (a purely fictitious post). Under the provisions of the Concordat, reinstated by the Third Republic, candidates for bishop are nominated by the pope, but the final appointment is made by a government official, the minister of cults. The choice of this plot element thus affords France the opportunity to depict the relations, both official and covert, between the Church and the Republic. This he does primarily through abbé Guitrel's encounters with the local prefect and his wife. Opposite the churchmen France places abbé Lantaigne's principal interlocutor, the secular educator M. Bergeret, professor (*maître de conférences*) at the Faculté des lettres of the nameless provincial town whose denizens and mores will provide the grist for France's satirical mill in the first three volumes of the series.

These portraits formed the contents of the chronicles France published in the *Écho de Paris* starting on January 22, 1895 and ending abruptly on April 9 of that year (Bancquart, "Notice" to *Contemporary History, Oeuvres* 2, 1321).[1] A year later France resumed the series, now under the title "The ideas of abbé Lantaigne." The stimulus was a remarkable coincidence that gave new impetus to France's antagonism to the 'new spirit.' For many years, he had been working on a study of the conditions that produced the mentality of Joan of Arc, and he had published a series of articles about supposed visionaries in *L'Écho de Paris* during the latter part of 1895 and the beginning of 1896. Then, in spring of that year an enormous sensation erupted in the Parisian press with the announcement of the existence of an alleged prophetess, a Mlle. Couedon who claimed she was visited by the angel Gabriel. For the writer, this was proof that the *ralliement* was reproducing in modern France the same noxious atmosphere of magic and superstition that had given rise to the visions of the Maid of Orleans (1321–22). What better way to bring out the danger to the Republic of the new spirit than to show the perplexity of the 'positivist' prefect Worms-Clavelin when confronted with this apparently inexplicable phenomenon? All the more so, since God has told France's fictional seeress, Mlle. Deniseau, through the voice of a saint, that misfortunes will befall the country as long as the Republic exists; good fortune will return only when the king is restored to the throne.

After the resumption of the episodes in 1896, the concept and structure of the work underwent a significant transformation, and in October of that year the series received its definitive title of *Contemporary History*. From then on, France purposely substituted the unforeseeable, chance occurrences of the daily news for any preestablished unity of character or plot, and he introduced more and more allusions to political events into the story. It became an improvisation, full of *l'imprévu* (the unforeseen; Levaillant 467).

The tongue-in-cheek apology for the disorder of his story France placed as a foreword to the March 23, 1897, episode—the narrative part of which was included in chapter VII of *Wicker Work Woman*—bears witness to the fact that by this time he was purposely making a virtue of what had at first been a real problem for him. Apologizing for having 'forgotten' about Mme. Bergeret and therefore having to disrupt the chronological order of his story in order to pick up the strand of her ruminations where he had left her several episodes before, France confesses that his tale is not as strictly lined up as the columns of the Louvre! But, he adds, neither are the Homeric epics, which are, after all, just a bunch of folktales stitched together by a talented raconteur. And if his chronicles lack the orderliness of *Remords d'un ange* (*An Angel's Remorse*)—a very long and very bad novel by one Adolphe Dennery or d'Ennery (real name Adolphe Philippe), author of several hundred plays who was famous in the nineteenth century as a kind of poor man's Scribe, the epitome of vulgar commercialism in the theater, and thus symbol of the facile organization known as the 'well-made play'—they conform completely to the pattern of such lesser works as *Don Quixote* and *Pantagruel!* So there is no shame in having to go back to Madame so long after the event. In fact, in all humility, he aspires to nothing more glorious than that his work be compared to that of the monk Raoul Glaber, who chronicled the plagues and famines of his times in the year one thousand, in what France terms a childishly candid little book as poor in style as in thought.

In the book version, France sustained his challenge to the narrative conventions of unity and order in other ways. The title of the series announces a temporal dimension to the challenge by juxtaposing past and present in the oxymoron of "contemporary history." That there are generic implications to this temporal dimension can be seen in the definition of the newspaper chronicle given in the Larousse *Grand Dictionnaire Universel du XIXe Siècle:* "certain articles or series, written day-to-day, published by newspapers, and which are, so to speak, the hour by hour reflection of everyday life. These hurried productions, forgotten as soon as they are born" (IV, 245–46). Dealing with the trivia of everyday life and thrown together in haste to meet a daily deadline, the newspaper chronicle is the quintessence of the ephemeral. It is the antithesis, therefore, of art as it was understood by virtually the totality of writers and critics in the nineteenth century, as is evident in the contrast implied between the disparaging terms used in the definition and their contraries—careful choice, studied craft, significant events, longevity if not the downright eternity associated with the beautiful. France distilled this quintessence in his novels by publishing them in book form with virtually no lag time, recounting the processes of change from the *ralliement* to the Dreyfus Affair at the very moment they were happening.

Disorder, randomness, transience, immediacy, insignificance: these qualities, or rather defects, make of the nineteenth-century newspaper chronicle the epitome of contingency. Why, then, attempt to force just these characteristics onto the apparently antithetical novel form? In joining his chronicles into novels, is France attempting to eternalize the random and ephemeral? Or is he striving to undermine the notion of timelessness, within and outside the domain of art? Does the oxymoron of 'contemporary history' mean that the literary purpose of the novel, as opposed to the original chronicles, was to develop a technique for treating the present as though it were past history (Sachs)? Or, on the contrary, does it intimate that the only genuinely historical mode of representation is that which eschews all attempts to find an eternal meaning in temporal events (Masson)? And do these contradictions apply only to the parts of the novels drawn from the chronicles published under the definitive title of *Contemporary History*?

As stated above, France wrote the first episodes of *Elm-Tree* in order to combat the dangerous 'new spirit' heralded in Brunetière's 1895 article about his visit to Pope Leo XIII. In that article, the dogmatic critic did more than simply endorse the pope's new politics; he outlined a series of arguments designed to supply an intellectual justification for the call for political *ralliement,* by establishing a parallel between the reconciliation of Republic and Church and a new agreement between science and religion. Now it turns out that the rationale Brunetière adduces for his truce between science and religion contradicts, on virtually every point, the ideological thrust of the chronicle.

It is this rationale that France attributes to one of the churchmen who represent the danger of Catholic ideology for the Republic, abbé Lantaigne. In broad strokes, Brunetière's argument is that science has recently lost some of its prestige, a claim he summarized in the catchphrase "la banqueroute de la science" (The bankruptcy of science"), since it has now been proven that it will never be able to dispel the three major 'mysteries' of life ("A Visit to the Vatican" 99): the origins of man, society, and morality (100); the law of his conduct; and his future destiny (103). Religion, on the other hand, has recovered some of its lost esteem, having proven its truth by the "continuity of its immutable dogma," and can regain even more by doing good in the world, establishing peace and harmony in the land through its reconciliation with the government and through its benevolent policies toward the poor working classes (106). The tenets of religion are matters of faith, which can neither be proved nor disproved, but only affirmed or denied; therefore, science has nothing to say to religion on this score. Likewise, religion can neither prove nor disprove scientific truths. Hence there is no room for intellectual conflict between the two (111).

All this peace and harmony, however, is only the hors d'oeuvre; the pièce de résistance of Brunetière's ideological feast is his treatment of the question that is obviously uppermost in his mind, the political implications of the 'law of man's conduct'; that is, the effect of this new harmony on social policy, or, what amounts to the same thing for him, morals. Even while protesting his great respect for science, Brunetière feels constrained to point out that the failure of science to solve the mystery of man's conduct disqualifies it from providing that independent morality so dear to the hearts of the Opportunist republicans. Morals, duty, can never be induced from nature (the proper domain of science), for all morality, indeed all civilization, consists precisely in separating man from (his) nature (117). Morals demand the sublime, the transcendent, the absolute; in short, God, as their foundation (111–12).

As the doctrine of original sin, reinforced by Darwinian science itself, teaches us, man's nature consists in selfish instincts, the antithesis of the social bond and the social good (117). Ergo, individualism, including the use of individual reason to criticize social institutions and to develop individual interpretations, especially of sacred texts (114), is a danger to society, no doubt the gravest danger (117–18). In Catholicism, all authority (the right to command) derives from God, and even though God has now changed His mind and decided, via the mouth of Leo XIII, that the Republic is a legitimate authority, obedience to authority is still the first duty of the individual (106–17). Q.E.D. Brunetière's final word, on the topic and in the article: "This is neither the time nor the place to oppose individual caprice to the rights of the community" (118).[2]

Like Brunetière, abbé Lantaigne criticizes the principle of individual interpretation of Holy Scripture (*Elm-Tree* 21). Like Brunetière, Lantaigne professes great respect for science—after all, human reason is one of God's creations—as long as it doesn't get in the way of Church doctrine (77–78). All duties, even secular ones, come from God, the good abbé informs us (102). For him as for Brunetière, the Church represents above all immutability and continuity: The unity and continuity of the *patrie française* derives from the institution of the bishops, whose power is spiritual and therefore stable; indeed, the homeland itself is "spirit, and completely contained in the moral and religious bond" (101–2). Most important, and most ironic, is the fact that Lantaigne too accedes to the pope's call to live in peace with the Republic (149), but he does so while openly proclaiming his adherence to the principle of monarchy, as though to say that the Church will accept the concept of democracy only to the extent that it doesn't infringe upon the interests of the Church. This impression is of course confirmed as the main thrust of the novel, when abbé Guitrel, who constantly protests his acceptance of the 'new spirit,' is finally named bishop of Tourcoing at the end of the third book and proceeds immediately to attack and insult the Republic, refusing to comply with its tax laws in blatant contradiction to his repeated promises to obey the legitimate government (*Amethyst,* chap. 26, 296–99).

Levaillant construes Lantaigne as the quintessence of the rigid, systematic spirit of Catholicism in its most narrow-minded sense and applied with the blindest of logic to everything—the "unity of faith" that Lantaigne declares to be the most important idea for a priest and the touchstone of true religion for all minds (*Elm-Tree* 14). He describes France's bête noire in the very terms that Barrès was using at the same moment to castigate the Kantian spirit of the Republic, as a "theorem," the epitome of "metaphysical unity," "scholastic abstraction" and "verbal rationalism" (Levaillant 474).[3] How better to challenge this systematic spirit he abhorred than with its opposites, just as Barrès was doing: the concrete, the individual, the transitory, the contingent?

But for France, Barrès's arguments prove the case against the monarchical principles of the Church. He assembles all the themes associated with Lantaigne in the final conversation between the priest and Professor Bergeret in *Elm-Tree*. The clergyman considers that the Republic is diversity incarnate and thus the principle of evil, for it is the very antithesis of the unity that characterizes true religion (150–51). In addition to its consequent lack of independence, permanence, and power, the Republic's lack of duration entails a lack of identity (*Elm-Tree* 808). For Lantaigne, the Republic is diversity, dispersion, discontinuity, weakness, transience, and dependency. And nonexistence, for the priest cannot restrain his vituperations, adding that the regime is a lack (of a prince), and an absence (of authority) (152). The Republic is 'essentially evil,' because it wants everything that God does not want: liberty, since he is the master; equality, since he established the hierarchy of dignities in heaven and on earth; tolerance, since evil is intolerable; the will of the people, since a multitude of ignoramuses should not prevail against the small number of those who act according to God's will; and of course it is evil in its religious indifference (158–59). The pretender to the throne, Henri Dieudonné, the Count de Chambord, last of the Bourbons who died in 1883, would have restored the principle of authority and human order along with divine order, hierarchy, law, rules, true liberty, and unity (155–56). In sum, for Lantaigne the Republic is everything we group together today under the name of difference, Otherness; Catholic monarchism, everything opposed to difference, what we might call the principle of indifference.

Lantaigne's condemnation of the Republic is even more sweeping than the foregoing considerations would make it appear, for along with unity and identity the regime has destroyed meaning itself. In the good old days, the sufferings of the French nation made sense; they were useful and even precious, because people recognized that they were punishments sent by God that contained lessons, merits, salvation, strength, and glory (153–54). But now suffering has no meaning, because, once faith in God has disappeared, without the absolute, the understanding of the relative is also lost, and even the sense of history (154). God, that is to say, unity and continuity, in and out of time, is the principle of intelligibility, without which there is no meaning of any sort, neither of the eternal (whatever that might be) nor of the transitory. All that is left, presumably, is disorder, randomness, transience, immediacy, insignificance—the realm of the meaningless that constitutes the bread and butter of the chronicle!

The form of the chronicle was therefore perfectly adapted to represent the ideology of the Republic France wanted to oppose to the principle of unity he discerned at the basis of Catholic doctrine and of the Church's new politics of *ralliement*. Still better was the novel stitching together a series of chronicles with varying focuses, changing characters, multiple levels, and unpredictable twists and turns of events that constantly belie the abstract unity and meaning Lantaigne champions. In some cases, France resorts to a rather facile irony to bring out the contradiction between lofty ideas and contingent realities, as when he relates the story of little Honorine, the poor thirteen-year-old orphan, miraculously cured of tuberculosis, who supposedly sees and hears the Virgin, only to reveal that this model of innocence and purity spends most of her time rolling in the hay with a little orphan boy who presses her to extract money and gifts from the rich Brécés who find her religious ecstasies so edifying (*Amethyst* 37–45). Or when M. Bergeret cites Jean de Launoy, a pious seventeenth-century Sorbonne scholar who provided historical evidence that the Saint Catherine whom Joan of Arc claimed to have seen in a vision never existed (*Elm-Tree* 103). France makes it clear that it is chance, not design, that brings about the most important event in the plot of *Wicker Work Woman,* when he has M. Bergeret, contrary to his habit, enter the drawing room of his apartment before going into his study, "for no particular motive or reason, without thinking" (86), and discover his wife's adultery. The tension between theoretical meaning and unforeseeable occurrence is compounded when Mme. Bergeret realizes, to her horror, "the entirely unforeseen results of such a trifling episode" (*Wicker Work Woman* 224).

Most directly related to the chronicle form, however, are the actual historical events that enter into the novel, such as the momentous failure, to which Lantaigne alludes, of the Count de Chambord's effort to restore the monarchy in the early days of Third Republic, due to the relatively trivial cause of his refusal to renounce the white Bourbon flag. Even more telling is the Americans' defeat of the very Catholic and monarchical flotilla of Spain, blessed by the pope and carrying the names of the Virgin and the saints, which, according to France's fictional reactionary military expert, General Cartier de Chalmot, goes against all the rules of military science recognized in the civilized world and is thus neither likely nor desirable (*Amethyst* 163–64).

France and Bergeret themselves became the victims of unforeseen circumstances when they were swept up in the unexpected torrent of events known as the Dreyfus Affair,[4] which would become a cause of national dissension belying Bergeret's sanguine assurances to abbé Lantaigne of the country's henceforth peace-loving nature and drag the writer along in directions he could have neither foreseen nor controlled, forever changing his life while giving a new sense to the title *Contemporary History.* Starting in the first chapters of *Amethyst,* the Affair encroached on the story of the competition to become bishop of Tourcoing, overshadowed that of Mme. Bergeret's adultery, and eventually swallowed up the entire plot of *M. Bergeret in Paris.*

France later confessed in a newspaper interview that the Affair justified beyond his wildest nightmares his original hostility to the *ralliement.* When he started his chronicles, he had no idea that the danger was so imminent. During the Affair, he witnessed the "black invasion" of "foreigners," the "Roman army" who "occupied" the homeland and controlled all its intellectual venues (interview of 1903, quoted in Levail-lant 520). This sense of the danger stemming from the clerical enemy within the Republic is increasingly present in the last two books of the tetralogy, rising in a frightening crescendo toward the end of *Paris*. In the penultimate chapter, M. Bergeret vents his considerable spleen against his new bête noire, Méline, an open anti-Dreyfusard and the politician who did most to confer an aura of respectability on the new right-wing nationalists in the eyes of bourgeois republicans (*Paris* 105). Head of the government (*Président du Conseil*) from 1896 to 1898 and influential leader of the center-right thereafter, he owed the unusual lon-gevity of his ministry to the coalition of centrist republicans and right-wing parties, including antirepublican royalists, who supported him (see J.-M. Mayeur, *Vie politique* 161–73). The catchword of his regime was 'appeasement' (*appaisement*), a slogan calculated as an appeal to national unity, but one that, in the aftermath of World War II, inevitably makes us shudder today. The parallel between Méline's appeasement and Chamberlain and Daladier's infamous visit to Hitler in Munich half a century later is in fact striking: His government would not prosecute the nationalists for their numerous illegal actions if they agreed not to disrupt the World's Fair of 1900 and prevent the merchants of Paris from making a good profit.

From the beginning of his ministry, Méline had denounced anti-clericalism, slowed the secularization of the schools to a snail's pace, and closed his eyes to the return of the oulawed Congregations. In the novel, therefore, France presents his policies as the natural extension of Spuller's new spirit, a revised version of the *ralliement,* which he had not foreseen when he started the series of chronicles, nor even when he wrote and published *Wicker Work Woman*. As a result, when the series is read from beginning to end in its present, definitive form, the events of *Elm-Tree* and *Wicker Work Woman* take on a meaning they did not have when those volumes were first published: The *ralliement* now appears to be the first step in the civil war that was to break out openly in the Dreyfus Affair. Later events thus conferred a sense on earlier occur-rences that no one could have, or at least that France had not in fact, foreseen when they were taking place.

For standard spiritualist criticism, the vice of the chronicle novel is that it is too shortsighted to allow accurate judgment of the meaning of the events it recounts. But this defect is just the obverse of the unique strength of the genre—its ability to stage the process of what Freud and Lacan called *Nachträglichkeit* (retroactivity), whereby the meaning of the past is periodically rewritten in light of the unforeseeable twists and turns of the historical present that no preconceived meaning can contain.

Desire or Unity?
The World according to Epicurus

If Father Lantaigne's main role was to expose the hypocrisy behind Father Brunetière's call for the conciliation of religion and science, Professor Bergeret's original function, even before France had made the decisive choice to follow the whims of the daily news, was to plead the case for the writer's Epicurean understanding of the contingency of the world (see his *Jardin d'Épicure* [1894]), in order to display the relation between theory and desire and thus to pry loose the veneer of intellectual legitimacy that the editor of the *Revue des Deux Mondes* wanted to spread over the power grab of the Church. At first a mere foil designed to goad abbé Lantaigne into expounding his 'ideas' for all to read, M. Bergeret soon begins to take on an autonomous existence in keeping with his professorial role as general commentator, explicator, and theoretician of the world.

Bergeret launches his independent career by intervening in the conversation of his fellow habitués of Paillot's bookshop. During the idle meanderings of their senseless chatter, Doctor Fornerol and M. de Terremondre, the latter a local property owner who will soon come to represent the mentality of the average supporter of the Opportunist Republic, discuss the old wives' tales that explain the various shapes and colors of birthmarks, called *envies* (wishing-marks), which were considered to be the result of the pregnant mother's sudden craving (*envie*) for raspberries, strawberries, or wine. Bergeret takes them to task for suggesting that pregnant women have such limited desires; that view is incompatible with "natural philosophy," which states that desire created the world, sustains it, and is its motive force. Like all other animate beings, women have "secret fevers, hidden passions, and strange frenzies," and the state of pregnancy "does not produce indifference, but . . . it rather perverts and inflames the deeper instincts" (*Elm-Tree* 142). Characteristically, M. Bergeret's first effort at interpretation is thus an exercise in disinterpretation, in removing the commonly accepted sense of phenomena.

Updating Epicurus and Lucretius with an admixture of Darwin and the science of their times, Bergeret and France oppose to the transcendent theological view of the universe an immanent and naturalist theory of the world that structures the professor's ironic commentaries as well as the writer's representation of the random course of events. Its first principle is of course the extraordinary power Bergeret attributes to desire here, in the inanimate as well as the animate world.

Later in *Elm-Tree,* France asserts the more general naturalist tenet that all human actions are motivated by the instincts of love and hunger (199). Hunger, in this context, is another name for the desire to destroy the other in order to assure one's own survival, and both he and the narrator repeatedly remark on man's instinctive lust for destruction. When old Mme. Houssieu, whose house is next door to Paillot's bookstore, is found slain in her bed, Bergeret argues that murder is completely natural, in man and beast (199). While on leave from his stint of military service, M. Roux explains that one of the reasons for the continual wars that plague humanity is the innate pleasure men take in shooting their rifles; he too enjoys this activity, even though he is a socialist, loves humanity, and believes in the fraternity of nations[!] (*Wicker Work Woman* 9–10). This pleasure is not restricted to army recruits and low-life murderers. The narrator wrings his metaphorical hands in delight as he notes the "profound instinctive desire to kill" (*Amethyst* 19) in the Duke de Brécé and his aristocratic guests when they see some pheasants in a clearing on his estate, and he then calls the duke's noble ancestors a pack of murderers for their exploits as hunters (*Amethyst* 39). Indeed, Bergeret includes in his indictment all civilized men, who think that their first social duty is to learn to kill their fellow men according to the rules of combat and that their greatest glory is that of carnage (*Wicker Work Woman* 169).

Nor is M. Bergeret himself, cultivated as he is, exempt from the enjoyment of destruction, for he too is the descendant of a long line of "men, apes and savage beasts" who have transmitted those same destructive instincts to the good professor (*Wicker Work Woman* 87). Upon discovering his wife's adultery, his first reaction—which lasts only a second, it is true—is that of "a simple, violent man and ferocious animal," who thirsts for carnage and wants to kill his wife and Roux (87). Instead of murdering the couple, however, a few moments later, after leaving the room where he found them, he vents his rage on Mme. Bergeret's poor, defenseless sewing form, crushing it with his bare hands, stomping on it, throwing the headless wicker work woman out the window, and watching it crash against the ground two stories below.

The problem for any naturalist theory of human behavior is to explain the existence of apparently noninstinctive modes of action, and first of all to show Brunetière and company that morality does not consist in setting oneself in opposition to nature; rather morality derives from nature. The positivists and their kin, as we have seen, responded to this challenge by asserting the existence of an innate "social feeling" that serves as the real basis of all forms of morality. M. Bergeret espouses a more malicious theory. For him, morality derives directly from the rage for destruction. Morality, in a word, is a form of cruelty. This derivation emerges in his second reaction to his wife's adultery. Immediately after his rather weak urge to kill has dissipated, his primitive instinct is replaced by 'social' ideas—a hodgepodge of religious and secular maxims, laws, and moral principles that fan the flames of his indignation and inspire in him notions of guilt, virtue, punishment, and justice: "After having wanted to kill Madame Bergeret and M. Roux by mere bloodthirsty instinct, he now wanted to kill them out of regard for justice" (88).

His real revenge, however, is subtler, more civilized, and more cruel. He simply treats Mme. Bergeret as though she does not exist, as absolute nothingness (936): He takes away from her the management of the household, looks right through her when she crosses his path, and, above all, never listens or speaks to her. In this way he does not simply kill her, he "annihilate[s] her" (128). A very sociable being, Mme. Bergeret cannot stand this cruel torture and begins to feel totally empty in this new state that resembles solitude and death (131). Euphémie, the Bergerets' servant girl, is not mistaken when she accuses him of being too mean. To her mind, all he had to do was beat his wife silly, then make up with her and continue as before. After mature reflection, Bergeret is delighted to agree with the girl that he is indeed being mean, for he has retained his "primitive instincts" that tell him that "the mere power of injuring and destroying were the motive force of living things, their essential quality and highest merit," and that life prospers only through murder, so that the best are those who wreak the most carnage (238). After some doubt, he concludes that he is indeed mean, because, while his enlightened principles make him theoretically indulgent toward a petty misdemeanor such as adultery, his actual conduct in punishing his wife as harshly as though he judged her guilty of some heinous crime, is "moral, but cruel" (241).

M. Bergeret is no more exempt from the power of love than he is from that of hunger. Like the pregnant women he invoked in his first panegyric to desire, he too is subject to 'secret ardors' and hidden lusts, in the form of Mme. de Gromance, an attractive and elegant young aristocrat who is notorious in the region for cheating on her husband. He sees her on New Year's Day and, grateful to her for bringing a ray of beauty and grace into his day, smiles at her, whereupon she cuts him dead. Nevertheless, he defends her to M. Mazure, the local archivist who revels in airing other people's dirty laundry, in exactly the same terms that he will subsequently utilize to excuse, in principle at least, his wife's transgression. Later in *Wicker Work Woman,* M. Bergeret muses to himself about the necessity of lying to others, or at least of keeping your thoughts to yourself. His prime example is his own "salacious, perverted, and grotesque" sexual fantasies about Mme. de Gromance.

If France takes pains to demonstrate that his man of high culture acts on the basis of these 'primitive instincts,' it is not only in order to include him in the general irony of the book, but also to emphasize the polemical lesson that civilization is not a separation from but a continuation of our immersion in the world of nature—and a hypocritical continuation at that, since it cloaks its character beneath a veneer of high-mindedness. Well before Foucault's *Discipline and Punish,* France takes aim at modern, humanitarian prisons. The day before Lecoeur, the butcher's boy who raped and murdered old Mme. Houssieu, is to be executed, Bergeret is in Paillot's bookstore with the usual cronies, discussing the death penalty and the penal system. Terremondre is proud of the new, progressive, 'humanitarian' cells in the local prison. Bergeret replies that a barbarian could never imagine the cruelty of locking men up in single cells, totally isolated from all social contact; "it required a philanthropist to conceive the idea of killing them [prisoners] with solitude" (152).

When Mazure, the Radical, chastises Bergeret for turning against his own friends, the republicans, and espousing the cause of his enemies, the clericals—Bergeret has just argued that both parties are equally desirous of freedom when out of power, because it strengthens the opposition, and just as despotic when in power, since nothing in the Constitution protects individual freedoms against national security—an allusion to the *lois scélérates* (black laws) passed after the recent anarchist bombings—the professor lays his ultimate trump card on the table, the argument France has designed to conflate and deflate the two parties simultaneously. Thrusting his stiletto through the very heart of the public disputes over the Ferry laws, the professor pops the bubble of official bluster by demonstrating that if the clericals were to replace the republicans in power, people's lives would not be significantly altered, because there is no difference between the religious and the secular moralities (247–48).

While it may at first seem as though Bergeret is simply repeating the Opportunists' protestations that there exists one single, universal morality, the reasons he adduces to support his assertion soon prove that impression to be mistaken. The gist of his naturalistic argument is that our moral ideas are effects, not causes, of our behavior; they are the result, or, better yet, the representation of the habits, the customs, the mores of a given time and place (248). As a consequence, there cannot be two rival moral systems at the same time and in the same place.

Poor M. Mazure comes close to bursting out in a rage, when M. Bergeret points out to him that he, a freethinker who believes that happiness is the goal of life, and M. de Terremondre, who is Catholic and believes expiation as the path to eternal life to be the principle of earthly existence, nevertheless both have the same morality. Both sides have the same traditions, the same prejudices, and are plunged in the same darkness.

Indeed, if the (anti-)ideal republic was the epitome of diversity, the real French Republic of the last years of the century adopted more and more the authoritarian principles of unity, command, and obedience dear to the hearts of its clerical opponents. Nowhere is this more evident than in the practice of obligatory universal male military service (adopted in 1872, modified in 1889). That is why *Wicker Work Woman* begins with Bergeret's ironic assault on the military in his conversation with M. Roux, on leave from his military service. The Republic will never renounce conscription, M. Bergeret informs his listeners, because the military teaches citizens obedience to authority, thus protecting the powers that be (23). General Cartier de Chalmot, the same shining light who confidently predicts the downfall of the American navy in its war against the Spanish, and who later asserts with aplomb, apropos of Dreyfus's conviction, that an army tribunal cannot make a mistake, assures his friends at the Duke de Brécé's château that the virtue of the army is the "sovereign and immutable" unity of its "one, unique" will (*Amethyst* 50).

In fact, the army is the perfect training ground for transmuting freedom-loving citizens into tyrants and slaves. In response to M. Roux's story of a Sergeant Lebrec, who curses the mother of a new draftee who fails to line up correctly; Bergeret comments, "[W]ere he dressed in the peasant's blouse this hero [Lebrec] would be thirsting for liberty, but clad in a uniform, it is tyranny for which he yearns, and to help in the maintenance of order" (*Wicker Work Woman* 25). Moreover, as M. Roux confesses at the start of their conversation, the lack of sleep and constant fatigue of boot camp make draftees incapable of entertaining general ideas and subtle thoughts, that is, of exercising the critical faculties necessary for freedom of thought. The army operates on the basis of the fear it can inspire in its members, and the sadistic enjoyment it can provide for its officers. The sergeant would have pitied the new recruits, "were it not that he thirsts to terrify them in order that he may enjoy his own sense of power"; "he is doubly perverted, both as slave and tyrant" (168–69).

The entire military code of justice constitutes an exercise in tyranny, since it seeks to 'maintain order' among the troups by the rule of naked fear. A holdover from the ancien régime designed for mercenaries and victims of forced conscription, which the Republic has neglected to amend now that it has citizen armies, Bergeret calls it a remainder of barbarity, for it mandates whipping, branding, and other cruel physical punishments for various offenses, and the death penalty for crimes ranging from theft to armed insurrection. Even before France became involved in the Dreyfus Affair, then, he saw that the military embraced by the republic after the shock of 1870 contradicted the very principles that same republic claimed to uphold against the monarchists and clericals.

Meaning and Desire:
An Essay on Indifference (in Matters of Politics)

The question France implicitly raises in the first two volumes of *Contemporary History* is: 'What has made the *ralliement* possible?' In other words, "How has it come about that the Republic has betrayed its principles and its very self?" The key to the answer he proposes is contained in M. Bergeret's speech on birthmarks: The state of pregnancy does not produce indifference; it stimulates the deepest instincts, the most diverse desires. The Republic, on the contrary, suffers precisely from the lack of desire that entails the lack of diversity, both of which Bergeret neatly combines in the one term—'in-difference.' Indeed the words 'indifference' and 'indifferent' are applied to almost every situation in the first volumes of the series, for indifference, the lack of desire, is the secret scourge of modern France under the Republic. Like the 'decadent' old men portrayed in works by Flaubert, Huysmans, Gustave Moreau, or Oscar Wilde, the Opportunist Republic has acquiesced in the *ralliement* because it has lost its desire to be (itself). It remains to be seen whether it will find a Salomé or Herodiade sufficiently stimulating to arouse that desire once again.[5]

In his great diatribe against the Republic, abbé Lantaigne excoriates its policy of religious "indifference" (which Ferry and friends called 'neutrality,' of course), a charge to which he returns with a vengeance in the second volume, this time armed with Lamennais's *Essay on Indifference in Matters of Religion*. Even though France is far from approving either Lantaigne or Lamennais's doctrine of expiation, he clearly prefers the abbé's forthrightness and conviction to the hypocrisy and indifference of the republican of the *ralliement* par excellence, M. de Terremondre.

Indifference is so important because France saw it as the force, or rather the absence of force, which had allowed the Republic to indulge in financial scandal after scandal with impunity. When M. Worms-Clavelin, the epitome of the Republican official in the novel, learns of Mlle. Deniseau's antigovernment prophesies, he thinks back to all the attacks the Republic has had to bear since the beginning of his career under President Grévy, who had to resign due to his complicity in the Wilson scandal. (Grévy's son-in-law, Daniel Wilson, was a corrupt journalist involved in selling official State honors). Having seen the Panama scandal come and go, and then come again (it was revived in 1895 with the arrest of Arton); having seen most of the financiers and engineers of his party end up in prison; having one senator and two deputies from his department under indictment for corruption, all without losing the support of the population, he had learned to be indulgent toward his fallible compatriots. As France puts it with exquisite irony, "events had enlarged his naturally limited intelligence. The vast irony of things had passed into his soul, making it easy-going, mocking, indifferent" (*Elm-Tree* 91–92). But, as an "honest civil servant," there are some affronts even he cannot tolerate, namely, those that risk preventing the government ministries from "peaceably enjoy[ing] that common attitude of indifference which, by gaining over their friends as well as their enemies, ensured at the same time both their power and their repose" (92).

In *Wicker Work Woman,* M. Bergeret directs his ironic wit against the government as well as the Church, taking over the function that had been for the most part reserved for the narrator in the first volume. Seated once again under the elms of the Mall, he discusses the latest government scandal with abbé Lantaigne, the arrest and imprisonment for corruption of the 'honorable' Senator Laprat-Teulier, leader of the Opportunist party in their town since the early days of the Republic. Bergeret's pastiche of government style in his rendition of Worms-Clavelin's reaction to this unfortunate event is as marvelous and as wicked as those France had given in *Elm-Tree* of Church style in the discourse of abbés Lantaigne and Guitrel:

[M. Worms-Clavelin] congratulates himself on the loyalty of their constituents [*ses administrés*—those who are passively 'administered,' rather
than electors who wield power], who remain true to the established
system, even when it seems the general wish to bring it into disrepute.
He declares, in fact, that [such] parliamentary episodes . . . leave the
working-classes of the department absolutely indifferent (188).

France's portrait of the honest civil servant is viciously funny and
unremittingly nasty, tinged by the kind of prejudicial stereotyping of
Jews typical of the times, despite France's public rejection of Drumont's
anti-Semiticism.[6] With neither superstitions nor homeland, empty, col-
orless, and hence 'free,' Worms-Clavelin is the prototypical man without
qualities, whose only motivating force is the desire to exist and who, a
pure exterior bereft of any inner being, can only exist by virtue of what
he can possess; in short, the negation of identity Barrès and his ilk
found so threatening in their phantasmagoria of the Jew. It is no doubt
because he has no convictions and no imagination that he must hang
on for dear life to the tangible facts that will make up for the identity
he lacks. In *Contemporary History* this combination of nullity and factu-
ality represents the 'rootless' Republic rather than a particular 'race' or
the dangerous foreigner per se, and specifically the Republic of the *ralliement,* which, being nothing in particular, having no desire other than
to survive, can all the more easily strive to be all things to all people,
under the reassuring banner of peaceful coexistence.

The official counterpart to the public's indifference is the government's policy of doing nothing, and France intimates that it is the combination of the two attitudes that was making the 'new spirit' acceptable.
M. Worms-Clavelin cloaks his selective inertia at first under the title of
liberal tolerance in his discussions with abbé Guitrel, which form a kind
of low-level parodic parallel to the genuine exchange of ideas between
Bergeret and Lantaigne. The prefect claims that he has shown his liberal
and tolerant attitude by closing his eyes when the Sisters and Brothers
returned to their convents and schools, and he offers this grotesque
justification for his application of the new Faure policy of friendship
toward the Church: "for if we vigorously uphold the essential laws of
the Republic, we hardly enforce them" (*Elm-Tree* 86)!

The policy of doing nothing has in fact been the key to the successful
survival of the Third Republic thus far, according to Worms-Clavelin.
Nothing could be further from M. Bergeret's mentality, who had just
a few pages earlier harangued Paillot about the "edifice" of the French

classical school curriculum, which has managed to withstand the test of time precisely because it has been constantly revamped, each period of history adding its own distinctive contribution. It would soon perish if people stopped changing it, repairing it, adding to it.

In a later scene, Worms-Clavelin's interlocutor is an artist and former Communard named Frémont, who translates his remarks as acquiescence in "fraud and iniquity." Once the liberator of peoples, the only rights France now cares to avenge are those of the stock- and bondholders. The Republic has supported the Turks in their battles against the Greeks in Crete and in their massacre of three hundred thousand Armenian Christians, ostensibly because of the recent alliance with the czar, who is in turn allied with the Ottomans, but in fact due to the influence of high finance, Jewish finance, which has lent millions to Turkey and has directed France in these matters to protect its interests. In abandoning the Armenians, "we have betrayed not only the interests of humanity, but our own" (*Wicker Work Woman* 145).

In a sense, then, Worms-Clavelin does represent a foreign power, that of international finance and banking, which was closely associated with the Jew in the doctrine of the anarchist, socialist, and communist left of the period. Bergeret considers this new "cosmopolitan" force present in all countries to have taken over where the Catholic Church left off. M. Bergeret points out more than once that no one supports the Catholic Church more strongly than the Jewish financiers, who see in it both an avenue to respectability and acceptance and a convenient force of repression, against the people in general and specifically against the bourgoisie's ultimate nightmare, collectivism. France emphasizes the cozy relation among government, Church, and Jewish finance through Mme. Worms-Clavelin's preoccupation with the Church, purchasing old Church vestments and objects used in mass, having her daughter baptized and educated in a convent school, and donating money to Catholic charities.

By doing nothing, the republican government is thus doing something, selling out the traditional identity of the French nation to the faceless power of big money that is as foreign to traditional French identity as to the political and physical nation, and it is the indifference of the people that allows those in power to do nothing without fear of reprisals. The result is the loss of identity that Worms-Clavelin symbolizes and that Frémont bemoans. The writer introduces another character to crystallize this theme, Commander Aspertini, an Italian legislator and intellectual who maintains a scholarly correspondence with M. Bergeret and who represents the spirit of Renaissance and Enlightenment humanism. The first time he appears, Aspertini explains that, if France has lost some of its prestige among the nations, it is not due to the defeat in the Franco-Prussian War nor to a supposed lack of intellectual production, but to its abandonment of its role as "apostle of brotherhood and justice," as liberator of humanity (*Wicker Work Woman* 29).

Eventually, Bergeret poses the question of popular 'indifference' and national identity explicitly, out of disgust with the venality and corruption of the officials of the Republic, and provoked by abbé Lantaigne's disparaging remarks contrasting public acceptance of immorality under the current regime with the active voice of public opinion under the Monarchy and the Empire. Unlike Barrès, however, Bergeret does not indict parliamentary government per se. Unable to discern the cause of the phenomenon, he imagines a scenario drawn from a Chinese folktale to explain the transformation of the French people. By some magic spell, an evil genie has replaced the brains of the French with those of "some tame, spiritless people, who drag out a melancholy existence without rising to the height of a new desire, indifferent to justice and injustice" (*Wicker Work Woman* 189–90). He soon decides, like Frémont, that the real perpetrator of the lobotomy that has excised the nation's historic desire for freedom and justice is "international high finance"; if the current mentality of the country is conducive to peace within and without, it is because, for the moment, "financial Europe is in a peaceful temper" (192).

Repetition and the Meaning of Meaning

This is not the first time the text has evoked the image of brain-dead people dragging out a dreary existence due to their lack of desire. Nonexistence and unremitting monotony are linked together in the silent treatment Mme. Bergeret finds so unbearable. Well before either of these episodes, however, the narrator had used virtually identical terms in *Elm-Tree* to describe M. Bergeret's reaction to an event that had occurred to him many times in the past. In the bookshop he frequents as a refuge from his mistreatment at the university, the hostility of the town's social circles, and his unhappy home life, Bergeret idly opens a book he has opened a thousand times before in the past six years, and always to the same page, the place in the *Histoire générale des voyages* that recounts Captain Cook's last voyage in search of the mythical Northwest Passage. In his diary, the captain observed that his failure allowed him to return to the Sandwich Islands and make the most important discovery by any European in the Pacific; to which the editor appends the sorry note that, unfortunately, the hopes aroused by Cook's words were never fulfilled. The 'fatal' repetition of this occurrence symbolized to the professor, so the narrator informs us, precisely the monotony and uniformity of the academic and provincial life that provide a foretaste of death and the dissolution of the body in the grave (143–44). These are the characteristics of an existence that consists of the repetition of the same things over and over again.

Significantly, this scene transpires just after Bergeret has delivered himself of his panegyric to desire, as though to underline the absolute contradiction between that life force and the dreariness, monotony, and uniformity that characterize a life of repetition without desire. It is not surprising, then, that the most knowledgeable commentators consider this scene—the only one to be repeated several times in the succeeding volumes of the series—to function as an allegory of the entire novel, articulating repetition as its main theme, central goal, and principle of construction (Levaillant 452–53; Sachs 120–22; Bancquart, *Anatole France*; France, *Oeuvres*, vol. 2, 1330–31).

These interpretations link repetition with two distinct concepts, fatality and chance. While the episode exists on two levels, that of Captain Cook and that of Bergeret, the question of repetition arises only for the unhappy professor, in whose hands the book 'accidentally' keeps opening to the same page. Captain Cook's fate may have been to fail to transmit his newfound knowledge to posterity, but it is not the result of repetition. He makes his great discovery by chance, as a result of a one-time occurrence, his failure to carry out his original purpose, and the discovery is also lost due to a single chance event, the unhappy fact that he and his men were murdered during their last visit to the Sandwich Islands. The question, then, is whether there is some connection between the singular events that befell the voyager and the repetitive occurrences that afflict the professor. In what sense can either one be construed as fate, as something inherent in the plan of an individual life or in the nature of the world? The answer is that the sense in question, the secret complicity between singularity and repetition, between chance and fatality, is that of non-sense.

Absurdity, futility, chance, all three are the others of that unity and continuity that constitute the theological version of truth and meaning espoused by abbé Lantaigne. Repetition could, under certain circumstances, be construed as the manifestation of a fatality opposed to chance, because, due to the apparent improbability of the same unmotivated occurrence happening repeatedly, it would seem to result from an underlying order or plan. But the underlying 'order' in this case is the Epicurean disorder of nature, according to which everything derives from the random collision of the atoms that form the primary building blocks of the universe. Bergeret alludes to this theory later when he muses on the parallel imperfections of his wife and his dictionary! It took nature millions of years to form both out of the molecules floating around in the primordial nebular cloud—France has adapted the theory of the ancients to conform with the physical science of his times—and yet both are still far from perfect (*Wicker Work Woman* 11). The point of his pessimistic excursus is that the universe is not organized according to a divine plan, à la Bossuet. It has neither direction nor meaning, as Bergeret's remarks later in the same chapter indicate, apropos of human history. In short, whether events are singular or repetitive, the fatality of Epicurean nature is that life makes no sense.

Moreover, the text implies, it would be a fate worse than death, or at least just as bad, if life did make sense. Bergeret's reading of this passage seems to indicate that the realization of abbé Lantaigne's ideal would result precisely in the reign of a kind of living death, for it is uniformity and monotony, two synonyms for the theological categories of unity and continuity, that characterize the provincial and university existence to which he feels condemned and that describe the (non)existence to which he condemns his wife. It was death, along with horrible suffering, that betrayed the meaning of the reign of meaning when the chance occurrences of real events led the writer to include a gruesome episode in his chronicles and in chapter XV of *Wicker Work Woman*. On May 4, 1897, there was a fire at the Charity Bazaar in Paris that took the lives of more than 100 people and injured more than 150, most of them high-society women. At the funeral services in Notre-Dame, Father Ollivier gave a sermon in front of the president of the Republic and other government dignitaries explaining that the calamity was a necessary expiation for a frivolous and perverted society (see Bancquart, *Anatole France* n1408). M. de Terremondre, the very Catholic government supporter, is horrified by this display of bad taste, whereupon abbé Lantaigne asks him: "How can you, one of the leaders of the Catholic party in our province, reproach him for telling the head of state and his ministers that France was wrong to turn its back on the Armenian Christians being slaughtered by the Turks, wrong to chase the true God out of its schools?" When Terremondre eventually retorts that Father Ollivier seemed to be making God responsible for setting the fire, Lantaigne remains silent, but Bergeret gets him to acknowledge that he accepts the doctrine of expiation expounded in Lamennais's *Essay on*

Indifference. When Terremondre protests that his cousin and his nieces who were burned in the fire did not deserve such a fate, Lantaigne can restrain himself no longer and bursts out that God was neither cruel nor unjust toward them, and that Christians have unfortunately lost the sense (*sentiment*) of sacrifice and the use of pain.

It would seem, then, that the living death of senseless repetition constitutes only an ironic 'progress' over the excruciating pain of theological meaning, and in any case the alliance of big money and big religion that is the *ralliement* joins the two together in an infernal round of suffering and apathy. That is no doubt why contemporary readers, both middle-of-the-road republicans and right-wing Catholic critics, found *Elm-Tree* unsettling. Despite its placid tone, they complained, it does away with all the prejudices that underlie the present social order (Gier 228). For the same reasons, *Wicker Work Woman* appeared even more threatening: In it France had undermined any basis for virtuous action (Gier 240); indeed, the book was nothing less than "a breviary of discouragement and a textbook on nihilism" (241).[7]

Liberation and Representation

It would be a mistake, however, to conclude that the alternative of fatal repetition or petrified meaning was France's last word on history, past, present, and future. For, although chance and repetition are both others of divine order, a certain tension between them persists nevertheless. If the whole purpose of *Contemporary History* is to represent the present as the past, to demonstrate the futility of human striving in the face of repetition, the absurdity of life in a totally deterministic universe, or human helplessness in the face of chance, why, then, adopt the chronicle form, whose special type of meaninglessness consists precisely in its openness to the unforeseeable vicissitudes of the present and future, as Levaillant and especially Masson argue persuasively?

In fact, once M. Bergeret emerges as the main character of the novel in *Wicker Work Woman*, the competition for the appointment as bishop of Tourcoing is pushed into the background. The main thrust of the series from then on, the plot behind its plot, becomes the struggle to break with the past, to escape from the tyranny of monotonous and uniform provincial life, to overcome senseless repetition without turning the events of history once again into a mere example of an eternal and immaterial meaning such as expiation (see Masson 16). Indeed, Levaillant construes the underlying structure of the first two volumes as "the contrast between the stifling universe of repetition and boredom and the hope for a distant opening, between the present truth of separation and the desire for participation" (492). But he points out that in those first two books, France's drama consists in "the desire for something unknown that each time immediately deteriorates into something only too well known" (492). The question then becomes: "Is it possible, in analogy with Kant's determination of the beautiful, to conceive of the course of events as a kind of unknown, that is, as 'meaningful without [reinstating a specific] meaning' (too well known)?" This, I would argue, is the central problem of France's *Contemporary History*, and the writer's attempt to come to grips with this seemingly insoluble conundrum on all levels gives the novel its special character and shape.

Since the dreary existence of French life under the Third Republic results from the indifference of its citizens, the only way to overcome that condition is to reawaken in them a new desire. Indeed, she who says 'plot' automatically implies the existence of a desire trying to reach satisfaction. But before this text can tell the tale of such a desire, it must recount the story of a subject striving to attain its desire. At first, therefore, the plot takes the form of a struggle between the two hostile forces of repetition and desire. Before Bergeret can form a positive desire, he must liberate himself from all the tyrannies, grand and petty, that imprison him in the worlds of meaning and repetition.

France finds a supremely clever way to bring out the dialectic between freedom and repetition. After Bergeret's first reactions of shock, fury, reflection, and dismay at his wife's adultery and the consequent loss of his home life, he wanders outside, and, after a visit to the shoemaker—who is of course looking for a wife—he winds up in his customary refuge, Paillot's bookstore. Naturally he opens once again the *Histoire générale des voyages* to the usual page, and it is while he is reenacting the primal scene of repetition, rereading the familiar passage about Cook's last voyage, that he hits upon the idea that will give shape to the rest of the book as well as to the rest of his fictional life: His wife's transgression has given him his moral freedom. France's text physically interweaves past and present, repetition and singularity, by interspersing the passage Bergeret is reading from the book with the professor's reflections about his current situation. Although the narrator informs us that Bergeret was not paying attention to what he was reading, the juxtaposition of the two textual threads confers an objective significance on the relation between the specific fragments of the book and the thoughts they seem to provoke. As Bergeret reads the part about Cook's failure to find the Northwest Passage, he tries out his usual 'philosophical' maneuver—the same one Sixte recommends to Greslou—of seeing his particular situation as a mere example of a universal law. It is only when he comes to the mention of the "discovery, albeit the last one," that the idea of his moral freedom occurs to him. Perhaps most significant is the fact that this time, unlike the first occurrence in *Elm-Tree* and the later one in *Paris,* he does *not* read the commentator's note about the disappointed hopes aroused by the explorer's announcement of his discovery.

As though to indicate his new optimism, Bergeret closes the book immediately after reading the lines from Cook's diary in which the explorer boasts of making his 'greatest discovery.' For reading about Cook's accomplishment has somehow aided the professor to make his own great discovery: of liberty and a new life. In a kind of reverse symmetry, in each case it is chance that breaks the grip of repetition. Just as Cook's failure led by chance to his greatest achievement, so Bergeret's failure, his chance discovery of his wife's betrayal, has led him to his greatest triumph, the recognition of the possibility of freedom from Mme. Bergeret's "despotic soul." It is the ability to take advantage of an opportunity opened up in the present by chance, that is, the capacity to see his situation in an entirely new light, which allows him—after (only?) ninety minutes, as the narrator points out waggishly—to reach a state of relative calm and 'wisdom.' Wisdom, for Bergeret, consists in the exact opposite of the traditional philosophical definition; it is the power *not* to see the present as a repetition of the past, *not* to reduce the singular to an instance of the universal. In this view, casting off the shackles of previously held ideas is the first step to liberation, emancipation is the first step to the formation of desire, and the pursuit of both becomes inextricably intertwined with the question of representation.

Usually vacillating and weak-willed, M. Bergeret is able to follow through on the resolution he forms, to free himself from his wife by 'extirpating' her from his household, because he is now motivated by a powerful desire, the pure desire unadulterated by hatred, never to see his wife again. For the first time in the novel, we see him develop a desire that leads him to take a particular action to improve his situation.

Bergeret's action is particular in that it is adapted to his wife's specific character and to his individual temperament. At the same time, however, it is a new variation on the age-old theme of murdering the offending wife. Similarly, his reading of the passage from the *Histoire générale des voyages* is not a straightforward repudiation of the use of the past as prototype, for it is precisely Cook's voyage in the distant past that serves as model for Bergeret's discovery in the present. Moreover, each time he reads the passage, this 'repetition of the same' is in fact slightly different.

Bergeret opens the book to the inevitable passage the second time just after Lantaigne's distressing dissection of the Republic's weaknesses and his own enumeration of all his failings and reasons for unhappiness. Appropriately enough for his despondent frame of mind, this time he reads only the first few lines, highlighting Cook's failure to find the Northwest Passage (*Elm-Tree* chap. XIV). The final occurrence, in the second chapter of *M. Bergeret in Paris,* is perhaps the most instructive, for that time he reads the entire text, diary entry plus commentary exactly as it was the first time, and the narrator accompanies it with a similar explanation of the impression it caused in Bergeret. Yet the sense of the passage is entirely different from all of the previous occurrences. Here the context makes it clear that the cause of his sadness is a kind of nostalgia provoked by the thought of relinquishing a part of his own past, and thus of his self. He is about to leave town for Paris, to take up his new appointment as a professor at the Sorbonne, and has come to bid adieu to Paillot the bookseller. The narrator makes a point of informing us that after scanning the familiar lines once again, Bergeret closed the book, never to open it again, as though to imply that, however gloomy it made him feel at the moment, the mentality of futile repetition it symbolized was a chapter in his life that he was closing forever.

France had built up the context for this interpretation of M. Bergeret's leave-taking in the previous volume of the series. Once his wife returns to her mother, Bergeret has completed the first step toward freedom; although he is not happy, he is no longer sad, for now he enjoys true independence, which is inner freedom of the soul. That the next step in his emancipation consists in detaching himself from the town and renouncing his ties to the past is brought out in the penultimate chapter of *Amethyst,* just after he learns of his appointment to Paris. As Bergeret looks around him on the street, all the familiar sights of the town suddenly appear strange. The city itself seems foreign, unreal, the mere image of itself. Analyzing his impressions, as he habitually does, he realizes that the reality of the town existed for him only insofar as he related the people and things in it to himself. Its sudden foreignness thus results from the withdrawal of his interest from this place where, as he remarks, he had spent the last fifteen years of his life.

Yet he still feels that he is tied to the things in town by invisible bonds, and he realizes that he also loves "his mother soil [*la terre de la patrie*] and the town" (*Amethyst* 289), so that he will feel a deep sense of loss upon leaving. It is in this ambivalent state of mind that Bergeret goes to say farewell to Paillot and Captain Cook, profoundly moved by the prospect of losing so important a part of his life, yet looking forward to a new phase of liberation in the metropolis where, in the last words of the chapter, he expects to find a few "minds which are sufficiently free to rid themselves of vulgar terrors and discover for themselves the veiled truths" (*Paris* 20).

That separation from his past is a necessary step in the process of mourning that will lead to his emancipation is confirmed a few chapters later in the novel. Looking for an apartment in Paris, Bergeret and his sister Zoé find out that the one they used to live in as children with their parents is for rent. They go to visit it, with the apparent intention of taking it for themselves once again. As they walk from room to room together, they are swept up in a torrent of childhood memories, of the objects and people they once knew, and above all of their parents. Classics professor that he is, M. Bergeret feels that, like Ulysses in the land of the Cimmerians, he is calling up the shades of his past. And yet, as Masson observes, "against all expectations, [Bergeret] tears himself away from the spell and resumes his search [for an apartment]" (171). The critic sees this turn away from the past as proof that France's protagonist, unlike the heroes of conservative fiction, wants to live his own life in his own time rather than repeat the life of a predecessor. And in fact, after they have inspected all the rooms, with what must be a cold shudder, Bergeret urges his sister to leave that realm of the shades. The land of memories, like the town in the provinces, is the realm of silence and death, as they perceive by the contrast with the noise and the bustling activity of life they encounter in the busy Parisian street below. Not for them, the Barresian conception of the ancestors as the source and support of the self.

CHAPTER 6

Contemporary History

✧⟨◉⟩✧

Filling the Emptiness Within

Commentary and the Subject

By inserting minor variations into the passage that serves as the paradigm of the repetition of the same, France seems to indicate that sameness is never total, difference never complete. It depends on the commentator—France, M. Bergeret, the reader—whether to see a given event as sameness or as difference; better, as difference or in-difference. This is not a matter of free choice, however; in keeping with his materialist principles, France constantly insinuates that his characters' interpretation of events, like a nation's morality, is determined by the material conditions of their lives at the time, and, in the case of individuals, especially by their prospects for success or their fears of failure.

And yet as early as *Elm-Tree* a chink appears in the armor of Epicurean determinism. Just after proclaiming that all our actions are motivated by love and hunger, and bemoaning the fact that in their constant blood lust men are like wild beasts, M. Bergeret adds: "But it still remains to inquire why I know this, and whence it comes that the fact arouses grief and indignation in me" (*Elm-Tree* 200). At this point he takes this knowledge and this reaction as proofs that there must also be goodness in the world, but a further implication is that this goodness must owe its existence to the possibility of separating oneself from the grip of nature, a theme that becomes explicit in the following book.

From the beginning, then, France presents a dialectic of freedom and determinism whose two poles are inextricably intertwined with the functions of commentary, meaning, and representation. With his questions, M. Bergeret has come upon the standard theme of the subject, common in Western thought at least since Descartes: I exist as a subject to the extent that I can stand outside the natural world in order to represent it to myself. But how is it possible for the mind to contemplate the natural universe in its entirety if it is itself a part of that universe? Being a fictional character, however, M. Bergeret does not trouble himself with finding an answer to this question. He simply lives out the conflicted role of the subject, whose claim to freedom is founded upon his ability to look at the world from a distance. By 'world' here is meant both the physical world and the world of human society, which is lived as a (second) nature by the child and the adult who never questions his or her beliefs. In *Contemporary History,* the function of the professor is to be the personification of the subject; the novel of education tells the story of the development of the subject and the formation of his desire in relation to the world he experiences as his object.

One of the basic functions of the nineteenth-century newspaper chronicle was in fact to subjectivize the reader's world by furnishing a commentary on current events (Levaillant 465–66), preferably one that was new, unexpected, and, if possible, amusing. The prevalence of this role forms the distinctive mark of France's tetralogy, as contemporary critics observed when they pointed to the preponderance of ideological discussions in the first two volumes. In the latter books, both the narrator and M. Bergeret indulge in all sorts of more or less fanciful commentary on the sentiments and motivations of the professor's new pet dog, Riquet. Similarly, in *M. Bergeret in Paris* France introduces the character Henri Léon, son of a banker ruined in the crash of the Union Générale and thus from a somewhat different social circle than that of the majority of right-wing youth, into the royalist and nationalist circles from which M. Bergeret is necessarily excluded. As skeptical and given to paradox as the professor, Léon can exercise the same function of critical commentator of the ideas and ambitions of the movements France deplores, with the added irony that France makes his criticism seem more objective, coming from a member of the group criticized. Indeed, virtually every event that occurs in the novels is immediately surrounded by a blanket of commentary supplied either by the various townspeople or by M. Bergeret. The direct opposite of Saint-Phlin's ideal in Barrès's novel, no event stands by itself; there is always a measure of distance between object and subject, between what happens and what people make of it. The world of *Contemporary History,* as of contemporary history itself as it appears in the chronicles, is the product of collective or individual interpretation, and the real action of the novel is not the events that take place but the struggle to eliminate or assign meanings.

Focalization

As M. Bergeret's role in the novels takes on greater proportions, the narrative enhances this subjectivization of the world by supplementing the conversations with internal focalizations. France first takes us into the meanderings of Bergeret's mind after the professor discovers his wife with M. Roux. Then, in the passage where he returns to Mme. Bergeret after supposedly having 'forgotten' her, the narrator shows us her thoughts as she tries to come to terms with her husband's silent treatment. In order to present another manner of dealing with an adulterous wife by which to weigh the severity of M. Bergeret's civilized cruelty, he then briefly takes us into the mind of Euphémie, the Bergerets' domestic, who looks at the matter from the peasant's point of view. Starting in *Amethyst,* the narrator reports the 'thoughts' of Riquet, M. Bergeret's new pet dog, who, acting first essentially as a more obedient replacement for Madame, sees the world from a simple, reverential, and 'natural' standpoint, then serves as an amusing caricature of the nationalist mentality.

The most instructive of these focalizations recounts the husband's various moves as he tries to cope with the trauma of his wife's adultery in *Wicker Work Woman,* for in it France deploys the technique best adapted to convey subjectivity as separate from the objective world precisely to display the entire panoply of methods M. Bergeret uses for distancing himself from events. Moving in the space of a few seconds from the ancient lust to kill to the civilized desire to punish the guilty parties with death, grabbing a brochure from the living room table to give himself a pretext both for entering and leaving the parlor, he retreats to his study. After a while he begins reading the brochure he picked up, but without comprehending its meaning. Nevertheless, the writer takes the trouble to include the text, which happens to deal with the problem of language. And it is language, in the form of the word 'adultery,' that suddenly comes to his lips, which begins to crystallize his experience for him, and, by bringing to mind the many nasty ideas associated with the word throughout the ages, allows Bergeret to see his situation as part of a general law (Levaillant 454), of which he therefore need not feel ashamed. Only then can he experience his pain, for the first time since the shock.

From simple verbalization and rapid reflection, Bergeret goes on to lengthy philosophical analysis, searching out the cause of the physical displeasure the sight gave him, and discovering what he takes to be the reasons for sexual modesty. As he sits in his study mulling over the question of sexual modesty, however, he is suddenly powerless to ward off the all-too-vivid image of M. Roux and his wife in their excessively immodest position on the couch. The narrator spares not a single adjective in his zeal to convey Bergeret's painful impression at that moment. Then he explains that the cruelty of this representation is not that it is too real but that it is too realistic. By reducing the degree of distance to zero and prolonging the image (another translation of the French *représentation*) indefinitely, this type of representation threatens to annihilate the subject entirely.

M. Bergeret's frantic efforts to tear his gaze away from this hypnotic image should therefore be understood as the attempt to stave off a kind of mental death. Eventually he is able to dissipate the fatal image and suppress it completely for the moment by the symbolic action of killing Mme. Bergeret in the effigy of her wicker sewing form. This second action soon proves to be as ineffectual as the first—picking up the book from the parlor table—for before long another visual image reminds him of his plight. While leaving the building, he notices for the first time a graffito of himself as cuckold that had been sketched long before. He deals with this new reminder by criticizing the quality of the drawing, then musing about graffiti from the days of the Roman Empire and wondering whether scholars in the thirtieth century will understand the one of himself, should it be preserved that long. Levaillant justly interprets these thoughts as a new way for Bergeret to distance himself from his situation by "submerging the present under the consideration of the past and the future" (455).

The structural principle underlying this sequence is the dialectical alternation between traumatizing visual images and distancing verbalized thoughts, punctuated here and there by attempts at action, as though to indicate that regardless of its specific content, the reality represented by those images dear to Barrès's heart is a danger to the existence of the subject. It is Piédagnel, the shoemaker looking for a wife, who revitalizes the impression for the last time, before Bergeret's reading of the Cook's voyage text finally lays it to rest. With each reincarnation the image becomes less vivid, the verbalization more detailed and articulated, until the latter wins the final battle in this ironic war of attrition between images of raw reality and symbolic assimilation that constitutes liberation for the intellectual M. Bergeret.

For it is well not to lose sight of the fact that France's tone is just as ironic here as in his caricatures of his adversaries, because his text is designed to make the reader keenly aware that Bergeret's intellectual wriggling and squirming is in part a sustained effort to repress the memory of the present by denying the reality of that situation. Like the critics of France's novel, the professor wants to do away with contemporary history. The mocking tone ceases, therefore, when Bergeret has his final revelation, for at that moment he is no longer intent on dissolving his awareness of his condition but has found a way to deal with it that reestablishes a certain subjective distance from the event while at the same time acknowledging its reality.

The Freedom of Fictionalization

Whether external or internal, however, commentary is only one component of the more general category that both structures the work and constitutes its content—fictionalization. Why did France choose to respond to Brunetière's visit to the Vatican with character portraits, stories, and then a novel, rather than with the expected polemical essays? If you are convinced that people's opinions derive from their material conditions, then the most effective way of rebutting the ideologies one opposes and supporting those one accepts is to embed them within the specific situations of lifelike characters who truly believe in them. In a more fundamental way, however, in establishing that on some level all people are true believers whose beliefs believe them, fictionalization is paradoxically designed to reverse the tendency it enshrines. By showing that beliefs say more about the believer than about the object of belief, more about the mind than about the world, it arouses the suspicion that one's ideas might be mistaken. France can then use fictionalization to attack the value of belief in general, making it the weapon of choice for the critique of religious faith that formed the original impetus in 1895 for what was to become *Contemporary History* and then acted as the reason for its continuation the following year.

The larger implication of the separability of belief and world is that human reality is, for the most part, a tissue of representations, of stories we tell ourselves—in short, of fictions. But if fiction thus inhabits our reality, it becomes possible to distinguish between the thinking subject and her ideas, to disengage the identity of the believer from the beliefs she holds that constitute her identity in the social world. The true freedom M. Bergeret seeks must therefore include both the ability to distinguish others from their ideas and a certain independence from his own representations. The dialectic of freedom and determinism thus turns on the question: 'Are we controlled by our representations, or is it we who determine them?' No greater contradiction to Barrès's nationalist conception of rooted identity can be imagined than France's notion here of true independence.

One effective technique for demonstrating the independence of thought from belief is to represent and bring together two or even a multiplicity of opposing views on the same topic without necessarily committing oneself to any one of them. That is, of course, the procedure that France employs when he stages the many conversations that populate his novel. In the early books of the series, M. Bergeret is thus able to dissociate ideas from the persons who hold them, so that, for instance, he can admire abbé Lantaigne's erudition and enjoy arguing with him, even though he execrates his views. A more radical method is to express contradictory positions about the same topic, as France did repeatedly. M. Bergeret does likewise in the text when he explains, with gusto and at some length to M. Goubin, his new favorite pupil, that he deems the notion of life on Mars quite plausible, whereas shortly before the professor had said just the opposite, that life was an anomaly in the universe, a kind of pustule fortunately limited to the planet earth. In flaunting this self-contradiction, France clearly indicates that what the critics take to be a flaw, he considers a virtue. This episode marks another step in M. Bergeret's emancipation, for it shows that he is not captive to his beliefs but has the freedom to look upon them as separate from his self.

The double irony for which France is renowned likewise could not exist without a prior level of fictionalization, and by virtue of this character it imposes on the reader the heady but disquieting experience of the process of de-identification—remaining suspended, at least momentarily, between two different views of the same object. As Jean-Yves Tadié explains, France's "irony consists in having [his characters] make perfectly plausible statements" and then leaving his readers in a moment of doubt as to whether the writer is for or against the ideas expressed, and especially as to whether they should react with indignation or with a smile (82).

This offshoot of Romantic imagination and Naturalist doctrine is not the Romantics' suspension of disbelief, but the more difficult and more dangerous Enlightenment suspension of belief, pushed to the limit in its radicalized Cartesian form as the temporary suspension of all belief. The experience may be exhilarating because, for a fleeting moment, it confers on the subject the sensation of total freedom and therefore of completely autonomous existence, yet at the same time it can be fraught with anxiety because, during the instant of hesitation, it empties out the subject by obliterating all its specific contents. In sum, it is the exact reverse of M. Worms-Clavelin's positivism: clinging to material facts in order to establish some kind of identity for himself.

It is not M. Bergeret, however, but the real Lieutenant-Colonel Picquart, the only military officer who defended Dreyfus's innocence, who comes to embody France's highest ideal of freedom in the novel. At the height of the Dreyfus Affair, described in the last volume of the series, the professor reads a newspaper editorial about Picquart to his pupils, an encomium that France had in fact published in *Le Figaro* August 16, 1899. Picquart was able to see and tell the truth about Dreyfus's innocence and Esterhazy's guilt, because he had a lively inner life and was therefore independent, free, in contrast to the crowd or the military conspirators.

This freedom has its price, however, as the destruction of Picquart's hitherto brilliant military career amply proved. In Bergeret's more humble case, separation from his self may lead to painful self-criticism and discontent, as the narrator points out in an early sketch of his character. Even in passages where the tone remains lightly ironic, as when Bergeret subjects himself to the same kind of scrutiny to which he submits his acquaintances, the process can lead to troubling results. Secretly flattered by Euphémie's accusation that he is a cruel man, M. Bergeret decides to apply his critical principles to his own ideas in order to verify his initial impression that she is correct, at which point he goes through a series of mental gyrations obviously motivated by his desire to prove what he wants to believe. The supposedly privileged understanding of the self provided by introspection controlled by the wary suspension of belief turns out to be as much a fictional construct determined by the very earthly desires of the thinker as the religious and political catchwords the naive believer accepts as truths.

Fiction and Idea

As these examples show, in France's tetralogy the relation between story and idea is infinitely more complex and interesting than in theories of the thesis novel as parable. At once a meditation on the problem of identity, an exploration of the paths to freedom, and a quest for the optimum distance to one's self as to the Other, fictionalization here is as much a matter of determining the share of narrative within general representations as it is of examining the relation of commentary to narration. As in all the more sophisticated novels of education, *Contemporary History* is in great measure a *mise-en-abîme* of the process of education through fiction: that is, of the relation among story, idea, teller, and listener. The characters in the novel are constantly telling or reading stories. These include the account of Cook's voyage, of course, but also the tale of one Philippe Tricouillard, the doctor's reports of the pregnant woman whose baby had a birthmark and of an injured peasant, the naval stories from the *Aeneid* that figure in M. Bergeret's research, and the episode of the sergeant and the recruit recounted by M. Roux. There is also the rumor of Bergeret's alleged cruelty, bruited around town by his wife, the fire at the charity ball in Paris, the tale of the evil Chinese genie, or the story of the first bishop of Tourcoing, one Saint Loup, that abbé Guitrel tells Mme. de Bonmont in chapter III of *Amethyst* while she pretends to listen but really thinks about her relation to Rara, i.e., M. Raoul Marcien, France's fictional version of Esterhazy (the man who actually committed the treason for which Dreyfus was condemned to Devil's Island), whom she loves passionately—a man who always has money troubles and makes love to all sorts of women.

Nor is M. Bergeret's role restricted to that of passive listener or reader. In the early volumes he accepts the priority of general ideas over particular events, so that when he tells a story about Napoleon III in *Elm-Tree,* he apparently follows the simple pattern so reviled by critics of the thesis novel, using the anecdote to illustrate an idea: Even absolute power has its limits. Yet on closer view it becomes apparent that the purpose of this story was not so much to 'prove' his idea as it was to criticize the accepted beliefs of his times. Elsewhere in *Elm-Tree* he often uses stories for the purpose of critique, as when he recounts the research of the pious scholar Jean de Launoy, who disproved the existence of the saint whom Joan of Arc claimed to have seen in one of her visions. In chapter I of *Wicker Work Woman,* he relates the tales of the Battle of Marathon and of Roman military campaigns in order to support his idea of the source of heroism. But that idea is controversial to say the least, since his claim is that heroism emerges only among the defeated and in routs, a point of view that was hardly popular in a period when the French were still smarting from the collapse of their armies in 1870–71, and when it was considered a patriotic duty to support the military. Once again, then, the thrust of the tale is to debunk received ideas more than to 'illustrate' a theory.

In the latter volumes of the series, once the Dreyfus case had become a national affair, M. Bergeret has increasing recourse to stories he recounts to his pupils; these stories, more clearly marked as texts within the text and lengthier than the generally brief references found in the earlier volumes, are designed to provide indirect representations of, or commentary on, the events and parties involved in the Affair. Bergeret's first appearance in *Amethyst* is as storyteller and educator teaching a lesson to M. Goubin about the figure of Hercules. The introductory passage to this interpretation of the Hercules myths makes it clear that the professor has made the Greek hero over in his own, at this point still pessimistic, image, lending him his own fatigue and doubts about the value of his work. Moreover, as though to express his own regrets about his new-found activity in ridding himself of his wife, M. Bergeret attributes to Hercules a heightened Epicurean sensitivity that makes him aware that, as Bergeret had phrased it in *Wicker Work Woman*, "to live is to destroy. To act is to injure" (190).

But it is also clear that Bergeret is using this story to counteract indirectly the versions of heroism circulating among the people of his town and the ethos of the anti-Dreyfusard aristocrats of the neighboring châteaux, which form the immediate context for his story. The towns-people have swallowed the myth of the ancient Gauls as virile, heroic, and civilized peoples who resisted the evil Roman invaders (*Amethyst*, chap. I), a widespread legend in the nineteenth century developed in plays, fiction, and sculpture especially since the defeat of 1870 (see Bancquart's bibliographical note on the topic, *Oeuvres*, vol. 3, 1166). The others have inherited the ancestral love of killing manifest in their taste for hunting and in their joy in punishing alleged evildoers.

M. Bergeret returns to the legends of Hercules once more, in one of the last chapters of *Amethyst*. This time, however, the adventures he ascribes to the hero correspond to nothing in Greek legend. He claims to be translating a newly discovered Greek manuscript from the Alexandrian period, a sure sign to the reader that the story is purely of France's invention. In fact, the tale is a transparent fable, a transposition of the Dreyfus Affair as it was unfolding when France composed this episode. M. Goubin remarks that it is a shame that the end of the story is missing, and M. Bergeret agrees, winking ironically to the reader once again: "[O]ne must have a change sometimes from present-day [*présentes*] affairs" (282; translation slightly altered).

This is a pattern France will increasingly follow in the final volume of the series. There, in chapter VIII, Bergeret reads to his pupil a chapter from a 'unique' sixteenth-century book that recounts the tale of "The Trublions, who arose in the Republic," a flagrant parody of the nationalist movement written in a droll pseudo-sixteenth-century French style imitated from Rabelais. 'Trublion,' as France explained in an article in *L'Écho de Paris*, is a Greek word meaning *gamelle*, a mess kit dish, the sarcastic nickname given to Philippe, Duke of Orléans, the new pretender to the throne of France in 1894, after he offered to enlist as a private in the French army. An ardent supporter of the nationalists and the Action Française in 1899, Philippe Gamelle sealed the unholy alliance of royalists and nationalists by intervening publicly in the Dreyfus Affair, as an anti-Dreyfusard, of course. The second leader of the Trublions is one Tintinnabule (= bell), famous for his *carmes mirifiques*, easily recognizable as Déroulède, author of the enormously popular *Chants du soldat* and exiled from France for his conspiracy to overthrow the republican government in the abortive coup of 1899; Robin Mielleux is Méline, the noted anti-Dreyfusard and quiet supporter of the nationalists; Gelgopole is General Mercier, the leader of the anti-Dreyfus movement; and so on. Together, they make such a horrible racket banging their metal dishes to attract the crowds to their movement that poor Minerva, the goddess of wisdom, must plug up her ears with wax in order to avoid having her eardrums shattered. Once again, France puts the allusive icing on the allegorical cake by having M. Bergeret end his reading with the comment: "'These old books,' he said, 'amuse and divert our minds, they make us forget the present day.' 'That is true,' replied Monsieur Goubin. But he smiled; a thing he seldom did" (*Paris* 77).

Toward the end of the novel, France varies the parodic formula by having the professor tell his disciple a parable about the loudmouthed Jean Coq and his docile friend Jean Mouton, apparently a sly allusion in this Shandyan context to Uncle Toby's cock-and-bull story. They noisily proclaim their adherence to the Republic, even while voting at every election, one for the Bonapartist candidate, the other for the royalist. Nationalists, imperialists, and warmongers, their prescription for foreign and civil war is "France to the French." The next time M. Bergeret speaks of them to his pupils, MM. Goubin and Denis, he drops all allegorical pretense and explicitly includes them, along with their friends Jean Laiglon and Gilles Singe, among the Trublions. They had reproached M. Bergeret for making them out to be bellicose, when they are merely military. They protest that they are in fact peace loving, although the peace they intend to establish once they become the masters will not be quiet and soft like the peace presently imposed on the nation; it will be a "terrible, clanking, spurred and booted, equestrian peace! We shall make a pitiless, savage peace . . . more frightful than the most frightful war" (235–36).

In chapter XXVI, M. Bergeret mysteriously discovers a second chapter in his sixteenth-century volume about the Trublions. After itemizing and exaggerating the various acts of street violence perpetrated by the nationalists, it tells the story of the "great fair held at Paris France," i.e., the World's Fair of 1900, the occasion of Robin Mielleux's great discourse on appeasement. As his family name indicates, Mielleux's words are designed to give a saccharine coating to a policy of tacitly encouraging the nationalists' brutality. The ones he intends to 'quiet down'—another possible meaning of *apaisement*—are the police and members of the justice system who obviously represent a threat to the land, along with anyone else who opposes the Trublions. May the latter receive, as soon as possible, the *apaisement* of eternal peace (144)!

While France had already used the same distancing mechanisms in the earlier volumes of the series, he greatly increases their frequency, especially that of parables, in *Paris*. The stories Bergeret now concocts are a type of action marking his transition from the position of lofty observer of the world to that of active participant in it. They serve not merely to try out ideas but to manipulate events through representation, giving the latter a character they would not otherwise have. The extensive use of far-fetched and transparent parables to narrate the history of the present highlights the fictionality of political representations, by exaggeration so to speak. No doubt a practical way of avoiding lawsuits, its main function is to point up the apparent arbitrariness of the nationalist's interpretation of the Affair. Specifically, the use of a specious sixteenth-century context and language to tell the tale of the Trublions emphasizes the grotesque anachronism of an ancien régime movement in the last years of the nineteenth century—royalism become nationalism. At the same time, the mocking humor of these tales forms a kind of criticism without violence, not even verbal violence, a gentle subjectivization that contrasts starkly with the brute force that, according to France, characterizes the nationalists.

Bergeret and the Crowd:
The Education of Anatole France

Readers have often criticized France for abandoning the stance of Olympian distance he had adopted in the early volumes of his tetralogy in favor of partisan attacks directed solely at his political opponents in *M. Bergeret in Paris*, when he had become personally committed to supporting Dreyfus (Bancquart, *Anatole France* 1223). In fact, as with determinism and contingency, a dialectic of distance and involvement is present from the beginning of the series, and if France paints total immersion within reality as a threat to the self, he is no less wary of the opposite extreme. While M. Bergeret ever prides himself on his superiority over the people around him as on his ability to draw abstract ideas from concrete experience and to engage in self-reflection and self-criticism, he constantly takes others to task for that other form of distance he calls "indifference," the total lack of desire. The danger of this state when pushed to the extreme emerges in the episode of his departure from the provinces for his new post in Paris at the end of *Amethyst*. As M. Bergeret is about to leave, he experiences the eerie impression that his town has lost its reality, has become a mere image. When, taken aback by this strange sensation, Bergeret indulges in self-observation, France cannot refrain from adding in his customary dash of irony, describing Bergeret's narcissistic reaction to himself in terms that exactly define his own relation to the fictional world of his novel: "[He] provid[ed] himself with an inexhaustible subject for surprise, sarcasm [*ironie*], and pity" (*Amethyst* 286).

The result of M. Bergeret's self-analysis is precisely to make him aware that he is the author of his world: "[The town] only existed in reference to myself. . . . I never knew that my mind was subjective to such a mad extent" (287). Excessive distance poses just as great a threat to the existence of the subject as does the stifling proximity of the object, for the reduction of the object to the status of mere image divested of its symbolic context propels the subject into the world of sheer madness as surely as the latter's occultation by an uncontrollable image of reality. This episode is both a ratification of Schopenhauer's contention that the world is my representation—and the 'I' of this 'my' is the product of the desire ('will') that determines me—and a caution against total capitulation to that notion, which France had formerly espoused and which was so widespread in the last third of the century. A counterpart to his critique of realism, Bergeret's unsettling experience condemns the exacerbated subjectivism of symbolist art as just as serious a menace to sanity as extreme realism.

The problem that confronts France and his protagonist is the modulation of distance rather than distance itself, and the distance in question is always that of the subject's relation to the Symbolic of his social world. Whenever that relation is disturbed, reality is reduced to one or more isolated images. In fact, M. Bergeret's relation to the Symbolic is always more or less troubled, because the assertion of distance from that world forms a crucial part of his identity as a subject. If the classical subject must prove its existence by separating itself from physical nature, the post-Enlightenment subject has the additional task of separating itself from the symbolic world of his society, which the majority of its inhabitants experience as though it were purely natural, a set of truths so evident as to escape all examination. In short, most people live in their Symbolic as though it were a nature.

It is logical, then, that the main thrust of M. Bergeret's efforts to affirm his independent existence should be to unmask the arbitrariness of his townsmen's and countrymen's beliefs, undercutting their prejudices and pretensions through a variety of verbal manipulations. When Doctor Fornerol, mimicking the claims of the Positivists and Opportunists, asserts that Christianity gives the people moral and human sentiments they would otherwise lack, M. Bergeret replies: "Popular opinions hold good as a matter of course, without analysis, and if they were inquired into, generally speaking they would not pass muster" (*Amethyst* 158). Similarly, M. Bergeret presents his great speech on the origin and significance of birthmarks as a correction of the popular superstitions of his times. It is one of the first indications of the role M. Bergeret will increasingly play in the novel, that of the outsider whose distance from society turns his world with its received ideas into a sad but droll spectacle and allows him to append a bemused and amusing ironic commentary onto every aspect of his environment, exposing "the emptiness of society, the inanity of a certain form of existence" (Levaillant 449). More generally, M. Bergeret uses irony and commentary to pry the accepted meanings loose from current events and then to assign them new ones of his own devising. Just as the professor must first detach himself from the tyrannies of his past involvements before trying to discover his desire, so he feels it incumbent upon himself to destroy the meanings that constitute the world of repetition in his provincial town. In this respect, as in so many others, the character is only doing within the novel what France is doing, or rather undoing, with the novel: dismantling one by one the presuppositions and conclusions of the authoritarian system of Brunetière, the *ralliement,* high finance, the monarchists, and ultimately the nationalists.

The role of outsider is, however, inherently unstable. M. Bergeret finds himself in an apparently inextricable dilemma: He cannot accept the ideas of the majority of the people around him, but he cannot bear to be cut off entirely from the human community he repudiates. Moreover, he needs the symbolic system he refuses, for he can assert his identity only by rejecting its terms. Starting from M. Bergeret's earliest appearances in *Elm-Tree*, France depicts him as persecuted by his family and his superiors at the university, and as unpopular with the members of his society, who, ironically enough, take him to be both clerical and anticlerical at the same time. Furthermore, he is the only person in town, other than abbé Lantaigne, who is interested in general ideas. Hence his refuge in antiquity, in books and in bookstores, as well as in his conversations with the learned abbé. But even Lantaigne does not share the "critical imagination" the professor uses to take his revenge on the society that excludes him.

M. Bergeret's famous irony is of course both the instrument and the proof of this capacity to observe, judge, and criticize everything in the world, including himself, as though he were not part of it. This is his strength but also his weakness. By his canny dissection of the views accepted in his society, he sets himself above his fellow townsmen, with the unfortunate but predictable result that he is quietly ostracized by many of those same worthy citizens, to whom his aloofness often appears as indifference to ordinary human concerns if not a lack of basic human feelings. In short, by setting himself apart, he makes himself different, and, as Stendhal observed, before Friedrich Nietzsche, "difference engenders hatred."

It is not just any difference, however, not singularity in itself that cuts M. Bergeret off from his fellows, but the particularity of a subject who reflects on the world and himself. Just how suspect this unfortunate propensity to think renders him in the eyes of at least a large and powerful segment of his society becomes evident in comparison to Bossuet's definition of the 'heretic' as "one who holds an opinion of his own; one who acts according to his own ideas and his own feelings" (*Amethyst* 22). In other words, it is all right to think, provided you think the same as everyone else, and everyone else thinks what they are told to think by the authorities. The context in which Bossuet's explanation appears is especially laden with irony, for its main theme is the justification of exclusion. The aristocratic elite of the town has gathered at the Duke de Brécé's mansion and, for the first time in the series, they mention the Dreyfus case, taking it as the pretext for violent anti-Semitic remarks. Abbé Guitrel explains that the Church has never considered the Jews to be heretics, because, never having accepted the divinity of Jesus or received his teachings, they cannot have rejected them. He quickly squelches any appearance of broadmindedness this theological quibble may have engendered in his listeners, when he points out that the proper term is 'infidels' and that God uses the Jews' 'obstinacy' as an example of what not to do, as a way of affirming Christian doctrine.

France emphasizes the tight connection between the religious dogmatism used to justify persecution of the heretic and the politics of the Dreyfus Affair by putting Bossuet's words into the mouth of Bergeret's old nemesis, the irascible, self-centered archivist, M. Mazure. Mazure is a Jacobin, which, in France's eyes, means that he is a staunch republican but also that he favors a strong central government; as a result, he is more than willing to renounce the republican claim to individual liberty in the name of 'patriotism.' He therefore eagerly joins the nationalists "for the unity and indivisibility of the Republic," parroting Barrès's assertions during the Affair that it makes no difference whether or not Dreyfus is guilty; the Dreyfusards are definitely guilty of betraying the nation by substituting their individual judgment for that of the legal system (*Paris* 79).

Good Romantic that he is, in the early volumes M. Bergeret sees only the defects and disadvantages of the society he nevertheless longs to join. The shabby black suit he must wear for the traditional New Year's Day visits makes him wish he were a man of the world. But then he wonders whether there really is a 'world,' inhabited by real 'men of the world,' and concludes, in chapter IV of *Wicker Work Woman,* that 'good society' is just a gilded mirage, like a rainbow. In fact, there is no such thing as a real community: People group together according to their prejudices and tastes, but the two often conflict, and chance mixes everything up. The community of good society depends on old money and leisure and consists merely of shared habits. Our real self is within us, closed off from the world. Society, that is, true human communion, is impossible because of its very nature, for humanity depends on an inwardness that contradicts the basic prerequisite of community, which consists of that which is shared with others, with the outside. And that which can be shared is precisely that which is external to the subject, namely, brute materiality. In short, here again, society has taken on the role of a second nature that, like the first, must be negated and surpassed in order for the subject to exist.

M. Bergeret is not alone in this judgment. France's narratorial voice also equates sociability with materiality, attributing Mme. Bergeret's need for social as well as sexual intercourse to her potbellied soul (*âme ventrue*), that is, the combination of her excess flesh and lack of inner life. The exact opposite of his ideal, Colonel Picquart, her total dependency on others contrasts with the officer's complete autonomy and resultant independence of judgment. It is for this reason that M. Bergeret's silent treatment is so well adapted to his goal of reducing her to nothingness. The perfect Barresian subject, she is nothing other than the others to whom she is attached. And it is for the same reason that her counterattack takes the form of attempting to persuade public opinion that she is the victimized party in the marriage. Since her identity consists solely of the image she sees of herself reflected in the eyes of others, Mme. Bergeret can restore her sense of existence only by rehabilitating herself in their thoughts and words.

The pervasive misogyny of the book—and *Contemporary History* is a terribly misogynistic novel—derives from the stereotyped equation of women with 'nature' in the two aspects defined above: materiality conceived as the drive for 'physical' pleasure coupled with the absence of 'spiritual' life, the latter specified in particular as the lack of thought that characterizes the second nature that is society—the tyranny of a public opinion dominated by a hodgepodge of mindless clichés. Mme. Bergeret is just one among a troop of unscrupulous women who betray husbands, promises, and principles for sexual pleasure, financial gain, or the ambitions of their lovers, from the teenage orphan Honorine to the octagenarian Mme. Houssieu, whose nineteen-year-old lover, Lecoeur, ends up strangling her in her bed one night. In between fall Mme. Worms-Clavelin, who gives up her courtesan past to marry the future prefect and seek the approval of the Church; Mme. de Gromance, "la belle ralliée" (in the words of M. Loyer, minister of cults), who takes on a parade of young lovers whose only distinguishing characteristic seems to be their right-wing political convictions; and, the prize of them all, Mme. de Bonmont, the converted Jewess whose affair with Rara symbolizes the ménage à trois of capitalism, church, and army.

While Mme. Bergeret is not directly associated with a specific political stance, all the others in the above list epitomize the views and actions of the right-wing parties the writer is at pains to caricature. Indeed, even Mme. Bergeret finds her staunchest defenders among the society ladies of the town, such as Mme. Dellion—whose son Philippe (France sometimes calls him Gustave) becomes Mme. de Gromance's lover in the last volume of the series—as though to intimate the coalition of false rumor with rightist convictions. Once the Dreyfus Affair enters the novel in *Amethyst,* France embellishes his caricatures of the women as a key part of his all-out attack on the unholy alliance of anti-Dreyfusards, the main butt of which is the hypocritical cloak of nobility they cast over their base motives. While amusing, these exposés would be rather trite and conventional, were it not precisely for the fact that the words

France puts into their mouths are direct quotes from the political and religious slogans of the times, and that he has the characters use these empty public clichés to justify their private transgressions.

Mme. de Gromance returns to the scene with M. Panneton (brother of a 'patriotic' supporter of the army who tries to get a deferment for his son), who is running for the Senate and promises to make her husband a deputy if he will run on Panneton's ticket and if she, needless to say, will come see his etchings. She agrees, on the pretext that if she shows up at the rendezvous, "it will be for the sake of the country and the army. We must save France" (*Paris* 194). Even Mme. Worms-Clavelin takes her turn with a certain Maurice Cheiral, head private secretary of the minister of cults, in an effort to ensure that abbé Guitrel will be named bishop of Tourcoing. All of this hanky-panky is of course meant to illustrate the selfishness and ambition, the lack of scruples and of true passion of the upper crust of society that provides the leaders of the royalist and nationalist parties, who cloak their petty self-interest under the guise of 'saving France.'[1]

The social self is thus at worst a cipher, a naught, the sheer absence of an inner life; at best a tissue of political slogans and convenient fictions. The fact that M. Bergeret nevertheless feels rejected by the human community shows that he needs to be a part of the symbolic world he spurns, just as his disinvestment of the provincial town is countermanded by his nostalgic sense of piety toward his homeland. Combining the ironic stance of the Enlightenment with the painful alienation of the Romantic hero, Bergeret refuses to renounce the distance that makes him what he is, even while he seeks to overcome the separation his irony produces. His problem, then—and it was of course France's as well—is to find a way back to the human community without compromising the critical thinking that constitutes the core of his singularity.

The author finds an ingenious way to combine these two apparently contradictory requirements by introducing Riquet, the pet dog, into M. Bergeret's life after his wife has left him. And it is not by chance that it is his new maid, Angélique, a member of the popular classes, who comes up with this answer to his isolation. Riquet shares the views and the subservience to authority of the masses—at least M. Bergeret imputes them to him in a most amusing way—but he does so in such a naive and endearing fashion that his master cannot find it in his heart to resent them as he does with the humans who surround him—especially since, unlike M. Bergeret's fellow citizens, the authority Riquet reveres most is precisely M. Bergeret. With his customary irony, the professor identifies with the little animal from the start, since he looked like the dog when he was a toddler; both have the same claim to immortality; and both have the same quantity of knowledge, compared to the infinity of absolute knowledge. Moreover, Riquet comes to Bergeret's aid and sympathizes with his pain when he falls off a ladder reaching for a book in his study, instead of laughing at him as a human being would have done. Bergeret concludes that despite the enormous difference between them, he and his dog are united by a sense of "universal brotherhood" (*Amethyst* 137).

Riquet is not M. Bergeret's only newfound friend. In the very next chapter of *Amethyst,* France unearths an unexpected comrade for his hero, a fellow whose only connection to the canine world would seem to be his name, M. Leterrier, the rector of the university. A philosophy professor and author of a textbook in which he judges all systems, Leterrier was previously anathema to M. Bergeret, who was repulsed by the fact that, bolstered by the certainties of official doctrine, he had no doubts about the beautiful, the true, and the good, while, for his part, Leterrier thought of Bergeret as a dangerous person. Now, however, much to Bergeret's surprise, the Dreyfus Affair has thrown the two of them together. Precisely because of his doctrinal spiritualism, Leterrier believes that the truth will win out and that Dreyfus's mistaken conviction will therefore be overturned. In addition to the basic fraternity of all living beings that ties M. Bergeret to Riquet, it is the communion of those opposed to the community of the compact majority that allows the ironic professor to overcome his isolation, for in each case he can maintain his distance from the dominant crowd, while joining with the oppressed minority of those who suffer.

Once he has found this new anticommunity of the excluded, M. Bergeret no longer needs to maintain his former attitude of universal aloofness and criticism, for now he has discovered a group whose ideas he approves. Instead of mocking the Republic and himself along with his personal and political antagonists, as he did before, he can turn his critique solely against those who oppose his views, or, rather, against those whose views he opposes—the Church hierarchy, the royalists, the financiers and industrialists, and the nationalists who unite them in opposition to Captain Dreyfus and the cause he represents to his defenders, a democratic and social parliamentary republic.

Having reached this point in his development, however, M. Bergeret finds himself in a terrible dilemma: How can he support such a republic when in fact the vast majority of his fellow citizens are violently hostile to Dreyfus? His quandary is all the more acute since his earlier opposition to the republican regime was based in great part on his conviction that international finance and banking had taken over from the Catholic Church as the foreign power responsible for dissolving the traditional identity of the French people, the very argument deployed by Barrès and company to justify their hostility to Dreyfus and the Jews in general. And if the thinking that separates Bergeret from the crowd defines his very being, how can he align himself with the principles of majority rule and the welfare of the greatest number without risking the dissolution of his self?

From the beginning, during his opposition to the *ralliement*, the question that has plagued M. Bergeret is why the masses, or the 'crowd' as he often calls them, fall for the slogans that to him seem so blatantly hypocritical. His explanation at that time, as we have seen, was their 'indifference.' But now, in the midst of the Dreyfus Affair, that explanation no longer holds water, for the crowd, thoroughly convinced of the Jewish captain's guilt, has acquired both a passion—their hatred of Dreyfus and those who champion his cause—and a concomitant desire to silence or eradicate all those who dare to oppose their view. Thus, while the nationalist crowd shouts army slogans and calls for the heads of Leterrier and Bergeret, the professor concludes his discussion with Doctor Fornerol about the moral value of Christian belief by stating that the most pressing concern of people united by a common faith is to exterminate those who think differently.

France calls upon both Leterrier and Riquet to present his solution to M. Bergeret's quandary. Several chapters after protesting about this hostility toward truth and justice, Leterrier returns to express his dismay at the public abuse he has been receiving as a result of his support of Dreyfus. Under the stress, he has begun to suffer from a series of physical maladies, and while he and the professor converse, the crowd not only screams its hatred but manifests its fury by throwing stones and breaking one of the professor's windows. Meanwhile, Riquet has greeted the rector with a fusillade of barks that seem to echo the howls of the mob outside. M. Bergeret obligingly explains that the little fellow is just obeying the indoctrination their human ancestors have given the canine race: namely, that the stranger is automatically the enemy. The pet dog has now become the image of the anti-Semitic mob,[2] convinced that the alien Jew is the enemy and therefore incapable of understanding the proofs of Dreyfus's innocence, but Riquet is the crowd with an appealing face, because it is clearly not his fault that he cannot discern the truth. He has been corrupted by the ignorance of our prehistoric ancestors, combined with his respect for authority and his love of his masters. In like manner, M. Bergeret explains that the average member of the masses, whom he jestingly calls *Pecus* (= 'herd,' or 'cattle'), likewise accepts what he is told uncritically and without malice.

The implication here is that the masses are divided into a good people and an evil, because corrupted, crowd.[3] It might seem that, in attributing all virtue, beauty, and glory to the people, Bergeret is repudiating everything he had implied about "Nature" in the criticism of his wife and that the writer had presented in his depiction of women in general in the series, not to mention the repeated assertions of mankind's alleged innate aggression. But there has been another, Rousseauistic strain running through the tetralogy as well. Bergeret's maid, Euphémie, was much less cruel than her master in her peasant idea of punishing the adulteress, precisely because she lacked his 'civilization.' Her replacement, Angélique, has no need of sophisticated reflection to find the right remedy for M. Bergeret's loneliness; her basic sense of humanity tells her that he needs a pet dog. The cobbler's son, Piédagnel, is the image of youthful innocence when he is unjustly expelled from the seminary by the learned but dogmatic abbé Lantaigne. For every Lecoeur, the butcher's boy who murders old Mme. Houssieu, there is a Pied-d'Alouette (nickname for an old vagabond named Seurin), who is wrongfully accused of a crime. Even the Honorines and Mlle. Deniseaus owe their duplicity to the enticements offered by the wealthy and the powerful whose prejudices they flatter with their visions of the Virgin and their predictions from the other world.

France's early apolitical attitude toward the people appears most clearly in Bergeret's encounter in chapter III of *Wicker Work Woman* with Pied-d'Alouette, whom the investigating magistrate has finally released from jail after holding him for six months without filing charges, on the vague hope that he might eventually come up with something against such an obviously dangerous character. M. Bergeret admires Pied-d'Alouette's resilience, his resourcefulness, his humility, and his apparent tranquility in the midst of genuine suffering. Above all, he feels drawn to him by his fellow feeling for "the unfortunate [*les misérables*]" (50), the same profound and painful sympathy that he expresses several volumes later in his encomium to Pecus. It is this Rousseauistic sense of sympathy for the poor, the downtrodden, and all those who suffer, that, running through the entire tetralogy, ties together M. Bergeret's attitudes toward the people and motivates his political evolution from the early to the later volumes.

France depicts the process that leads to Bergeret's changed attitude through his analysis of the professor's motivations. In the chapter following his conversation with Pied-d'Alouette, as M. Bergeret contemplates the threadbare condition of his Sunday suit and muses on the superficial reasons that bring people together in communities without communion, he feels the same pity and sympathy for himself as he does for the unfortunate. He identifies with those who are unhappy, because he is convinced that no one loves him. This feeling is only increased when Bergeret discovers his wife's adultery, so that the self he contemplates at that time becomes, as we have seen, an "inexhaustible subject of pity." It is this sense of exclusion, misunderstanding, and persecution by the powers that be that forms the bridge between himself and Pied-d'Alouette and will continue to connect him in his thoughts to Riquet, Pecus, and, no doubt, Captain Dreyfus himself. Here, in sympathy for shared weakness, suffering, and lack is the only true communion, the only true social bond. The ultimate irony, then, is that it is the lack of thought of the people—the root cause of their poverty and weakness— that forms their bond of solidarity with the intellectual, whose isolation and consequent weakness are due precisely to his excess capacity for reflection and critique.

This ability to feel sympathy, the source of morality in Enlightenment ethics that is present in M. Bergeret from the start, will constitute the basis of his subsequent political evolution toward socialism. Not by chance, then, does M. Bergeret's sense of sympathy become most acute after his discovery of his wife's betrayal, at the moment of his greatest suffering, at the same time that he decides to take action against the tyrannies that have previously ruled his life. Having overcome his attitude of ironic distance toward himself, he no longer approves of the resignation of the people, either. While in *Elm-Tree* his sympathy and admiration for Pied-d'Alouette led him to hope that the poor man had become reconciled to his state, renouncing all desire, in chapter XII of *Wicker Work Woman,* M. Bergeret now envisions a fresh workers' revolution that will soon usher in an era of socialism, "for there will be a socialistic Europe . . . if indeed that unknown power which is approaching can be rightly called Socialism" (193). Just as he is now ready to seek his own private desire, so he imagines that those oppressed by the capitalist system that supports the Opportunist and Radical Republic will throw off their shackles and find their own political and economic identity.

This somewhat vague hope reaches the intensity of an almost physical need when the *ralliement* morphs into appeasement, and the Dreyfus Affair changes the indifferent populace into a blind and violent mob. Now, as he is about to move into his new apartment in Paris, Bergeret agrees with Lamennais, who charged that the present order of society rests on the resignation of the poor. No longer does he think of the people as the refuge of mindless prejudice and superstition alone. In the following chapter of *Paris,* M. Bergeret calls in a carpenter named Roupart, a member of the working classes who is clearly superior to all those depicted in the earlier volumes. Here it is the artisan who plays the role of teacher, the professor that of student, as the former answers his questions about the finer points of building shelves. Then the carpenter avows his admiration for M. Bergeret, for he knows that he has abandoned his 'caste,' the army and the clergy, and has taken up Dreyfus's defense. Roupart bemoans the split in the socialist camp, between the hard-line position of Guesde—take no stand on the Affair, rather let the capitalists kill each other off, starting with the Jews—of which he disapproves, and that of Jaurès, whose arguments in favor of Dreyfus he paraphrases, to the effect that true socialism can exist only when justice and goodness reign. Therefore, we socialists must fight all tyrannies, hate war, and ignore religious differences, loving the whole human race.

Now the professor has a mission that will mark him for the rest of his days, that of aiding the masses to free themselves from violence and blindness, helping to transform the crowd into the people, and the example of Roupart proves to him that it is possible to do so. In order to accomplish this task, M. Bergeret must combine the two opposite elements personified in Riquet and Leterrier: Riquet, the simple people whose lack of critical thinking makes them susceptible to being led astray; Leterrier, the honest intellectual whose respect for evidence, logic, and truth override class interests and group prejudice.

If the French people have strayed from their historical mission in recent years, it is because they have been misled, at times by people as ignorant and fearful as themselves, lately by a handful of ill-intentioned manipulators intent on consolidating wealth and power in their own hands. And they have been misled so easily because, respectful and loving but also ignorant and unreflective like Riquet, they have lacked the inner life that makes critique and distance possible. In this logic, the vacuity of the social self embodied by Mme. Bergeret derives from another, complementary nothingness, that of ignorance. In the words of a socialist named Bissolo who takes part in a counterdemonstration against the nationalists: "In the brain of the working-man, in the place where the bourgeois carry their inept and brutal prejudices, there is a great cavity." Armed with this conviction, Bergeret does not scruple to repeat the catchword of reactionary intellectuals opposed to universal (male) suffrage since the Second Republic: "A stupidity repeated by thirty-six millions of mouths does not for that reason cease to be stupid.

Majorities, as a general rule, display a superior capacity for servitude." But unlike the Flauberts of the world, his remedy for the empty self is to fill the cavity with knowledge (*Paris* 118).

France's answer to the trauma that the Affair was for Bergeret was to deploy the force of the secular logos, a desire consistent with his profession and his earlier ironic stance, yet utterly different in practice from his previous attitudes of lofty amusement and sad resignation. On New Year's Day, 1900, M. Bergeret welcomes the brand-new century by unfurling before the eyes of his daughter Pauline his vision of the new society, governed by speech and reason (*Paris* 174). Bancquart, in her "Notice" to *M. Bergeret à Paris,* points out that France broke with Jaurès over the issue of granting amnesty to all parties, including the military men who had framed Dreyfus and then lied to cover up the frame, in order to calm the public waters. France joined Clemenceau, arguing that education was the instrument both necessary and sufficient to effect progressive social change,[4] whereas political appeasement, for whatever reasons, meant abandoning truth and justice halfway, throwing the guilty in with the blameless, with no official acknowledgment of Dreyfus's innocence, and all in the name of an expedience that played into the hands of the bourgeoisie, making the Affair into the culminating repetition of the politics of the *ralliement.*

It was of course unthinkable for France to accept such a policy, since his very existence as a subject depended on the possibility of avoiding repetition, the repetition of mindless clichés, and, still more important, the repetition of historical events that imprisons the nation in the status quo. The entire thrust of the two final volumes of his novel was the effort to overcome repetition, to construct a present and a potential future that would not be the simple copy of the past. Contemporary history must neither recount nor relate but construct the contingent, the unpredictable, the hitherto unknown power. That is why, when M. Bergeret foresees the victory of socialism after the demise of the reign of capitalism in *Wicker Work Woman,* he adds the clause, "if indeed that *unknown* power which is approaching can be rightly called Socialism" (emphasis added). That is also the sense of the numerous parables and indirect representations of contemporary events M. Bergeret narrates to his pupils in those last books of the series. Those are the words that are designed to "change the world," as Bergeret puts it to his daughter, who is no doubt his main hope for the future. Henceforth, as a result of the Dreyfus Affair, the intellectual has become an actor in public life. The novelist, having taken on the role of historian of contemporary affairs, now tells stories that give new and unexpected meanings to current events, without predetermining their future course. France purposely avoids the closure of a definitive meaning by ending the final volume of the series in the middle of the story, as it were, when the outcome of the Affair was still very much up in the air. In the last scene, the nationalist leaders are eagerly awaiting the end of the truce of appeasement called in honor of the World's Fair, so that they can unleash the crowd once again against the government. France allows Henri Léon, the voice of skepticism, to prevail, however. Citing the socialist Bissolo, his former companion and archrival in street demonstrations, Léon cautions his coconspirators that it is not easy to control the people and warns them that Paris will not rise up against the Republic. To be continued.

The one factor capable of uniting all M. Bergeret's variables into a single equation is indeed education. Through education he can overcome his isolation by bringing the crowd to him, rather than dissolving back into it, as the nationalist program urges. Instead of trying to impose national unity by castigating those who think for themselves, as Bossuet/Mazure/Barrès recommend, France proposes establishing national harmony by enabling all to think for themselves. Through education the malicious and bloodthirsty 'crowd' created by the coalition of Church, capitalists, royalists, and nationalists can be liberated from its corrupters and returned to its original state of being the 'people.' Perhaps most important, through education the people will acquire that inner life that is the sine qua non of a substantial identity, as opposed to the 'nothingness' of the social self that is a mere mirror image of others. Moreover, this mode of identity-formation is not dependent on opposition to what is considered to be alien or foreign. The stranger need no longer be automatically taken for the enemy. In what we might call 'educative socialism,' France felt he had found a means of answering the need for identity without falling into the nationalist trap of identity politics. (See Joan W. Scott's excellent article on the dangers of this snare in our contemporary world, "Multiculturalism and the Politics of Identity.") The socialist revolution that M. Bergeret calls upon is no longer a matter of unseating the foreign power of capitalism; it is not its foreignness but the regime of ignorance, injustice, and inequality it inflicts on its people that must be overthrown.

Education and the New Republic

The question remains, however, how exactly education will lead to the establishment of the "new republic," and specifically how it will bring about the realization not only of M. Bergeret's desire, but of that of the people as well. Can a genuine society arise out of an assemblage of people who define themselves as outsiders? Or will their identities collapse and their communion turn into the aridity of bland conformity, once there is no inside, no leaders who oppress them nor a crowd that excludes them? If all their demands were met, if everyone worked for the community and each received the fruits of his own labor, would some at least be impelled to rebel out of 'spite,' as Dostoyevsky's man from underground protests, in order to preserve their autonomy, their desire to be subjects?

It is clear that the goal of education for M. Bergeret is not simply the inculcation of the capacity for sympathy and independent, rational judgment, in accordance with the Enlightenment principles of truth and justice, although it is certainly partly that. Despite his earlier protestation that socialism is the unknown future that will follow the downfall of capitalism, in chapter XVII, on the first day of the new century, M. Bergeret does give some content to his hopes. To be sure, he continues to insist that the future must remain an unknown quantity, forever invisible to those who nevertheless work to bring it about. He does not recant his objections to the idea of a transcendent meaning of history. History will have the meanings that people give to it through their efforts, whose effects and success are never predictable.

In their conversation, Bergeret's daughter Pauline becomes the spokesperson for the objections he himself as well as his political adversaries bring to his new republic. When she exclaims, with perhaps just a touch of irony, that in this brave new world everyone will be happy, he scotches that idealized hope, noting that physical and psychological suffering are part of the human condition and will therefore continue to exist no matter how society is reorganized. Moreover, without suffering the most important human quality, sympathy, would atrophy, and with it our humanity as well. What Bergeret does aim to accomplish is the elimination of the needless, artificial evils that result from specific social arrangements. This will arise in part due to the advances of science and technology that will make life easier for everyone. More significant, but infinitely more difficult to achieve, will be the voluntary transformation of the bosses of the world into simple workers who demand no special privileges nor take any more of the common wealth for their intellectual labors than those who work with their hands. Since the community is the necessary precondition for the existence of private property, there is no inconsistency in extending it to society as a whole and entrusting it to the State.

Pauline remarks without undue alarm that this is a prescription for collectivism, and before her father can answer his own rhetorical question, "What is the State?" she chimes in with the objection that the State is a pitiful, boorish fellow sitting behind a counter, to whom no one would willingly give up his property. M. Bergeret attempts to counter this most telling critique of communism with the theory of the disappearance of the State once collectivization is completed. Here, in a move reminiscent of Spinoza's pantheism,[5] the dialectic of the universal and the particular that subtends the arguments of both the nationalists and the republicans finds its resolution. To the liberal objection that the freedom of the individual vis-à-vis the State depends on the possession of private property, M. Bergeret replies that once the State has become everything, has been universalized, it will no longer need anything more and will therefore have no reason to oppress the individual. To the Barresian nationalist who protests that those who want to reshape society according to an abstract plan ignore the realities and necessities of the historical life of diverse communities, he retorts that by dissolving the State into social activity, it is he, not they, who replaces abstraction with that which is most concrete, the very life of the community the nationalists claim they want to protect. Finally, Bergeret comforts all those anarchists (like himself!) who fear that the power of the State will crush all individual identity in a sea of mindless conformity, with the thought that once it becomes everything, the State will lose its independent existence, and having become a nonperson, will no longer be able to threaten anyone.

In this, his version of the end of history, the professor describes at the same time the endpoint of the trajectory of his desire. The keystone to this whole edifice is the disappearance of the desire of the Other, and it is that disappearance which makes possible the fulfillment of M. Bergeret's desire along with that of the members of the society he envisions. Only if in becoming everything the State really does become nothing, only if it becomes a nonperson, losing its identity as an independent source of will and power, will it cease to limit and control the desires of its citizens. M. Bergeret will have rid himself of his greatest burden throughout the book, the sense of being excluded from the group, both willingly and unwillingly, once the group no longer exists as such. Indeed, from the beginning, M. Bergeret's desire has been defined in terms of his relation to the desire of the Other, which itself consists in the collusion of two others: on the one hand the mass of his fellow citizens, and on the other the powers that be, which maintain themselves in being by manipulating the desire of the populace. As the leaders of the bourgeois Republic guide the crowd from selfish indifference to fear and violence to appeasement, M. Bergeret moves from lofty distance to involved concern to educational commitment. If education will allow each member of society to form his or her own desire, only the vanishing of the desire of the Other will allow those individual desires to flourish.

Starting from the first volume of the series, M. Bergeret's ideal had always been stoic *ataraxia*,[6] the attempt to reach total autonomy by suppressing all desire, for desire depends on the Other for its fulfillment. As Lacan points out, this is therefore a specific desire, namely, the desire not to desire (*Four Fundamental Concepts of Psychoanalysis* 235). The professor's misogyny no doubt derived from the same source, for to desire a woman is to make oneself dependent on the woman's response, or lack thereof. In the later books, having freed himself from bondage to his wife and his provincial town, confronted with the Dreyfus Affair and the rise of nationalism, M. Bergeret had developed the positive desire to intervene in public affairs by educating the people. But he can imagine succeeding in this enterprise only by giving an ironic twist to the theme of *ataraxia*, transferring it from himself onto the Other, the State.

The basic fantasy that undergirds France's politics and structures his perception of the world—on the face of it, the exact opposite of Barrès's—consists of a system of mutual sacrifice: *ataraxia* for the State, and total abnegation for the subject: "We truly give only when we give our work, our minds, our genius. And this splendid offering of one's whole self to all men enriches the giver as much as the community" (*M. Bergeret in Paris* 172). The secret of communism, according to France, is not that it's going to satisfy all the desires of the people, the subjects, but that it's going to satisfy all the desires of the community taken as a whole, the State, the Other—at which point the Other will no longer make incomprehensible or impossible demands on the subject. Ultimately, then, France's recipe for utopia boils down to killing the Other with kindness. His socialist society is going to fulfill every possible desire of the State, in the frantic effort to fill up the frightening nothingness of the social self and thereby assure its absolute plenitude. France's ideal is totality, the impossible *jouissance* of the Thing, as opposed to that of the partial objects that constitute reality (see Copjec 38–40). The hope is that this satiation will prevent it from sapping the being of its citizens.

It remains an open question as to whether in this situation everyone wins or everyone loses. If the State becomes nothing by becoming everything, what then happens to the subject? Ultimately, France's construction, which of course derives from Jaurès's reading of Marx, will rise or fall with the validity of the supposition that under the void of the social self there lurks, or can be formed, a substantial inner self. But if desire is the desire of the Other, as Lacan maintains, then the collapse of the desire of the State would cause the collapse of that of the individual as well. The outcome would be the dissolution of the subject into the State, with virtually the same result as in the nationalism France despised.

The enemy within the people is thus the emptiness within them, the great void of ignorance nourished by the education in superstition and resignation they receive in the Congregationist schools of the Church and the lack of critical thinking and inner life imparted in the secular schools. In his capacity as university professor, M. Bergeret would ordinarily have little opportunity to influence the masses. His only direct contact with them would be to participate in the new popular universities being organized around the turn of the twentieth century, in large part as the intellectuals' response to the Dreyfus Affair.[7] The main vehicles for implementing the project of educating the masses under the Third Republic, however, were the newly reformed primary schools. It is for that reason that Zola, France's comrade-in-arms and the most outspoken of those intransigent Dreyfusards who refused anything that smacked of appeasement, took schoolteachers (*instituteurs* and *institutrices*) as the subject of his education novel, *Vérité* (*Truth*).

CHAPTER 7

Truth, by Émile Zola

Zola's Daymare and the Truth of *Vérité*

Larbin de la juiv'rie,
Zola jusqu'à sa mort
Gueulait contr' la Patrie
Criait tant et plus fort
Et pour Dreyfus le traître,
(Ce fameux bout coupé)
Il allait fair' paraître
Le roman *Vérité* . . .

Flunkey of Jewry
Zola up to his death
Mouthed off against the Homeland,
Screamed so much and so loud
And for Dreyfus the traitor
(That well-known capon),
He was going to publish
The novel *Truth*
— Song sung by anti-Dreyfusards at Zola's
funeral; Bedel 83

From the Dreyfus Affair to the Simon Affair

When *Vérité* (*Truth*) was first published, reviewers immediately read the novel as a fictional transposition of the Dreyfus Affair, in which the Jewish schoolteacher Simon Lehmann, who is twice falsely convicted of a heinous crime, plays the role of Captain Dreyfus, while his fellow *instituteur* and defender, Marc Froment, plays that of Zola. The plot is launched by the discovery of the crime: the rape and murder of Simon's nephew and ward, Zéphirin, who lives in the public schoolhouse where his uncle teaches, in the village of Maillebois, a town whose government, in symbolic fashion, is evenly divided between Republicans and reactionaries (*V* 49).[1] It is Simon who is soon accused of the crime, although, in deference to Zéphirin's Catholic mother, the boy attended a Congregationist school. (The Congregations were loose organizations of brothers [and sisters] attached to the Church but not ordained priests [or nuns]).

Marc hears of it while visiting his in-laws in Maillebois and soon suspects that the allegations against his colleague are specious, the result of a conspiracy instigated by the local Church hierarchy, who manage to turn the townspeople against Simon by playing on their ignorance, their self-interest, their fears, and, above all, their anti-Semitic prejudice. After convincing himself of Simon's innocence, Marc speaks out on the latter's behalf, thereby exposing himself to vilification by the clerical party and its followers in public, and estrangement from his religious wife, Geneviève, in private. He then devotes his life to waging a campaign to overturn Simon's conviction and to preventing a future outbreak of the same madness by teaching respect for truth and justice to the children in his primary school, the future citizens of the Republic. In the latter part of the book, Zola imagines that Simon has been exonerated (whereas Dreyfus was not acquitted until 1906, four years after the publication of the novel and Zola's death) and that the ideal Republic has been established, thanks in large part to the efforts of Marc and his colleagues around the country in spreading Enlightenment among the people.

But this reading raised serious questions about the scope and validity of the work. In an otherwise highly laudatory review in *La Raison*, May 10, 1903, Gustave Téry wondered whether Zola had betrayed the national significance of the Affair by reducing it to a private matter. By replacing a case of treason with a crime of passion, had he not sacrificed the political themes of patriotism, militarism, and nationalism that played such an important role in the actual Affair (Mitterand, "Notice" 1499)? Working from Zola's preparatory notes for *Truth*, recent commentators have sought to respond to these criticisms by tracing the evolution of Zola's thinking as he mulled over his plans for the novel. Henri Mitterand quotes the writer's statement that "the entire story [of the crime] is only secondary. It is the point of departure, the incident that shows Marc the need for truth, so that the people may become just" (1496). Citing further passages from the *Preliminary Sketch* (*Ébauche*), Mitterand argues that *Truth* is not in fact a paraphrase of the Dreyfus Affair; its subject is the ideological battle between clericals and secularists in 1901–1902. The Affair was included simply because it was the most recent example of the effects of the ignorance that formed the greatest obstacle to justice. Uppermost in Zola's mind were problems of morals and sociology rather than the history of the Dreyfus Affair. After the *ralliement,* the Opportunist politicians had pushed their opportunism to the extreme of welcoming the prodigal back into the fold, relinquishing their original policy of relentless combat against the Catholic educational system, and had used the Church and the army as support for a moderate political program. Hence their fall from power after the Dreyfus Affair, and the rise of the Radicals. In Zola's view, national institutions such as the army, the judicial system, and Parliament were doing the opposite of what they should. The moral and intellectual bases of the country remaining fragile, the only solution was to uproot the causes of these evils from the national mentality. From this perspective, the history of the struggle between the lay and Congregationist schools was more important than the Affair itself, especially since the latter led to a revival and intensification of the battles that had taken place in 1880–81, when the anticlerical Ferry educational reforms were first promulgated.

Citing the same passage from Zola's notes, Jean-Claude Cassaing agrees that the Simon Affair is just a "pretext": the novel "is not a rewriting of the Dreyfus Affair, but the political history of the Third Republic" (308). The main target in *Truth* is not the Church per se, but the self-styled republicans who, once in control, have allied themselves with the Church in order to maintain themselves in power and to enjoy their wealth without having to fear the people's demands for social and economic justice. The Dreyfus Affair, and especially the amnesty granted to all parties in December 1900, showed most clearly that the Republic had abandoned its own principles and with them the enlightenment of the people that had been the goal of the Ferry educational reforms in 1880–81.[2] In the novel, therefore, the school will not be the site of propaganda or knowledge, but the guardian of the moral principles—freedom, truth, and justice—that the bourgeoisie has abandoned in its selfishness, greed, and fear of socialism. Cassaing recalls Zola's contention in his letter to President Loubet that Dreyfus was an allegory of the disinherited, the oppressed, the sacrificed. The Affair could have been a powerful *leçon de choses,* an exemplary demonstration of true republicanism for the people, had the bourgeoisie not encouraged their infection with the lies, calumnies, filth, and insults that were driving it mad.[3] Cassaing concludes that the Dreyfus Affair simply offered Zola a model of judicial error, while the real subject of the novel is the struggle of the primary schools with the Congregationist schools to shape the popular way of thinking, a struggle used as a means to conduct the political battle of the true, social Republic against the compromising, and compromised, antidemocratic bourgeois republic of the Radicals and Opportunists.

Zola's transposition of the Dreyfus Affair into the Simon case in *Truth* was thus meant to supply the object lesson the republic had failed to provide, by detecting and exposing the reasons for the popular acceptance of injustice condoned by the false republic of *la défense nationale*. In the broadest sense, that cause was the perpetuation of the mentality of the ancien regime resulting from the persistent influence of the Catholic Church with its training in irrationality and its insistence on the believer's subservience to unquestioned authority, which facilitated the exploitation of the credulity of the ignorant. The remedy was therefore the spread of enlightenment among the people through the secular education in the experimental method to be provided by the primary schools. But while Zola considered the dissemination of knowledge and the observational method necessary for the establishment of the social republic, he did not think it was sufficient by itself. The selfishness of the well-educated bourgeoisie was convincing proof of the need to complement knowledge with morality.[4] In the language of the times, it is *éducation* (upbringing) even more than *instruction* (education) that preoccupies Zola, because, as Laville concludes from the fact that he rarely describes classroom activities in the novel, school interests him only as "the place where future citizens are trained" (Laville 272). The emphasis on political morality that Mitterand and Cassaing discern in Zola's notes derives ultimately from the writer's concern with the revamping of French national identity, from monarchical subject to republican citizen (see Chaitin, "Transposing the Dreyfus Affair" 430–32).

The irrationality of religion that plagued the country thus was not just an external threat to morality and justice; it was a parasitic enemy within the self of the nation, menacing its identity and its sanity. Here, as so often, art was an improvement over life. Spying for a foreign country, as the case of Esterhazy showed, would have been motivated by the rational self-interest of monetary gain; the crime of passion Zola chose for his fictionalization of the Dreyfus Affair allowed him to make the crime itself into a dramatic figure of the madness infecting the people of France which was responsible for the subsequent miscarriage of justice masterminded by the leaders of the army and the Catholic teaching orders, with the collusion of the press and the officials of the courts and the government. Although his novel does not embrace the themes of patriotism, militarism, and nationalism explicitly, as Zola's notes show, the involvement of the Church hierarchy in the Simon Affair serves as an analogue of the military's involvement in the Dreyfus Affair, while the "confidentiality of confession" invoked by Father Philibin in his (false) testimony before the court replaces the "secrecy of national security" General de Boisdeffre cited at Zola's trial in refusing to divulge the details of the (nonexistent) letter General de Pellieux claimed proved Dreyfus's guilt (*V* 151, and n2). Father Philibin plays the roles of Major Henry and General de Pellieux (see *V* 43 n2), Brother Fulgence that of Du Paty de Clam (*V* 149 n1), and Brother Gorgias is the Esterhazy of the Affair (folio 421; quoted in *V* 43 n2). Moreover, Zola's very choice of crime implicitly challenged the nationalists' explanation of the problem in France, replacing the contention that French identity was being undermined by Jews and foreigners who had infiltrated the nation with Zola's own anticlerical view that the inner enemy was the irrationality promoted by religious education, and that it was this foe that was violating the identity of the republican citizen.

The Detective's Nightmare

As important as Zola's preparatory notes are for the understanding of this complex novel, they only tell half the story unfolded in the actual text. The Simon Affair is not just an example of the ignorance that made injustice possible nor a mere pretext for a narrative of recent political history, although it is clearly both of these. In the process of writing the novel, Zola fused the fantasy scenario of the rape and murder with a network of ideas, metaphors, and narrative links that crystallize the writer's conception of the Dreyfus Affair as a traumatic event that threatened the roots of identity, both individual and national. In fact, I would suggest that it is precisely the relation between narrative, fantasy, and ideology that forms both the texture and the principal topic of the novel.

Zola begins *Truth* as a detective story, a genre whose conventions had been more or less codified by the end of the nineteenth century with the publication of Arthur Conan Doyle's Sherlock Holmes mysteries in the 1880s and 1890s.[5] The text starts with the account of a crime that seems inexplicable. At the end, the detective always manages, nevertheless, to solve the mystery and put together a coherent narrative of the crime. In Lacanian terms, the crime constitutes the trauma that tears asunder the fabric of everyday reality, that is, the real of desire that interjects itself into the Symbolic, while the solution represents the restoration of the Symbolic to its previous state of apparent whole-ness by cordoning off desire in the single individual who committed the crime (see Žižek, "Two Ways"). According to the standard critical view, the detective is the embodiment of bourgeois scientific rational-ism, who applies to the human world the same methods of objective observation as the scientist does to the determination of the facts and laws of nature. He does this generally in victorious competition with the police, whose methods are too mundane to penetrate the mysteri-ous circumstances surrounding the crime. Given Zola's long-standing commitment to positivism and his desire to demonstrate its exceptional status as sole conduit to the truth in this novel, we should expect that Marc would assume precisely the role of objective, scientific observer in his investigation of the crime against Zéphirin. And indeed, to a certain extent Marc's inquiry into the crime does conform to this code. The detective story thus forms the perfect vehicle for the presentation of the wider themes of the novel indicated in its title: The search for the truth of the crime quickly evolves into the general problem of distin-guishing truth from falsehood. In ever-widening circles, Marc's inquiry becomes an attempt to expose the lies spread by the Church, which in turn leads to an inquiry into the credulity of the people that allows them to accept that deception, which then opens out into the even larger question of the social ills that make this possible, and ultimately to the means for correcting those problems. Combining the roles of detective and schoolteacher, Marc becomes the perfect allegory of the naturalist writer turned social reformer.

In order to solve the crime, exonerate the innocent Simon, and remove the causes that made his conviction possible, Marc must delve into the "*détraquements*" (breakdowns) of society and humankind. This investigation will inevitably force him, in imitation of the Zola of *The Experimental Novel*, to "work on spoiled subjects, descend into the midst of human misery and folly" (*Roman expérimental* 133), which in this novel are condensed into the vicious crime against Zéphirin and the still more vicious repetition of the crime in the mad persecution and cruel punishment of Simon that reveal the hitherto secret folly of the nation. And, again like the experimental novelist, Zola's goal will be to "pre-sent the documents whose knowledge is necessary to control good and evil" (133), that is, to correct the miscarriage of justice and establish the reign of the utopian Republic in France. By connecting the Simon Affair to the theme of scientific inquiry, the detective story format thus allows Zola to unite the three main plots of the novel: the investigation of the crime and its cover-up; the struggle between the Catholic and secular primary schools for control of the minds of the French; and the duel between Marc, the positivist freethinker, and Mme. Duparque, the ultra-Catholic matriarch, for the love and allegiance of Geneviève (Bory 1002).

There is one significant difference between the scientist and the detective, however, which seems to elude Zola, no doubt because his positivist principles prevent him from seeing it. As Slavoj Žižek points out in his compelling article on the detective story, in a sense the detective is always faced with a kind of deception, for the scene of the crime is usually a false image, arranged by the criminal in order to mislead those who would try to track him down ("Two Ways" 53). Unlike the natural scientist, the detective is involved in an intersubjective relation, and his primary role in reestablishing the truth concerns the field of meaning rather than that of natural phenomena. He "unmask[s] the imaginary unity of the scene" (53), rearranging its details in order to undo the deception and restore their true significance.

In the standard nineteenth-century detective story, it is the criminal who attempts to cover his tracks by creating a false impression of the crime scene, but while there is something similar in *Truth*—the top edge of a handwriting model found in Zéphirin's room has been torn off—in Zola's text it is the authorities of the Church and the Republic who attempt to perpetrate the deception. In addition, the ineptitude of the police typical of Poe's or Conan Doyle's fiction is replaced here by the corruption of the Church that cooks up the false scenario and of the government officials who go along with the cover-up and frame-up of Simon. To make matters worse, in addition to the deceiving Other of the Church, the hero is subjected to the intense pressure of the deceived Other, the masses who are both the victims and the collaborators of the Church.[6] Unlike the standard detective, then, Marc is not faced with a simple rent in the fabric of the Symbolic that can be stitched together by the solution of the enigma posed by the crime. He is confronted with a symbolic system that has gone haywire; the nightmarish quality he senses from the start derives from a distortion of the entire structure and leads him into a fun-house hall of horrors. His role is not simply that of the guarantor of meaning but rather that of producer of a substitute system of meaning (see Chaitin, "Le cauchemar de [la] *Vérité*").

Zola's detective thus takes on the role of the modern subject, like M. Bergeret, a lone seeker after truth whose path to knowledge is opposed not only by the inherent difficulty of the task but also and mainly by the obstacles placed in his way by the self-interest of the people and the powers that be, as well as tradition and social convention represented by a corrupt legal system and the government behind it. Once he makes his decision to pursue his mission of truth, his story becomes one of increasing isolation: detested by the clericals, rejected by the towns-people of Maillebois, left to fend for himself by the republicans who are his supposed allies, given only verbal support by the school hierarchy, regarded with contempt or fear by his fellow teachers, forced by public opinion to sever relations with the girls' teacher and kindred spirit Mlle. Mazeline, and, his most painful ordeal, abandoned by his wife. These trials, which echo those of Florent in *Le ventre de Paris* or of Étienne in *Germinal,* resonate with the isolation from the human race that Zola took to be the most severe punishment of Captain Dreyfus (*La vérité en marche* 18).

In his article, Žižek points out that this type of situation is charac-teristic of the "hard-boiled" detective of the 1930s and 1940s. For this new breed, it is the identity of the detective himself that is jeopardized by the "dialectic of deception": "caught in a nightmarish game whose real stakes escape him . . . the detective himself . . . undergoes a kind of 'loss of reality,' . . . finds himself in a dreamlike world where it is never quite clear who is playing what game" (63). Now while Marc is very far from the heroes of Raymond Chandler or Mickey Spillane in most respects, once he becomes involved in the Simon case, he is indeed drawn into a dreamlike world that imperils his identity. The night the crime is discovered, Marc is unable to sleep. Haunted by the thought of the crime and the feverish craving to know what happened, he finds himself enmeshed in what he calls a waking nightmare (*V* 68). Zola inti-mates that more is at stake here, for the protagonist and for his society, than a simple crime, when from the start he has Marc sense behind the murder "threatening murky depths, an entire dark abyss" (*V* 67). The young teacher's train of thought moves from his own pangs of doubt and the anguish of ignorance to his wife's family when, hearing Genev-iève laugh in her sleep, Marc is somehow reminded of her grandmother, Mme. Duparque, the martinet and religious fanatic who had admon-ished him earlier that day not to get involved. Now he thinks of his wife's Catholic upbringing and her latent tendency to revert to absolute ideas, superstitions, and the Catholic "God of selfishness and cruelty" (*V* 68). The crowd's reaction at the Congregationist school that after-noon forms the bridge between what he thinks of as "that monstrous, mysterious, enigmatic crime his intellect must grapple with" (66) and the God of cruelty and selfishness, for the rumor immediately spreads among the townspeople that one of the teaching Brethren must have committed the deed. The broader thesis of the novel—that is to say, its truth—is thus discreetly evoked without the need for any commentary by the narrator or pontificating by Marc as the spokesperson character of the novel.

Zola makes it crystal clear that Marc's very existence is at stake in the investigation of the crime, for the inability to discern the truth causes him acute physical and mental anguish. The question remains, however, why he becomes so involved in this particular search for the truth, instead of remaining at a cool distance, like a Sherlock Holmes or the objective scientist he professes to emulate. That Marc should feel horror at the brutality of the crime and that he should sympathize with his former schoolmate and fellow schoolteacher Simon at the loss of his nephew is not surprising; nor is it surprising that he should want to find out who did it and why. In themselves, however, these reactions do not explain the nightmarish quality of his brooding that first night. To be sure, he uses the word 'nightmare' only after waking the next morning, astonished that before falling asleep he had had "nightmares wide awake [*des cauchemars tout éveillé*]" (68), an expression that echoes the standard term for a daydream (*rêve éveillé*), as though to dismiss his nocturnal worries as an insubstantial fantasy, unworthy of serious consideration. But even if his anxieties were just fleeting will-o'-the-wisps, our understanding of the protagonist and his function in the novel is considerably enhanced by discovering the precise nature of the fears capable of throwing him into such turmoil. In fact, we soon find out that Marc's worst nightmares become realities, so that whether we take his ruminations as an insight into the psychology of the character or as an authorial device designed to unify the text by planting the seeds of future events in the mind of the reader, it is apt to say that this 'mere fantasy' structures the entire text.

In his richly evocative exposition of the major themes of the novel, Zola describes several events of the previous day capable of turning Marc's daylight concerns into powerful and apparently unrealistic anxieties about the murky implications of the crime (see Petrone). Mme. Duparque's warnings give him a perfectly legitimate reason for fearing that his attempts to clear up the mystery will bring him into conflict with his wife's family and thus destroy the peace and "perfect understanding" (*V* 68) he has had up to then with Geneviève. But this unpleasant anticipation is also intensified by several indirect intimations of what is to come. When Geneviève is upset by the insinuations and threats of violence against the Brethren, she asks Marc, "Will there be a fight? [*Est-ce qu'on va se battre?*]" (*V* 65). He reassures her, but, given the hostile atmosphere already dividing the members of Mme. Duparque's household along religious lines, the wonderful ambiguity of the little word *on*, which could mean 'they' or 'we,' at least suggests the possibility that Geneviève is worried as much about dissension between herself and Marc as about the danger of street-fighting between clericals and anticlericals in the town of Maillebois. To ambiguity is added denegation. Marc's half-conscious suspicion that he will find himself opposed to the Church in this affair must have increased in intensity when that afternoon he heard Mme Duparque's servant Pélagie, the faithful echo of the clerical rumor-mill of Maillebois, loudly proclaim that in any case Brother Gorgias could not be the culprit, since on the night of the assault he walked her nephew Polydor to his home far outside of town and thus could not have returned in time to attack Zéphirin in his room at the schoolhouse in the center of town.

For these reasons, it is understandable that when his thoughts turn to his wife and her family, Marc should review his relationship with her and recall the "revivals of her lengthy Catholic education, ideas of the absolute that clashed with his, superstitions, relinquishments of her will to the hands of a God of selfishness and cruelty, which sent a chill to his heart" (*V* 68). Although he tries to set his mind at rest by reminding himself of the harmony in which they've lived together until then, Marc nevertheless foresees the possibility of having to oppose the ideas of his in-laws and the consequent disruption of his marriage. Marc's anxiety that night thus derives in part from the rift he foresees in his marriage, which symbolizes the greater division between Catholic and freethinking France.

The marital discord Marc anticipates is not only a foreshadowing of the future; it is also a repetition of the past, namely, of the divergence between Zéphirin's parents, the Jewish Daniel Lehmann and his Catholic wife, Marie Prunier, at least as the latter interprets their life. When the child was six years old, his father died in a horrible industrial accident, which Marie understood as divine punishment for falling in love with a Jew. When the boy later began to develop a hunchback, his mother took this as further evidence of "the implacable vengeance of heaven" hounding her, because she could not tear the memory of her beloved husband out of her heart (*V* 39). To add to Marc's discomfort, when Mme. Duparque learns that local workers and peasants are accusing one of the Brethren teachers of the local Capuchin school that Zéphirin attended, she repeats her admonition to Marc and caps it off with the threat that God will exact vengeance on the enemies of His faithful.

These ominous words, the last ones Marc hears before he goes to bed, confirming the message of divine vengeance Zéphirin's mother read into her boy's nascent hunchback, cannot help but mobilize the enlightened teacher's most irrational fears, precisely the ones he has rejected as a freethinker and so cannot acknowledge within himself. This effect is all the more probable because one of the most prominent themes of his reflections about his relationship to Geneviève is that, like Zéphirin's parents, he too is part of a 'mixed' marriage—not between Catholic and Jew, to be sure, but between Catholic and militant, anticlerical freethinker, which may be even worse in the eyes of Mme. Duparque's God. The similarity between the two couples is reinforced by the fact that Zéphirin's terrified mother too is "won back by the religion of her youth" (*V* 39), much as Geneviève will be pulled inexorably back to the faith of her childhood. In a belated attempt at reparation and repentance, from then on Marie sends the boy to the Catholic school. After her death, when Simon takes him in on behalf of his wife's family, the Jewish teacher allows his nephew to continue with the Capuchin brothers. Indeed, when Mme. Duparque first hears of the murder, she has trouble understanding how God could have permitted such a thing to happen to a good Catholic boy, but then she decides that some families are just "accursed" (*des familles maudites*; 29).

In Marc's ear, as in that of any Frenchman of the period, this expression must have echoed the epithet the Catholics used to describe the Jews, "accursed people" (*peuple maudit*).[7] Mme. Duparque made the theme of Catholic anti-Semitism explicit later in the day, when she recalled an event that took place in her youth: The body of a kidnapped child was found in front of the church, cut in four, "and only the heart was missing. . . . They accused the Jews of needing it for their Passover matzoh" (60). Marc tries to shake off the suggestion that Zéphirin was the victim of a ritual sacrifice, by calling the story despicable nonsense (*ces stupidités infâmes*), but he surely understands Mme. Duparque's tacit allegation that Simon the Jew is the guilty one. He is all the more ready to perceive her insinuation because he has just heard a similar idea expressed by Férou, the anarchist teacher in the neighboring village of le Moreux who minces no words about what will happen. The "dirty" crew of priests will blame the "dirty Jew" schoolteacher in order to beat up on us schoolteachers, "the laic perverters, poisoners" (57). They will not scruple to accuse Simon of violating and strangling his nephew. Marc has a thoroughly plausible reason for dismissing these dire predictions, for they are issued by a fellow who is intelligent but embittered by his life of privations and therefore given to violent rancor and extreme ideas. He reproaches Férou for 'going too far,' and exclaims, "You must be out of your mind!" But when the other snickers at Marc's naïveté and insists that the clericals will not care a fig for the truth, Marc feels an icy shudder (*V* 58). Férou's remarks had thus already planted in Marc's mind the admittedly irrational idea that since Simon's Jewishness and Marc's secularity put them both in the same guilty category in the eyes of the Church, Marc's mixed marriage would be just as likely to suffer God's vengeance as Daniel Lehmann's. At the same time, his colleague's comments arouse the apprehension, equally unfounded at the time, that the Church will use these attributes to mount a case against Simon in the court of public opinion.

Marc's nightmare, then, is not only irrational fear but also fear of the irrational, in the form of the "despicable nonsense" of anti-Semitism, for he senses that he will have to battle against it if the Church decides to launch a campaign against Simon. As with his anxiety about the disruption of his marriage, these fears of course prove to be entirely justified. The day after his restless night, Marc learns from Pélagie that "people" are accusing Simon of the crime. Having neither families nor homeland, Jews commit evil for the sheer pleasure of it, in league with the devil, and Marc realizes, in the free indirect discourse typical of this text, that the people are resuscitating the ancient accusation of ritual murder.

After Simon is convicted, his name becomes "the accursed name that brought misfortune" (170), and the pious ladies of Maillebois broadcast the idea that "education without God was the cause of all stains [of sin] and all crimes" (169), exactly like de Broglie, Bourget, Caro, and Feuillet, while the general populace, represented by the peasant Bongard, the worker Doloir, and the office worker Savin, wallows in the mud of anti-Semitism. Bongard is convinced that the Jews go around poisoning the wells in the area in order to sicken the peasants' animals; Doloir explains that those citizens of nowhere (*sans-patrie*) are determined to destroy the army, so they can sell France to the Germans. Savin is just as delusional (*délirant*) as the others, but his madness takes a different form; he knows that Simon was a scapegoat, sacrificed in order to hide the corruption of *all* French schools, public and parochial (*V* 170–71). Zola thus offers a pastiche of the propaganda of the anti-Dreyfusards, spread by the newspapers—*Le Petit Beaumontais* and *La Croix de Beaumont* in the novel—but ultimately traceable to the teachings of the Church. *Le Petit Beaumontais* is a takeoff on *Le Petit Journal,* the paper with the highest circulation during the Third Republic, while *La Croix de Beau-*

mont is a representation of the various local versions of *La Croix,* the organ of the Catholic Congregation of the Assumption which, with *Le Petit Journal* and Drumont's *La Libre Parole,* was the most anti-Semitic newspaper of the last decades of the nineteenth century.[8] Its main accusations against the Jews were that they are a deicide people, murderers of Jesus; a people cursed forever by God for that crime; a people that has signed a pact with Satan; a people that practices ritual murder of Christian children; a people that persecutes Christians [!] and that aims to pillage France and destroy all Christians; the internal enemy of France and the enemy of religion and the homeland (Sorlin 138–58).[9]

Several of these themes, especially those of the deicide people and the accursed people, were not limited to the Assumptionists or the nineteenth century but have been parroted by Church dignitaries and historians from Bossuet (*Discours sur l'histoire universelle,* chaps. XX–XXI to Lamennais (during his orthodox period, in his *Essai sur l'indifférence*) and beyond, and have their source in the writings of the Church Fathers. They had been drummed into the heads of the faithful through their repetition in the Easter liturgy and the textbooks used in Catholic schools for centuries (Isaac, *Jésus et Israel* 360–82), just as Zola portrays the transmission of prejudice and superstition through the concept of the hereditary flaw (*tare héréditaire*) in *Truth.* (Happily, the Catholic Church began to change its teachings about the Jews in the 1950s [Démann 18–19]; unhappily, not everyone has gotten the message yet.) In the text, Marc describes this process as "a continuous supply of the stupidities currently circulating, the deep, overlapping layers of popular prejudices, the viruses of superstitions and legends amassed over the years, which destroyed all reason" (*V* 171).

The War of the Wor[l]ds:
Madness and Interpretation

Marc's fears that first night thus adumbrate the wide-ranging and fundamental battle that saturates every aspect of the text, the constant clash of two irreconcilable symbolic systems, that is, two patterns of intelligibility couched in two separate languages pitted against each other. This structure is already visible in the account of the circumstances leading up to Zéphirin's murder, which juxtaposes two parallel but contradictory explanations of events, the one 'rational' and 'scientific' according to the discourse of the novel, the other 'irrational' and 'religious.' The latter, presented in the ideas of the boy's mother and Mme. Duparque, makes subjectivity, the personal God of authority and vengeance, the basis of the causality that rules life and the entire universe. Its principle is obedience and reward or transgression and punishment, so that the individual must attempt to put himself into accord with divine will by adhering to Church doctrine. In this system, the repetition that plagues the Lehman family, then the Froment clan, curse of the Atrides style, results from the cycle of transgression and vengeance: Marrying outside the faith brings on the father's death and his son's hunchback, while the ritual murder of Catholic children by treacherous Jews causes the demise of the son. The first system, championed by Marc and, of course, Zola, puts impersonal objectivity at its center, with the determinism of natural law as its causal principle. Here the wise person must use observation and logical deduction to discern the truth, generalize from it, and use the laws so discovered to enhance the fraternal solidarity and material progress of humankind. Daniel Lehman's death must then be explained as the result of the social milieu, namely, his dangerous working conditions, combined with chance perhaps; his son's hunchback is the result of an "hereditary flaw" (V 39); and the hereditary 'instincts' of cruelty and "the madness of passion" at work within the murderer lead to the boy's death (cf. "a sudden burst of madness" [*une folie brusque*] [V 305], "his old madness" [*sa folie ancienne*] [V 602], etc.).

Marc's nightmare is that the irrational system should prove to be the true explanation of phenomena, so that the crime against Zéphirin would be justified as retribution for disobedience to the divine law. It would then be repeated endlessly, unless everyone involved, and Mark first of all, were to bow down to God's will. But for the freethinking subject, such obedience would itself amount to the repetition of the crime, with himself in the role of victim and God the Father in that of aggressor, a kind of spiritual violation and murder involving passive submission to an overwhelming authoritative and personalized force. For Mark this would be subjective death, the overthrow of all autonomy and rationality—in short, madness (see Chaitin, "Le cauchemar de [la] *Vérité*").

It is not Marc alone who is thus threatened. 'Madness' and its equivalents—*la folie* (madness), *fou* (crazy), *la démence* (insanity), *le délire* (delusion), *délirant* (delirious/delusional)—haunt every aspect of life in the France Zola conjures up in this text, whenever the crime or the religious system of explanation is at stake. It is the nation driven mad by the Dreyfus Affair Zola envisions in his letter to President Loubet after the grotesque outcome of Dreyfus's second trial in Rennes: "[A]s long as this frightful act of iniquity [the repeated conviction of the innocent Dreyfus] has not been rectified, it will continue to plunge France into the delirium of horrible nightmares" (*V* 154). Marc describes the new worship of the relics of Saint Anthony of Padua as the epitome of stupidity, cupidity, and laziness depending on the "caprice of a god of irony and iniquity" (*V* 183). And he adds that it is "complete insanity, an irresistible stampede of the faithful" (*V* 185). When Geneviève feels she can no longer live with Marc but must return to the Catholicism of her youth, he tells her, "Then go to your madness, follow it until it is exhausted, since there is no other way to cure you of it" (*V* 344). And shortly after Simon's conviction, when a conspiracy of silence about the case reigns, the text characterizes it as society's hidden insanity.

The common thread running through these various manifestations of *la folie* is a capricious, irrational subjectivity: that of the fearful, credulous, and often self-centered members of the unenlightened people; that of the furious erotic and aggressive impulses that overcome the criminal in a moment of sudden and uncontrollable passion; that of the capricious God of cruelty and selfishness who cares more for his own grandeur and his believers' subservience than for truth or justice. This same subjectivity forms the bond between religion and the politics of the Third Republic. As early as the Versaillais slaughter of the Communards, Zola had insisted on the distinction between the idea and official ideology of the republic, and the reality of political action. This critical analysis reached its culmination in the articles he published in the antirepublican *Figaro* in 1879–81 and later collected in *Une campagne,* the gist of which was to elevate letters to the level of the eternal while relegating politics to the dustbin of ephemerality and irrationality. As Roger Ripoll has cogently observed, Zola assimilated politics with hunger, aggression, and sexual desire, the domain of the irrational instincts (48). Literature and science are at the summit of human accomplishment, because they confer life and immortality; literature is the eternal and the absolute, while politics is merely the fleeting and the relative of human affairs (Pagès 49–50, quoting passages from "La haine de la littérature" and "Adieux"). But that is only true of the objective artist; "the personal feeling" of the artist, unless it is a simple 'hypothesis,' a starting point for the work of art to be checked by objective knowledge, is, on the contrary, the source of madness. And Zola gives the example of an artist who might be 'crazy' enough to represent people walking on their heads, simply because that was his 'personal idea' (*Roman expérimental* 94, 96).

If the country concedes too much importance to the politicians, it will risk breaking down; Zola uses his favorite verb, *se détraquer* (to break down), to indicate both physical and mental breakdown ("Adieux" 873). And that is just what he claims has happened during the Dreyfus/ Simon Affair. The ultimate cause of the potential collapse is the utter void at the center of unleashed subjectivity ("Adieux" 321). Marc's violent rejection of the religious system stems from the same icy dread, that the Other upon which it depends has no substance at all, that at bottom it is mere nothingness. The faith to which Geneviève reverts, the superstition that moves the faithful in Maillebois and enriches the Capuchin monks, the creed that Brother Gorgias avows in his final confession, all are characterized as being totally empty. In art as in politics or religion, for Marc as for the Republic, the supreme peril is subjectivity gone wild, that is, the danger that the outside world has the void at its heart, for in that case the individual subject would lose the connection to the phenomenal world on which identity and sanity depend. The emptiness around which the irrational system is built threatens madness because it dissolves the object which alone can serve, in the positivist perspective, as the firm foundation necessary to the life and equilibrium of the self. It is the vacuity of God the Father that dominates the French society Marc comes to know and makes it possible for the people to believe anything whatsoever, no matter how irrational or hateful. And it is dread of this same emptiness that explains why Marc is convinced he must, at all costs, eradicate this system and replace it with positivist objectivism.

Marc's efforts to find the truth and to make his conception of it prevail thus become part of the wider confrontation between secular education, with the positivist notion of truth and the neo-Kantian doctrine of secular morality and justice that supported it, and the religious education of the catechism, Catholic dogma, and moral training based on divine authority. "The struggle appeared terrible and immediate to Marc, who had never felt with such strength the need for France to kill the Church, if France did not want to be killed by it" (*V* 191). *Ceci tuera cela* (This will kill that), in the phrase Zola had already adopted from Hugo's *Notre-Dame de Paris* in *Le ventre de Paris* (see Zarifopol-Johnston, "Ceci tuera cela"), a fight to the finish between secularism and Catholicism that was necessary, in Zola's eyes, to establish the true Republic. On this level, the novel is a Manichaean battle between two diametrically opposed and mutually exclusive forces that is played out in the novel's three plots. In the dispute about the Simon case, the competing theses are tested by their ability to discover factual information, the true identity of the criminal. The touchstone in the competition between the secular and parochial primary schools is the capacity to establish justice in the nation. The struggle between Marc and Mme.

Duparque for Geneviève's heart measures the power of the two systems to foster love and thereby life, peace, and harmony. In each case, of course, the scientific method wins out.

The goal in these plots is not simply to outdo the competitor, but, as in many a political contest, to eliminate the rival at any price. This murderous urge becomes all the more imperative the more the two competing forces resemble each other, and it is remarkable to what extent Zola's conception of Marc's endeavor mimics the system he is trying to oust. In this respect, however, he is merely following the lead of the anticlerical campaign undertaken by the journalists of *l'Aurore,* who accused the Church, especially the Jesuits, of exactly the same misdeeds as the latter did the Jews: organizing a secret "syndicate," pumping millions of francs into its campaign to seize control of the nation, doing the insidious work of a foreign power, plotting nefarious crimes designed to bring about the death of the 'true France.' This specularity is just as apparent in the religious vocabulary and the narrative framework of the novel, which, as the title of the series proclaims, imagines the promotion of science and the social state as a latter-day gospel replete with missions, myths, and martyrs. Indeed, Zola did aim to create a new religion of science capable of killing off Christianity (Laville 345, 463–64). Here again he was simply embracing the strategy of the Opportunist Republic, which from its inception had adapted the ideology of Catholicism to its own purposes by replacing the God of the catechism with the republican homeland in its primary school textbooks.

Discerning the meaning of events becomes the principle that underlies the structure of the last book of the novel as a series of rereadings of the past. The narrative flow is interrupted while the principal characters look back on their lives and those of their communities, recapitulating their main events and meditating on the significance of their experiences. As Evelyne Cosset (*Les* Quatres Évangiles *d'Émile Zola*) points out, these moments of deliberation allow the author to assess the present situation in light of the past events of the novel, making that past intelligible while conferring plausibility on the lesson of progress that forms the writer's thesis. According to Cosset, these recalls of the past serve the rhetorical purpose of making believable the utopian future Zola envisions, by showing precisely how it has evolved from the historical reality of the country he has depicted realistically in the first three sections.

Marc's project of spreading enlightenment, however, is not just a matter of reviewing preexisting meanings. Like all genuine educational undertakings, it involves forming new meanings or replacing those that already exist. In short, it is a matter of changing people's minds, and, as Marc soon finds out, changing people's minds quickly entails changing their identities. The fundamental purpose of the Ferry school reforms that Marc strives to put into practice was in fact the performative function of making meaning, since, as we've seen, they were designed to create the new national identity of the loyal republican citizen. For Zola and Marc, as for the Republic, the objectivism of Opportunist ideology was just the starting point for the process of identity formation; it is the subjective processes of inculcating and altering belief, and thus of controlling the subject's adherence to the symbolic systems of his or her society, that comprise the core of their endeavor as of the novel as a whole.

Yet it is apparent that even in *Truth*—especially in *Truth*—Zola is not willing to concede this point where his own positivist discourse is concerned. Marc's truth must remain untainted by the virus of performative language; it must be the rock-solid bed of objectivity compared to which the other systems of interpretation are flimsy vapors of insubstantial subjectivity. The text is thus pulled in opposite directions, riven by the tension between mimetic realism with its premise of an objectively given nature to which it refers, and performative art with its constructivist notion of the power of language to create its own object—the ideal citizen of the ideal Republic.

Saving the Republic, from Nothing

The battle of interpretations reaches a dramatic climax in each of Simon's trials, but it pervades the entire novel and finds its most vivid expression in the disunion of Marc and Geneviève. In fact, the two plots are artfully intertwined, for Geneviève's return to her grandmother's home and religious influence and her subsequent departure are precipitated by Marc's involvement in Simon's case. The local representatives of the Church and Mme. Duparque, who slavishly follows their lead, want to coerce Marc into abandoning his defense of Simon by persuading Geneviève to leave him if he persists in broadcasting the Jew's innocence. Geneviève eventually does leave Marc soon after he discovers new, damning evidence against the real culprit, Brother Gorgias, and begins clamoring for a new trial. Likewise, Geneviève's return to her husband results from Simon's second conviction in the fictional town of Rozan, a transparent allusion to Dreyfus's second trial in Rennes. The evidence produced there causes Geneviève to recognize Simon's innocence, and it leads her mother, Mme. Berthereau, to realize that religion, in the person of the Church authorities behind Simon's conviction, is responsible for his inhuman suffering on Devil's Island. Sensing a parallel with the living death she suffers through religious renunciation of earthly happiness, she defies Mme. Duparque and warns her daughter not to allow the same thing to happen to her.

The married couple's relationship represents the theory of the "two Frances" promoted by *l'Aurore* at the turn of the century but already widespread in the 1870s in the notion of the "two groups of youths" (*deux jeunesses*) being created by the two parallel but opposed educational systems (Mona Ozouf 19; Prost 37). Just before Geneviève walks out on Marc, the only thing the two agree on is that they no longer agree about anything!

> —"What troubles me the most is that we can no longer get along with each other [*nous entendre*]" she concludes, and he continues:
> —It's true. . . . we can no longer understand each other [*nous entendre*]. Words no longer have the same meaning for us, so everything I reproach you for, you reproach me for. (*V* 281)

So wide is the cleft between them, that is, between the positivist and the Catholic notions of the world, that they now speak two different languages; or, what is worse, they speak the same language, but it has a different meaning for each of them. To make the lack of understanding more poignant, when Marc repeats Geneviève's very words in this exchange—*nous entendre*—he gives this seemingly last remnant of their "perfect understanding" (*entente parfaite*) of former days a different sense from his wife. For him it bears its more literal, material, we might say positive(ist), meaning, of understanding words spoken, whereas she meant it in the more figurative, psychological sense of mutual understanding and harmony.

The main lesson that emerges from the drama of Marc's troubled relation to his wife is that it is a battle between something and nothing, presence and absence, fullness and lack. Zola turns this abstract conflict into narrative action, portraying it in terms of contradictory emotions and conflict among characters that develop over time. The bridge figure between the older and younger generations of women in her family, Geneviève's attraction to religion and to nature is evenly balanced, leaving her to vacillate at different moments between the faith of her childhood, embodied in Mme. Duparque and her house in Maillebois opposite a former Capuchin monastery now used as a Catholic school, and her love for her husband, Marc, and his dwelling in the secular republican schoolhouse. Book Two ends with Geneviève's departure from her husband to return to her grandmother and to the Catholicism of her youth; in the climactic scenes that end Book Three, spurred on by her mother's urging to take advantage of life while she still can, Geneviève renounces both and is reunited with Marc, soon to become a schoolteacher herself.

From the start, Geneviève is caught between her grandmother and her husband. Mme. Duparque had always been violently opposed to the marriage on religious grounds, accusing Marc of "stealing her granddaughter's soul" (*V* 31). Less than a week into their annual summer visit to her childhood home in Maillebois, Geneviève urges Marc to take her away from the influence of her grandmother's devoutness, sensing that "the ideas and feelings of her childhood were coming back to her [*lui revenaient*]" (*V* 106). Geneviève's faith thus acts as the *revenant,* the gothic element, so frequently present in Zola's earlier novels, which manifests the return of a nighttime past that refuses to die, haunting the daylight world of the present.

Two years later, the rift between the spouses becomes manifest, when Marc, now the teacher in the Maillebois primary school, feels firmly entrenched enough to brave the local clericals by taking the crucifix down from the wall of his classroom. (The executive order [*circulaire*] of November 2, 1882 forbade the display of all religious emblems in the public schools.) Geneviève catches him in the act, and when she reproaches him, it seems as though an alien personality has taken over her identity, as though she is literally not herself. As Marc watches this transformation, he is seized with gothic horror. Like the victim of a demonic possession, Geneviève is being slowly dragged back toward her "pious youth," a return to the past that estranges them ever more (233–34). As Marc later realizes, Geneviève is "possessed by another, filled with an indestructible past" (274).

It is as though Mme. Duparque has stolen back the soul of her granddaughter. In fact, Marc does identify this alien presence as Mme. Duparque, who threatens to take his daughter Louise back as well, but the text notes that he had caught a glimpse of a more sinister presence in his wife's eyes, a presence which is really an absence, "the mystical darkness of the beyond" (*V* 233). For the positivist Zola, the darkness of mysticism derives from its invisibility, itself a consequence of its nonexistence, and the basis of all religious belief is ultimately mystical. He repeatedly equates it with emptiness, nothingness, and the imaginary when analyzing Geneviève's religious aspirations and their consequences for her identity: She insists on proclaiming her happiness with the "void of her chimera"; refuses to admit "the nothingness" of her prayers (*V* 477); and, in her parting speech to her grandmother, asks, "[W]hy God has not filled the frightful nothingness of my being?" (*V* 488). For Zola and his protagonist, the nothingness of the mystical is the essence of the irrationality the Church implants in its followers (see Chaitin, "Le cauchemar de [la] *Vérité*").

The disillusionment Geneviève expresses to Mme. Duparque is in fact that of a frustrated lover whose "mystical" desire is never fulfilled. When Marc begins to sense that he is losing his wife, he reconstructs her life story in an attempt to determine the causes of her disaffection. The crucial moment, he decides, was the preparation for her first communion, combining darkness, mystery, perverse desire and mystical curiosity, which disturbed her reason forever. The Church exercises its sway over women, and through them over their children and husbands, by manipulating and perverting their sexual desire, seducing them into a precocious sexual initiation, displacing the object of their desire from mere human beings to the divine lover, and promising them a jouissance beyond all earthly satisfactions from which they will never be able to free themselves (272).[10] In short, behind Mme. Duparque lurks a much more powerful agent calling Geneviève back: the lure of divine love.

As the rift between Marc and Geneviève widens, like so many divorcing couples they play out their hostility in disputes over the education of their daughter, Louise. Until this point, Marc has allowed her to attend catechism class, despite his atheism, in large part to keep the peace with his wife. But now that Louise has reached the age of twelve, the priest insists she must begin going to confession if she is to continue with her religious instruction. Geneviève is adamant, but Marc categorically refuses to allow it, not only because he does not want to risk his daughter confessing to one of the small number of disturbed priests whose vow of chastity might lead him to all kinds of sexual aberration, nor even because such a colloquy is a kind of moral violation of a young girl whose senses are just awakening; no, the prime reason is that confession is a kind of rape, a trauma whose aftereffects will enslave the girl throughout her life. From then on she remains her confessor's thing, Marc goes on to say (in free indirect discourse), an obedient instrument of servitude.

Marc's fears for his daughter are justified by Geneviève's experience, torn between "the reality of her love for her spouse" and "the deceitful nothingness of her mystical education" (*V* 482) that incites her to desire the impossible. The nothingness of Geneviève's "mystical" desire is thus its ultimate lack of object, the longing for union with a beyond that does not exist. When she finally does leave Marc and return to her grandmother's house, she is never satisfied; her hopes of finally feeling in her flesh Jesus's blood and flesh are always disappointed.

Still more perverse than the attraction of the beyond is the insidious effect Zola discerns—and here he goes beyond both the pleasure principle and the analyses of Michelet and his other anticlerical predecessors—in the mental violence the rigid practice of Catholicism exercises on women (and therefore on the men they marry and the sons they raise). By first criminalizing sexuality to awaken guilt within its victims, then imposing blind obedience to the authority of the Church, it actually creates a specifically feminine sensual enjoyment that cements the bond between women and the Church. Mme. Duparque not only enjoyed the caressing words and unctuous gestures of her confessor, she received a thrill of delight from his harsh reproaches, his threats of hell with its horrible torments of the flesh. The Church's hold over women is no longer the result of ignorance, dis-education and fear of the devil alone. As a consequence of centuries-long experience, subservience to authority has become a source of pleasure, enslavement the object of a love that makes the task of liberation all the more formidable.

Zola's diagnosis of Geneviève's condition—and by implication that of women in general—is simple: She has abandoned "the only natural human pleasure possible" (V 477). For Zola, human sex is the only real, because "natural," fulfillment of desire. The "mystical" teaching of the Church is perverse in that it arouses desires that can never be satisfied, because they have no real object. The ultimate goal of Marc's crusade of enlightenment is thus to stamp out insatiable desire, the desire for "something other."

Zola's method for achieving this aim is to allow the adult Geneviève to compare the imaginary pleasures of her youth to the mature sexual and emotional fulfillment she knew with her husband during the happy years of their marriage. By enacting rather than resisting the return of the repressed indicated by the gothic overtones of these episodes, Geneviève manages to free herself from the iron grip of her first lover, the one who "deflowered" her.[11] It is precisely because she has tried to recapture the intoxication of the pious practices of her childhood that those practices have lost their charm and their hold over her, dispersed, one by one, like so many mirages. As Geneviève learns that the mystical beliefs of her "chimerical" youth can no longer fulfill her desire, her dreams grow pale and weak. The clear implication is that "mystical" passion for the beyond could have exercised a hold over her and the women of the nation only because the Church instilled it into them before they had any concrete experience capable of satisfying their desires for happiness and sexual union, and the memory of that passion can continue to hold them in thrall only if its vacuity is not exposed to the light of day.

Now, as David Baguley has observed, all the heroines of Zola's *Évangiles* (*Gospels*) represent the Republic that the apostolic hero must save from "the harmful influences that endanger the country" ("L'Evangile républicain de Zola" 109). Geneviève's story is thus an allegory of the nation's attempt to achieve freedom by expelling the "poison" of the irrationality, the love of ignorance, and the lure of imagined satisfactions inculcated into its citizens by Catholic education, the shackles of Church teachings. Marc characterizes the irrationality of her religious faith as the "ancient flaw" that comes back to haunt her (*V* 476), thereby combining the gothic theme of the return of the repressed with the naturalist concept of the "hereditary flaw" that determines so much of human behavior in the writer's earlier novels. Unlike in the *Rougon-Macquart* series, however, the flaw is understood here in an historical and textual sense as the inscription of Catholicism into the nation's psyche through the long ages during which it was dominated by that religion, and its return is described as an atavism: that is, the recurrence in the present of an ancient primitive trait.[12] Zola reinforces the connection by having Mlle. Mazeline, who has become Marc's primary interlocutor during his wife's stay in Mme. Duparque's home, console him with the argument that Geneviève is the victim of the heredity of Catholic education that goes back countless generations beyond her grandmother.

Geneviève's liberation from the influence of Catholicism, and, by implication, the emancipation of the nation from the covert interference of Rome, consists in chasing away the alien personality that had regained its hold over her body and mind in the scene of taking the crucifix down from the schoolroom wall. Through this exorcism, as the critics are fond of putting it, Zola thus implies that there was something potentially salutary in the national trauma of the Dreyfus Affair, if it could shock the country into reliving its past and thereby make it capable of surmounting its hereditary flaws. Book Three and the "realistic" plot come to an end when Geneviève and the two children rejoin Marc and reconstitute the family that had been torn apart the way the nation was divided into the "two Frances." Her return signifies the reunification of the nation that prepares the way for the final, utopian section of the novel. Book Four begins with Marc succeeding in having Geneviève appointed teacher of the girls' school in Jonville, the town of his own new assignment, so that they would be completely united, in "perfect understanding" once again (*V* 500, 507–8).

The text treats the healing process made possible by this catharsis as a matter of nature taking over once the "poison" of mysticism has been extracted. The parasitic identity having been cast out, the "true" identity of the republic is free to emerge and prevail. No longer warped by the irrational teachings of Catholicism, the people will be automatically attracted to truth and justice, the positivities of concrete evidence, mutual solidarity, and the pursuit of happiness, in accordance with their nature. Zola's formula for healing the nation, his solution to the problem of creating national unity and identity, is thus the exact opposite of those of Burke, Taine, Renan, or Barrès, for it consists not in identifying with the past but in mourning, reviving and then disengaging oneself from one's past attachments. To paraphrase Santayana, one might say that, for Zola, those who cannot repeat the past are condemned to live it.

CHAPTER 8

Truth

❦

True Treason, or the Rape of the Republic

> You Senators are traitors
> the ministers are traitors
> the President of the Republic is a traitor.
> And when you have voted in this law [of amnesty]
> You will have done the work of traitors.
> — Zola, *La vérité en marche* 141

The Sins of the Fathers

Marc must verify his positivist system of interpretation and disprove that of his Christian adversaries, because the greatest threat to his identity and sanity is the possibility that the nation is in the grips of a capricious and malicious Father who condones Simon's frame-up, one who is an updated version, with nineteenth-century anti-Semitism thrown in, of Descartes's evil genie (*malin génie*). Like the Cartesian subject, the hero's being depends on his ability to find a certainty that the existence of such an Other would render impossible (*V* 66). His first inklings of the relation between the father and the world gone berserk were aroused the day of the crime. His colleague Férou's contention that the Church will accuse Simon echoes the fleeting suspicion that must have crossed his mind a few moments earlier, when he had the "rapid intuition" that Zéphirin must have known the killer, since he didn't cry out when the latter entered his room (50). For it takes no great imagination to conclude that the murderer must therefore have been either one of the Brethren or Simon himself.

Marc's worst nightmare, an irrational and entirely unfounded accusation, is that the brutal criminal is the boy's own protector, indeed his

219

surrogate father. Earlier in the day, during the judicial inquiry, Simon had consoled his wife, Rachel, in public by first kissing her "as a lover and a father," then reminding her that they have treated Zéphirin like their own child (55). As in earlier passages, negation is used to suggest and then reject an idea, or rather two: first, that the boy's death was in some sense the responsibility of his guardians; that, as several witnesses more or less imply or deny, it was due to their negligence in letting the child sleep in a room with a window opening directly onto the street that the crime could have been committed; and second, as a response to the first, that they were indeed his substitute parents, that Simon therefore in practice was tantamount to being his father.

Of course, Marc's horror can be accounted for by his sympathy for the victim of such vileness and injustice rather than his suspicion that Simon is the killer, and there is no direct textual evidence prior to the nightmare scene that he ever had the thoughts I impute to him. It might be more accurate, then, to say that they exist in the text and, as a result, in any reader familiar with the Dreyfus case. But the following day, when Marc first gets wind via Pélagie of the smear campaign the Church and the newspapers are beginning to pump up against Simon, this very doubt does enter his mind: "Could Simon be guilty?" he asks himself feverishly (75). At this point he rethinks all the evidence presently available about the case and tells himself (in free indirect discourse) that reason, deduction, and observation have made him certain that Simon cannot have committed the crime (75–76).

Yet the only serious argument he adduces, and it is a negative one, is that Simon had no motive. The really telling evidence against the Congregationist (Capuchin) school and Brother Gorgias—the handwriting model, the torn-off corner, the precise manner in which it came into Gorgias's possession that night—will not come to light for several years. Marc's unshakable certainty is all the stronger precisely because it is not based on evidence—which can always be interpreted in various ways and therefore inevitably leaves at least some room for doubt— but almost entirely on plausibility (*vraisemblance*) and deduction. The only place observation enters Marc's review is in his own evaluation of Simon's character, situation, and demeanor while recounting the story of the fatal night. But Zola himself knew very well from his own mistakes concerning the roles of Major Du Paty de Clam and Major Henry in the Dreyfus case how misleading such appraisals of character and testimony can be. Later in the novel, he will have Marc and Delbos, Simon's lawyer, repeat that error with regard to Brother Fulgence and

Father Philibin. Even though Marc turns out to be right about Simon, if he protests the latter's innocence so loudly and with so little justification, it must be that he feels it imperative to exclude at all costs what he dreads the most, the possibility of the father's complicity in the crime against the child.

That conclusion becomes even more compelling when the crime is repeated at the end of the book. This time it is Marc's great-grand-daughter, Rose, who is assaulted by a would-be kidnaper right in front of Zéphirin's old room, but she manages to escape with only a broken arm and emotional shock when the protagonist happens along to save her (619). Unhesitatingly, Marc sees this event as an uncanny reprise of the earlier crime, as though the gothic repressed he thought had been laid to rest forever with Geneviève's return had come back to haunt his utopia (620). But when, to complete the resemblance with the past, the girl's father, François, is mistakenly accused of the crime, like Simon previously, the townspeople, having been trained in the interim to communal solidarity and the love of truth by Marc and his battalion of *instituteurs*, come forward this time to provide the eyewitness reports and evidence that soon lead to François's exoneration and the identification of the real criminal, the brother of the young woman he had run off with.

Once again (strange coincidence!), it is precisely the father who is accused, only this time it is the child's 'real' father, and all the evidence points in his direction—the material evidence of his handkerchief found at the scene of the attempted kidnapping and, above all, the eyewitness testimony of his own daughter, the intended victim. Once again the theme of the nightmare is evoked, only this time there can be no mistake about its cause, the guilt of the father: "But it was her father, she was haunted by that nightmare, born perhaps from the suffering she saw in her mother since the departure of the unfaithful husband" (623). Moreover, it turns out that François really is involved in the assault, although indirectly, because it is his lover, Colette, who cooks up the scheme, and her brother, Faustin, who carries it out, or rather bungles it. The text insinuates that the secular educational system is once again succumbing to the seduction of the Church, perhaps unwittingly this time, for Colette is reputed to be the illegitimate daughter of Father Théodose, one of the fieriest preachers and most predatory confessors of Maillebois. In fact, the whole episode is attributed to a last, desperate effort of the Congregation to smear the secular schools, and even though there is no evidence to support this hypothesis, 'everyone' is convinced of it (633). None of that, however, has the slightest effect on Marc, the devotee of factual truth, empirical observation, and logical deduction. Like the neighbors of a mass murderer interviewed on television the day after his conviction, who regularly express their disbelief that such a nice, quiet, respectable fellow could do such a thing, Marc is once again unshakably convinced that his grandson could not have committed the act, since he had no motive and was always such a loving father (*père tendre*; 624), the very idea Simon had used to protest his innocence of all responsibility for the calamity that befell Zéphirin: "'It's impossible, it's crazy!' Marc repeated" (623). "'No! No!' Despite Rose's assertion, despite the handkerchief recognized as his, François was not the guilty party; it was a moral impossibility, there were arguments [*raisonnements*] stronger than evidence" (625). The townspeople may have learned a greater respect for empirical truth in the interim, but it seems that Marc has not. He has his preconceived idea and he will stick to it, no matter what.[1] Of course, once again Marc is right. But what does that mean other than that Zola was as concerned as his character to prove beyond a shadow of a doubt that it was just a waking nightmare, that the father could not possibly be guilty? (See Chaitin, "Transposing the Dreyfus Affair" 439–41.)

He had good reason to be so concerned. One of the smear tactics the army used just before his libel trial for the charges he roared out against military officers in his "J'accuse" article was to release apparently damning papers from François Zola's military file to a certain M. Judet. Judet used them to publish a malicious article about Zola's father in *Le Petit Journal*, asserting that François's request for permission to resign his commission in the Foreign Legion in 1832 was denied so that he could be held in military prison for stealing from his company's funds. Zola immediately expressed his outrage in an article in *L'Aurore* of May 28, 1898, titled "My Father" (*Mon père*), later collected in *La vérité en marche* (169–76). He followed this up in January 1899 with three articles designed to clear his father's name, also republished in *La vérité en marche*, simply called "François Zola," written after he had gained access, by dint of prolonged and difficult maneuvers, to his father's military dossier. There would be little point in rehearsing all the details of the case here, but one passage shows the same inclination that we've seen in the text of *Vérité*, to value reasoning above factual data when it comes to absolving the father: "[W]hile I was copying the important documents in the dossier . . . a conviction [of his innocence] formed within me. It is obviously my personal [belief] and is based only on reasoning [*raisonnement*]" (194).

But Zola's desire to save his father's reputation does not explain why he chose these particular crimes for his transposition of the Dreyfus Affair, although the theft imputed to François would have been a betrayal of trust. There is certainly an enormous gap between Dreyfus's alleged crime of spying for a foreign country, on the one hand, and rape and murder, on the other. Some have suggested that Zola simply took over the stereotyped attacks on the morals of monks and clergy spread by anticlerical propaganda since the Restoration (and dating back well into the Middle Ages), recently brought into public view by the 1899 government survey of conditions in the monasteries and the subsequent campaign of leftist publicists and newspapers such as *l'Aurore* and *La Petite République,* which circulated charges against Church officials of sadistic punishments and sexual abuse of children (Laville 195–96). No doubt there is a good deal of truth in this theory, but a more probing interpretation, while not contradicting the first, relates the charge of treason brought against Dreyfus to the dimension of betrayal so prominent in the novel: "The capital offense—treason [*trahison*] for an officer—for a schoolteacher is violating one of his pupils: scandalous 'betrayal' [*trahison*]" (Bory 1002). The verb *violer* being just as ambiguous as *trahison,* we can surmise that Zola chose a *viol* (rape) as crime to intimate as graphically as possible that Catholic education was violating the trust of its pupils as of the country at large. And, as his notes explicitly state, Zola wanted an exemplary crime that would act as a *leçon de choses* for the people of France to bring home the point that ignorance and an inability to think rationally inevitably lead to the miscarriage of justice (see Cassaing 302; Mitterand, "Notice" 1495–96).

These explanations, true as far as they go, do not, however, account for the specifically traumatic effect of the crime, the abhorrence Marc feels for the repeated implication, however quickly repudiated, that the fault may lie with the father. This crucial element of the transposition, I would argue, derives from Zola's experience of a trauma in his own life that could act as a refractor for the larger trauma of French life that was the Dreyfus Affair. Like Rose's father and accused kidnaper, Zola's father was named François. Like Zéphirin, Zola was the child of a 'mixed' marriage, between a French woman and a foreigner, the Italian Francesco Zolla (a fact Barrès did not neglect to emphasize in his xenophobic witch-hunts during the Dreyfus Affair). That victim of the first crime, Zéphirin, is marked with the letter *Z* that inevitably calls to mind the famous name of Zola. Moreover, the original name of the criminal in Zola's notes also began with a *Z*, Zacharias (although this name was probably an allusion to Esterhazy as well). All these little clues point to the fact that, according to police archives, Émile Zola was sexually molested at the age of five by a twelve-year-old babysitter whom his father, François, left in charge of him at a hotel in Marseilles where he was staying while on a business trip (Mitterand, *Olympia* 93; Brown 23–25). In this novel called *Truth*, in his effort to depict the crisis of the Republic with which he identified, Zola came closer to articulating his personal truth than anywhere else in his long career.[2]

The repercussions of this traumatic experience could be traced through virtually all of Zola's life and fiction, and, I would argue, it supplied one important motive for his decision to intervene so decisively in the Dreyfus case as well as furnishes a key to understanding *Truth*. What makes an event a trauma is not what actually happens, it is the disruption it causes in the subject's symbolic world after the fact. Little Émile was not murdered, he did not have his arm broken, he probably was not raped—the legal term *attentat à la pudeur* covering a multitude of sins when exercised against a minor—and the assault was certainly not committed by his father (or a churchman), but these must have been some of the fantasies he wove around the actual occurrence, like a dark pearl crystallizing around an intrusive grain of sand. He probably did suffer the mental shock he attributes to little Rose in the novel, and he must have asked himself the questions, "How could father have allowed this to happen?" "Was he not the one who chose this servant to mind me?" "If father let this happen, even wanted it to happen, then anything is possible, even the worst." Zola transposes the agonizing conflict between the conviction that the father is guilty and the desire to believe such guilt impossible into the experience of little Rose, who accuses her father and then is horrified by her apparent mistake. When François learns of her attempted abduction, he immediately returns home, all the more easily because his lover, Colette, has left him in the interim. Rose compares her father's appearance to that of the man who attacked her, realizes that his beard and the shape of his body are different from those of her assailant, and retracts her accusation (632).

As grave as the teacher's 'treason' toward his pupil may be, a much greater betrayal of trust is that of a father turning on his child. It is so great that it threatens the fundamental intelligibility of the world, for, like the detective who solves the crime, the father acts as the guarantor of truth. The end-of-the-world scenarios of *Germinal* and *La débâcle* are there to attest to the cataclysmic effects of this loss of the subject's confidence in the system of representation that sustains his mental life. For Zola, the Dreyfus Affair was already a repetition—of his childhood trauma.

The Rape of the Republic

The symbolic system at stake in *Truth* is of course the political ideology of the Ferry educational reforms in their attempt to secularize the schools and wrest control from the Catholic educational system run by the so-called Congregations, loose organizations of brothers (and sisters) attached to the Church but not ordained priests. As Mitterand and others have shown conclusively, this struggle for control of the minds of the young had abated in the following decade, but was revived with a vengeance by the Dreyfus Affair (Mitterand, "Notice" 1492, 1494). The renewed strife led, on the one hand, to the 1901 law that for all intents and purposes outlawed the Congregations, and then to the official separation of Church and State in 1905; on the other, to a deep rift among the Dreyfusards, between Jaurès and the socialists who supported the government of Waldeck-Rousseau in celebrating the victory of the Republic over the authoritarian enemies of parliamentary democracy, and Clemenceau and the journalists of his newspaper, *l'Aurore*, who insisted that there would be no real republic until the people were educated to understand and respect democratic values (Cassaing 304; Mitterand, "Notice" 1493–94). Zola came down on the side of Clemenceau, concluding that secular education designed to turn the 'crowd' into the 'people' must come first if social, economic, and political reforms were to be feasible.

The keystone of the republican ideological edifice was, as we have seen, the claim that there exists a universal secular morality capable of taking the place of the Christian moral system and replacing the believer's subservience to unquestioned authority with the promotion of the citizen's freedom of inquiry. Zola's choice to begin his novel with the commission of a crime presented a subtle challenge to that claim, beyond the obvious parallel to the false accusations and anti-Semitism of the Dreyfus Affair, and the equally obvious attempt to tar the religious right with the same brush of immorality the latter used in politics and in fiction to attack secular education. By locating the crime within the walls of a public school, Zola seems to hint that although the crime was committed by a Catholic teacher, a share of the guilt belongs to the republican school system. The idea that the secular schoolteacher is partly to blame is made explicit when the townspeople suggest that Simon allowed the crime to happen by housing his nephew on the ground floor, almost inviting intruders to enter the boy's room. The very fact that he, an *instituteur* in the reformed primary schools, should permit his Jewish ward to continue attending the Catholic school indicates a certain degree of complicity between the secular and the religious schools. Far from promoting the universal morality at the heart of the theoretical definition of republican identity, as the new primary schools were supposed to do, in reality they cooperate with the Church education that makes the crime and its cover-up possible, and this collaboration is the source of the *mal social* that Marc senses from the start.

When, nonplussed by the people's refusal to acknowledge the evidence of Simon's innocence, he reflects on the reasons for their obtuseness, Marc asks himself how that is possible in a Republic a third of a century old. Shouldn't the wise reforms of the primary schools have produced "a conscious democracy, freed at last from the age-old errors and lies" and "a freer and freer people, won over to reason and logic, capable of certainty and justice" (179)? As expected, at first he puts all the blame on the shoulders of the Church, its recognition of the importance of controlling popular education, and especially its latest stratagem, the *ralliement,* "using free laws in order to keep locked in the jail of its dogmas the millions of children whom those same laws were supposed to liberate" (179). But the real culprit is not the *ralliement* in itself; no, it is the founders of the Republic who have fallen for the *esprit nouveau* and appeasement (180).

The result of the 'new spirit,' as Zola saw it, was that the irrational mode of thinking not only persisted in France but was allowed to flourish in the very bastion of secularism, the new Ferry primary schools. Among the articles Zola clipped out while preparing his novel was one titled "Le cléricalisme est au coeur de l'école laïque" (Clericalism is in the heart of the laic schools; *V* 41, n2), and he announces this theme in his initial description of Mlle. Rouzaire, the *institutrice* of Maillebois's supposedly secular girls' school at the time the crime is committed, who has her pupils recite the catechism and is completely at the service of the local priest, abbé Quandieu (41). After Simon is convicted, when the influence of the Church is at its peak in Maillebois, Marc's replacement, a weak fellow named Méchain, gives in to Mlle. Rouzaire's pressure and institutes daily morning and evening prayers for the boys. In order to put a stop to that practice and to reassert republican principles in the school, Marc's mentor, Salvan, the director of the departmental normal school he attended, invites him to take over the job of *instituteur* in Maillebois.

Méchain is not the only member of the public educational hierarchy to bow to the Church's pressure. As the campaign to dishonor Simon reaches a fever pitch just before his first trial, there is a mass defection of hitherto reliable anticlerical teachers, whose patriotic zeal and love of the military after the defeat of 1870 make them easy prey to the nationalist anti-Semitic propaganda spewed forth by *Le Petit Beaumontais* (123). More dangerous than the *instituteurs* are Mauraisin, the primary school inspector, who, in Salvan's words, becomes a "traitor to the Université, won over to the Congregation . . . in the certainty that the Church would be victorious," and Depinvilliers, the principal of the *lycée* in Beaumont, the departmental capital, who delivered the republican school over to the Jesuits (125).

The fight to the finish between science and religion that Zola depicts in *Truth* is therefore not merely a face-off between two external enemies, each determined to eradicate his adversary. The target of the educational crusade that Mark undertakes as his mission is an internal foe, the religious system that already holds the nation in its grip through its control of education. Now the language Zola uses to describe this situation that he is at pains to oppose is highly significant:

> In sum, I'm taking the moment of the apparent failure of the Republic. *Republicans* who helped to found the republic, who counted on the schools to found it yet *who unwittingly allowed themselves to be penetrated by scheming clericalism*, the much vaunted new spirit. (*Ébauche* folio 413, *V* 649; emphasis added)[3]

The traumatic plight of France that Zola takes as the main subject of his novel is none other than an ideological rape, the insidious penetration of the republicans, and the Republic, by scheming clericalism. At the origin of the novel there is thus a parallel between physical and mental violation, and in both cases the ultimate danger is the incursion of what one would like to consider the external enemy into the interior, of the body, of the mind, of the nation. And of woman. Zola attributes the growing disunion between Marc and Geneviève to the machinations of the clerical party, who want to prevent the teacher from proving Simon's innocence and Brother Gorgias's guilt, which would of course discredit the Church and transfer authority and power to the public schools. It is just when he has discovered new evidence against Gorgias that the clericals provoke the physical separation of the couple. As we have seen, they employ the age-old tactics of the Church to dominate women and thereby to control their husbands and sons. Their chief maneuver is to use the first confession and communion of a young girl as a kind of spiritual penetration, a defloration whose effects are designed to last throughout life.

The fundamental fantasy of the novel derived from Zola's personal experience thus acts as the link between the crime that launches its plot, the anticlerical tradition, the fight to extricate religion from the secular schools, the theme of women's enslavement and liberation, and the political situation at the time of the Affair. In each case, it is a matter of a literal or metaphorical rape, by a religious or secular father.

Now, as Cassaing astutely points out, Zola divided the characters in *Vérité* into three groups in his *fiches-personnages,* rather than the two that would be expected in a purely Manichaean confrontation between clericals and republicans: the clericals, the bourgeois republicans who have permitted the Catholic invasion of the Republic, and the socialist republicans who are genuinely committed to driving Catholicism out of the Republic and replacing it with the secular faith (Cassaing 311). In the text Zola repeatedly stresses that it is the bourgeoisie whose complicity in iniquity has allowed the crime and the false conviction of Simon to take place. Nelly Wilson points out that it is "the silent majority, the ignorant masses, the cowardly politicians, the fearful good citizens [*bons bourgeois*] [who] are responsible for widening the Simon case into the Simon Affair" ("Mise en fiction" 489). She notes that Marc calls the policy of the republican authorities "the hidden will to do nothing," an apt description of the official world of the novel. Darras, the mayor of Maillebois, avowed republican, anticlerical, and friend of Simon, complains that if only he had a more solid majority in the town council, he would certainly have acted courageously "instead of being reduced to the most diplomatic opportunism." The local deputy, Lemarrois, former friend of Gambetta, a good Radical and firmly ensconced in power, is nevertheless afraid to do anything to jeopardize his position as a committed defender of the Republic in the department in the upcoming elections. Not surprisingly, after he is reelected, he is unwilling to bring up the Affair, for fear of compromising important legislation and the survival of the republic itself. The Mélinist prefect, Hennebise, like so many of the officials of the Third Republic, denies the very existence of an "Affair," while the young careerist deputy Marcilly makes it a policy to please all his constituents by playing the Simonist with the teacher's supporters, the anti-Simonist with his opponents (Wilson, "Mise en fiction" 490–91).

That the ignorant masses should be easily duped or stirred to hatred does not surprise Marc, however much it saddens him; but how is it, he wonders, that whether out of fear, hypocrisy, naked self-interest, caution, or political savvy, the inaction of the entire clan of republican officials cooperates with the Church in perpetrating a conspiracy of silence about what has become the Simon Affair? In his response, Marc uses the same words, 'iniquity' and 'crime,' earlier applied to Zéphirin's tragedy and Simon's conviction, thus linking the complicity with the Church and anti-Semitism to the bourgeois's desire to oppose the rise of the workers and socialism at all costs.[4] It is this denial of social justice that belies the politicians' declarations about the universal morality of their republic. The Simon Affair thus serves as the 'object lesson' that illustrates this general state of injustice.

The bourgeoisie and its political representatives are therefore both the victims and the perpetrators of a *trahison* infinitely more pernicious than anything Captain Dreyfus was accused of, let alone did in reality. The true treason, Zola implies, was not the sale of some minor military secrets to the Germans, nor even the conspiracy mounted by the army and abetted by the Church, but the betrayal of the Republic by its French political fathers. In this sense, the reviewers who saw the novel as a failed attempt to transpose the Dreyfus Affair into fiction completely missed the point. And the critics who rely almost exclusively on the preparatory notes give some of Zola's remarks too literal a reading, not taking into account the fictional transposition of the ideological themes into the novel form. While it is true that Zola thought of the Simon case as the pretext for his portrayal of the political and social situation of the Republic at the turn of the twentieth century, in the text Zola plays on the ambiguity of the word *trahison,* making the crime and the ensuing Affair act as the metaphor of the treason committed by the republican authorities that made the Dreyfus Affair possible.

Truth is all about the Dreyfus Affair, for it is *trahison,* treason and betrayal, that forms the bridge between Zola's personal trauma, the national trauma of the Dreyfus Affair, the disintegration of Marc's marriage, and the primary ideological conflict of the text. In Zola's eyes, the general amnesty the government granted participants in the Dreyfus Affair was itself a betrayal of the Republic. In his "Letter to the Senate" during its debates on the amnesty, he accused the entire French government of treachery (*La vérité en marche* 141). Why? Because, for the sake of appeasement, the amnesty was designed to "save the skin" of the real enemies of the Republic: the nationalists who call Jews traitors because they have no country and call their defenders traitors because they put truth above the army; the Church that exploits anti-Semitism to bring the nation of nonbelievers back to Catholicism by arousing ancestral hatreds based on the claim that the Jews betrayed Jesus and can never be forgiven for that crime (138–41). Worst of all, the amnesty will close off the last opportunity to bring the truth out into the open (145). But that public betrayal was also a personal trauma for Zola, the individual, for, he charged, the amnesty was designed to silence him and the others who were defending justice by putting them in the same bag with the true criminals. That was the ultimate lie (*équivoque;* 135). Colette Becker and Véronique Lavielle assert that healing this "deep wound" was one of Zola's principal motivations for writing the novel ("Préface" 10; see also Cassaing 302–4).

What infuriated Zola most about the amnesty was that it deprived him of the opportunity to clear his name. For him personally it was a denial of justice (134). It was himself as well as the fathers, then, whom Zola was anxious to vindicate through his text, a desire apparently magnified by his own sense of guilt. It seems as though he felt that he too shared some responsibility for the crimes he attributed to the fathers, his own and those of the Opportunist Republic, for he ascribed a degree of complicity in the policy of *apaisement* that made the rape of the Republic possible to even the most exemplary educators in the novel. Simon was guilty of allowing the Catholic teacher to intrude into his nephew's room, and he sent Zéphirin to the Congregationist school, even though he and the boy's father were Jews. While the critics tend to exempt Marc and his mentor, Salvan, from the general condemnation of the characters who renege on their obligations to the Republic (see, for instance Becker and Lavielle's "Préface" 17), in fact they too compromise with the Church. During the period when Geneviève has left Marc, Salvan, the one who first introduced him to Geneviève, confesses his complicity openly, reproaching himself for his action "in consenting to marry free thought with the Church" (428). Salvan thus represents the retrograde Republic that has invited the enemy into the fortress by arranging the unholy matrimony of big money with big religion, bourgeois State with monarchist Church.

Moreover, Marc himself is guilty of the same "treason," since he not only consented to the marriage but fell in love with the very Catholic Geneviève! Was he not attracted to her, in truly specular fashion, precisely because she was the object of desire of the Other, of her Catholic family and of Catholicism in general? Is that not the secret of his struggle with Mme. Duparque for Geneviève's allegiance? Right from the first night, as Marc ruminates over his relation to Geneviève, he admits that his "tolerance" of her convictions in allowing their daughter to be baptized is an act of appeasement, stemming from his desire to "live in peace with the ladies [Geneviève's mother and grandmother]" (67). (Zola of course did the same with his daughter, although perhaps for different reasons; i.e., allowing the girl the freedom to choose, care for her future.) This small hint is amplified enormously once Geneviève has left him. Marc bitterly regrets his fear of ruining the "sweet peace through love" they enjoyed (273), he, the committed republican teacher who has educated everyone in the area except his own wife. Thus he castigates himself for doing nothing to combat her religious faith, the source of their discord: "If he was suffering now, it was from his prideful illusion, his laziness and his selfishness in not acting, through cowardly fear, at bottom, of spoiling his happiness in love" (275). Even now, although he is resolved to fight, the respect for the other's freedom and sincere beliefs prevent him from using any weapons other than persuasion, discussion, the example and the logic of life (275). But are they sufficient to prevent his daughter Louise from falling onto the "mortal error" of Catholicism (275)?

Zola makes the connection among the corruption of the Republic, Geneviève's defection, and Marc's inactivity explicit when he has Marc include himself in the guilt for the injustice done to Simon: "It was a pain, a shame from which he could not recover, which haunted him as though it were a crime in which he had participated" (165). Zola makes Marc's identification with Simon explicit by having him literally take the Jewish teacher's place, as the *instituteur* in Maillebois's primary school.[5] Here, then, is added impetus for Marc's desperate need to quell his doubts by unearthing the truth of the crime: He himself has abetted the betrayal of the Republic on which his identity depends. In *Truth* as in the stories Žižek analyzes, there is a dialectic between two different truths, the objective truth of the facts of the case that point to the one perpetrator, and the subjective truth that everyone is guilty of the murder in their unconscious desire. The detective thus "discharges us of all guilt for the realization of our desire" (59).

That Marc does harbor murderous desire is evident from his unceasing efforts to eradicate the Church. He can allow himself to indulge this urge openly, because he considers it a matter of survival, the Republic's and his own. What he cannot admit is the existence within himself and his colleagues, the proponents of secular rationality, of a seemingly gratuitous drive to rape and kill that has no 'rational' basis, that is acted upon for mere enjoyment. Marc's ultimate nightmare is that such an irrational impulse should function within him the way the Church now operates inside the Republic, destroying it from within. This is the truly devastating fear that turns the detective's world into a hall of horrors. Now if his fellow *instituteur* Simon could have had such a concealed desire, then so could he, Marc, especially since the two share the guilt of propitiating the Church. Marc must shift all blame from Simon to

Brother Gorgias, from the rational republican to the irrational churchman, for the same reason he must dedicate himself to eliminating the
Church from the education of the children of the people. In both cases
it is a matter of expelling from within the hidden desire to enjoy the
rape that is undermining the mental integrity, of Marc as of the French
nation.

Utopia and the Trauma of Desire

Marc's mission, as he understands it, is to undo the betrayal that has
authorized the rape of the Republic, by expelling the enemy from its
stronghold within the gates of the nation in order to restore the integrity
of the symbolic system upon which its identity and that of its citizens
depend. Convinced by the Simon Affair that the bourgeoisie is rotten
beyond all redemption, he sees the only hope for the regeneration of
the nation in the people (498). It is this conviction that justifies Marc's
mission as a schoolteacher and explains Zola's reason for choosing an
instituteur as his hero (498). Only by breaking the link between the
bourgeois government and the Church can Marc prevent the continued
reign of injustice in the nation (204).

But is he right? Does the spread of education prevent the repetition of iniquity? It would seem so. The first three books of *Truth* paint
a rather grim picture of the divided France of the Dreyfus Affair era,
while Book Four depicts the ideal republic of the future, in which the
goals of liberty, equality, truth, and justice are realized. Zola marks the
transition from the present to the future partly through the progress
made in women's liberation. The theme permeates Zola's novel of education, first, because he was convinced that education was both the root
of the problem of women's dependency and its solution, and second,
because, as Marc comes to realize (338–39), he believed that independent and enlightened women were the key to a free, healthy, and unified
republic.

One of Marc's closest collaborators in his campaign of educating
the French people is Mlle. Mazeline, the enlightened schoolteacher
appointed to the girls' school next to Marc's in Maillebois. She illustrates both the progress and the limits of Zola's notion of liberation,
which is, in most respects, identical to that of the Opportunist authorities such as Ferry, Sée, or Félix Pécaut, for whom the ultimate goal of
women's liberation was to prepare good republican mothers and wives
(161). However independent she herself may be, Mlle. Mazeline agrees

with Michelet that the most important goal of women's education is to overcome the disunity of French families in which progressive republican husbands are estranged from their pious and reactionary wives (353).

While Mlle. Mazeline has sacrificed her personal desires for love and maternity in order to devote herself to her mission, women of succeeding generations aim to reach the promised land that she can only gaze upon from a distance. Zola brings this evolution to life for the reader by producing a snapshot of the four generations of women in the family of Marc and Geneviève, at the moment when her mother is on her deathbed, pleading with Geneviève and Louise to leave the house of the family matriarch, Mme. Duparque. The younger each is, the closer she is to health, life, and liberty. Mme. Duparque, seventy-eight years old, the incarnation of intransigent, authoritarian Catholicism in the novel: She is gaunt and yellowed with age, with rigid features matching the narrow Catholic piety that stifles all impulses toward warmth, light, and life. Mme. Berthereau, aged fifty-six, is softer and more supple than her mother, but unable to free herself from her religious training. Geneviève herself is caught in the conflict between her love calling her back to her husband and her Catholic upbringing that prevents her from returning to him. Eighteen-year-old Louise, "freed at last, having escaped from the priest's stranglehold on women and children," has returned to "happy nature, to the glorious beneficence of the sunlight, with a cry of youth and health" (482–83). Louise remains a transitional figure, nevertheless, who is allowed to make up her own mind about taking catechism lessons and first communion, but who, by virtue of this very choice, is not free to avoid following the wishes of either her Catholic mother or her freethinking father.

It is Louise's daughter, Thérèse, who represents the truly emancipated woman of the following generation in the utopian future Zola imagines to conclude his gospel. Liberated by law (in the fictive world of Zola's utopian Republic) as well as by upbringing, Thérèse is also financially independent, for, like her mother and grandmother, she is herself an *institutrice* who earns a generous salary from the grateful Republic of Zola's dreams. As a result, she really can act on her own initiative, refusing to take back her adulterous husband despite her grandparents' desires and advice to the contrary.

This record of progress is measured according to a system of simple binary oppositions, cold versus warmth, darkness versus light, authority/obedience versus individual will/freedom, and, ultimately, life versus death. All these are exemplified, and in fact controlled by one other dichotomy, sexual love versus Catholic faith. A kind of reverse Emma Bovary, Mme. Duparque turned to religion at the age of thirty, because her husband was unable to satisfy her sensual needs or her desire for love. Too strict to take a lover, she gleans whatever sensual pleasure she can from her "mystical rendezvous with the blond Jesus" (478). Her daughter did know love with her husband, but he died suddenly, and, forced by poverty, at the age of twenty-nine Mme. Berthereau moved back in with her mother, now a widow herself. Always pious, she becomes as strict a Catholic as Mme. Duparque, but with a certain gentleness due to her awakening to love and life. Her devoutness cannot erase the memory of her husband's love, however, and she suffers from the despair of lost happiness (30). It is this sentiment that motivates her on her deathbed to implore her daughter and granddaughter to leave Mme. Duparque's house before they too succumb to the living death of a sexless and loveless existence.

Other proofs of France's "renewal" (532) some thirty years after the Affair abound. Geneviève resumes her profession as schoolteacher, a role she had abandoned before the opening of the story because she was unable to find a job in the same community as her husband. Simon's rehabilitation begins when his son Joseph is named as assistant (*adjoint*) to Joulic, the *instituteur* in Maillebois after Marc and Geneviève have moved back to teach in the town of Jonville, where Marc began his career. Now Simon's socialist lawyer, Delbos, who had been virtually ostracized after his defense of the Jewish teacher, finally wins an election as deputy, a sign that the times have changed, "like an annunciation" in the prophetic discourse of this gospel text, that the people are becoming strong and will soon overthrow the bourgeoisie (533). The narrator takes obvious pleasure in enumerating the good fortunes of each of the pupils of the secular schools, before concluding that each succeeding generation lives more happily than its predecessors, thanks to the improved education they receive (537).

Eventually, in Zola's ideal world, the *Cour de cassation* (analogous in this function to the United States Supreme Court) revokes Simon's conviction, and the townspeople agree to finance a monument to him, a house to be built for him facing the newly constructed public park, as reparation for the guilt of Maillebois (564). Chapter 3 combines Simon's official exoneration and triumphant return to Maillebois with another exorcism (Cassaing 314); that is, Brother Gorgias's public confession of his crime, this time with all the sordid details of his mad, 'unnatural' passion (603). The implication is of course, as proponents of Enlightenment have argued since the eighteenth century, that perverse desires flourish and drive men mad when their 'normal' sexual desires are frustrated. Like the mystical desires the Church fosters in women, the ascetic teachings and practices of Christianity will inevitably produce intolerable sexual frustration in the faithful. The vow of celibacy and the isolation from the community at large are as noxious for men as first communion and confession are for women. The difference is that men will act out their frustrations.

As in a standard detective story, at last the various strands of evidence, intuition, and logical surmise are rewoven into a coherent narrative in Gorgias's confession. As though to confirm the cathartic effect of this restoration of meaning, Simon makes his appearance just as the monk is finishing his speech, causing the mood of the crowd to swing from hatred to joy. Even the mitigated repetition of the crime that opened the story, the assault on Rose outside Zéphirin's old room, seems to confirm the efficacy of Marc's action, for this time, it will be recalled, the townspeople put into practice the lessons in truth and justice Marc and his band of *instituteurs* have taught them. They refuse to believe the "accursed family" theory the Church tries to revive concerning François, Simon's grandson, and they speak up to identify the real offender. Thus, as Laville argues, the episode is designed specifically to confirm the thesis of the novel, that secular education of the people in the primary schools of the Republic leads directly to the reign of truth and justice in the nation and thence to an increase in the happiness and general well-being of the populace (Laville 247–48).[6]

With the source of the evil so thoroughly uprooted, it would seem that little remains for Marc other than to inventory his successes and his succession. Yet in fact the novel does not end with this happy denouement, and the utopia Zola imagines is not quite so tidy as some critics would have us believe. There is one loose end that is not tied up by the progress of enlightenment: When François returns home after the kidnapping attempt, Thérèse must decide whether to take him back. Ostensibly in order to help her make up her mind, but actually to ensure that the peace and harmony of his utopia will remain unbroken, Marc calls a great family reunion in the schoolhouse. This meeting quickly degenerates into a session of gloating about the progress accomplished since the Simon Affair, with special emphasis on the recently accomplished—in the fictional world of the story—legal and moral emancipation of women that leaves Thérèse free to make up her own mind about her husband. Marc's indulgence in self-congratulation is brought to a sudden halt, however, when Thérèse's deliberations bring her into direct conflict with his vision of utopia. Not at all certain of loving her husband still, Thérèse exercises her newfound equality and autonomy by refusing to take François back. Her choice thus exposes the inherent contradiction between two aspects of the republican utopia: the assertion of individual autonomy and the institution of social harmony through unity.

Now it would have been easy for Zola to maintain that this fly in the ointment of utopia was simply the result of its as yet imperfect establishment, and that after a sufficient number of generations, such defects would vanish. Instead, he offers quite a different explanation, through the mouth of Thérèse, who thereby complements her legal emancipation with the assertion of her intellectual resistance to Marc's version of the perfect society. When Marc advises her to take François back in order to spare both of them needless suffering, she replies that suffering will always be with us, especially that caused by thwarted passion (638).[7] This final episode, the direct aftermath of the repeated crime, constitutes the declaration of independence of woman, but also of suffering and irrationality, from patriarchal laws and customs but also from the Enlightenment reason and unity those laws represent in the modern world of Zola's ideal Republic.

Even before the attack on his great-granddaughter took place, Marc was forced to acknowledge that the frustration of celibacy is not the only cause of men's irrational behavior, when he learned that François had run off with Colette (617–18), a deed whose similarity to Gorgias's behavior Zola underlines by having Marc call it an "act of passion-induced madness" (624). Thérèse reiterates the idea that man's irrationality is ineffaceable when she attributes François's "folly" to the "eternal madness" of the human heart (637).

Here Zola is harking back to a major theme of the *Rougon-Macquart* series, emphasized notably in *Nana:* Desire is that aspect of human life that refuses to obey the rules of rationality, self-interest, ambition, fortune, and even physical and mental well-being. In her probing analysis of truth in *L'Assommoir,* Françoise Gaillard brought out the fact that the role of irrational, antisocial desire was often attributed to the people, precisely because they remain outside the pale of bourgeois norms (23).[8]

The social order not only tries to erase the heterogeneous; once the difference is erased, society wants to ensure that this Other will be forgotten entirely by creating in its members a desire not to know. In the days of *L'Assommoir* and *Nana,* because the bourgeois republic identified both its own particular social order and literary truth with universal morality (Gaillard 18), it desired not to know about the promiscuity, alcoholism, and despair endemic to the Parisian working classes. Zola of course insisted on bringing these very things to light in his working-class novels. The parallel situation in *Truth* (170) as in reality at the time of the *Évangiles* consisted in the efforts of the government of appeasement to "bury" the Dreyfus Affair, to "dig a deeper hole and throw the amnesty in on top" as Zola puts it in his "Letter to the Senate" (140), coupled with the writer's determination to unearth the truth about it.

But there the parallel stops. In *Truth* it is not only the powers that be who want to hear nothing about the social wound, it is the people's desire not to know that allows the original crime to be blown up into an Affair in which the fate of the nation is at stake (see Cosset 107). In *Truth,* it is precisely their heterogeneity, their unenlightened ignorance, superstition, and irrationality that Zola aims to eradicate through education. Given his treatment at the hands of the mob during the Affair, it is not surprising that the image of the people in the early parts of this socialist novel should be highly unsympathetic, especially in contrast to *L'Assommoir* or *Germinal,* because this time they are in connivance with the oppressors. Yet in a sense they are also portrayed as victims, of Catholic education and nationalist newspaper propaganda. But whether victims or oppressors, the path to utopia necessarily means that they must not only be instructed in the experimental method but also divested of their irrational hatreds. Whereas the heterogeneity of the people (and of women, as the example of Nana demonstrates) in the *Rougon-Macquart* novels corresponded nicely with Zola's empiricist stance at the time, according to which the observational facts of human behavior were expected to remain independent of preconceived idealist notions of human nature, it no longer squared with the thrust of *Truth,* where knowledge is often attained by pure logic, and facts merely confirm the truths of reason.

The goal of republican education for utopia is to eliminate heterogeneity, if at all possible. Nowhere is this ideology of universalism more apparent than in the solution to anti-Semitism proposed in the text. Zola's utopia is the ultimate melting pot, in which everyone will be the same. In order to end sectarian prejudice and ensure national unity, he makes a special point of marrying the two Jewish Simon children, Sarah and Joseph, to two non-Jews, Sébastien Milhomme and Louise Froment (see 529 n1). After several generations of this practice, the result is that there remain neither Catholics nor Jews nor religious differences. The paradoxical result of this plethora of mixed marriages is that eventually there can be no more. However satisfying this outcome may be to Marc or Zola, both of whom suffered in one way or another from their involvement in mixed marriages, it is ironic that, in the end, the Enlightenment solution is not so different from that of the bigot.

But stamping out all difference is no simple matter. The very structure of the novel indicates the nagging presence of a residue that refuses to permit utopia to reach completion. No matter how many times the ghosts of irrationality are exorcised, they still come back to haunt the world of the living. Book Three would seem to achieve narrative closure: Simon has been pardoned; Geneviève has been freed from her ghosts. Yet Zola felt compelled to add a fourth book, in order to represent the new generation completely imbued with Enlightenment values, Simon's triumphant return to Maillebois after his official acquittal and the narrative closure of Gogias's confession revealing the complete truth of the crime. These loose ends are knotted up at the end of chapter 3 of Book Four, yet once again Zola felt it necessary to add a fourth, antiutopian chapter, in reverse symmetry to the utopian fourth book he appended to the three realist Books of the text. The three parts plus one composition of the fourth book of the novel is thus itself a repetition in miniature of the structure of the entire text, as though no matter how much the novel displays, there will always be something that lies beyond its capacity for representation.

Changing people's minds, remaking their identities, eliminating the ghosts of the past, nothing is sufficient to eradicate irrationality, for it inhabits the rational symbolic system as such. As Marc admits, if it is a pity that people will always be 'mad' enough to suffer from their irrational passions, then it would be truly mad to try to eliminate madness altogether (617). The goal of republican education, in Jules Ferry's original plan or in Zola's revised socialist version, reaches its limit in the nonnaturalness, or excessive naturalness, of human "instinct," passion, madness.[9]

In *The Four Fundamental Concepts of Psycho-Analysis,* Lacan explains this insistent residue as a trauma that repeats itself until it can gain full recognition. In particular, the beyond of representation indicates the secret connection between a father and his son's dead body, namely, as Kierkegaard argues, the father's sin (34). Lacan goes on to claim that in Shakespeare's tragedy, Hamlet's father cannot find rest in the other world because he was killed in the flower of his sinning. The play is not about the prohibitions the father imposes but about the son's profound doubt of this "too ideal father."

In any given real instance, those 'sins' would be specific actions or omissions in the life of the father, and there is good reason to believe that in Zola's case, it was the boy's molestation and the father's untimely death experienced in the unconscious as an abandonment. But there is a trauma that no one can escape, because it is built into the structure of every symbolic system: the message from the beyond, the beyond of representation, that is, is that the particularity of the subject's being cannot be spoken (Lacan, *Le désir et son interprétation* 266), especially in the universalizing system of the enlightened republic. The neo-Kantian system, with its universally human person, and the positivist system, with its self-effacing subject of scientific objectivity, both exclude the individualized subject. In his role as support of the symbolic system, the "father" has successfully "stolen the soul" of his "offspring." This threat to the very existence of his children is the fundamental assault and murder.

As we have discussed, the nemesis of Marc the positivist is emptiness, that which is omitted from the logos. In all logic, then, his project must be a more or less frantic attempt to plug up the holes in the signifying system guaranteed by the fathers of the ideal Republic, for that is the only way he can consolidate his own identity. As Lacan explains, the *manque à être* is not only the lack of being, it is also, as in the English translation Lacan himself proposed, a "want-to-be."

Marc's solution to the problem of the gap in the Other is to assume the role of father himself. Unable either to accept the passivity necessary to joining the social order as an obedient citizen, or to identify with the power of that order to subjugate its subjects as do the authoritarians, the good republican must take on the fantasmatic role of the fecundating father who sows his seed to create a new world in his own image. As Baguley observes, Zola's utopian solution in the *Évangiles* is the narcissistic proliferation of his self in the form of the many descendants he confers upon his protagonists ("Du récit polémique au discours utopique" 118). I would simply add that he resorts to this remedy because the danger he is striving to overcome is the grave injury to that same narcissism represented by the initial trauma. *Truth* in fact repeatedly evokes the imagery of Hugo's "Saison des semailles" to describe Marc's pedagogical activity, advertising the fantasy of paternal creation as antidote to the dread of filial helplessness in a rhetorical appeal to potential educators of France. Zola thus grants to the *instituteurs* and to those who support republican Enlightenment the vocation of author, in the strong sense of absolute creator given the term by the Romantics, and which he had always attributed to himself as novelist. This is the fantasy incentive designed to compensate for the alternating fear of the fathers and the attempt to clear them of any guilt.

The text thus acknowledges what it nevertheless denies, that since, like the rumors and legends it aims to supplant, it too produces its own object of reference, its system of artistic and political representation comes from and is imposed by a particular subjective stance and is therefore as violent as the one it seeks to discredit. If Zola nevertheless insists on grounding his utopian Republic in a universal scientific truth allegedly independent of any human will or idea, that is due to his need of an imaginary community of the enlightened that can safeguard his identity against the threat of pure nothingness.

It is in the context of this dread of the beyond of representation that the choice to end the novel on the topic of women's liberation takes on its full significance. From the start the theme of nothingness gravitates around the female figures of the novel. The mystical object of Geneviève's childhood education and desires is *le néant* (nothingness), as we have seen. But in addition, in accordance with the most traditional patriarchal ideas, women, at least those who have been raised in the traditional manner, are themselves conceived as having no inner shape or personality, as being a kind of 'nothing' waiting to become something thanks to the form-giving masculine (and artistic) principle, as in the Aristotelian tradition. Both Marc and Salvan take it for granted that it is the husband's paternalistic duty to 'form' his new wife in his own image, an 'artistic' duty Marc reproaches himself more than once for neglecting to carry out due to his complacency, inertia, and fear. Salvan expresses this fantasy of paternal omnipotence when he "concludes" with his student that in a loving marriage the man is the god who recreates the girl he marries (274), and Geneviève agrees that she is the "work" (*œuvre*) that he has begun (492).

Ventriloquized first by Mme. Duparque and Catholicism, Geneviève still remains a puppet after returning to her husband, only now it is the positivist line that she follows in her role as *institutrice* (508) and parrots in her final words to her husband at the family reunion (635). The threat of nothingness is its allure, the almost irresistible attraction that the mystical beyond exerts, along with its promise of the enjoyment of total subjection. In making Geneviève into a copy of himself, Marc is striving to repudiate the ultimate danger to his identity, feminine desire, especially the desire to acquiesce in passive enjoyment. As long as "woman" is the name of the traumatic nothing that haunts the positivist imagination from the beginning of the novel to its end, Geneviève's emancipation from the one father, the Church, can only lead to the filling of that void with the seed of another, her husband, the artist, the (re)producer. As long, that is, as Zola equates subjectivity with nothingness, nothingness with femininity, and femininity with rape, madness, and annihilation, the liberation of women and of the Republic can only mean turning them into the opposite of all that, that is, into replicas of men. That is equality with a vengeance.

The Truth of *Vérité*

Due to Zola's overt aim of passing judgment on the contemporary political situation, critics have generally categorized *Truth* as a thesis novel, saddled with many of the notorious defects of that genre. Even enthusiastic and well-informed Zola specialists, such as Baguley, Cosset, and Laville, feel they must first acknowledge the typical flaws of the thesis novel in Zola's *Évangiles* and apologize for them, before showing that the novels nevertheless have some strong redeeming social or literary value. Like Zola's other *Gospels*, they argue, *Truth* departs from the canons of the naturalist narratives of the *Rougon-Macquart* series, in which it is the objective facts rather than any subjective idea that structure the story; observation and documentation precede all general conclusions; and in any case the narrator abstains from interpreting his story, leaving it to the reader to draw her own conclusions about its meaning and its potential implications for action.

The trouble with this neat dichotomy is that its two sides simply cannot be held apart. While the distinguishing traits of the *roman à thèse* are indeed to be found in *Truth,* it would be an easy matter, space permitting, to show that, with the exception of the narratorial pronouncements, every one of them is also present in Zola's naturalist fiction. It is not just the continuity of themes or the preoccupation with education that link the later novel to Zola's earlier works, as several of the best scholars have pointed out (e.g., Mitterand, Borie, Laville); nor is it only a matter of returning late in life to the method of his beginnings, when he illustrated the theses of Michelet and Taine in *Madeleine Férat* and *Thérèse Raquin* (Borie, *Mythologie de l'hérédité*); nor even the use of isolated familiar techniques such as the introduction to the milieu of the novel through the eyes and the free indirect discourse of a 'stranger'—Marc in *Truth,* like Florent in *Le ventre de Paris,* Denise in *Au Bonheur des Dames,* or Étienne in *Germinal* (Cosset, Laville). As the preface to the *Rougon-Macquart* series attests, in the heyday of his career, as before and after, Zola conceived of the novelist's task as didactic through and through, a fact that has not entirely escaped the eyes of the critics either.[10] Moreover, the actual structure of *Truth* appears to be a direct application of the procedure Zola outlines in his well-known description of the naturalist novel in *Le roman expérimental:* "We seek out the causes of social ills [*le mal social*]; we perform the anatomy of classes and individuals in order to explain the breakdowns that occur in society and in people" (133). What is bothering Marc the night after the rape and murder of Zéphirin are discovered, if not the mysterious *mal social* he senses behind the crime committed against a defenseless schoolboy? What stimulated Zola to change the subject of his projected novel from a portrait of his "ideal Republic" to an analysis of the present-day society that produced the Dreyfus Affair and its temporary conclusion in amnesty for all parties, if not his determination to unearth the causes that made these 'breakdowns' possible? In *Truth,* the crime, the ensuing Simon Affair, and the rampant anti-Semitism that feeds it are presented as symptoms of a wider social evil, the infiltration of the Third Republic and its educational system by the Church, just as the plots of *L'Assommoir* and *Nana* are arranged so as to demonstrate that alcoholism and prostitution are symptoms of the general plight and the vengeance of the working classes under the Second Empire.

Even the use of Marc as spokesperson for the writer's theories is not a radical departure from Zola's practice in the naturalist novel: Étienne in *Germinal,* Denise in *Au Bonheur des Dames,* Claude in *L'oeuvre* (and in *Le ventre de Paris*), Pascal in *Le docteur Pascal* (and already in *La fortune des Rougon*), to name just a few prominent examples, all serve a similar purpose. The crucial difference between the *Rougon-Macquart* series and the *Évangiles* consists in the textual consequences of Zola's avowed aim in the latter not only to identify the causes of the social evil that forms the heart of his 'experiment,' but also, as he puts it, to 'heal the wound.' Whereas previously Zola had been content to let his experiments speak for themselves and to leave it up to society to continue or to alter the conditions producing the situation described,[11] in *Truth* he takes matters into his own hands and actually represents the process of the 'cure' and its results. To paraphrase Levaillant's characterization of Anatole France's political development, Zola moved from 'narrative as spectacle' to 'narrative as intervention.'

The most obvious divergences from the earlier works resulting from this modification are the depiction of an imagined, utopian future state of the nation, and the unambiguous identification of Catholicism as the root of the evil with the consequent overt, single-minded and violent battle waged against it in word and plot. In order to bring about the desired end, a third change becomes necessary: Zola must have his protagonist attain his own truth at an early stage. In the climactic moment at the end of Book One, much like Étienne Lantier deciding to stay and fight after his first day in the mine in *Germinal,* Marc receives the 'revelation' that determines his mission and his identity (188–89): Rome has divided France into two warring factions in its battle against Enlightenment, and the most noble mission in a new democracy is to educate the people (194). But, unlike Étienne, Marc has once and for all overcome all hesitations and doubts about the causes of the evil, the proper remedy, and the means of effecting the cure. Although Zola's schoolteacher does undergo a harsh process of political education in the first part of the novel, in which growing insight is matched by personal suffering, much like the living nightmare Zola endured as a result of his intervention in the Dreyfus Affair, *Truth* abbreviates the period of qualms and indecision that plague Étienne throughout *Germinal,* the array of mutually contradictory social and political theories he must strive to assimilate and sort out, the vagueness of the enemy he wants to combat, and the difficulty of formulating an effective plan of action against it—in short, all the ambiguities and complexities that constitute the intellectual component of that book's lasting appeal.

Looking beyond the customary debates about Zola's use of utopia to criticize present-day France and the desirability of the image he projects of the nation's future, Baguley puts his finger on a problematic aspect of utopia that escapes most of the critics. The defect of Zola's narratorial interventions is not simply that they are fundamentally separate from the story and attempt to control its interpretation, as the standard criticism of the thesis novel would have it, but that they are themselves utopian in that they create a world totally independent of reality ("L'Evangile républicain de Zola" 121). The critic thus condemns in one stroke two of the favorite bêtes noires of realist writers like Flaubert and Henry James, authorial intervention and utopian imagination. But it is only according to the standards of realism that the relation Baguley so shrewdly discerns constitutes a fault. In fact Suleiman, the most widely recognized authority on the genre to whom Baguley, Cosset, and Laville all refer for their critiques and apologies, uses this very argument to claim that *Truth* is not a genuine thesis novel. Thesis novels are by definition realist texts that give themselves out as pure, that is, as innocent renditions of reality (*Authoritarian Fictions* 72), whereas *Truth* contains prophetic speech and utopian situations and calls attention to its fictional status by referring to an absent text, that of the actual Dreyfus Affair. The result is that the novel requires a double reading whose discovery depends on the reader, unlike the standard canonical novel, which, in authoritarian fashion, imposes an explicit and univocal interpretation of the story in the primary text ("Passion/Fiction" 97–98). Suleiman classifies Zola's third Gospel as a "transposition," a genre she invents in order to describe narratives that employ the indirect speech typical of allegory, yet represent traumatic historical events in more realistic style than is found in most satirical and allegorical texts (96).

Suleiman admits that only a fine line demarcates the transposition from the allegory, and we may add the same qualification about the distinction between the genre she defines and the thesis novel. The important point is that *Truth* has many of the characteristics of allegory, not the least of which, as Baguley noted, is the national significance of Geneviève's story. In *The Language of Allegory,* Maureen Quilligan endorses the view that "allegories do not need [exegetical interpretation] because the commentary is already indicated by the text" (31). Here is one more respect, then, in which the thesis novel resembles allegory and other parabolic narratives. But, Quilligan adds, "[the author's] 'commentary' of course is not discursive, but narrative . . ." (53). By that statement she refers to her theory that the key to allegory is "the generation of narrative structure out of word play" (22). The action of the first book of Spenser's *Faerie Queene,* for instance, is built around the polysemy and homonymy of the words 'error'—errant, wandering, sin—and 'despair'—dis-pair, pair, em-pair, re-pair (33–42).

Now, although Zola does not indulge in the complex, extensive, and often exuberant verbal play found in Spenser's masterwork, he does generate the main actions of his novel out of discursive signifiers. The gothic element that plays so important a role in Geneviève's story is a narrativization of the verb *'ramener'* as used in the following commentary: "execrable anti-Semitism, this revival of religious hatreds, this Catholicism exacerbated and masked, with which they hoped to bring back [*ramener*] to the priests the non-believing people, who had deserted the churches" (191). Geneviève is literally, that is to say, metaphorically, dragged back involuntarily to the Catholic faith, and along with her, the nation at large. That action is, in turn, a metaphor of the political policy of the *esprit nouveau.* Moreover, the connection established in the passage between being pulled back and the anti-Semitism that ensures Simon's conviction is mirrored in the concordance between the alterations in Geneviève's beliefs about his guilt and the changes in her relation to Marc. On a larger scale, it is the words *trahison, traître,* and their meanings of treason, betrayal, and treachery that govern the three main plots of the novel. Finally, the most general and the most particular metaphorical dramatization is that of the word *pénétrer,* which generates the original crime, undermines the claim of universal morality, embodies the fear of feminine passivity, and makes palpable the rape of the Republic.

It makes no sense, then, to assert that the idea distorts the story, or that the story is a mechanical application of the idea. In fact, the text is a far-reaching exploration of the various meanings and implications of the key signifiers that generate its action. In this context, it is worth noting that the passage Baguley cites, in apparent condemnation of the *Évangiles,* comes from a book by Louis Marin in which the latter argues that the ability of utopian discourse to reveal the constructive power of language is a virtue rather than a failing. The utopian text opposes the mimetic notion of realism in that it overtly designates itself as the intervention of the Other into reality. It is performative in that, while it forms part of a signifying system and denotes a being outside language, as does the realist text, the being it designates is the product of its own operation (Marin 122). Quilligan's theory of allegory explains exactly how Zola's utopia, and his entire text, manifest the creative power of language.

This power, too, is transformed into narrative action: The entire mystery of the Simon Affair turns on a bit of text, the torn-off corner of the handwriting sample found in Zéphirin's room. This piece of evidence is of course Zola's transposition of the *bordereau* (memo) that played such a key role in Dreyfus's conviction, but that is all the more reason to believe that fictive language is as powerful in historical as in textual reality. In fact, the intertext for *Truth,* the traumatic historical event at its origin, is not the Dreyfus Affair in itself, whatever that might mean, but its textual representations, the discourses of the Church, the government, and the various political factions, the newspapers of his enemies—*Le Petit Journal* and *La Croix*—and of his friends—especially the *Aurore*—and his own writings—his articles, letters, and preparatory notes (not to mention his *Bête humaine*). Likewise, Zola's mode of operation as a writer, and Marc's as an educator, are purely verbal—persuasion, discussion, and examples drawn from life as Marc puts it during his struggle against Mme. Duparque, a stark contrast to the exploitation of personal seduction that defines the Barresian educator's power. Moreover, although Marc's identity is at stake in his search for the truth, it is by intellectual effort, not immediate experience, that he attains his goal. The allegorical structure of the text works against the overtly didactic aspects of the text, inviting the reader to imitate the hero's learning process by exploring the implications of its generative terms in order to understand, to penetrate, the true sense of *trahison.* In this respect, *Truth* functions as an 'analytic' rather than a transferential novel, a text in which the subject is forced to find her own way through the labyrinth of signification in her search for her truth. Like the other major novels of education of the period, *Truth* is a *mise-en-abîme* of the novelist's didactic role, in this case that of the naturalist writer.

Yet *Truth* is not a wholehearted work of allegory. From the positivist perspective espoused by Zola and the ideologists of the Third Republic at the turn of the century, any such performative use of language violates the tenets of the experimental method and of realist representation that define Zola's naturalism and form the basis of Marc's project of education. The key to the fundamental contradiction between what the text says and what it does lies in the naturalist conception and function of desire in its relation to subjectivity. Zola certainly made no secret of the fact that in his *Gospels* he gave free rein to his dreams and desires. Utopian discourse, narratorial interventions, the interpretation of the story included in the text, all these traits associated with thesis novels bear witness to the operative force of authorial subjectivity in *Truth*. Yet this open avowal of the role played by authorial desire blatantly contradicts the positivist ideology expressed in the text, in Marc's thought, and in the events of the plot. As Geneviève's struggles show, the most formidable adversary of the hero's project of Enlightenment, because the antithesis of realism on every level, is precisely the irrational desire for something other, for that which is lacking in reality, exemplified for the secular republic by the mystical union with Jesus that cannot be consummated.

The contradictions in *Truth* are strictly analogous to those in the political project of creating new republican citizens. The text thus unwillingly exposes to view a *trahison* still more fundamental than all those discussed so far: it is not only that Enlightenment universalism leaves no room for difference or dissent, as Baguley, among others, observes ("L'Évangile républicain de Zola" 119), but that in using language to remake people it cannot help contradicting in its practice the principles, of universal cognitive objectivism, of positivism, or of the equally universal neo-Kantian subject of cognition and morality, which define its justification and its objectives.

The peculiar virtue of Zola's thesis novel resides precisely in these contradictions. What Baguley calls the "fantasmatic character" of representation in the novel is not restricted to its utopian aspects. All representation in the novel is fantasmatic, not in the sense of the imaginary, the unreal, but in that every major plot line branches out from a set of fantasies understood as particular relations of the republican subject to the symbolic system and the fathers who support it. The overarching plot of the novel consists in the battle to expose the treachery of one set of fathers who undermine certainty and identity, and the effort to replace them with another who will guarantee the subject's being. These are the fantasies designed to attract Zola's readers to the political position he champions. *Truth* thus brings into the light of day a truth that is purposely repressed in the practice of more traditional realist and art for art's sake narrative as well as in political literature and philosophy, the inextricable bond between fantasy and ideology in real literary and political movements.

CONCLUSION

The Erotics of Politics

❦

The Crisis of Authority

The Republic of the republicans staked its legitimacy on the universality of the democratic principles it claimed to uphold, and the avowed goal of its program of educational reforms was to transform the identity of its citizens by inculcating those same principles into their minds. Although mandated by the government rather than a disenfranchised group, this program followed the lines of populist politics analyzed by Ernesto Laclau in his book *On Populist Reason* (2005): Isolate an internal enemy in order to undermine the latter's claim to govern and even to be a legitimate member of the populus; promote one demand to the status of general representative of all discontents in order to unite various, often incompatible factions; and thereby produce a political identity claiming to be the legitimate representative of the entire population.

From the start, opponents on the right challenged that program precisely because of its dependence on universal principles, which, by virtue of their generality, were alleged to be too abstract to inhibit the perverse natural "instincts" of mankind, and, due to their objectivity, to ignore the concrete feelings that prevent people from acting cruelly toward their fellow human beings. At the end of the nineteenth century, the new, right-wing nationalism renewed and modified these attacks with the claim that republican universalism ran roughshod over the historical and regional particularity that constitutes the real core of human identity, both of individuals and of the communities they form. Moreover, harking back to Vallès's criticisms in his Jacques Vingtras trilogy, they blamed the Republic for creating a group of alienated *déclassés,* people who had profited from the opportunity for upward social mobility the regime offered to all citizens in the name of universal equality, but who had thereby lost the secure identity of their origins without obtaining an alternative sense of belonging and empowerment in its place.

Meanwhile, in the wake of the Dreyfus Affair, critics on the left chided the Republic both for being too universalist and for not being universalist enough. For many moderate socialists, the republic betrayed its own principles by condoning the violation of truth and justice in its prosecution of Captain Dreyfus, by shirking its duty to educate the populace at large in the methods of objective inquiry, and by ignoring the economic bases of the freedoms it promised its citizens. Anarchists on the left accused its educational system of robbing its pupils of their spontaneity and individuality by imposing upon them a universal moral- ity that utterly neglected the real particulars of their conditions and their lives. Some made the still more radical argument, similar to that of the right in this respect, that parliamentary government, through its sys- tem of representation that reduces individual voters to mere numbers, deprived the members of society of their right to self-government.

The ideology of the Third Republic was composed of two appar- ently incompatible doctrines, positivism and Kantianism. Their fusion was made possible by the fact that each was more or less consistent with the liberal principles of 1789; each proposed a program of education and politics consonant with the interests of the new industrial and finan- cial bourgeoisie; and, above all, each was a reaction to what has been variously called the crisis of authority, of legitimacy, or of government that the new republican leaders faced. The crisis of authority has been attributed to a variety of factors both by participants in the ideologi- cal battles of the times and by later commentators. For Comte it was the lack of social consensus, the mental, social, and political anarchy fomented by the Revolution that, from the beginning of his career as a follower of Saint-Simon, his doctrine of sociology was designed to rectify by producing a unity of ideas among the population that would restore the social coherence necessary for the establishment of order. In this respect at least, virtually all Comte's disciples remained faithful to his thought until the end. The neo-Kantians Renouvier and Pillon looked to both the social and intellectual upheavals of the century that, in uprooting traditional French customs and beliefs—by which they obviously meant Catholicism—had undermined the nation's spiritual authorities, and to more proximate political and historical causes, especially the military defeat at the hands of the Prussians and the brutal suppression of the Commune, which had discredited the country's temporal authorities. Clarisse Coignet argued that the political instability of the nineteenth century had arisen because of the disparity between the democratic secular institutions of the country and its mores, which had remained for the vast majority monarchical and religious (*De l'éducation dans la démocratie* v). Like Michelet, Ferry, and Sée, she saw the struggle between these two forces dividing the family, with progressive husbands confronting traditionalist wives. And in accord with the positivists, she deems that societies need strong convictions and a common ideal in order to form a strong social bond (viii). That is why Coignet concludes that, with religion no longer serving this function, modern society needs a morality that arises from within the experience of the individual conscience, which can thus serve as the basis for self-rule (viii). And, of course, for Gambetta and Ferry, it was the dogma and temporal power of the Church that undermined the intellectual and political authority of the secular state.

To these perceptions of the proponents of liberal ideology must be added those of its critics, for opposition pressure also contributed to compressing Kantianism and positivism into an ostensibly cohesive amalgam. By the middle of the century, according to some historians, the administrative centralization started by Napoleon I, along with accelerating industrialization, had led to the demise of the local organizations and customs that had previously made up the texture of people's lives. Now they faced only the impersonal, modern, anonymous, centralized State (Tison-Braun 42–43). While this description echoes the reproaches brought against the Third Republic itself, especially by conservative critics like Taine, Bourget, and Barrès, and while more recent data tend to prove that these effects did not become widespread until the last two decades of the century (see Weber 41–42, and throughout), it is not far-fetched to imagine that they had already become visible in the more advanced regions of the country during the Second Empire. Others, with an interest in political history, add that the state had lost prestige due to the repeated changes of regime during the century and the stinging loss of face resulting from the defeat in the war. These effects were compounded by the fact that the republic was voted in by a very slim majority and by the ensuing internecine battles among the factions during its first years of existence. In the eyes of the masses, the State had lost its aura of sacredness with the demise of the monarchy and the disappearance of a prince who sat on the throne by the grace of

God (Arendt 46). In the early years of the Republic, monarchists and conservatives saw the defeat by the Prussians as a punishment from God for the luxury, excesses, and corruption of the Empire and called for a regime of penitence and moral austerity in order to regenerate France and its army (Mayeur and Reberioux chap. 1). Many intellectuals—one might think of Zola in this context, as well as the Kantians—repeated the same reproach and the same call for moral renewal, but instead of begging God for forgiveness through processions, miracles, and pilgrimages, on the contrary they identified Catholicism with the decadent Empire and blamed it for the defeat (Digeon 333–36).

Beyond their differences, however, all agree that the crisis derived in large part from the aftereffects of the Revolution and the disputes between secularism and religion, whose most evident manifestation in the nascent Republic were the Ferry reforms of education. In *The Disciple* Bourget put his finger on the fundamental problem that gave rise to these political and ideological clashes: It was the advent of modern science embedded within the Enlightenment theory of the subject that destabilized individual and national identity. The ultimate meaning of scientific objectivity is the desubjectification of nature, that is, the refusal to admit the existence of a personal presence operating within the universe. The paradox of the science taught in republican schools was its basic presupposition that the world is intelligible yet devoid of intelligence, design without a designer; and Kant's mere "postulates of reason," as he calls them in the *Critique of Practical Reason*—God and the afterlife—do not satisfy most people's craving for a guarantor of existence.

The void in the heavens gives rise to several traumatic themes, the first of which is the inadequate or treacherous father-educator of the Republic. In Sixte and his philosophy, Robert Greslou seeks a surrogate father who will protect him from the overwhelming sexual desires that threaten his identity, but the master of republican psychology proves inadequate to the task. As in a typical *Bildungsroman*, Sturel, Roemerspacher, and their comrades from the Nancy *lycée* leave home hoping to find the leader who will solidify their identities by replacing their roots—Bouteiller, Taine, Hugo, Napoleon, Boulanger—only to find that their true fathers are the ancestors they had a left at home. In *Contemporary History* it is the prefect Worms-Clavelin and the corrupt Republic he represents, along with the fathers of the Church and the aristocracy, who fail in their duty to uphold truth, justice, and equality. The subtext of *Truth* is the hidden and disavowed guilt of the fathers: the republican fathers, who are too weak to resist the penetration of the

Church into their ranks; Simon, who lets his ward attend the Congregationist school and allows the crime to be committed on school grounds;
François, who is falsely accused of attacking his daughter; Gorgias and
the Church, of course; and even Marc's mentor, Salvan, who encourages
him to marry a good Catholic girl.

The same attacks and counterattacks on the Other's Other undermined the stability of representation, for it too cries out for a firm
basis on which to stand, and it was this crisis that formed the context
for the flourishing of the novel of ideas at the turn of the century. I
would suggest that the primary thrust of the newly codified genre was
to present both the predicament opened up by the lack in the Other
and its remedy. Bourget articulated the problem in his *Essais:* Reading in
the modern world leads to mental confusion because it is overburdened
with a multiplicity of points of view, a welter of interpretations, and the
sheer weight of previous literature. According to Bourget, "each of us
perceives, not the universe, but *his* universe; not naked reality, but what
his temperament allows him to appropriate from that reality" (*Essais*
I: 130; emphasis in original). Jean Moréas, for his part, announced
that "objectivity is nothing but pure semblance, empty appearance" (*Le
Symboliste* 7 [October 1886], quoted in Ouston 55 n37). "Reality varies
with each one of us, since it is the sum of our habits of seeing, feeling
and thinking," Barrès informs us in *Sous l'oeil des barbares* (29). Mansuy
sums up the prevailing view among these and other fin de siècle symbolist and antipositivist writers, such as Vogüé or Wyzewa, as follows:

> The world as we perceive it, the outside world no longer appears as
> supreme reality, but as a subjective creation, for it reaches us through
> the senses and the categories of the understanding. The ultimate truth
> must not be sought in phenomena but in the thinking subject, in the
> organizing intellect. (431)

While there are significant philosophical differences among these
antiobjectivist views—Kantian formalism, Schopenhauerian vitalism,
something approaching Nietzschean perspectivism, and a more or less
naive subjectivism—they all concur that every notion of reality is the
result of human interpretation. Whether this plethora acts as the impetus to an exhilarating liberation, as for many symbolists, or leads to
mental confusion and despair, as Bourget would have it, the literary critics of positivism were united in rejecting the claim of a single, objective,
and therefore innocent reading of the world.

Armed with this conviction, the novelist now conceives of her task in very different terms from that of the realist writer. No longer a matter of representing reality, the goal of the fin de siècle novel will be the self-reflexive task of exploring the process of representation itself, the ways in which the variety of particular points of view, including the one that gives itself out to be objective and universal, are constructed as specific interpretations (Raimond 76). But, if that is the case, then it is equally impossible for any narrative, no matter how it is recounted, to be totally idea free. An innocent narration is just as unthinkable as an innocent reading, for it must be recounted from a narrative stance that entails specific ideological—although not necessarily political—presuppositions. The main corollary of this position is that the radical distinction between narrative and idea or thesis, on which virtually every criticism of the thesis novel is based, is untenable and is, in fact, the result of the so-called realist illusion. By its very simplification of the relation between story and idea, the genre makes visible the fact that meanings inform reality and it forces its readers to recognize the fundamentally ideological nature of all fiction. If the critics justifiably perceive many thesis novels as authoritarian, that is because such texts magnify the ever-present but more hidden coercive force of every symbolic system that functions within or like a language.

Neither the novel of ideas nor novels dealing with education origi-nated in the Third Republic, but the Ferry reforms precipitated a new combination of both these traditions in the form of the novel of educa-tion. From the earlier novels with a thesis it drew the techniques the genre had developed to hone realist fiction into a trenchant weapon of ideological polemics. It called upon the many prior works of satirical fiction devoted in whole or in part to taking potshots at the teachers and institutions of French education for a series of standard themes and characters to adopt, adapt, or attack. It often appropriated the form of the *Bildungsroman,* in which a young hero is brought to maturity, usu-ally through the influence of one or more mentors who instruct him or her in the ways of the world and reveal the ideas that give shape and coherence to his or her experience.

In their form and structure the novels we have studied counter the pretensions to autonomy of *l'art pour l'art* and the claims to objectivity of positivist realism, which imply either that the text contains its own meaning or that it has none. The genre lays bare the inevitable process of making meaning through the self-reflexive inclusion of an educator figure within the text, who mirrors the act of didactic interpretation performed from a specific point of view by the narrator or the spokesperson character and the similar act of reading by the younger character and the audience. As Suleiman observes, in the thesis novel the action of the hero most often consists in learning how to interpret, how to discover the 'right' meaning of experience (*Authoritarian Fictions* 78). Whether the reader makes meaning or meaning makes the reader, in either case it becomes evident that there must be such a process, that meaning in narrative is neither automatic nor avoidable. The pertinent questions are not, therefore, whether ideas have infiltrated, contaminated, and perverted the story, but which ideas are in bed with which stories, and what is the relationship between the two in a particular text or genre.

Unlike the contemporary decadent and symbolist movements, the novels of education take the potential multiplication of ideological points of view, with no transcendent standpoint from which to deliver the unvarnished truth of the world, as a wound to be healed. Just as the Republic was striving to confer transcendent status onto its particular ideology by claiming for itself the prestige of universal morality, so the thesis novels attempt to legitimize their right to assume the role of pedagogue by defining for themselves a privileged, if not necessarily objective, point of view which the narrator or spokesperson loudly asserts to be the one correct meaning of the narrative. For Bourget it was the logical necessity of proper induction from observation to law, for Barrès the French national standpoint, for France the autonomous judgment provided by a rich life of the mind, and for Zola the eternal truth of science.

These assertions of privilege correspond to the disavowed performativity made evident in *Truth*. Each of these claims to truth is a polemical attempt to produce the transcendent social unity to which the proponent aspires, rather than to express a preexisting, inherent, factual, or potential unity (Laclau 29). In Laclau's terms, this is the beginning of the process of naming the demand one wants to promote as the object of social desire. Naming allows one demand to take on the role of representing the social goal as a whole, the totality of society and its unity through a metonymic process of association, and this always involves affective investment (26). This object, Lacan's *objet petit a,* or a-object, as I translate it, is supposed to fill the lack that is undermining national and individual identity and unity.

Laclau goes on to point out that, because of the logic of the a-object, there is always a "mutual contamination of universality and particularity" (25). A specific, limited object takes on the role of the totality, becoming what he calls, after Antonio Gramsci, a "hegemonic forma-tion": "History is . . . a discontinuous succession of hegemonic forma-tions" (25). Only the signifiers of particular demands can become the representation of the fulfilled society, of universality; there is nothing else, no ideal perfection, as in Kant or Marx; no Hegelian teleology toward which society strives or moves; no universal ground in being, in the way things are, or in the existence of a specific set of characteristics (25).

We have seen that neither our novels nor the Republic itself were able to escape this mutual contamination of the universal and the par-ticular. As noted in chapter 1, the contradiction between the Republic's theoretical universality and practical particularity existed on multiple levels. Barrès, and to a lesser extent Bourget, reverse this process, mak-ing particularity into a universal value for individuals, regions, and the nation. Zola follows the lead of the Republic, taking its official pro-nouncements literally and using them to impose a particular ideology onto the public at large. France is the most interesting case. M. Bergeret prides himself on his appreciation of general ideas, and his conception of truth requires abstraction from the real for the purpose of making disinterested judgment possible. Yet he lauds the concern for particular-ity of the Republic, in opposition to the monolithic universality of the Church's ideology, and combines the two in his vision of communist society in which the State disappears and the totality of society becomes nothing more or less than the activity of its individual members.

Culture Wars and National Identity

As early as 1927 Julien Benda recognized that in the modern era, politi-cal wars would entail the new phenomenon of culture wars, as every nation "hugs itself and sets itself up against all other nations as superior in language, art, philosophy, civilization, culture" (14). What Benda failed to appreciate was that the exacerbated promotion of national cul-tures was a response to the undermining of the traditional guarantor of existence, due in large part to the very Enlightenment principles he was defending.

Just as the Enlightenment depersonalized the universe, so scien-tific objectivity desubjectified the individual. Yet disinterested objectiv-ity is, paradoxically, a subjective stance in itself. Each of our novels enacts one of the dilemmas of the modern subject by posing a varia-tion on the question: What would happen if people were to apply the principles of the Enlightenment subject taught in the republican schools to the realm of human affairs and interpersonal relationships? Bourget's disciple takes this question literally, attempting to live by disinterested observation and experimentation alone. France wonders what it is like to live the life of the Cartesian subject, a being abstracted from the world and thus isolated from his fellow human beings yet obliged to live and develop a desire within his society. In keeping with his Decadent beginnings, Barrès asks what life is like for those who, denying the existence of any overarching, objective, point of view, must settle for what is just one of a series of apparently equal, specific, limited points of view. By pushing universalism and objectivity to their outer limits, Zola's hero unwittingly posed the republican subject's dilemma in its most acute form: How can he be both the abstract Cartesian subject and an agent for change in the world?

The Enlightenment subjects of the nineteenth century suffered from these dilemmas because without the guarantee of Descartes's god of truth, the abyss of nothingness opened up beneath them—and within them. The fantasy scenarios in all four texts indicate that it was the glimmering suspicion of the otherness within the self that motivated people to reject with all their might what they felt to be the enemy within.[1] For writers on the right, the contingencies of history, region, and family were the bulwark against the ravages of universalism and the incursion of governmental power into the life of the subject, but also against the presocial instincts that threaten to expose the void at the heart of the self. So much for the fear. The lure was the more or less surreptitious gratification of sadistic impulses in eradicating the hated foreign element that had infected the body politic, which represented the simultaneous elimination of their own, otherwise uncontrollable desire.

Both writers on the left agreed that the Catholic Church was the enemy inside the Republic and the minds of its citizens, but their conceptions of the nothingness it fostered and the remedies they proposed were different. For France the danger was authoritarian rule and the emptiness of the externally controlled social self that renders the masses indifferent to principles, incapable of finding the truth, and vulnerable to hate campaigns. His solution was twofold: to fill the void in the individual's mind with education, with the promise of a satisfying inner life that would guarantee individual judgment and the ability to develop one's own desire; and to fill that of the Other by satisfying its every desire, thereby freeing its members from the psychological and economic pressure of society and the State. The nothingness the positivist

Zola feared was that of the 'mystical' because nonexistent supernatural, that which exercises uncanny attraction and power precisely because its functioning and the enjoyment it holds out to its believers allegedly escape observation and reason. For him, contingency represented the arbitrary capriciousness of a senseless world, in which the dark forces of the passions run wild. The remedy was therefore the establishment of universal intelligibility, so that all mysteries could be solved. To do so required replacing the inadequate, deceitful, or corrupt fathers of the Church and the Opportunist Republic. The new schoolteachers, starting with Zola's persona Marc, would be compensated by the opportunity to become the fathers of the new Republic of truth and justice.

Ultimately, it was the dread of nothingness provoked by the challenge of science to the Symbolic that paved the way for culture wars by producing the need to rely on society or culture, and hence on politics, for a guarantee of existence, even as it opened up the possibility for literary texts to play a major role in the battle to define and determine those conflicts. The political strategy of identifying a noxious internal enemy can no doubt be traced back through history in various civil and religious wars, and it was certainly present during the Revolution, with the attempt to root out alleged counterrevolutionaries. What distinguished the Third Republic was the use of that strategy in combination with the quasi-official adoption of Enlightenment ideology and its dissemination in the new Ferry schools. It was this combination, along with the upheavals due to the recent defeat and the Commune, which triggered the fears of lost identity, emotions that were spread and magnified by the polemics in learned journals and the mass press. The political identification of the internal enemy thus triggered fears of the alien enemy within the self.

In short, what made the political battles of those times and of ours into culture wars was and is the unwitting or deliberate politicization of extimacy. The achievement of our four novels of education was to bring to light this coupling of the internal enemy with threats and promises of identity through the exposure of the fantasy scenarios accompanying the political programs.

APPENDIX A

Chronology of Historical, Intellectual, and Literary Events

1774   Johann Gottfried Herder, *Another Philosophy of History Concerning the Development of Mankind*

1788   Immanuel Kant, *Critique of Practical Reason*

1789, French Revolution

1789   Declaration of the Rights of Man and of the Citizen

1792–1804, First Republic

1790   Edmund Burke, *Reflections on the Revolution in France, and on the proceedings in certain societies in London relative to that event*

1792   Marie Jean . . . Condorcet, *Report on Public Education . . .*

1800   Louis de Bonald, *Analytical Essay on the Natural Laws of the Social Order*

1804–14/15, First Empire

1806   Creation of the *Université,* national administration of all secondary and higher education

1814/15–30   Restoration of Bourbon Monarchy

1814   Joseph de Maistre, *Essay on the Generating Principle of Political Constitutions*

1830–48, July Monarchy

1830–42   Auguste Comte, founder of positivism, *Course on Positive Philosophy* (6 volumes)

1840   Pierre-Joseph Proudhon, *What Is Property?*

1848–51, Second Republic

1848   Comte, *A General View of Positivism*

1848   Charles Renouvier, *Republican Manual of Man and of the Citizen*

1848   Ernest Renan, *The Future of Science* (first published in 1890)

1850   Edgar Quinet, *The Education of the People*

1850   Falloux laws giving control of education to Catholic Church

1851–70, Second Empire

1858   Proudhon, *On Justice in the Revolution and in the Church*

1860   Étienne Vacherot, *Democracy*

1865–70   *La Morale Indépendante*, Alexandre Massol, journal editor

1866   Ligue de l'enseignement founded by Jean Macé

1869   Clarisse Coignet, *Independent Morality in Its Principle and Its Object*

1870   Jules Ferry gives Salle Molière speech, April 10

1870   Hippolyte Taine, *On Intelligence*

1870   Théodule Ribot, *Contemporary English Psychology*

1870–71   Franco-German War

1870–1940, Third Republic

1871   Paris Commune, March–May

1871	Founding of the neo-Kantian journal *La Critique Philosophique,* Renouvier & François Pillon, editors
1871	Gambetta campaign speech in Bordeaux, June 26
1874	Émile Boutroux, On the Contingency of the Laws of Nature
1875	Republican Constitution
1875, 1876	Ferry gives speeches to Freemasons
1875	Renouvier, *Short Treatise on Morals for Use in Laic Primary Schools*
1876	Jules Vallès, *Les réfractaires*
1876–94	Taine, *The Origins of Contemporary France*
1877	French translation of Eduard Hartmann's *Philosophy of the Unconscious*
1877	Republican majority in Chamber of Deputies
1878	Vallès, *The Child,* first volume of Jacques Vingtras trilogy
1880	*Evenings at Médan,* Émile Zola editor of collection of naturalist short stories
1880	Zola, *The Experimental Novel,* manifesto of naturalist literature
1882	Republican majority in Senate
1880–82	Jules Ferry, minister of public education, introduces laws establishing obligatory, free, and laic primary schools; Camille Sée introduces laws establishing public secondary schools for girls
1881	Founding of École Normale Supérieure for women at Sèvres, first director Mme. Jules Favre
1882	Renan, *What Is a Nation?*
1882	Paul Bert, *Civics Education in the Schools*
1883	Ferry, *Letter to Primary Schoolteachers*
1883	Elme Caro, *Monsieur Littré and Positivism*
1883	Ferdinand Brunetière, *The Naturalist Novel*
1883	Death of Henri Dieudonné, the Count de Chambord, last of the Bourbons
1885	Death of Victor Hugo (born in 1802)
1886	Octave Feuillet, *Aliette*

1886–89	Boulangist threat to the Republic
1883	Paul Bourget, *Essays in Contemporary Psychology*
1885	Bourget, *New Essays in Contemporary Psychology*
1886	Eugène-Melchior de Vogüé, *The Russian Novel*
1887	*The Manifesto of the Five,* attack on Zola and his novel *Earth*
1889	Henri Bergson, *Time and Free Will: An Essay on the Immediate Data of Consciousness*
1889	Bourget, *The Disciple*
1887	Wilson scandal, Daniel Wilson, son-in-law of Jules Grévy, president of the Republic, accused of selling state honors
1888–91	Maurice Barrès, *Cult of the Ego* trilogy
1892	Pope Leo XIII's encyclical calling for French Church to rally to Republic
1893	Founding of the new spiritualist journal, *Revue de Métaphysique et de Morale*
1894	Eugène Spuller, minister of public education, fine arts and cults calls for "New Spirit" of reconciliation with Church
1892–93	Panama Canal scandal; legislators accused of taking graft to support financing of canal
1895	Brunetière, "After a Visit to the Vatican"
1896–98	Méline president of the Council of Ministers
1897	Anatole France, *The Elm-Tree on the Mall,* and *The Wicker Work Woman,* first two volumes of *Contemporary History*
1897	Barrès, *The Uprooted,* first volume of *The Novel of National Energy*
1897–1900	Dreyfus Affair (see appendix B)
1898	Spanish-American War
1899	France, *The Amethyst Ring,* third volume of *Contemporary History*
1899	Pierre Waldeck-Rousseau president of the Council of Ministers
1899–1900	Policy of Appeasement
1900	World's Fair in Paris

1901   France, *Monsieur Bergeret in Paris,* Book Four of *Contemporary History*

1901   Émile Zola, *La vérité en marche,* collection of articles about Dreyfus Affair

1900   Barrès, *Appeal to the Soldier,* second volume of *The Novel of National Energy*

1902   Zola, *Truth* (published posthumously)

1902   Bourget, *L'étape*

1902   Barrès, *Their Faces,* third volume of *The Novel of National Energy*

1902   Barrès, *Scenes and Doctrines of Nationalism*

1905   Émile Combes's laws separating Church and State

The Dreyfus Affair

❧⟨◉⟩❧

Main Participants

Major Esterhazy	The actual traitor, author of the memo (*bordereau*) used as main evidence proving Dreyfus's guilt
Major Henry	Military intelligence, forged a note indicating Dreyfus's guilt
General de Pellieux	Directed inquiry into Esterhazy's involvement that absolved him of any guilt; witness at Zola's trial, designated Henry forgery as 'absolute proof' of Dreyfus's guilt
Major Du Paty de Clam	Military intelligence, examining magistrate in Dreyfus's initial court-martial
General de Boisdeffre	Chief of staff at beginning of Dreyfus Affair
General Gonse	Deputy chief of staff
General Mercier	Minister of war at the beginning of Affair
Colonel Sandherr	Head of military intelligence at beginning of Affair, intercepted *bordereau* sent to German military attaché, Schwartzkoppen
Captain Alfred Dreyfus	Accused of passing military secrets to the Germans
Mathieu Dreyfus	Alfred's older brother, worked tirelessly to clear his name

Major (Lieutenant-Colonel) Picquart	Replaced Colonel Sandherr as head of military intelligence, defended Dreyfus to his fellow officers, imprisoned, career ruined
Auguste Scheurer-Kestner	Vice president of the Senate, defended Dreyfus's innocence, brought case before Parliament
Bernard Lazare	Anarchist, waged a campaign in the papers and among intellectuals to prove Dreyfus's innocence

Chronology

October 15, 1894	Dreyfus, identified as author of *bordereau* (letter to German military attaché Schwartzkoppen announcing dispatch of secret military documents), is arrested for spying for the German government
November 1, 1894	*La Libre Parole,* anti-Semitic newspaper, names Dreyfus as traitor
December 19–22, 1894	Dreyfus is court-martialed, found guilty of treason, sentenced to deportation for life
January 5, 1895	Military degradation of Dreyfus
April 13, 1895	Dreyfus is placed in prison on Devil's Island
March 1896	Major Picquart discovers *petit bleu* (message from German embassy to Esterhazy)
April 6, 1896	Picquart is promoted to lieutenant-colonel
August 1896	Picquart discovers that Esterhazy wrote *bordereau*
Autumn 1896	*L'Éclair* and *Le Matin,* large-circulation newspapers, draw attention to supposed proofs of Dreyfus's guilt; Bernard Lazare circulates his document about Dreyfus's innocence
October 26, 1896	Picquart is ordered to duty in North Africa
November 2, 1896	Henry hands forged letter, 'proving' Dreyfus's guilt, to General Gonse
November 6, 1896	Bernard-Lazare publishes his pamphlet, *A Judicial Error,* in Brussels
December 1896	Henry adds more forged documents to Dreyfus's file
May 18, 1897	Picquart writes letter of protest to Major Henry

June 29, 1897	Picquart gives his material to his lawyer, Maître Leblois
July 13–14, 1897	Leblois shows Picquart's material to Scheurer-Kestner, vice president of the Senate, who then informs his colleagues that he thinks Dreyfus innocent
Autumn 1897	Esterhazy and general staff—Gonse, Henry, and du Paty under the protection of General de Boisdeffre—conspire to avoid his conviction; Esterhazy writes three letters to the president of Republic accusing Picquart of forging the *petit bleu*
November 16, 1897	Mathieu Dreyfus publishes his accusations against Esterhazy in *Le Figaro*
January 11, 1898	Esterhazy is acquitted at the court-martial he requested
January 13, 1898	Zola's "J'accuse" is published in Clemenceau's *L'Aurore;* Picquart is arrested and imprisoned
February 23, 1898	Zola is convicted of libel in criminal court (Cour d'Assises)
February 26, 1898	Picquart is dismissed from the army
April 2, 1898	The Cour de Cassation (Supreme Court of Appeal) annuls Zola's conviction
May 23, 1898	Zola is retried by court-martial at Versailles
July 7, 1898	Minister of War Cavaignac reads out supposed proofs against Dreyfus, thus precipitating rebuttals and exposure of Henry's forgeries
July 12, 1898	Esterhazy is placed under arrest
July 13, 1898	Picquart is arrested and prosecuted
July 18–19, 1898	Zola is convicted once again; he flees to England
August 13, 1898	Henry's forgery is discovered
August 31–September 1, 1898	Major Henry's arrest and suicide; Esterhazy is dishonorably discharged from army, flees from France; General de Boisdeffre resigns
June 3, 1899	The Cour de Cassation sets aside conviction of 1894, leading to new court-martial in Rennes
June 5, 1899	Zola returns to France

June 9, 1899	Dreyfus leaves Guiana; Picquart is exonerated and freed
September 9, 1899	Once again, Dreyfus is convicted of treason
September 19, 1899	President Loubet signs pardon of Dreyfus
June 2, 1900	Senate votes general amnesty, which takes effect December 27, 1900
July 12, 1906	The Cour de Cassation sets aside Rennes conviction, thus clearing Dreyfus
July 13, 1906	Dreyfus and Picquart are reinstated in army; Dreyfus is promoted to major, Picquart to general

NOTES

Introduction

1. Ferry was already Minister of Public Education and retained that portfolio when he was named Président du Conseil des ministres in December 1880.

2. See my "Education and Political Identity: The Universalist Controversy" for a more comprehensive review of the literature that follows.

3. All translations from the French in this book are my own, unless otherwise specified.

4. I refer specifically to the production of literary texts that offer representations of the questions of pedagogical theory and practice. For the teaching of literature in the schools, see Ralph Albanese, *Molière à l'École républicaine* and *La Fontaine à l'École républicaine,* and M. Martin Guiney, *Teaching the Cult of Literature in the French Third Republic.*

5. Bourget is referring here to the tradition of British philosophy and psychology going back to Locke and especially to Hume and his popularizer Hartley, as well as to their nineteenth-century followers such as Mill, Bain, and Spencer. Théodule Ribot's *La psychologie anglaise contemporaine,* first published in 1870, was the main source in French for information about this trend, along with Taine's attempted fusion of Hegelian thought with positivism, *De l'intelligence,* also of 1870, in which he adopted Mill's view of the self as nothing more than the series of its states. It was Ribot, however, who became the leading authority in France on the new experimental psychology in the latter third of the century.

6. Earlier in the century, critics and writers spoke of 'novels with a thesis.' It was only at the end of the century that the term *roman à thèse* became the name of a subgenre.

7. In 1902, Bourget published a second novel of education designed, like Zola's *Truth,* to draw the lessons allegedly taught by the Dreyfus Affair, titled *L'Étape* (see Charle, *Paris fin de siècle* 201–26, for a comparison of Bourget's novel with Zola's *Truth*). While the book shows the changes in Bourget's politics since 1889, it adds little to his interpretation of the flaws in republican education or the latter's effect on national identity; hence my decision not to include an analysis of it in my text.

8. In his comparison of *Vérité* and *L'étape,* Charle points out that recent scholarship has shown that the Republic was actually quite stable at the time, and he argues that the crisis actually occurred in the field of the intellectuals rather than in the nation at large (*Paris fin de siècle* 213–15). As the present-day division between red and blue states in the United States illustrates, however, it is quite possible for the members of a nation to feel they are in crisis, even though the government is stable. And the millions of readers whom the popular press—*Le Petit Journal* and the various regional versions of *La Croix,* especially—whipped up into a frenzy of anti-Semitism during the Affair were certainly not all intellectuals; on the contrary.

9. Throughout the decades bracketing the turn of the century, a public debate raged in France over the role of the "intellectual" as educator, a category that included professors and journalists as well as novelists (see Charle, *Naissance des intellectuels;* and Datta, *Birth of a National Icon*).

Chapter 1

1. Actually, with the exception of the crucial elections of the National Assembly in 1871, the republicans had been steadily gaining ground over their opponents since the latter days of the Second Empire, and had held majorities in both houses at various times before the dates mentioned (see J.-M. Mayeur, chaps. 1–2).

2. In reference to nineteenth-century Catholicism, the term "liberal" designates the wing of the French Church that accepted the Concordat treaty, which placed the Church hierarchy under the rule of French law and allowed the existence of other religions, thus rejecting the dogma that there was no salvation outside the Catholic Church. In politics, these were Orleanists, supporters of the monarchical pretensions of the Count of Paris and the rule of the traditional, or 'dynastic,' bourgeoisie that had reigned supreme during the July Monarchy (1830–1848).

3. Church hostility to the Republic lasted well beyond the publication of the encyclical. At the same time, many Catholics saw the call for *ralliement* as the Church's capitulation to Enlightenment ideology.

4. Under the Falloux laws, primary schoolteachers had to submit to the involvement of priests in their classes, were forced to serve as cantors or sacristans in the local churches, and had to teach catechism classes (Compagnon and Thévenin).

5. See Phyllis Stock-Morton's *Moral Education for a Secular Society* for a comprehensive history of the development of what was alternately called 'social morality,' 'independent morality,' or 'laic morality.' Stock-Morton rightly observes that the vital link between Condorcet and Quinet was the philosopher and minister of public instruction under the July Monarchy, Victor Cousin, whose separation of ethics from religion was the basis for all later arguments about independent morality and its teaching in the schools (29–40).

6. This was a change from Comte's earlier position in the *Cours de philosophie positive,* where he argued that it is unnecessary to teach morality in a separate course, since it would result naturally from the eventual victory of positivism in the public mind and from the teaching of sociology (Legrand 29–30).

7. This biographical information on Coignet is taken from the summary of a study by Janine Joliot on file in the Bibliothèque Marguerite Durand in Paris.

8. See Désiré Nolen, "Kant et la philosophie du dix-neuvième siècle" (cited in Digeon, 335 n2). Stock-Morton declares that "although Durkheim completed the theoretical development of *morale laïque,* we must conclude that the last moral philosophy actually accepted by the French for use in education was that of Renouvier" (173).

9. Digeon mentions a host of writers who maintain that, for better or for worse, Kantianism dominated the Third Republic and its schools—A. Cresson, *La morale de Kant* (1897; cited in 334 n2); Victor Basch (cited in 334 n2, itself a citation from Maurras's *Quand les Français ne s'aimaient pas*), as well as L. Daudet, Julien Benda, and Abel Hermant.

Digeon also refers to many writers who attacked Kantianism—Th. Funck-Brentano; Barrès, of course; Fouillée; and especially members of l'Action française, such as H. Vaugeois (336 n2).

10. In 1806 Napoleon established the Conseil de l'Université, an institution designed to organize and govern all secondary as well as higher education in France. In nineteenth-century texts and common parlance the term 'Université' most often designated the public secondary schools (see, for instance, Daudet's widely read novel *Le petit chose* [1868], in which the hero goes to work for the Université as a monitor in a *collège*).

11. For a representative overview of their ideas about morality and education, see Steeg, Buisson, and Pécaut. See also Mona Ozouf 87. In accord with the general thesis of *Teaching the Cult of Literature in the French Third Republic*, that Republican education imitated the Catholic education it sought to overthrow, Guiney contends that the education they instituted owed little to Protestantism; on the contrary, it came to resemble the Catholic education they were replacing (86–88). My point here is simply that the notion of morality they introduced into the schools was heavily influenced by Kantian ideas.

12. Guiney provides ample evidence for the view that the calls for teaching either Latin or literature in the secondary schools were based on the claim that these topics conferred a moral sense on the students through their apprenticeship and appreciation of form rather than content; the cultivation of "taste" was thus both moral and national, in the sense of imbuing pupils with the appreciation of specifically "French" style. This is summed up in Fouillée's pronouncement: "Considered philosophically, grammar has its own morality" (quoted on p. 180).

13. There is some dispute as to Boutroux's impact on Bergson. Parodi, Chevalier, and Scharfstein assert the importance of Boutroux's thesis for the development of Bergson's ideas; others, such as Barthélemy-Madaule in her *Bergson*, deny it any significant role, relying on Bergson's airy dismissal of Boutroux's teaching as being too Kantian (Barthélemy-Madaule 8–9). On the other hand, it is clear that Boutroux's admiring pupil Durkheim adopted his professor's basic mode of reasoning in giving precedence to the social over the individual in *Les règles de la méthode sociologique* (1895). Stock-Morton summarizes the argument as follows: "just as the chemical properties of atoms were insufficient to account for physiological phenomena, so the nature of individuals was insufficient to explain social phenomena" (131).

14. In thus combating rationalistic natural science by linking contingency and freedom to the notion of a voluntaristic God, Boutroux was reviving a tradition which goes back to the thirteenth century, when Bishop Étienne Tempier declared the principles of Averroism, i.e., Aristotelian rationalist philosophy and science, to be heretical (see Gilson). A more immediate predecessor was Jules Lachelier, who argued in his thesis, *Du Fondement de l'induction*, that all causality is subordinate to purpose and therefore to contingency. Bergson stated that he considered Lachelier to be his teacher even though he never took a course with him, so great was the effect of reading *Fondement* while at the rue d'Ulm (Bergson, *Essais et témoignages* 358).

15. On the level of epistemology, despite his reputed "irrationalism," Bergson's main objection to Kant was the latter's restriction of scientific knowledge to phenomena, whereas for Bergson, as for the spiritualist realism of Ravaisson, "the mathematical and physical sciences tend to reveal reality in itself, absolute reality" (quoted in Scharfstein 134).

16. Recall, for instance, Renan's harangue against democracy in *La réforme intellectuelle et morale de la France* as the antithesis of rationality because it represents the triumph of number, "that is, of stupidity and spinelessness" (Digeon 197).

17. Irvin Edman, in his foreword to the Modern Library edition of *Creative Evolution* (1944); Zeev Sternhell, in *Maurice Barrès et le nationalisme français* (1983); and Anna Boschetti, in *Sartre et "Les Temps Modernes,"* all document Bergson's adoption by the political right, even while they skirt the claim that the philosopher himself drew the political conclusions the right attributed to him (see Chaitin, "From the Third Republic to Postmodernism" 783–85). See also R. C. Grogin (85–88).

18. In another textbook, *Livre de lecture et de morale* (1894), Émile Devinat has the children recite the following lesson titled "You love your country": "I love France, my country, because its inhabitants are my brothers, children of the same race, with the same blood and the same ancestors. . . . France is my mother: in my heart there will never be anything above her" (83).

19. This substitution was not complete, however. Despite the complaints of Catholic critics about the vagueness of the religious content of the courses on morals and civics (see numerous articles in *La Réforme Sociale*, e.g., de Metz Noblat, "L'instruction civique à l'école d'après G. Compayré"), most primary schoolteachers and authors of textbooks in the 1880s and 1890s were, as Ferry pointed out to Parliament, believers of some sort, and they included specific references to God in their teachings (Katan 421–22). The only significant function of the God taught in the schools, however, was to guarantee the physical order of the universe, the moral order of the self, and hence the social order of the human world. Thus, even when this conception of divinity was retained, it easily merged into the purely secular versions of independent morality (Steeg, *Cours de morale;* Buisson, *La religion, la morale et la science;* Rauh, *Psychologie appliquée à la morale et à l'éducation; Cours de morale à l'usage des jeunes filles;* Katan 425).

20. In *Molière à l'École républicaine* and *La Fontaine à l'École républicaine,* Albanese details many of the ways the schools of the Third Republic attempted to use the study of the so-called classics to inculcate in their pupils a sense of national identity and unanimity (*Molière* 4–6); and to teach them the morals that undergirded the regime's claims to legitimacy (*La Fontaine* 100).

21. Anderson in fact notes, in a general way, the coincidence of the rise of nationalism with the weakening of religion in Europe and points out that the nation serves the same purposes as religion (18–19).

Chapter 2

1. All references to *The Disciple* are to the anonymous T. Fisher Unwin translation, reprinted by Howard Fertig Publishing. I have occasionally modified the translation after comparison with the French.

2. See Ferdinand Brunetière, "A propos du Disciple"; A. France, "Paul Bourget: *Le disciple,*" and "La morale et la science."

3. The notion of a theory of the subject goes back of course to Descartes, Kant, and especially Hegel, but in nineteenth-century France it was Littré who bemoaned the lack of an empirical theory of the subject in Comte's philosophy, an omission he set out to remedy (Caro, *M. Littré et le positivisme* 125, citing Littré's *Auguste Comte et la philosophie positive*).

4. The French term *revanchard* indicates anyone who aims to take revenge, especially for a military defeat. It was used extensively after the defeat by Prussia in 1870–71 to refer to militaristic French patriots intent on recovering the lost provinces of Alsace and

Lorraine from the Germans. In the novel, Count André is considered a hero for having participated in the war and killed a German soldier.

5. In fact, Greslou compares himself to Faust (147, 172). It should be pointed out that 'pity for human suffering' was enjoying a great vogue at the time in France, contributing to the popularity of George Eliot (just after her death) along with that of Charles Dickens and Charlotte Brontë, and especially of the Russian novel starting with the translation of *Crime and Punishment* in 1884, as well as the publication of several critical studies preceding and including Vogüé's *Roman russe* (Mansuy 429–30).

6. Like Goethe's Charlottes, both the fictional and the real one, Chambige's mistress was also an "older" woman who was married and had children. From the biographical perspective, Bourget's Charlotte can be seen as a replacement for Chambige's maternal Mme. Grille.

Chapter 3

1. These novels have not been translated into English. All translations are mine.

2. Barrès announced a study of contemporary nihilism—by which he meant the poets Baudelaire, Verlaine, Mallarmé, and Rimbaud—in the initial issue of *Taches d'encre* (1884), the first magazine he edited as a young man in Paris. Bourget had just made the term stylish in his *Essais* of 1883. In succeeding years, the word became a commonplace among writers and intellectuals. Édouard Rod makes Renan the great priest of nothingness (*du néant*) in his *Idées morales du temps présent* (1891) (73). Théophile Funck-Brentano, a professor at the recently created École des Sciences Politiques, wrote a book titled *Les sophistes allemands et les nihilistes russes* (1887), in which he blames all the ills of "Western civilization," by which he means every movement dedicated to the modification or overthrow of the political status quo in Europe, on Kant and his successors. As early as 1799, the German theologian and philosopher F. H. Jacobi had labeled Kant's philosophy "nihilism" in a letter to Fichte.

3. A more distant source of these ideas is found in Barrès's reading, at the age of sixteen, of an article about the "young Hegelians" by Saint-René Taillandier in the *Revue des Deux Mondes* of July 15, 1847: "The Ego of Max Stirner" eliminates "everything that is not the ego" (261). "I alone exist, I alone, outside of myself I can know nothing and believe nothing" (258–59). Stirner, he says, "boldly preaches the religion of the ego," "celebrates egoism as the only form of complete freedom" (264; quoted in Frandon, *Barrès précurseur* 54). "No more God, no more human race, no more homeland, nothing outside my being any more, not a general idea, not an absolute principle" (70). The same article condemns the young Hegelians' "exaltation in nothingness" (262).

4. At least, so Barrès seems to imply. In fact, the model for Bouteiller, Auguste Burdeau, was born in 1851. In 1859, when he turned eight, France was still under the Second Empire. Since Bouteiller, like Burdeau, fought and was wounded in the Franco-Prussian War in 1870, his early education could hardly have been carried out under the Third Republic. No doubt Barrès would reply, with Taine, that ever since its institution under the first Napoleon, the University had been an instrument of centralization and deracination (see the last completed volume of Taine's *Origines*, titled *L'école*).

5. Sternhell points out, however, that Barrès's admiration for Soury dates at least from 1888 (*M. Barrès et le nationalisme français* 256; see "La jeunesse boulangiste," *Le Figaro*, May 19, 1888). In her *Orient de Maurice Barrès*, Frandon argues plausibly that in fact Barrès started attending Soury's lectures as early as 1886 (39; also 378 n7).

Chapter 4

1. This image of Jewish immigrants recalls the fact that large numbers of poor, working-class, ghetto Jews fleeing the pogroms in Russia and Eastern Europe had settled in France in the 1880s and 1890s. If the anti-Semitic literature of the period is any judge (e.g., Renan; Drumont), they appeared much more alien to the French than those from Alsace (Wilson, *Bernard Lazare* 75–76). Bernard Lazare himself, during his early anti-Semitic period, exclaimed: "Open an anti-Semitic book at random, and you will hear people cry out, for good reason usually, against the Frankfurters, the Galicians, the Rumanians, the Russians, who are swooping down onto our country like locusts" ("La solidarité juive," *Entretiens Politiques et Littéraires* (October 1890), quoted in Bredin, *Bernard Lazare* 110). Barrès seems to be assimilating the two groups in order to compound revanchism with anti-Semitism.

2. The elements in Frege's set are those things that are identical to themselves; everything real presumably. The empty set contains those things which are *not* identical to themselves, i.e., nothing, which is why it is empty. But if it contains nothing, nevertheless it is itself something, a signifier, a set, the first element in that other set, the series of integers; it is the zero term that acts as the starting point necessary to launch the infinite series.

3. Strictly speaking, this should be termed a 'hypnotic' rather than a transferential theory, according to Freud's analysis in *Group Psychology and Ego Analysis*. Likewise, Barrès's fiction should be classified as hypnotic rather than transferential narrative, since the speaker (the hypnotist) is the authority rather than the listener (the psychoanalyst) (see Chaitin, "Psychoanalysis and Narrative Action" 284–301, 293–94). It is Lacan's notion of the analyst as the "subject supposed to know," developed in his 1964 seminar on *The Four Fundamental Concepts of Psychoanalysis,* which Felman then elaborated into a theory of narrative in which it is the storyteller, or the author, who becomes the object of the reader's transference, in "Turning the Screw of Interpretation." Lacan himself, however, reverted in 1967 to something closer to the Freudian idea, claiming that the true subject supposed to know(ledge) was the analysand, not the analyst (see Chaitin, *Lacan and the Rhetoric of Culture* chap. 5). I have retained the term 'transference,' nevertheless, since, in the last analysis, for both Freud and Lacan the transference is a kind of spell that must be broken in order to attain a degree of mental health and autonomy.

Chapter 5

1. Scholars generally give one of two reasons for this interruption: either France wanted to downplay France's opposition to the Church during his candidacy for the Académie Française (which was successful), or he was distracted by the trips he took at the time to Italy and the North Sea (Levaillant 442; Bancquart, "Notice" to *Contemporary History* 1321; Sachs 118). Bancquart adds a third possibility: France simply could not see how to organize his individual scenes into a larger whole, on the one hand, and, on the other, his characters were so closely related to each other that he could not separate them into discrete short stories ("Notice" 1324).

2. In many ways, these arguments constituted a reprise of those Brunetière had brought forth in the dispute over *The Disciple,* in which he and France had locked horns half a decade before. It is more than a little ironic, then, that neither one of them realized at the time that Bourget's main intention in that novel was precisely to allow for

the conciliation of science and religion via Spencer's 'unknowable' (see chap. 2 in this volume; see also Levaillant 291–98).

3. As France well knew, Brunetière was far from being the sole perpetrator of these ideas. Levaillant refers to a series of Church publications and doctrines, especially a recent encyclical distinguishing theological from scientific truths aimed at eliminating scientific textual biblical criticism, and which, presumably, a well-informed contemporary reader would have recognized (473–74).

4. In November 1897, France published two articles—one in *L'Aurore,* the other in the *Écho de Paris* (the latter adapted from *Amethyst*)—questioning the judgment against Dreyfus (Bancquart 228).

5. This was the standard argument of the anarchists, at that time and even after 1905, when they judged that the experiment in mass education represented by the Ferry reforms of primary education had been a failure: "Look at the anarchists, who see the French as a spineless, mindless, submissive, indifferent mass. The artisan of this cowardly resignation is of course the schoolteacher, that champion of conformism who has replaced, and even 'surpassed his religious rival' (it's *le Libertaire* of October 1909)" (J. Ozouf).

6. In her "Notice" to the first two volumes of *Contemporary History,* Bancquart tries to assess France's attitude toward the Jews before the Dreyfus Affair, given the negative portraits he paints of Worms-Clavelin and his wife, who, unlike the other caricatures in the book, have no redeeming qualities. She argues that the prefect is really very antipathetic, like the Jewish bankers of Maupassant and Zola, even though all three were opposed in principle to anti-Semitism (1343–44). She attributes this to a 'diffuse' anti-Semitism, "wariness, a sense of difference," combined out of the prosperity and visibility of the well-known Jewish financiers, plus the inclusion of numerous Jews in the government and civil service since the rise of the 'republic of the republicans,' and their support of the Opportunists, who gave them much greater freedom than in other regimes and other countries (1345). Bancquart concludes that France really did feel hostility toward Jews, especially those who renounced their own heritage, but that he was nevertheless opposed to anti-Semitism. See Pierre Birnbaum's *Les fous de la République* (translated as *The Jews of the Republic*) for a comprehensive history of the Jews who participated in the government during the Third Republic and the anti-Semitic reaction of the period. Birnbaum gives detailed information about Ernest Hendlé, the prefect who came to symbolize the Jewish republican prefect capable of entertaining good relations with the Church hierarchy and whom France took as model for his Worms-Clavelin (32–33).

In her "Notice" to *Amethyst,* Bancquart points out that, with the onset of the Affair, France dropped Worms-Clavelin and transferred his satire onto the rich capitalist Jewish converts to Catholicism, Mme. de Bonmont and her family (1156).

It should be noted that in *Amethyst,* at the height of the Affair, France makes a point of debunking the anti-Semites' racist claim that "Jews and Frenchmen cannot live together. The antagonism is ineradicable, it is in the blood," as M. de Terremondre puts it—to which M. Bergeret responds that the Jews are the most adaptable people on earth and that "the daughters of our Jewish financiers marry nowadays the heirs to the greatest names in Christian France" (142), admittedly a typical double-barreled critique of both groups.

7. Needless to say, anarchists like Adolphe Retté and younger readers such as Adrien Chevalier, Georges Rodenbach, and Léon Blum were delighted by the same qualities. Retté notes with glee that France "demolishes present-day society by undermining: the army, the administration, the clergy, not to mention the family" ("M. Anatole France: *L'orme du mail," La Plume* 8 [1897]: 251ff.; cited in Gier 229); Blum heartily approved

France's "powerful critique of the State, of society, and of everything generally [considered] respectable" (*Revue Blanche* 12 [1ᵉʳ semestre 1897], "Les Livres," 144–47 [*L'orme du Mail*, 146–147]; cited in Gier 229).

Chapter 6

1. I should add that it is not just the women who display this venality and lack of principle. It occurs to Mme. de Bonmont's son that he should try to make Guitrel a bishop in order to be invited to the Duc de Brécé's prestigious hunts. He thinks of Loyer, minister of public education and churches, who therefore appoints bishops and whom he thinks he can influence via Mme. de Gromance. He meets Gustave (later called Philippe) Dellion, son of one of the leading aristocratic families of their home town (Dellion's wife used to be Mme. Bergeret's defender), and who owes Bonmont a lot of money. Gustave is Mme. de Gromance's lover, which is why Bonmont is unaccustomedly nice to him. Bonmont asks him to ask Mme. de Gromance to ask Loyer to make abbé Guitrel Bishop of Tourcoing, more or less promising to buy an automobile for Dellion if he succeeds. This imbroglio is meant of course to illustrate the absurdity of the chain of causes leading to Guitrel's appointment as bishop, in the manner of Voltaire's *Candide*.

2. There are several passages in *Paris* about Riquet's defense of the premises against the interloper, in which M. Bergeret makes the dog out to be a member of the anti-Dreyfus crowd (as Levaillant points out, 252). But then his master recognizes Riquet's virtues, such as goodness and protection of the household. Above all, Riquet/the people is governed by fear, the age-old gods of fear and violence; and ignorance.

3. In his reception speech to the Académie Française in 1841, Victor Hugo distinguished the *peuple* from the *populace* and then from the *foule*. The latter became traditional in the ideology of the left and was often invoked during the Dreyfus Affair to explain away the contradiction between the appeal to the people and the reality of the masses' violence and anti-Semitism. Cf. Séverine, "La Foule" for the identical argument distinguishing between the good, robust 'people' and the evil 'crowd.'

4. Cassaing (303) cites several contributors to Clemenceau's organ, *L'Aurore:*

Clemenceau: "What we need to change, to reform, is the sovereign people. . . . We must *educate* our master with a thousand heads."

Gustave Geoffroy: "How can we conquer this crowd? . . . Everything shows us that the problem to be solved is that of *educating this crowd,* helping it to conquer its right to life, to a complete life, to a life of the body and a life of the mind." (emphasis in original)

And of course, Zola, as we will see in the following chapter.

Levaillant gives a similar quote, from Emile Duclaux: "[If we suffer from this type of crisis,] it's only because people lack critical sense and the masses have not been educated"; [therefore we must cooperate] on the rational education of people's minds" (525, n180).

5. Just as Spinoza's God is immanent in the universe—is all beings, rather than an independent entity, source of all being, outside of or beyond the universe—so the communist State dissolves into the set of all the people that constitute society. Interestingly enough, M. Bergeret cites Spinoza immediately before the passage quoted, but in reference to an apparently totally different topic—that intellect and comprehension often hinder action.

6. M. Bergeret seeks this ideal in the quintessential representative of the goodness of the people, Pied-d'Alouette. He returns to this theme in relation to himself after the

departure of his wife, when he feels "unmoved by either love or hate" (*Wicker Work Woman* 129). In the subsequent volume, he comes upon Mme. de Gromance in the street and is delighted to find that, although he knows she will never be his, "he was not sad, because his wisdom approached the happy state of ataraxy, without, however, finally attaining it" (*Amethyst* 114–15).

7. In reality, Anatole France devoted much time and energy to launching these universities, for he believed that by teaching science and economics to the working classes, they could become the instrument for changing bourgeois society into a society of social justice (Bancquart, "Notice" to *M. Bergeret à Paris* 1216).

Chapter 7

1. All references to *Truth* are from the Livre de Poche edition, which is the most accessible and has the best critical apparatus. In a few cases, I have corrected obvious typos by comparing the text to that of the François Bernouard edition. References to the Livre de Poche edition will be marked by the letter *V* in italics. An English translation is available (see bibliography), which I have consulted, but it has so many omissions and inaccuracies that I prefer to use my own translations.

2. Cassaing argues most convincingly that Zola espoused the line of Clemenceau and the *Aurore* team, that the secularization of education must precede political and economic reform, against the conciliatory stance taken by Jaurès and his socialist party toward the Waldeck-Rousseau government (303).

3. Zola repeats this point almost verbatim in the text of the novel: "[Marc harbored] regret for not having been able to draw an admirable object lesson from this prodigious Simon Affair, one which would have taught the people. . . . In a few months, the Simon Affair would have done more to emancipate the people and to establish the reign of justice than a hundred years of ardent politics" (quoted in Cassaing 302).

As for the idea of the people's 'infection,' in his review of *Truth* in the *Revue mondiale* of February 15, 1903, Georges Pellissier had already observed that the Simon Affair was just an episode that brought to light "all the deep, latent infection hidden in the soul of a people odiously deprived of thought by ignorance, vitiated by prejudice and fanaticism" (480–81).

4. "I know that it [knowledge] alone makes people capable of justice. Everywhere the bourgeoisie is educated and how it acts in keeping everything. So knowledge is not enough, you have to be brought up right, have morals" (Zola's preparatory notes, quoted in Laville 221).

5. *The Adventures of Sherlock Holmes* was published in 1891–1892, *The Memoirs of Sherlock Holmes* in 1892–1893.

6. In *The Four Fundamental Concepts of Psycho-Analysis,* Lacan points out that the correlative of the Freudian subject is the deceived Other; that is, the fear that the Other can be deceived and therefore will not understand the meaning of his or her symptom (233).

7. A custom that persisted in France even after World War II, according to Jules Isaac: "To those who deplored Auschwitz and the fate of innocent Jewish victims, how many times has a Christian responded: 'What do you expect, they are an accursed people [*un people maudit*]'" (*L'antisémitisme a-t-il des racines chrétiennes?* 36).

8. In his "Letter to the Senate," Zola wrote: "The most serious, the most painful thing is that they have allowed the country to be poisoned by the vile press that has impudently gorged it on lies, calumnies, filth and outrages, to the point of driving it mad" (*La vérité en marche* 138).

9. At the height of the Dreyfus Affair, *La Croix* published calls to violence: "Eviscerate him" [apropos of Zola]; "All this will end badly for them [the Jews]. . . . If the police and government remain powerless, the citizens in their disgust will have to mete out justice themselves" (Sorlin 120). And to cap it all off, Sorlin writes:

> The issue of 21 July [1898] reproduces, filling an entire page in bold-face type, a poster published by the Committee on Justice-Equality of Montpellier . . .
> Judas Dreyfus sold out France
> The Jews have grabbed everything, dirtied everything, destroyed everything
> The Jews are turning France upside down for the greater profit of world-wide Kikedom.
> *Let us unite to turn Jewish omnipotence upside down and kick the Jews out of [France]* (120; emphasis in original).

Moreover, it would seem as though the Assumptionists' efforts met with a certain degree of success, since, according to modern scholars, two anti-Semitic masons, unable to disembowel Zola, had to settle for murdering him by stuffing up his chimney and asphyxiating him (see Bedel; Mitterand, *Olympia* 93; Brown 23–25).

10. The idea of the indelible imprint left upon a woman by her first lover is, of course, the Michelet theory from *L'amour et la femme* that Zola used as the thesis of his early novel, *Madeleine Férat* (1868).

11. In this respect, then, *Truth* is the answer to Michelet and *Madeleine Férat,* rather than their repetition.

12. In a sense, Zola had always espoused a kind of Lamarckian theory of the inheritance of acquired characteristics, since the descendants on the Macquart side of the family inherit their destructive tendencies from their immediate forebears: Étienne Lantier, for example, inherits the alcoholism of his mother, Gervaise. The difference in *Truth* is that, perhaps in response to the current nationalist ideology of the soil and the dead, Zola extends the range of operation of heredity to include the entire nation and its past from the beginnings to present. Zola uses the language of writing when he has Geneviève protest that in her the hereditary flaw seems to be "indelible" (*V* 493).

Chapter 8

1. Marc's conviction about the identity of the real criminal is just as independent of the evidence as his reasons for refusing to believe in the guilt of the fathers. Even after receiving the piece of evidence that clinches the guilt of Brother Gorgias, he insists that reason alone can determine the truth: "All the facts illuminated each other, they all led to the same conclusion. Even outside the material evidence that they were beginning to possess, there was a certainty like the demonstration of a mathematical problem, which reasoning alone was sufficient to solve" (I: 302, 311).

Like his adversaries then, Marc judges the world by his ideas, his representation of it. His relation to phenomena is every bit as 'subjective' as that of his opponents, in the sense that it depends on mental constructs, even though it is not the least bit capricious nor even self-serving.

2. Zola's recent biographers do not make a connection between his molestation and *Truth*. Brown sees the event as the origin of Zola's later puritanical moralism and a possible source for *Thérèse Raquin* (a very plausible suggestion) (24), while Mitterand denies categorically that he "retained the slightest trauma from it," except that it may have favored his later transgression of prudish taboos (*Olympia* 93).

3. Zola is echoing here the party line of *L'Aurore* in response to the amnesty. In the number of October 2, 1899, Clemenceau had denounced the amnesty as a betrayal (*trahison*) of the Republic, because it delivered the republican government over "to the barracks and the sacristy" (Cassaing 301).

4. Earlier in the novel, while mulling over the causes of the Church's newfound power and arrogance, Marc had already expressed his views on the role of the bourgeoisie:

> The bourgeoisie, which used to be liberal, non-believing and rebellious, now has been reconquered by its retrograde spirit, out of the terror of being dispossessed, of ceding its place to the rising tide of the people. (190).
>
> In 89, victorious over the dying nobility, the bourgeoisie had replaced it; and for a century it had kept its booty, refusing its just share to the people. Now its role was finished, it confessed it itself by going over to reaction, hysterical at the idea of giving back, terrified by the rise of democracy that was going to sweep it away. (172; 192)

5. It was all the easier for Zola to identify with the Jewish captain, since not only was he vilified as a Jew lover during the Affair, but many years before, Octave Mirbeau, in his early anti-Semitic days, had assimilated naturalism to Judaism, because both "lacked metaphysics and mystery," were materialistic and "pornographic," and, in Zola's case, involved the large-scale commercialization and industrialization anti-Semites associated with Jewish capitalism ("Le théâtre juif," in the short-lived anti-Semitic journal, *Les grimaces* [November 3, 1883]; cited in Wilson, *Bernard Lazare* 71–72). (But note that Mirbeau later changed sides completely and became a friend of Bernard-Lazare and an ardent Dreyfusard.)

6. Cosset makes a similar point, but in a more nuanced way. She evaluates this episode as just one example of Zola's artful representation of the relation between reality and utopia, present and future, in the novel as a whole: "The constant criss-crossing between a discourse about a 'pre-utopian' past and a discourse about the utopian present constitutes a form of argumentation that undermines myth and aims toward making utopia plausible" (141).

7. It is true that both Thérèse and Marc then attempt to justify the necessity of suffering with various standard theological and scientific arguments, but even the characters themselves seem unconvinced by these half-hearted rationalizations. The inevitability of physical and mental suffering was, in fact, one of the tenets of turn-of-the-century socialism, as we have seen in France's *Contemporary History*.

8. Zola, and Gaillard, are of course simply echoing a view at least as old as Plato's *Republic*. The main force of *L'Assommoir* stems not from the stereotyped idea, but from the detailed picture Zola paints of the ways the working people of Paris go about finding their enjoyment.

9. "If you can enlighten mankind," Becker and Lavielle explain, "the 'human beast' (*la bête humaine*) remains, despite everything, crouching in the shadows, ready to drive people to crime, to rape, to uncontrollable passions" ("Préface" 28). Indeed, Mitterand contends that *Truth* is a rewriting of the novel titled *La bête humaine* (*L'honneur* 738–39).

10. See Jean-Louis Bory's introduction to *Vérité* 999, and Laville 131, both of whom emphasize the first words of that preface, "Je veux expliquer."

11. "I've often said that we don't have to draw conclusions from our works, which means that our works carry their conclusions in themselves. An experimenter does not have to conclude, precisely because the experiment concludes for him. . . . It's always up

to society to produce or not to produce the phenomenon, if its result is useful or danger-ous" (*Roman expérimental* 79).

Conclusion

1. I should point out that the education novels of the period written about, and especially by, women show different concerns: attaining autonomy, developing their in-tellectual and artistic potential, and achieving professional success, while maintaining their desire for sexual, emotional, and maternal fulfillment. No longer do they want to be identified only as saints, wives, and mothers, forced to choose between sexual and professional gratification. For the women, the question of identity is a matter of their relation not to a transcendent Other, but to the immanent Other of social definitions and restrictions.

BIBLIOGRAPHY

Acomb, Evelyn M. *The French Laic Laws (1879–1889)*. New York: Columbia University Press, 1941.

Agulhon, Maurice. "Introduction." In *Manuel républicain de l'homme et du citoyen*, 9–28. Paris: Garnier, 1981.

———. *Marianne au pouvoir: L'imagerie et la symbolique républicaines de 1880 à 1914*. Paris: Flammarion, 1989.

Albanese, Ralph, Jr. *La Fontaine à l'École républicaine: Du poète universel au classique scolaire*. Charlottesville, VA: Rookwood Press, 2003.

———. *Molière à l'École républicaine: De la critique universitaire aux manuels scolaires (1870–1914)*. Saratoga, CA: ANIMA Libri (Stanford French and Italian Studies), 1992.

Anderson, Benedict. *Imagined Communities: Reflections on the Origin and Spread of Nationalism*. London: Verso, 1991.

Arendt, Hannah. *The Origins of Totalitarianism*. New York: Harcourt, Brace & World, 1966.

Athanasius of Alexandria. *The Festal Letters of Athanasius*. Edited by William Cureton. London: Society for the Publication of Oriental Texts, 1848.

Autin, Albert. *"Le disciple" de Paul Bourget*. Paris: Société Française d'Éditions Littéraires et Techniques, 1930.

Baguley, David. *"Fécondité": roman à thèse, évangile, mythe*. Toronto: University of Toronto Press, 1973.

———. "Du récit polémique au discours utopique: l'Evangile républicain de Zola." *Cahiers Naturalistes* 54 (1980): 106–21.

Bakhtin, Mikhail. "Discourse in the Novel." In *The Dialogic Imagination: Four Essays*, edited by Michael Holquist, 259–422. Austin: University of Texas University Press, 1981.

Bancquart, Marie-Claire. *Anatole France: Un sceptique passionné*. Paris: Calmann-Lévy, 1984.

———. "Notice" à *L'anneau d'améthyste. Anatole France: Oeuvres*. Vol. 3: 1133–60. Paris: Gallimard, 1991.

———. "Notice" à *Histoire contemporaine. Anatole France: Oeuvres.* Vol. 2: 1319–48. Paris: Gallimard, 1991.

———. "Notice" à *M. Bergeret à Paris. Anatole France: Oeuvres.* Vol. 3: 1209–29. Paris: Gallimard, 1991.

Barrès, Maurice. *L'Appel au soldat.* In *Maurice Barrès: Romans et voyages,* 755–1048.

———. *Les déracinés.* In *Maurice Barrès: Romans et voyages,* 493–754.

———. *Du sang, de la volupté et de la mort.* In *Maurice Barrès: Romans et voyages,* 341–479.

———. *L'ennemi des lois.* In *Maurice Barrès: Romans et voyages,* 259–332.

———. "Examen des trois romans idéologiques." In *Maurice Barrès: Romans et voyages,* 15–31.

———. *Un homme libre.* In *Maurice Barrès: Romans et voyages,* 87–185.

———. "L'influence de M. Taine." *Le Journal* (March 6, 1893). In *Taine et Renan: Pages recueillies et commentées par Victor Giraud.* Paris: Bossard, 1922.

———. *Le jardin de Bérénice.* In *Maurice Barrès: Romans et voyages,* 186–258.

———. *Leurs figures.* In *Maurice Barrès: Romans et voyages,* 1049–1214.

———. *Maurice Barrès: Romans et voyages.* Edited by Vital Rambaud. Paris: Robert Laffont, 1994.

———. *Mes cahiers 1896–1923.* Paris: Plon, 1994 [1963].

———. *Mes mémoires. Oeuvres complètes* T. XIII. Paris: Club de l'Honnête Homme, 1968.

———. "La mode russe." *La Revue Illustrée* 1.4 (1886): 123–26.

———. *L'oeuvre de Maurice Barrès.* Ed. Philippe Barrès. Vol. 4. Paris: Au Club de l'honnête homme, 1965.

———. "Préface de l'édition de 1904 d'*Un homme libre.*" In *Maurice Barrès: Romans et voyages,* 186–258.

———. "Réponse à M. René Doumic." In *Maurice Barrès: Romans et voyages,* 179–85.

———. *Scènes et doctrines du nationalisme.* Paris: Éditions du Trident, 1987.

———. "La sensibilité d'Henri Chambige." *Le Figaro* (November 11, 1888).

———. *Sous l'oeil des barbares.* In *Maurice Barrès: Romans et voyages,* 27–86.

———. "Taine" (response to survey). *La Revue Blanche* (1897).

———. "Taine." In *Taine et Renan,* 114–15. Paris: Bossard, 1922.

Barthélemy-Madaule, Madeleine. *Bergson.* Paris: Le Seuil, 1967.

Becker, Colette, and Véronique Lavielle. "Préface." *Vérité.* Paris: Livre de Poche, 1995. 7–28.

Bedel, Jean. *Zola Assassiné.* Paris: Flammarion, 2002.

Bellet, Roger. *Jules Vallès journaliste: du Second Empire, de la Commune de Paris et de la IIIe République.* Paris: Les Éditeurs français réunis, 1977.

Benda, Julien. *La trahison des clercs.* Paris: Bernard Grasset, 1977 [1927; 1958].

———. "L'oeuvre nécessaire." *Le courrier social illustré* (November 1, 1894).

Bergson, Henri. *Essai sur les données immédiates de la conscience.* Paris: F. Alcan, 1889.

———. *Essais et témoignages.* Ed. Albert Béguin. Paris: Le Seuil, 1965.

———. *Les deux sources de la morale et de la religion. Oeuvres.* Paris: Presses Universitaires de Paris, 1970 [1932].

Berman, Sandra. "Looking to Particulars: Feminism and the New History." *Yearbook of Comparative and General Literature* 39 (1990–91): 100–112.

Bernard-Lazare. "Les Livres." *Les entretiens politiques et littéraires* 6, no. 43 (May 25, 1893).

Bert, Paul. *L'instruction civique à l'école.* Paris: Picard-Bernheim, 1882.

———. *Lectures et leçons de choses, à l'usage de l'enseignement primaire et des classes élémentaires des lycées et collèges; Cours élémentaire et moyen.* 12th ed. Paris: Picard et Kaan, 1902 [first edition with Picard et Bernheim, in 1887].

Berthelot, Marcellin. "La science et la morale." *Revue de Paris* (February 1, 1895): 449–69.

Bhabha, Homi. *The Location of Culture*. New York: Routledge, 1994.

Birnbaum, Pierre. *Les fous de la République: Histoire politique des Juifs d'Etat de Gambetta à Vichy*. Mesnil-sur-l'Éstrée: Fayard, 1992.

———. *"La France aux Français": Histoire des haines nationalistes*. Paris: Le Seuil, 1993.

Bluysen, Paul. "Un drame décadent." *La République Française* (November 7 and 8, 1888).

Bonald, Louis de. *Essai analytique sur les lois naturelles de l'ordre social*. Paris: A. Le Clere, 1800.

Borie, Jean. *Mythologies de l'hérédité au XIXᵉ siècle*. Paris: Galilée, 1981.

———. "Préface." In *Les déracinés*. Paris: Gallimard (Folio), 1988.

Bory, Jean-Louis. "Introduction." In *Vérité*. Paris: Cercle du Livre Précieux, 1968.

Boschetti, Anna. *Sartre et "Les Temps Moderns."* Paris: Minuit, 1985.

Bossuet, Jacques Bénigne. *Discours sur l'histoire universelle*. Paris: Garnier-Flammarion, 1966.

Bouglé, Célestin. "L'éducation morale et l'école." *Encyclopédie française* 15, no. 40 (1939): 10–12.

Bourdieu, Pierre, and Jean Claude Passeron. *Reproduction in Education, Society and Culture*. Baltimore: Johns Hopkins University Press, 1976.

Bourgeois Léon. "Le projet de loi sur les universités devant le sénat." *Revue Internationale de l'Enseignement* 23 (January–June 1892): 263–305.

Bourget, Paul. "Avant-Propos de 1883." *Essais de psychologie contemporaine*. xv–xviii.

———. "Avant-Propos de 1885." *Essais de psychologie contemporaine*. xix–xxvii.

———. *Le disciple*. Paris: La Table Ronde, 1994 [1889].

———. *The Disciple*. New York: Howard Fertig, 1976. Reprint of 1901 edition, published by T. F. Unwin, London.

———. *Essais de psychologie contemporaine*. 2 vols. Paris: Plon-Nourrit, 1901.

———. *Mensonges*. Paris: Plon, 1901 [1887].

———. *Pages de critique et doctrine*. Vol. 1. Paris: Plon-Nourrit, 1912.

———. "Réflexions sur Octave Feuillet." In *Pages de critique et de doctrine*, vol. 1 (1912): 116–20.

———. *Solidarité*. Paris: Armand Colin, 1906 [1896].

———. "Théories politiques: Un élève de Taine." In *Essais de psychologie contemporaine: Études littéraires*, 169–71. Paris: Gallimard, 1993.

Boutmy, Émile. *Quelques idées sur la création d'une faculté libre d'enseignement supérieur.* Paris: A. Lainé, 1871.

Boutroux, Émile. *De la contingence des lois de la nature*. Paris: Alcan, 1921 [1874].

Bredin, Jean-Denis. *Bernard Lazare*. Paris: Éditions de Fallois, 1992.

Brown, Frederick. *Zola: A Life*. London: Papermac, 1997.

Brunetière, Ferdinand. "A propos du *Disciple*." *Revue des Deux Mondes* (September 15, 1889, and July 1, 1889): 214–27.

———. "Après une visite au Vatican." *Revue des Deux Mondes* (January 1895): 97–118.

———. *Le roman naturaliste*. Paris: Calmann Lévy, 1883.

Buisson, Ferdinand E. *La foi laïque: Extraits de discours et d'écrits (1878–1911)*. Paris: Hachette, 1912.

———. *La religion, la morale et la science: Leur conflit dans l'éducation contemporaine*. Paris: Fischbacher, 1900.

Burgelin, Claude, ed. *Lectures de Sartre*. Lyon: Presses Universitaires de Lyon, 1986.

Burke, Edmond. *Reflections on the Revolution in France*. London: Penguin, 1986.

Burke, Peter. *The Fabrication of Louis XIV.* New Haven, CT: Yale University Press, 1992.

Calhoun, Craig, ed. *Social Theory and the Politics of Identity.* Oxford: Blackwell, 1994.

Carassus, Émilien. "De l'Affaire Chambige au Jardin de Bérénice." *Littératures* 24 (1991): 115–25.

Caro, Elme. M. *Littré et le positivisme.* Paris: Hachette, 1883.

———. "La morale de la guerre: Kant et Bismarck." *Revue des Deux Mondes* (December 1, 1870).

———. *Le pessimisme au XIXᵉ siècle.* Paris: Hachette, 1878.

———. *Poètes et romanciers.* Paris: Hachette, 1888.

Carroll, David. *French Literary Fascism: Nationalism, Anti-Semitism, and the Ideology of Culture.* Princeton, NJ: Princeton University Press, 1995.

Cassaing, Jean-Claude. "Vive la République!" *Cahiers Naturalistes* 54 (1980): 299–316.

Chaitin, Gilbert D. "Le cauchemar de (la) *Vérité:* Ou le rêve du revenant." *Cahiers Naturalistes* 82 (2008).

———. "Education and Political Identity: The Universalist Controversy." *Yale French Studies* 113 (Spring 2008): 77–95.

———. "'France Is My Mother': The Subject of Universal Education in the French Third Republic." *Readings in Nineteenth-Century French Prose* 32.1 (Spring 2005): 128–58.

———. "From the Third Republic to Postmodernism: Language, Freedom, and the Politics of the Contingent." *MLN* 114, no. 4 (September 1999): 780–815.

———. *Lacan and the Rhetoric of Culture.* London: Cambridge University Press, 1996.

———. "Psychoanalysis and Narrative Action: The Primal Scene of the French Novel." *Style* 18.3 (1984): 284–301.

———. "Transposing the Dreyfus Affair: The Trauma of Identity in Zola's *Vérité.*" *Australian Journal of French Studies* 38.3 (September–December 2001): 430–44.

Champfleury [Jules-François-Félix Husson]. *Les souffrances du professeur Delteil.* Paris: Michel Lévy frères, 1857.

Charle, Christophe. *Naissance des intellectuels, 1880–1900.* Paris: Éditions de Minuit, 1990.

———. *Paris fin de siècle, culture et politique.* Paris: Le Seuil, 1998.

Charles-Brun, Jean. *Le roman social en France au XIXᵉ siècle.* Genève: Slatkine, 1973. [Reprint of Paris: Giard et Brière, 1910 edition.]

Chevalier, Jacques. *Henri Bergson.* Paris: Alcan, 1926.

Citti, Pierre. *Contre la décadence: Histoire de l'imagination française dans le roman 1890–1914.* Paris: PUF, 1987.

Clark, Linda L. *Schooling the Daughters of Marianne.* Albany: State University of New York Press, 1984.

Coignet, Clarisse. *Cours de morale à l'usage des écoles laïques.* Paris: L. Le Chevalier, 1874.

———. *De l'éducation dans la démocratie.* Paris: C. Delagrave, 1881.

———. "De l'enseignement laïque en France et en Angleterre." *Revue Politique et Littéraire (Revue Bleue)* (March 29, 1873): 928–31.

———. "De l'enseignement de la morale. Plan, méthode et esprit de cet enseignement: Instruction secondaire des jeunes filles." *Revue Politique et Littéraire (Revue Bleue)* (July 24, 1880): 73–82.

———. *La morale indépendante dans son principe et dans son objet.* Paris: Germer Baillère, 1869.

Colloque sentimental entre Émile Zola et Fagus. Paris: Société libre d'édition des Gens de Lettres, 1898.

Compagnon, Antoine. *La Troisième République des lettres, de Flaubert à Proust.* Paris: Le Seuil, 1983.

Compagnon, Béatrice, and Anne Thévenin. *Histoire des instituteurs et des professeurs, de 1880 à nos jours.* Mesnil-sur-l'Estrée: Éditions Perrin, 2001.

Compayré, Gabriel. *Éléments d'éducation morale et civique, degré moyen et supérieur.* Paris: P. Garcet, Nisius et Cie, 1880.

Comte, Auguste. *Cours de philosophie positive.* Vol. I. Paris: Baillière, 1864.

———. *Discours sur l'ensemble du positivisme.* Paris: Flammarion, 1998 [1848].

———. *A General View of Positivism.* Translated by J. H. Bridges. Stanford, CA: Academic Reprints, n.d.

Condorcet, Marquis de. *Rapport et projet de décret sur l'organisation générale de l'instruction publique, présentés à l'assemblée nationale, au nom du comité d'instruction publique.* Paris: Assemblée nationale de la [Première] République, 1792.

Copjec, Joan. *Imagine There's No Woman: Ethics and Sublimation.* Cambridge, MA: MIT Press, 2002.

Cosset, Evelyne. *Les* Quatre Évangiles *d'Émile Zola: espace, temps, personnages.* Geneva: Droz, 1990.

Cresson, A. *La morale de Kant: Étude critique.* Paris: F. Alcan, 1897.

"Le crime littéraire." *La République Française* (November 12, 1888).

Crubellier, Maurice. *L'école républicaine, 1870–1940.* Paris: Christian, 1993.

Curtius, Ernst Robert. *Maurice Barrès und die geistigen Grundlagen des französischen Nationalismus.* Bonn: Friedrich Cohen, 1921.

Darlu, Alphonse. "Réflexions d'un philosophe sur les questions du jour: Science, morale, religion." *Revue de Métaphysique et de Morale* 3 (1895): 239–51.

Datta, Venita. *Birth of a National Icon: The Literary Avant-Garde and the Origins of the Intellectual in France.* Albany: State University of New York Press, 1999.

Dauriac, Lionel. *Contingence et rationalisme.* Paris: Vrin, 1924.

De Maistre, Joseph. *Essai sur le principe générateur des constitutions politiques.* Paris: 1814.

Démann, Paul. *La catéchèse chrétienne et le peuple de la Bible: Constatations et perspectives.* Paris: Cahiers Sioniens, 1952.

De Metz Noblat, A. "L'instruction civique à l'école d'après G. Compayré." *La Réforme Sociale* 4 (1882): 337–42.

Derrida, Jacques. *Who's Afraid of Philosophy? Right to Philosophy I.* Stanford, CA: Stanford University Press, 2002.

Devinat, Émile. *Livre de lecture et de morale.* Paris: Larousse, 1894.

Devolvé, Jean. *Rationalisme et tradition: recherches des conditions d'efficacité d'une morale laïque.* Paris: Félix Alcan, 1910.

Digeon, Claude. *La crise allemande de la pensée française (1870–1914).* Paris: Presses Universitaires de France, 1959.

Dupanloup, Félix-Antoine-Philibert. *L'élection de M. Littré à l'Académie Française.* 1871.

Durkheim, Émile. *Éducation et sociologie.* Paul Fauconnet, ed. Paris: Félix Alcan, 1922.

———. *L'évolution pédagogique en France.* Paris: PUF, 1969 [1938].

———. *Les règles de la méthode sociologique.* Paris: Flammarion, 1988 [1895].

Duruy, Victor. *Discours prononcé par M. Duruy au Sénat, séance du 22 mai 1868 au sujet d'une pétition relative à l'enseignement supérieur.* Paris: Ch. Lahure, 1868.

Du Val, Thaddeus Ernest, Jr. *The Subject of Realism in the* Revue des Deux Mondes. Philadelphia: University of Pennsylvania, 1936.

Duveau, Georges. *Les instituteurs.* Paris: Le Seuil, 1957.

Edman, Irwin. "Introduction." Henry Bergson. *Creative Evolution,* i–xxv. New York: Modern Library, 1944.

Eros, John. "The Positivist Generation of French Republicanism." *Sociological Review* 3 (1955): 255–77.

Falloux, Frédéric-Alfred de. *De l'unité nationale*. Paris: A. Sauton, 1880.

Favre, Julie. *La morale des stoïciens*. Paris: Alcan, 1888.

Felman, Shoshana. "Turning the Screw of Interpretation." In *Literature and Psychoanalysis. The Question of Reading: Otherwise*, edited by Shoshana Felman, 94–207. Baltimore: Johns Hopkins University Press, 1982.

———. *What Does a Woman Want?* Baltimore: The Johns Hopkins University Press, 1993.

Ferry, Jules. "Discours sur l'égalité d'éducation." Salle Molière, April 10, 1870. Reprinted in Legrand, 217–37.

Feuillet, Octave. *Histoire de Sibylle*. Paris: Calmann-Lévy, 1877 [1863].

———. *La morte*. Paris: Calmann Lévy, 1886.

Finkielkraut, Alain. *La défaite de la pensée*. Paris: Gallimard, 1987.

———. *The Defeat of the Mind*. New York: Columbia University Press, 1995.

Flaubert, Gustave. *Bouvard et Pécuchet*. Edited by Claudine Gothot-Mersch. Paris: Gallimard, 1979.

Fletcher, Dennis. "Sartre and Barrès: Some Notes on *La nausée*." *Forum for Modern Language Studies* 4, no. 4 (1968): 330–34.

Fouillée, Mme. Alfred (pseudonym G. Bruno). *Le tour de la France par deux enfants, devoirs et patrie: Livre de lecture courante*. Paris: E. Belin, 1877.

France, Anatole. *The Amethyst Ring*. Translated by M. P. Willcocks. London: Bodley Head, 1926.

———. "Bouddhisme." In *La vie littéraire*, vol. 3: 330–37. Paris: Calmann-Lévy, 1892.

———. "Le colonel Picquart." *Le Figaro* (August 16, 1899).

———. "Un crime littéraire—l'affaire Chambige." *Le Temps* (November 11, 1888).

———. *The Elm-Tree on the Mall*. Translated by M. P. Willcocks. London: Bodley Head, 1923.

———. *Le jardin d'Épicure*. Paris: Calmann Lévy, 1895.

———. *Monsieur Bergeret in Paris*. Translated by M. P. Willcocks. London: Bodley Head, 1925.

———. "La morale et la science. M. Paul Bourget." In *La vie littéraire*, vol. 3: 46–68. Paris: Calmann Lévy, 1925.

———. *Oeuvres*. Vol. 2. Edited by Marie-Claire Bancquart. Paris: Gallimard, 1987.

———. *Oeuvres*. Vol. 3. Edited by Marie-Claire Bancquart. Paris: Gallimard, 1991.

———. "Paul Bourget: *Le disciple*." *Le Temps* (June 23, 1889).

———. "Les Trublions." *L'Écho de Paris* (November 29, 1898).

———. *The Wicker Work Woman*. Translated by M. P. Willcocks. London: Bodley Head, 1924.

Frandon, Ida-Marie. *Barrès précurseur*. Paris: Fernand Lanore, 1983.

———. "Fait divers et littérature." *Revue d'Histoire Littéraire de la France* 84, no. 4 (1984): 561–69.

———. *L'orient de Maurice Barrès, étude de genèse*. Genève: Droz, 1952.

Freud, Sigmund. "The Economic Problem of Masochism." *Collected Papers*. Vol. 11: 255–68. London: Hogarth Press, 1949.

———. *Group Psychology and Ego Analysis*. Translated by James Strachey. New York: Norton, 1975.

Funck-Brentano, Théophile. *Les sophistes allemands et les nihilistes russes*. Paris: Plon, 1887.

Gaillard, Françoise. "A chacun sa vérité." *Cahiers Naturalistes* 52 (1978): 17–26.

Gambetta, Léon. *Discours et Plaidoyers Choisis*. Edited by Joseph Reinach. Paris: Charpentier, 1886.

Gauchet, Marcel. "Préface." In *Benjamin Constant: Écrits politiques*. Paris: Gallimard, 1997.

Germain, Marie-Odile. "Genèse d'un roman: *Les Déracinés*." In *Barrès: Une tradition dans la modernité*, edited by André Guyaux, Joseph Jurt, and Robert Kopp, 31–40. Paris: Honoré Champion, 1991.

Gide, André. "A propos des *Déracinés*." In *Prétextes, Suivi de Nouveaux prétextes*, 29–33. Paris: Mercure de France, 1990 [1903; 1911].

Gier, Albert. *Der Skeptiker im Gespräch mit dem Leser: Studien zum Werk von Anatole France und zu seiner Rezeption in der französischen Presse, 1879–1905*. Tübingen: Niemeyer, 1985.

Gilson, Étienne. *La philosophie au moyen âge*. Paris: Payot, 1944.

Girardet, Raoul. *Le nationalisme français. Anthologie*. Paris: Le Seuil, 1983.

Giraud, J. Didier. *Émile Masson: professeur de liberté*. Chamalières: Canope, 1991.

Gleizes, Albert. *Tradition et cubisme vers une conscience plastique. Articles et conférences, 1912–1924*. Paris: J. Povolozky, 1927.

Goodrick-Clarke, Nicholas. *The Occult Roots of Nazism*. New York: New York University Press, 1992.

Grand dictionnaire universel du XIXᵉ siècle. Vol. 4. Paris: Larousse, 1868.

Gregh, Fernand. Review of *Histoire contemporaine*. *La Revue Bleue* (February 23, 1901).

Grogin, R. C. *The Bergsonian Controversy in France 1900–1914*. Calgary: University of Calgary Press, 1988.

Guiney, M. Martin. *Teaching the Cult of Literature in the Third Republic*. New York: Palgrave Macmillan, 2004.

Hartmann, Édouard de. *Philosophie de l'inconscient*. Translated by D. Nolen. Paris: Germer Baillière, 1877.

Harvey, David. *The Condition of Postmodernity*. Cambridge, MA: Blackwell, 1989.

Hauser, Arnold. *The Social History of Art*. Vol. 4: *Naturalism, Impressionism, the Film Age*. London: Routledge, 1999.

Hegel, Georg Friedrich. *Natural Law: The Scientific Ways of Treating Natural Law, Its Place in Moral Philosophy, and Its Relation to the Positive Sciences of Law*. Philadelphia: University of Pennsylvania Press, 1975.

Idt, Geneviève. "Modèles scolaires dans l'écriture sartrienne." *Revue des Sciences Humaines* 174 (April–June 1979): 83–103.

Irigaray, Luce. "How to Define Sexuate Rights." *The Irigaray Reader*. Ed. Margaret Whitford. Cambridge, MA: Blackwell, 1991.

Isaac, Jules. *L'antisémitisme a-t-il des racines chrétiennes?* Paris: Fasquelle, 1960.

———. *Jésus et Israel*. Paris: Fasquelle, 1959.

Janicaud, Dominique. *Une généalogie du spiritualisme français. Aux sources du bergsonisme: Ravaisson et la métaphysique*. The Hague: Martinus Nijhoff, 1969.

"La jeunesse boulangiste." *Le Figaro*, May 19, 1888.

Johannet, René. "L'évolution du roman social au XIXᵉ siècle." *Revue de l'Action Populaire* (September 20, 1908): 513–39.

Kant, Immanuel. *Critique of Practical Reason*. Translated by Lewis White Beck. New York: Macmillan, 1993.

Kaplan, Alice Yaeger. *Reproductions of Banality: Fascism, Literature, and French Intellectual Life*. Minneapolis: University of Minnesota Press, 1986.

Karr, Alphonse. *Fort-en-thème*. Paris: aux bureaux du "Siècle," 1850.

Katan, Yvette. "L'enseignement de la morale et de l'instruction civique de la IIIᵉ République jusqu'en 1914." In *Études dédiées à Madeleine Gravitz*, 419–37. Paris: Dalloz, 1982.

Kristeva, Julia. "Women's Time." *The Kristeva Reader*. Ed. Toril Moi. New York: Columbia University Press.

Lacan, Jacques. *Le désir et son interprétation.* "Compte rendu" de J.-B. Pontalis. *Bulletin de Psychologie* 13 (1959–60): 263–72.

———. *The Four Fundamental Concepts of Psycho-Analysis.* New York: Norton, 1978.

———. "Kant with Sade." Translated by James B. Swenson. *October* 51 (Winter 1989): 55–75.

———. *The Seminar. Book 7. The Ethics of Psychoanalysis.* Translated by Dennis Porter. New York: W. W. Norton, 1992.

———. *The Seminar. Book 17. The Other Side of Psychoanalysis.* Translated by Russell Grigg. New York: W. W. Norton, 2006.

Lachelier, Jules. *Du Fondement de l'induction.* Paris: Pocket, 1993 [1871].

Laclau, Ernesto. *On Populist Reason.* London: Verso, 2005.

Lacoue-Labarthe, Philippe, and Jean-Luc Nancy. *Le mythe nazi.* La Tour d'Aigues: Éditions de l'Aube, 1991.

Laville, Béatrice. "L'éducation et ses enjeux à la fin du dix-neuvième siècle: 'La Vérité' d'Emile Zola." Doctoral thesis, Université de Paris III, 1991.

Lavisse, Ernest. *A propos de nos écoles.* Paris: A. Colin, 1895.

———. "Louis Liard." *Revue Internationale de l'Enseignement* 72 (1918): 88–89.

Le Bon, Gustave. *Les lois psychologiques de l'évolution des peuples.* Paris: F. Alcan, 1894.

———. *La psychologie des foules.* Paris: F. Alcan, 1895.

Lebovics, Herman. *True France: The Wars over Cultural Identity.* Ithaca, NY: Cornell University Press, 1992.

Legrand, Louis. *L'influence du positivisme dans l'oeuvre scolaire de Jules Ferry: Les origines de la laïcité.* Paris: Marcel Rivière, 1961.

Lemaître, Jules. *Impressions de théâtre.* Dixième série. Paris: Société Française d'Imprimerie et de Librairie, 1898.

———. Review of Octave Feuillet, *La morte. Revue Politique et Littéraire (Revue Bleue)* (February 6, 1886): 177.

Levaillant, Jean. *Les aventures du scepticisme. Essai sur l'évolution intellectuelle d'Anatole France.* Paris: A. Colin, 1966.

Liard, Louis. *Morale et enseignement civique à l'usage des écoles primaires.* Paris: L. Cerf, 1883.

Limayrac, Paulin. "Du roman actuel et de nos romanciers." *Revue des Deux Mondes* (September 1, 1845): 937–57.

Loué, Thomas. "Les fils de Taine entre science et morale: A propos du *Disciple* de Paul Bourget (1889)." *Cahiers d'histoire: Revue d'histoire critique* 65 (1996): 45–61.

Luc, Jean-Noël. *L'invention du jeune enfant au XIXᵉ siècle.* Paris: Belin, 1997.

Lukàcs, Georg. *Theory of the Novel.* Cambridge, MA: MIT Press, 1971.

Lyotard, François. "Le manifeste des cinq." *Le Figaro* (August 18, 1887).

———. *The Postmodern Condition. A Report on Knowledge.* Translated by Geoff Bennington and Brian Massumi. Minneapolis: University of Minnesota Press, 1984.

———. "Universal History and Cultural Differences." *The Lyotard Reader.* Ed. Andrew Benjamin. Cambridge, MA: Blackwell, 1991.

Mansuy, Michel. *Un moderne: Paul Bourget de l'enfance au Disciple.* Paris: Les Belles lettres, 1960.

Marin, Louis. *Utopiques: jeux d'espaces.* Paris: Minuit, 1973.

Marion, Henri. *Leçons de morale.* Paris: A. Colin, 1890.

Massis, Henri. *La pensée de Maurice Barrès.* Paris: Mercure de France, 1909.

Masson, Pierre. *Le disciple et l'insurgé: Roman et politique à la belle époque.* Lyon: Presses Universitaires de Lyon, 1987.

Mayeur, Françoise. *L'enseignement secondaire des jeunes filles sous la 3e République.* Paris: Presses de la Fondation Nationale des Sciences Politiques, 1977.

Mayeur, Jean-Marie. *La vie politique sous la Troisième République*. Paris: Le Seuil, 1984.

Mayeur, Jean-Marie, and Madeleine Reberioux. *Les débuts de la Troisième République*. Paris: Le Seuil, 1973.

———. *The Third Republic from its Origins to the Great War, 1871–1914*. Translated by J. R. Foster. Cambridge: Cambridge University Press, 1984.

Mézières, Alfred, and Charles Rinn. *Morale et patrie: Lecture à l'usage des écoles primaires*. Paris: C. Delagrave, 1885.

Michelet, Jules. *Le peuple*. Paris: Flammarion, 1974 [1846].

———. *Le Prêtre, La Femme, La Famille: Les Jésuites*. Paris: Flammarion, 1845.

———. "Tableau De La France." In *Histoire De France. 1833*, vol. 1, edited by Claude Mettra, 291–352. Geneva: Edito-service, 1987.

Miller, Jacques-Alain. "Extimacy." In *Lacanian Theory of Discourse: Subject, Structure, and Society*, edited by Mark Bracher et al., 74–87. New York: New York University Press, 1994.

———. "Suture." *Screen* 18.4 (1977/78): 24–34.

Milner, Jean-Claude. *De L'école*. Paris: Le Seuil, 1984.

———. *L'oeuvre claire: Lacan, la science, la philosophie*. Paris: Le Seuil, 1995.

Mitterand, Henri. "La bête humaine. In*Étude" de La Bête humaine. Les Rougon-Macquart*. Vol. 4: 1704–1757. Paris: Gallimard, 1967.

———. "Notice." In *Vérité*, 1495–1500. Paris: Cercle du Livre Précieux, 1968.

———. *L'honneur 1893–1902*. In *Zola*. Vol. 3. Paris: Fayard, 2002.

———. *Sous le regard d'Olympia, 1840–1871*. In *Zola*. Vol. 1. Paris: Fayard, 1999.

Monod. "De la possibilité d'une réforme de l'enseignement supérieur." *La Revue Politique et Littéraire* 5 (1873–1874).

Moréas, Jean. *Le Symboliste* (du7 au 21 octobre 1886): n.p.

Mosse, George L. *The Crisis of German Ideology: Intellectual Origins of the Third Reich*. New York: Grosset & Dunlap, 1964.

Mouffe, Chantal. "Feminism, Citizenship, and Radical Democratic Politics." In *Feminists Theorize the Political*, edited by Judith Butler and Joan W. Scott, 369–83. New York: Routledge, 1992.

Munteanu, Basil. "Episodes kantiens en Suisse et en France sous le Directoire." *Revue de Littérature Comparée* 15 (1935): 387–454.

Nolen, Désiré. "Kant et la philosophie du dix-neuvième siècle." *Revue Bleue* (January 27, 1877): 717–24.

Nye, Robert A. *The Origins of Crowd Psychology: Gustave Le Bon and the Crisis of Mass Democracy in the Third Republic*. London: Sage, 1975.

Ordinaire, Dionys. "Chronique." *La République Française* (November 13, 1888).

Ouston, Philip. *The Imaginatin of Maurice Barrès*. Toronto: University of Toronto Press, 1974.

Ozouf, Jacques, ed. *Nous les maîtres d'école*. Paris: Gallimard, 1973.

Ozouf, Mona. *L'école, L'église et la République, 1871–1914*. Paris: Cana/Jean Offredo, 1982.

Pagès, Alain. *Émile Zola, un intellectuel dans l'affaire Dreyfus: Histoire de "J'accuse."* Paris: Séguier, 1991.

Parodi, Dominique. *La philosophie contemporaine en France*. Paris: Alcan, 1919.

Payot, Jules. *Avant d'entrer dans la vie: Aux instituteurs et institutrices, conseils et directions pratiques*. Paris: A. Colin, 1897.

Pécaut, Félix. *L'Éducation publique et la vie nationale*. Paris: Hachette 1897.

Pellisier, Georges. Review of Émile Zola, *Vérité*. *Revue mondiale* (February 15, 1903).

Pernot, Denis. *Le roman de socialisation, 1889–1914*. Paris: Presses Universitaires de France, 1998.

Petitbon, Pierre-Henri. *Taine, Renan, Barrès: Étude d'influence.* Paris: Belles Lettres, 1935.

Petrone, Mario. "Structures oniriques dans *Vérité.*" In *Il terzo Zola: Emile Zola dopo i "Rougon-Macquart,"* edited by Gian Carlo Menichelli, 409–17. Naples: Istituto Universitario Orientale, 1990.

Pillon, François. "Le principe d'autorité." *La Critique Philosophique* 1.10 (April 11, 1872): 145–51.

Pinto, Louis. "La vocation de l'universel." *Actes de la recherche en Sciences Sociales* 55: 23–32.

Pois, Robert A. *National Socialism and the Religion of Nature.* New York: St. Martin's, 1986.

Prost, Antoine. *Histoire De L'enseignement en France 1800–1967.* Paris: Armand Colin, 1968.

Proudhon, Pierre-Joseph. *De la justice dans la Révolution et dans l'Église.* Paris: Garnier frères, 1858.

Proust, Marcel. *The Past Recaptured.* Translated by Frederick A. Blossom. New York: Albert & Charles Boni, 1932.

Quilligan, Maureen. *The Language of Oratory: Defining the Genre.* Ithaca, NY: Cornell University Press, 1979.

Quinet, Edgar. *L'enseignement du peuple. 1850.* Paris: Hachette, 1895.

———. *Le génie des religions.* 2nd ed. Paris: Chamerot, 1851.

Raimond, Michel. *La Crise du roman, des lendemains du naturalisme aux années vingt.* Paris: J. Corti, 1966.

Rajchman, John, ed. *The Identity in Question.* New York: Routledge, 1995.

Rambaud, Vital. "Barrès et 'le sens du relatif.'" *Mesure* 4 (October 1990): 183–96.

Rauh, Frédéric. *Psychologie appliquée à la morale et à l'éducation; Cours de morale à l'usage des jeunes filles.* Paris: Hachette, 1900.

Ravaisson, Félix. "Métaphysique et morale." *Revue de Métaphysique et de Morale* 1 (1893): 1–25.

Reclus, Maurice. *Jules Ferry 1832–1893.* Paris: Flammarion, 1947.

Reid, Martine. "L'orient liquidé (Barrès, *Les déracinés*)." *Romanic Review* 83, no. 3 (May 1992): 379–88.

Rémond, René. *L'anticléricalisme en France. De 1815 à nos jours.* Bruxelles: Éditions Complexe, 1985.

Renan, Ernest. *L'avenir de la science. Oeuvres complètes de Ernest Renan.* Tome III. Paris: Calmann-Lévy, 1949. 715–1121.

———. *The Future of Science.* Boston: Roberts Brothers, 1893.

———. *Qu'est-ce qu'une nation? Ernest Renan, texte intégral: littérature et identité nationale de 1871 à 1914: textes de Barrès, Daudet, R. de Gourmont, Céline.* Edited by Philippe Forest. Paris: Bordas, 1991.

———. *La réforme intellectuelle et morale de la France.* Paris: Union Génerale d'Éditions, 1967 [1871].

Renouvier, Charles. "Le credo politique de la France et des races latines." *La Critique Philosophique* 3, no. 31 (1874): 65–79.

———. "La doctrine républicaine, ou ce que nous sommes, ce que nous voulons être." *La Critique Philosophique* (August 8, 1872): 1–16.

———. *Manuel républicain de l'homme et du citoyen.* Paris: Garnier, 1981 [1848].

———. "Petit traité de morale à l'usage des écoles primaires laïques." *La Critique Philosophique* 4.35 (September 30, 1875): 128–30; 4.49 (1876): 366–68.

———. "La raison d'État en 1872." *La Critique Philosophique* 1.12 (April 25, 1872).

———. *La science de la morale.* Paris: Ladrange, 1869.

Renouvier, Charles, and François Pillon, "La doctrine républicaine ou ce que nous sommes, ce que nous voulons être." *La Critique Philosophique* (August 8, 1872): 1–16.

Réval, G. [Gabrielle Logerot]. *Les Sèvriennes*. Paris: Ollendorff, 1907 [1900].

Ribot, Théodule. *Maladies de la volonté*. Paris: G. Ballière, 1883.

———. *La psychologie anglaise contemporaine*. Paris: G. Baillière, 1875.

Ringer, Fritz. *Fields of Knowledge: French Academic Culture in Comparative Perspective*. Cambridge: Cambridge University Press, 1992.

Ripoll, Roger. "Littérature et politique dans les écrits de Zola (1879–1881)." *Cahiers Naturalistes* 26 (1980): 41–53.

Robiquet, Paul, ed. *Jules Ferry, Discours et opinions*. Vol. 4. Paris: Armand Colin, 1896.

Rochet, Marie-Claudette. "L'instituteur dans les romans publiés entre l'établissement de la IIIᵉ République et 1914." Sorbonne maîtrise de lettres classiques, 1969.

Sachs, Leon. "Finding *l'École républicaine* in the Damnedest of Places: François Bégaudeau's *Entre les murs*." *Yale French Studies* 111 (2007): 73–88.

Sachs, Murray. "The Present as Past: Anatole France's *Histoire contemporaine*." *Nineteenth-Century French Studies* 5, nos. 1, 2 (1976–77): 117–28.

Said, Edward. *Orientalism*. New York: Random House, 1979.

Sartre, Jean-Paul. "L'universel singulier" [1964]. In *Situations, IX*, 152–90. Paris: Gallimard, 1971.

Scharfstein, Ben-Ami. *Roots of Bergson's Philosophy*. New York: Columbia University Press, 1943.

Scott, Joan Wallach. "Multiculturalism and the Politics of Identity." *October* (1993): 12–19.

———. *Parité! Sexual Equality and the Crisis of French Universalism*. Chicago: University of Chicago Press, 2005.

Scott, John A. *Republican Ideas and the Liberal Tradition in France 1870–1914*. New York: Columbia University Press, 1951.

Séverine [Caroline Rehn]. "La Foule." *Le Journal* (September 1, 1900).

Sorlin, Pierre. *"La Croix" et les juifs 1880–1899: Contribution à l'histoire de l'antisémitisme contemporain*. Paris: Bernard Grasset, 1967.

Soucy, Robert. *Fascism in France: The Case of Maurice Barrès*. Berkeley and Los Angeles: University of California Press, 1972.

Soury, Jules-Auguste. *Campagne nationaliste*. Paris: Imprimerie de la Cour d'appel, 1902.

Steeg, Jules. *Cours de morale à l'usage des instituteurs*. Paris: F. Nathan, 1885.

Sternhell, Zeev. *La droite révolutionnaire, 1885–1914: Les origines françaises du fascisme*. Paris: Le Seuil, 1978.

———. *Maurice Barrès et le nationalisme français*. Bruxelles: Éditions Complexe, 1985.

Stock-Morton, Phyllis. *Moral Education for a Secular Society: The Development of Morale Laïque in Nineteenth Century France*. Albany: State University of New York Press, 1988.

Suleiman, Susan Rubin. *Authoritarian Fictions: The Ideological Novel as a Literary Genre*. New York: Columbia University Press, 1983.

———. "Passion/Fiction: L'Affaire Dreyfus et le roman." *Littérature* 71 (October 1988): 90–107.

Tadié, Jean-Yves. "Jean Santeuil et L'anneau d'améthyste: Deux romans de l'affaire Dreyfus." In *Anatole France: Humanisme et actualité*, edited by Marie-Claire Bancquart and Jean Dérens, 79–85. Paris: Bibliothèque Historique de la Ville de Paris, 1994.

Taine, Hippolyte. *De l'intelligence*. Paris: Hachette, 1870.

———. *Derniers essais de critique et d'histoire*. 2nd ed. Paris: Hachette, 1896.

———. *L'école. Les origines de la France contemporaine*. Paris: Hachette, 1876–1894.

————. *Les origines de la France contemporaine.* Paris: Hachette, 1876–1894.

————. *Les philosophes classiques.* Paris: Slatkine Reprints, 1979 [1888].

————. *La révolution jacobine. Les origines de la France contemporaine.* Paris: Hachette, 1876–1894.

Thibaudet, Alfred. *Le bergsonisme. Trente ans de vie française.* Vol. III. Paris: Gallimard, 1923.

Tison-Braun, Micheline. *La crise de l'humanisme: Le conflit de l'individu et de la société dans la littérature française moderne (1890–1914).* Paris: Nizet, 1958.

Maître Trarieux. "L'Affaire Chambige." *Gazette des Tribunaux* (November 9, 1888).

Vacherot, Étienne. *La démocratie.* Paris: F. Chamerot, 1860.

Vallès, Jules. *Le bachelier.* Paris: Livre de Poche, 1985 [1881].

————. *The Child.* Trans. Douglas Parmée. New York: New York Review Books, 2005.

————. *L'enfant.* Paris: Livre de Poche, 1985 [1878].

————. "Les Victimes du livre." *Le Figaro* (October 9, 1862). Article reprinted in Jules Vallès. *Les Réfractaires.* Paris: Les Éditeurs Français Réunis, 1973. 161–86.

————. *Les réfractaires.* Paris: Éditeurs français réunis, 1955 [1876].

Viereck, Peter. *Conservatism from John Adams to Churchill.* New York: Van Nostrand, 1956.

Vogüé, Eugène-Melchior de. "La ligue démocratique des écoles." *Revue des deux mondes* 117.63ᵉ année, 3ᵉ période (May 1, 1893): 214–25.

————. *Le roman russe.* Paris: Plon-Nourrit, 1886.

Weber, Eugen. *Peasants into Frenchmen: The Modernization of Rural France, 1870–1914.* Stanford, CA: Stanford University Press, 1976.

Weisz, George. *The Emergence of Modern Universities in France, 1863–1914.* Princeton, NJ: Princeton University Press, 1983.

West, Cornel. "The New Cultural Politics of Difference." In *Out There: Marginalization and Contemporary Culture,* edited by Russell Ferguson et al., 19–36. Cambridge, MA: MIT Press, 1990.

Wilson, Nelly. *Bernard Lazare: Antisemitism and the Problem of Jewish Identity in Late Nineteenth-Century France.* Cambridge: Cambridge University Press, 1978.

————. "La mise en fiction de l'Affaire Dreyfus: quelques réflexions sur *Vérité.*" In *Il terzo Zola: Emile Zola dopo i "Rougon-Macquart,"* edited by Gian Carlo Menichelli, 487–503. Naples: Istituto Universitario Orientale, 1990.

Winock, Michel. *Nationalism, Anti-Semitism and Fascism in France.* Translated by Jane Marie Todd. Stanford, CA: Stanford University Press, 1993.

Wittmann, Jean-Michel. *Barrès romancier: Une nosographie de la décadence.* Paris: Champion, 2000.

Wyzewa, Théodore de. *Nos maîtres: études & portraits littéraires.* Paris: Perrin, 1895 [1887].

Zarifopol-Johnston, Ilinca. "Ceci tuera cela: The Cathedral in the Marketplace." In *To Kill a Text: The Dialogic Fiction of Hugo, Dickens, and Zola,* 176–91. Newark: University of Delaware Press, 1995.

Žižek, Slavoj. "Sur le pouvoir politique et les méchanismes idéologiques." *Ornicar?* 34 (July–September 1985): 41–60.

————. "Two Ways to Avoid the Real of Desire." In *Looking Awry,* 48–66. Cambridge, MA: MIT Press, 1991.

Zola, Émile. "Adieux." *Une Campagne.* 872–77.

————. *Une campagne. Émile Zola: Oeuvres complètes.* Vol. 11: 695–885. Paris: Nouveau Monde, 2005.

————. "Lettre au Sénat." *La vérité en marche.* 147–63.

―――. *Le roman expérimental*. Paris: Garnier-Flammarion, 1971.

―――. *Truth*. Translated by Ernest Vizetelly. Amherst, NY: Prometheus Books, 2001. Reprint of 1903 edition published by John Lane, New York.

―――. *Vérité*. Paris: Livre de Poche, 1995.

―――. *Vérité*. *Oeuvres complètes*. Edited by Maurice Le Blond. Vol. 41. Paris: François Bernouard, 1927.

―――. *La vérité en marche*. *Oeuvres complètes*. Edited by Maurice Le Blond. Vol. 42. Paris: François Bernouard, 1927.

INDEX

Democracy (Vacherot), 260

deracination. *See* uprooting

Déracinés, Les (Barrès), 81, 82–100, 105, 107, 111, 116, 118, 120, 121, 123, 129–34, 137, 262

Déroulède, Paul: *Chants du soldat,* 176

Derrida, Jacques, 3

Descartes, René, 168, 271n3

desire, 66–73, 107, 122, 124, 126–28, 137, 150–51, 159, 163, 173, 179, 187, 189, 191–94, 200, 216, 223–24, 229, 230–32, 246, 256; to be, 155, 157; bestial, 69; civilized, 169; feminine, 240, 279; formation of, 164, 168; frustrated, 121; for identity, 114; incestuous, 123; insatiable, 129, 122, 216; irrational, 98, 236, 246; to kill, 151, 185, 231; to know, 9; lack of, 155, 159–60, 178; to live, 97, 111, 117; for love, 234; man of, 106; maternal, 279n1; mystical, 215; not-to-know, 236–37; of the Other, 77, 192–94, 230; perverse, 215; for power, 69; protection from, 73–74; sexual, 72, 78, 209, 215–16, 279n1; social, 254; for something other, 122, 216, 246; unconscious, 231; for vengeance, 117

despotism, 26, 27, 87, 153, 164

details, small human, 50, 60, 63

detective, 199–202, 224, 231; story, 199–202, 235

determinism, 35–36, 61, 76, 77, 80, 90, 91–93, 95–96, 98–99, 101, 104, 106, 110, 111, 167–68, 172, 178, 208

Devinat, Émile: *Livre de lecture et de morale,* 271n18

dictatorship, 17, 18, 19, 22, 39, 43, 81, 87

didacticism, 81–82, 102, 123, 241, 245–46, 253

Dieudonné, Henri, Count de Chambord, 147, 261

difference, 4–6, 24, 30, 32, 36, 119, 127, 135, 147, 167, 180, 188, 236, 237, 238, 246, 274n6

dignity: through democratic education, 24; human, 26, 69, 84, 88; of the individual, 25–26, 67; of moral being, 30; of a rational being, 2; social, 88

dilettantism, 8, 101

Disciple, Le (Bourget), 11, 45–78, 83, 98, 131, 140, 141, 251, 262, 271n1, 271n2, 273n2 (chap. 5)

discontinuity, 146

Discours sur l'ensemble du positivisme (Comte), 23

discourse: on appeasement, 177; cognitive, 13; free indirect, 102–3, 206, 215, 220, 241; of identity, 81; of the Master, 4; of morality, 10; narratorial, 82; of the nation, 42; of the novel, 102; of philosophy, 10; positivist, 212; pre-utopian, 278n6; prophetic, 234; of religion, 10; of the Republic, 114; of rootedness, 127; of the University, 4, 127; utopian, 245, 246, 278n6

disinterestedness, 3, 5, 10, 21, 48, 65, 67, 70–71, 78, 255–56

disorder, 91, 106, 122, 143, 144, 147, 161. *See also* chance; randomness

distance, 124, 137, 168, 170–71, 174, 177–79, 183, 184, 187, 188, 193, 203

diversity, 4–5, 8, 92, 129, 146, 154, 155

Le docteur Pascal (Zola), 242

dogma, 2, 20, 24, 29, 31, 34, 39, 41, 87, 145, 181, 210, 226, 250, 269n2

Dostoevsky, Fyodor; *Crime and Punishment,* 56, 272n5

doubt, radical, 92

Doumic, René, 11, 135. *See also* "Réponse à M. René Doumic"

Dreyfus Affair, 1, 11–13, 79, 81, 96, 100, 104–5, 108, 112, 118, 139, 144, 148, 149, 155, 173, 175, 176, 180–81, 182, 184, 185, 187, 189, 193–99, 208, 210, 217, 220, 222, 223, 224, 225, 229, 232, 237, 242, 243, 245, 249, 262, 263, 264–67, 268n7, 274n4, 274n6, 275n3, 277n9

Dreyfus, Alfred (captain), 28, 174, 178, 181, 184–85, 187, 188, 189, 195, 196, 202, 208–9, 223, 229, 275n2, 277n9

Drieu La Rochelle, Pierre, 79

Du Fondement de l'induction (Lachelier), 270n14

Dupanloup, Félix Antoine (bishop), 19, 31

duration, 36–37

Durkheim, Émile, 42, 80, 97, 269n8,

Revue Illustrée, La, 56
Revue Occidentale, La, 22
rhetoric, 23, 82, 123, 125, 137, 211,
239; nationalist, 18; of reconciliation, 141
Ribot, Théodule: *Les Maladies de la
volonté,* 68; *La psychologie anglaise
contemporaine,* 98, 268n5
rights, 20, 25, 28, 30, 68; of citizens,
59; civil, 3, 31; of the community,
145; human, 12, 26, 76, 81, 113;
of illegitimate children, 30; of stock-
and bondholders, 158; universal, 32.
See also Declaration of the Rights of
Man and of the Citizen; individual,
rights of
Ringer, Fritz, 60, 64, 83, 88, 89, 92,
113
Ripoll, Roger, 209
Rod, Édouard, 11; *La course à la mort,*
55; *Les idées morales du temps présent,*
272n2
Rodenbach, Georges, 274n7
Roman de l'énergie nationale, Le. See
Novel of National Energy, The
Roman expérimental, Le (Zola), 9, 200,
209, 242, 261, 279n11
Roman naturaliste, Le (Brunetière), 48
Roman russe, Le (Vogüé), 48, 85, 262,
272n5
Romanticism, 3, 8, 36–37, 56, 68, 72,
119, 124, 130, 172, 181, 183, 239
rootedness, 93, 112, 127–28, 172. *See
also* nationalism
Rosenberg, Alfred, 118
Rougon-Macquart novels (Zola), 217,
236, 237, 241–42
Rousseau, Jean-Jacques, 43, 85, 130

S

Said, Edward, 4
Saint-Simon, Henri de, 28, 135, 249
Salle Molière Speech (Ferry), 17, 23,
32, 260
sameness, 80, 114–15, 165, 167, 237
Sand, George, 7, 9
Sarcey, Francisque, 54
Sartre, Jean-Paul, 5, 10, 35; "Existential-
ism Is a Humanism," 35
Sartre et "Les Temps Modernes" (Boschet-
ti), 271n17
Scenes and Doctrines of Nationalism

(Barrès), 13, 81, 89–90, 96, 110,
112, 118, 119, 263
Schlegel, Friedrich, 10
School: Catholic, 1, 25, 40, 205–7, 213,
225–26; Congregationist, 20, 30–31,
141, 194, 196–97, 202, 204, 220,
230, 252; German, 19; for girls,
1, 24, 29–30, 217, 226, 232, 261;
laic, 26, 31, 71, 194, 221, 226, 228,
234, 261; Lemonnier, 26; modern,
6; normal, 226; primary, 20, 23,
29–33, 39, 65, 71, 194, 196–98,
201, 210, 211, 214, 225–27, 231,
235, 261; public, 7, 23, 206, 214,
225, 227; secondary, 1, 2, 13,
20, 24, 28, 29, 32, 69, 132, 261,
270n10, 270n12; without God, 2,
31. *See also* education
schoolteacher, 20, 29–30, 33, 41, 71,
115, 194, 195, 200, 203, 205, 214,
223, 225, 232, 234, 243, 269n4,
271n19, 274n5
Schopenhauer, Arthur, 8, 53, 54, 80, 93,
126, 178, 252
science, 2, 8–9, 14, 17, 20–22, 23–24,
27, 33–36, 41, 43, 47–48, 54,
56–57, 59, 61–65, 67–71, 72–78,
95–97, 119, 123, 125, 144–45, 148,
150, 161, 191, 200, 207, 209, 211,
227, 239–40, 251, 254–55, 257,
270n14, 270n15, 274n2, 274n3,
276n7, 278n7. *See also* ethics, of
science; morality, science of; religion,
science and; religion, of science;
responsibility, of science; subject, the,
of science
Scott, Joan Wallach, 5, 190
Scott, John, 28
secular education. *See* education, laic
Sée, Camille, 1, 261
self, 66, 95, 111–14, 155, 165–66, 167,
172, 187, 271n19; analysis of, 51,
53, 178; annihilation of, 113; childhood, 9; conscious, 113; control of,
70; criticism of, 64, 173, 178; desiring, 127; disappearing, 113; distance
from, 174; divided, 54, 58–59, 61,
64, 70, 75; in duration, 37; empty,
189, 256; enemy within the, 15, 69,
126, 198, 257; equilibrium of, 210;
extimate, 15; 110; freedom of the,
110; individual, 110, 113; inner, 8,
111, 114, 194; limits of, 70; loss of,